Peasants and Capital

HAU Books is published by the
Society for Ethnographic Theory (SET)

www.haubooks.org

Peasants and Capital

Dominica in the World Economy

Michel-Rolph Trouillot

Reprint

With a new introduction by **Ryan Cecil Jobson**

Afterword by **Schuyler Esprit**

Hau Books
Chicago

Peasants and Capital was first published in 1988 by The Johns Hopkins University Press

Cover design: Daniele Meucci
Layout design: Deepak Sharma, Prepress Plus Technologies
Typesetting: Prepress Plus Technologies (https://prepressplustechnologies.com)

ISBN: 978-1-914363-22-1 [paperback]
ISBN: 978-1-914363-24-5 [e-book]
ISBN: 978-1-914363-23-8 [PDF]
LCCN: 2025940319

Hau Books
Chicago Distribution Center
11030 S. Langley Ave.
Chicago, IL 60628
www.haubooks.org

Hau Books publications are printed, marketed, and distributed by The University of Chicago Press.
www.press.uchicago.edu

Printed in the United States of America and the United Kingdom on acid-free paper.

for Jean-Philip
for Claude

Contents

List of Maps ix
List of Tables xi

INTRODUCTION
Anthropology and the Banana Wars:
Michel-Rolph Trouillot's Dominica by Ryan Cecil Jobson xiii

Preface and Acknowledgments xlv

CHAPTER 1
Peasants as Part-Economies 3

PART I: THE NATION

CHAPTER 2
Space: A Patchwork of Enclaves 31

CHAPTER 3
Time: An Island in the World Economy 59

CHAPTER 4
The Evolution of the Peasant Labor Process:
The Past in the Present 77

CHAPTER 5
Factions and Strategies 115

CHAPTER 6
"I Can Always Eat My Fig" 141

PART II: THE WORLD

CHAPTER 7
Working for Capital 163

CHAPTER 8
The Making of a Transnational 191

PART III: THE VILLAGE

CHAPTER 9
Wesley Ville La Soye 211

CHAPTER 10
"Neither Here nor There": The Ethnography of Mediation 231

CHAPTER 11
The Impact of the World: Hard Cash and Small Change 269

CHAPTER 12
Peasants, Part-Peasants, and Change: The Banana Children 311

CHAPTER 13
Contemporary Peasantries: Illusions and Hard Choices 333

AFTERWORD
by Schuyler Esprit 349

Notes to Peasants and Capital 357
Bibliography to Peasants and Capital 383
Index to Peasants and Capital 413

Maps

2.1 A Nation of Enclaves
2.2 The West: From Scotts Head to the Layou River
2.3 The West: From Layou to Portsmouth
2.4 The North
2.5 The East: From Anse du Mai to Castle Bruce
2.6 The East: From Castle Bruce to Grand Bay

10.1 Central Wesley
10.2 Residential Wesley
10.3 Peasant Purchases of Plots from the Londonderry Estate, 1915
10.4 The Greater Wesley Area

Tables

2.1 Population Trends by Parish, 1970–1980
3.1 Coffee Export Quantities, 1833–1896
3.2 Estimated Distribution of Slaves by Type of Activity in 1810, 1820, and 1830
3.3 Quantities of Sugar Exports in 1852, 1862, and 1866
3.4 Export of Sugar and Sugar Byproducts, 1870–1874
3.5 Sugar Exports, 1883–1896
3.6 Value in Percentage of Major Export Commodities to Total Exports, 1882–1896
3.7 Quantities of Cocoa Exports, 1839–1896
3.8 Early Exports of Lime Juice
3.9 Value in Percentage of Lime Products to Total Exports, 1900–1924
3.10 Main Export Values, 1950–1963
4.1 Historical Configurations of the Peasant Labor Process
4.2 Distribution of the July–November Decrease according to Crops Cultivated
4.3 Distribution of the July–November Decrease according to Size of Labor Force before Emancipation
4.4 Distribution of the July–November Decrease according to Labor Conditions
4.5 Crops and Labor Conditions in November 1838

4.6 Estates with Extreme Losses
4.7 Estates Gaining Laborers
8.1 Geest Industries: Capital and Profits after Taxation, 1972–1980
8.2 Geest Holdings Limited: Main Subsidiaries for the Years 1972–1973 and 1980
8.3 Major Branches and Activities of Geest Holdings
8.4 Geest Holdings Limited: Profits (or Losses) by Sector or Activity, 1976–1980
9.1 Slave Owning in Saint Andrew South in 1821
9.2 Population and Houses of the Saint Andrew South Estates, 1891
9.3 Acreage and Lime Production of the Estates in Saint Andrew South, 1916
11.1 District 17, Wesley Area: General Outlook on Banana Production and Income, 1976–1980
11.2 Average Banana Income of Wesley's Growers Grouped according to Estimated Acreages in Bananas, 1977–1978
11.3 Producer/Consumer Ratio in a Type One Household
11.4 Producer/Consumer Ratio in a Type Three Household
11.5 Banana Incomes of Three Yeomen, 1976–1979
11.6 Population of 207 Households according to Gender of Head of Household

INTRODUCTION

Anthropology and the Banana Wars: Michel-Rolph Trouillot's Dominica

Ryan Cecil Jobson

"The wonder about 'peasants' is their continuing existence." So opens the first chapter of Michel-Rolph Trouillot's debut English-language monograph, *Peasants and Capital: Dominica in the World Economy*. Trouillot turned to Dominica in search of an empirical resolution to a conceptual impasse. If capitalism represents a progressive stage in world history that supplanted a feudal order of bonded serfs and free tenants, what can explain the persistence of peasants *after* the proliferation of plantation capital in the Caribbean?

Hailing from Port-au-Prince, Trouillot's political exile from Haiti compelled him to seek answers to the predicaments of his native land elsewhere in the Caribbean. The "reconstituted peasantry" formed by formerly enslaved Africans after emancipation in the nineteenth century was by no means unique to Dominica. As Trouillot would later observe when he turned his attention back to the country of his birth, "the history of the peasantry in Dominica, Jamaica, and Haiti can be read as a continuous struggle between those committed to this labor process and the local and international forces that tried to destroy it" (1990: 39). But in Dominica, Trouillot personally encountered this labor process and reconstructed its historical and philosophical contents.

The fact of peasant persistence in the Caribbean rests at odds with the rapid disappearance of Trouillot's foundational text on the same topic. First published in 1988 by The Johns Hopkins University Press in its storied Atlantic History and Culture imprint, *Peasants and Capital* appeared primed for an enduring influence over the study of the Caribbean and the practice of anthropology writ large. In his review for *Nieuwe West-Indische Gids / New West Indian Guide*, William Roseberry praised the intellectual range charted by Trouillot's study of a small, Eastern Caribbean island:

> Read one way, this book is a contribution to theory, a reflection on labor processes within capitalist processes of accumulation. Read another way, it is one of the few available accounts of Dominican history and society. Read another way, it is an ethnography of the village of Wesley Ville la Soye, a banana producing village on Dominica's northeast coast. Read yet another way, the book offers an account of the relationships between Dominican banana producers and the British firm of Geest Holdings Ltd., outlining the manner in which Geest controls trade and documenting the process of capital accumulation at Geest at the expense of Windward producers. (Roseberry 1988: 165)

Indeed, *Peasants* is an ethnography years ahead of its time. By applying the methodological toolkit of anthropology to a frame as vast as the "world system," Trouillot followed the lead of his Hopkins dissertation advisor, Sidney Mintz. Three years earlier, in *Sweetness and Power: The Place of Sugar in Modern History*, Mintz traced circuits of sugar production and consumption from Caribbean plantations to European metropoles. In doing so, Mintz eschewed the classical anthropological preoccupation with a "pristine primitive" to chart a sweeping history of the Atlantic World (Mintz 1985: xxv). Where Mintz drew on decades of fieldwork in Puerto Rico, Haiti, and Jamaica to scaffold his *magnum opus*, Trouillot sought to do so in his first academic book. Conducting fieldwork in distinct locations along the commodity chain of bananas—from the mountain plots cultivated by independent farmers to the state-directed Dominica Banana Growers Association to the corporate headquarters of agricultural multinational Geest Industries in London—Trouillot carried the teachings of his mentor to their logical conclusion: a historical ethnography of the world system with the small place of Dominica at its center.

Paradoxically, Roseberry's praise for *Peasants* helps explain its rapid disappearance from print. Trouillot's study is relatively light on ethnographic description. It is, at once, a history of colonial Dominica and a critique of metropolitan political economy from what appears to be its most remote peripheries. Confronted with a discipline still steeped in debates between world systems analysis and thick descriptions of peoples and cultures, Trouillot dared to do both. As a result, he continues to be read as a figure too historical for the tastes of anthropologists and too anthropological for those of academic historians. In his brazen disregard for disciplinary commonsense, Trouillot crafted a book that fell between the "boundary spaces" of history and anthropology.[1] To revisit *Peasants and Capital*, then, is to consider what anthropology might have become if its novel historical ethnography had become paradigmatic rather than falling unceremoniously through the cracks of our intellectual tradition.

Still, there is another and perhaps more consequential reason for the premature disappearance of *Peasants and Capital*. Trouillot's subsequent works, by contrast, have not disappeared at all. If anything, they enjoy a renaissance in scholarly and public engagement. His historical ethnography of the Haitian state and Duvalier dictatorship, *Haiti: State Against Nation, the Origins and Legacy of Duvalierism* (1990), remains in print and is celebrated by contemporary scholars in Caribbean Studies and political anthropology alike. His meditations on anthropological theory collected in *Global Transformations: Anthropology and the Modern World* (2003) are a mainstay on undergraduate and graduate anthropology syllabi. His best-known work, *Silencing the Past: Power and the Production of History* (1995), is an undisputed classic recently blessed with a commemorative twentieth anniversary edition. Finally, three of Trouillot's students from The University of Chicago—Yarimar Bonilla, Greg Beckett, and Mayanthi Fernando—anthologized a selection of his writings in the 2021 volume, *Trouillot Remixed: The Michel-Rolph Trouillot Reader*.

To understand the disappearance of *Peasants and Capital*, then, we must properly diagnose the trends in world anthropologies and international geopolitics since its publication. When Trouillot embarked on his Dominica field research in the summer of 1979, the English-speaking Caribbean sat in the crosshairs of US counterinsurgent operations in the Americas. A few months prior, the New Jewel Movement had seized

1. On the concept of "boundary spaces" and the discipline of anthropology, see Stocking 1995 and Jobson 2023.

power in Grenada and installed the People's Revolutionary Government of Maurice Bishop. The Grenada Revolution pressed forward until it collapsed in 1983 under the weight of conflicts within the party's central committee, the assassination of Bishop, and the subsequent US military invasion of Grenada in Operation Urgent Fury.

Reaganomics touched the Caribbean, too, easing trade and tariff restrictions for select Caribbean and Central American countries under the Caribbean Basin Initiative, a program launched in 1984 to counter a Soviet sphere of influence in the hemisphere. By the time of its publication in 1988, *Peasants and Capital* entered a world of *détente* closely followed by German reunification, the dissolution of the Soviet Union, and the Cuban *período especial*. In this new landscape, anthropological research on the English-speaking Caribbean withered in concert with intelligence and national security dictates. Firmly absorbed into a resurgent Washington Consensus, the English-speaking Caribbean began to retreat from anthropological view as federal funding in the social sciences was redirected toward militarized frontiers opened by a post-Cold War order of US assaults on Iraq, Somalia, and Sudan.

Caribbean anthropology did endure in this climate of an inchoate War on Terror. But it did not emerge unscathed. Historically, Caribbean Studies drew many of its signature concepts and categories from its smallest territories and most remote regions. Indeed, the dual value system of "reputation and respectability" familiar to Caribbean social scientists developed out of Peter Wilson's fieldwork on the island of Providencia (Wilson 1973). Elsewhere, studies of peasant labor, rural social organization, and Maroon communities predominated. After Trouillot parlayed his research on a small Eastern Caribbean island into a flourishing academic career with stops in Durham, Baltimore, and Chicago, the study of the Caribbean rapidly shifted to encompass new anthropological preoccupations with urbanization, garrison politics, informal commercial importers, and efforts to "study up" among Caribbean middle classes and in theaters of office and factory and work.[2] Peasants began to disappear from Caribbean anthropology at the very moment that *Peasants and Capital* fell out of print.

In the 1990s, the easing of restrictions on US researchers in Cuba directed anthropological interest toward another geopolitical hotspot in the region. Likewise, the democratic transition (and subsequent US covert interventions) in Haiti garnered renewed attention from

2. See Freeman 2000; Jaffe 2024; Kivland 2020; Lewis 2020; Thomas 2011.

security experts and social scientists. Alongside these tidal shifts in the hemisphere, the decline in monograph-length ethnographic studies of Dominica, Providencia, and their *smallest* island kin is a symptom not of their lack of intellectual vitality but of the "electoral politics" that dictate who or what is awarded resources and credentials in academia today.[3]

This backdrop helps us understand why Trouillot is remembered more for his extensive writings on Haiti than for his early field research in Dominica. This is not to say, however, that *Peasants and Capital* disappeared entirely from the consciousness of Caribbean letters. The novel structure of *Peasants and Capital*—split into three distinct sections on "the Nation," "the World," and "the Village"—has earned a reputation all its own. In her classic ethnography of race and nationalism in Jamaica, *Modern Blackness*, Deborah Thomas credits *Peasants and Capital* with the inspiration behind her modified analytical trinity of "the Global-National," "the National-Local," and "the Local-Global" (2004:19). Likewise, in her ode to the late Trouillot titled "Bodies in the System," Vanessa Agard-Jones proposes that we supplement his framework with the addition of the body as a unit of study that serves as "a nexus, a conjuncture, and a site from which we might read an ever-evolving genealogy of power" (2013: 187).

These homages to Trouillot ensure that *Peasants and Capital* persists in our collective memory even if not in print. Accordingly, it is a book often invoked but less often read due to its apocryphal status. For many, including this author, it became a text passed between interlibrary loan holdings, shuttled in fragments via xeroxed pages or hastily scanned digital files. Its return to print is an occasion then to behold its innovations in content as well as form. The reverence for Trouillot's model of multisited and multiscalar analysis has often come at the expense of a robust engagement with his political insights into the Dominican peasantry, its perseverance, and its uncertain future. The impending banana wars and the decline in banana production were fresh on the mind of a young Trouillot during his Dominica field trips in the late 1970s and 1980s. It is Trouillot and the "banana children" he toiled with that we turn to next.

3. On Trouillot's concept of "electoral politics" in academia, see Trouillot 2021a. On the epistemological erasure of small islands in the Caribbean history and social science, see Baker 2024.

Peasants and the State

By the time The Johns Hopkins University Press published *Peasants and Capital* in 1988, Trouillot had already distinguished himself as an artist and intellectual of considerable repute. In 1968, Trouillot followed the parade of Haitian émigrés fleeing the Duvalier dictatorship to join the *jaspora* in Brooklyn, New York. His earliest intellectual adventures were framed explicitly by his status as a Haitian exile. In the Kreyòl-language literary magazine *Lakansièl*, Trouillot published poetry and a serialized history of the Haitian Revolution under the nom de plume, "L. Raymond." This account, which championed the revolutionary capacity of the peasantry over and above the storied military generals Toussaint Louverture and Jean-Jacques Dessalines, was collected and published as *Ti difé boulé sou istoua Ayiti* in 1977. The lyrical panache of *Ti difé boulé*—modeled after Haitian oral traditions of storytelling—extended beyond his written word, too. In Brooklyn, Trouillot formed the theater troupe Tanbou Libèté with fellow Haitian exiles and applied his talents as a singer and songwriter to challenge noiriste appropriations of the Haitian folk. As Bonilla observes (2021: 4), this renaissance in Haitian language, music, and folk idioms labored to demonstrate that "peasant traditions were not intrinsically linked to the Duvalierist project and could serve as both a site and a vehicle for political reform."

Trouillot's leap from the tinderbox of Haitian diasporic *kilti libète* to the apex of North American academe was not preordained. While enrolled as an undergraduate student at Brooklyn College, he drove a taxi to finance his studies. An encounter with the anthropologists Sidney Mintz and Richard Price—who had been invited to conduct an external review of the anthropology department at Brooklyn College—inspired Trouillot to follow them to Baltimore and begin his doctoral studies at Johns Hopkins (Price 2022: 95).

At Hopkins, Trouillot continued his inquiry into Caribbean Maroons and peasantries under the tutelage of the veteran ethnographers Price (who had conducted extensive fieldwork in the Saamaka Maroon territory of Suriname) and Mintz (whose aforementioned résumé included research in Puerto Rico, Jamaica, and Haiti). Unable to return to Haiti under the reign of Jean-Claude "Baby Doc" Duvalier, Trouillot selected Dominica as a case study of peasant persistence and its role in the building of a "new state" that attained political independence less than a year before his initial field trip in May 1979. In preparation, Trouillot conducted library research on the history of land tenure and development in Dominica which he presented at the Fourth Annual Caribbean Studies Association Conference in Fort-de-France, Martinique (Price 2022: 121). Facilitated by acquaintances of his Hopkins professor, Price, Trouillot departed Martinique from Petit Anse by a fishing boat to complete his first crossing of the northern channel to Dominica (Price 2022: 121).

The Commonwealth of Dominica, for Trouillot, was an "odd and ordinary" Caribbean geography (Trouillot 2021b). This initial period of research during the summer academic holiday sharpened the focus of Trouillot's research on the relationship between peasants and the nation-state in the Caribbean. In his dissertation proposal, "Yeomanry and Nationhood: The Case of Dominica," Trouillot observed a tendency of anthropologists to define peasants "in terms of their opposition to the state and the 'larger society.'" Trouillot's initial observations of state building in Dominica led him to chart an alternative to the pathbreaking studies authored by Robert Redfield and Eric Wolf.

To do so, Trouillot engages in a lyrical play befitting of his talents as a songwriter. The term "peasant" is not commonly used by Dominican cultivators themselves. In Dominica, those who engage in the peasant labor process are regarded as "smallholders" or, more often, "small farmers." To insert this class of laborers into the orbit of global peasantries was deliberately provocative, following the example of Mintz. If the small farmers of the Caribbean could be defined as peasants, this unsettled Marxist historical materialism and its teleological stages that proceed from feudalism to capitalism to socialism. For Trouillot, the taken-for-granted opposition of peasants to capitalism and the state represented an analytical and political error. If he was correct, what did this portend for the future of Dominica as an independent nation-state?

Instead, he observed that the transition to independence in Dominica placed peasant cultivators in direct contact with the new state. With the export market for bananas governed by a state outfit in the form of the Banana Growers Association—which deducted fees from producers before selling on to the European distributor, Geest—small farmers subsidized the growth of the independent Commonwealth of Dominica and the London-based multinational. In his early estimation, it was the peasant who supplied the laboring foundation of the Dominican state and its capacity to deliver goods and services to a citizenry scattered across disparate residential enclaves.

In his dissertation proposal, he identified "banana days" as the principal locus of Dominican statecraft. On these occasions, banana cultivators carried their products to state-run distribution depots known as boxing plants. Since peasants regularly faced the new state through their encounters with the Banana Growers Association, Trouillot hypothesized an expanded role that the peasantry could assume in national political affairs. The character of this role would hinge on ordinary cultivators' awareness of their subsidizing of the state treasury. Trouillot proposed an ethnography of the banana day to "determine the extent to which the very staging of the 'banana days' can be said to contribute to the awareness of surplus extraction as a national event" (n.d.a: 3) At this stage of his study, peasants' consciousness of this surplus extraction remained an open question. He did underscore, though, the popular slogan of the Dominica Farmers' Union that circulated during his fieldwork in 1979: "We Feed the Country." Whether this slogan referred only to nutritional sustenance (in the form of staple crops of green bananas) or included the sustenance of state revenues and infrastructural power was not yet clear. Moreover, the devastation of Dominica by Hurricane David in August 1979, mere weeks after his first fieldwork, interrupted the political momentum of small farmers.

Here, Trouillot's concern with the abuses and appropriations of the Haitian peasantry loomed large, even if silently, over his dissertation research. To what extent could peasants not simply craft lives outside the state, but *become* the state at a moment of political transition and economic change in the Caribbean? Did the militarized incorporation of Haitian peasants under the Duvalier dictatorship inevitably await their counterparts in Dominica? Could the peasants of Dominica chart another path forward for Haiti and the Caribbean? How and when could a political consciousness emerge from the peasantry of its essential role in the construction of a new Caribbean state?

The Cooking of History

Even as Trouillot proposed a relatively modest ethnography of the "banana day as ritual," the heterodox historian who had written *Ti difé boulé* would soon intervene in his study of Dominica. *Peasants and Capital* does arrive at the ritual event of the banana day—or "fig day" in local creole parlance—but not before unearthing the rise of bananas and tracing the historical contours of the nation in Dominica.

The country of Dominica, Trouillot reminds us, is less a taken-for-granted unit of analysis than a patchwork of "scattered villages and uneven enclaves" separated by mountain peaks and dense rainforests in the island interior ([1988] 2025: 56). At the time of his fieldwork, the enclaved character of Dominican towns and villages persisted with communities disconnected by unsparing terrain and treacherous road passages. Insular communities cleaved to specific linguistic heritages (of French or English-based creoles), religious traditions (of Protestantism or Catholicism), and patterns of crop cultivation or animal husbandry. The opening section of *Peasants and Capital*, "The Nation," testifies to the uneven application of this category to a geography beset by topographic and social divides.

If not religion or language, Trouillot contends that the ubiquity of banana production unites the nation of Dominica. This is not to say that the cultivation of bananas is practiced in the same way throughout the island. Neither does it suggest that the predominance of bananas was guaranteed. On the contrary, it is the incidental rise of bananas to which he alerts us first. The story of the Dominican nation is best told through a "succession of crops" cultivated for export ([1988] 2025: 61). Trouillot locates the first boom in the plantation economy of Dominica in the fourth decade of the eighteenth century, when the introduction of coffee established the first in a series of cash crop experiments that would unfold in the centuries after. The formal concession of Dominica by France to the British Crown in 1763 established Dominica as an exception to the sugar plantation colonies of the British West Indies. Instead, coffee production continued to command the greatest share of enslaved labor in Dominica through the conjuncture of emancipation in 1834–38.

In the mid-nineteenth century, blight conditions plagued coffee crops; advantageous markets for sugar inspired planters to reinvest in cane production. Sugar reigned as an export monocrop in Dominica for the rest of the century. It would be imperiled, though, by the withdrawal of protective tariffs for British West Indian sugar producers and competition from beet sugar in Europe. The decline of sugar, too, imperiled free Africans after emancipation. Trouillot argues that "the material quality of life may have declined in the second half of the nineteenth century" ([1988] 2025: 68). The pursuit of replacements for sugar inspired short-lived experiments in cocoa and lime cultivation before the revelation of bananas.

Bananas did not only provide an opportune market to reverse the decline of sugar. Unlike sugarcane, bananas can serve as a staple of laborers' diets. This crucial difference allowed bananas to outlast their predecessors in the consciousness of peasants themselves. Unlike sugar, which remained entirely dependent on metropolitan markets, bananas served as a ballast against economic crisis on the Caribbean periphery. In contrast to the bleak decades of the late nineteenth century when the retreat of sugar markets besieged Dominica with extreme poverty, the rise of bananas collapsed the distinction between the production of crops for export and the cultivation of plots for household consumption. For Trouillot, this informed Dominican peasants' perception of themselves and their relative independence: "[bananas] merged at the cognitive sphere inasmuch as tenants and yeomen never felt that this new cultivation was imposed on them from the outside to fulfill the needs of a faraway market" ([1988] 2025: 156). With bananas, the labor processes of the plot and the plantation converged. When metropolitan markets wavered, the banana growers could consume the fruits of their labor to weather the crisis.

Late nineteenth-century colonial reformers concurred with this assessment even if they did not appreciate its full implications. In 1897, the Crown convened the West India Royal Commission to inquire into the conditions of Britain's sugar-producing colonies in the Caribbean. Sparked by economic depression and the uprisings of sugar workers in British Guiana and St. Kitts, London sought a market solution to the problem of social unrest. Her Majesty's Government had to provide stable work if it did not want riots to recur elsewhere. For Dominica, the Commission recommended unanimously that this could be found in an export trade in fruit—first to markets in the United States and then, potentially, to Great Britain as well.

The report of the Royal Commission of 1897 identified Dominica and St. Vincent as the model colonies from which to develop a successful fruit trade. But the transition from sugar plantation work to peasant agriculture required vast material investments. The construction of roads to service the Dominican interior, the extension of low-interest loans to peasant cultivators, and the commission of cargo steamships to carry fruit crops to market in New York were the first orders of business.[4] While the commission's report is understated in its assessment of the social value of this economic transformation, subsequent dispatches from colonial administrators underscore their association of the fruit trade with the liberal values of colonial uplift.

My own research in the Colonial Office Records at the National Archives of the United Kingdom in Kew sheds additional light on the temperament of colonial officials. Upon receiving a print copy of the report in October 1897, the curator of Botanic Station in Dominica,

4. *Report of the West India Royal Commission, 1897* (London: Her Majesty's Stationary Office, 1897), 51.

Joseph Jones, penned a response to the Assistant Director of the Royal Botanical Gardens in Kew:

> The scheme for settling labourers on Crown lands will not receive much sympathy from the large proprietors for obvious reasons, but if the matter is worked with Imperial funds the planters cannot complain. *In my opinion it will be the first real chance the Dominican negro has ever had* and I think it will be found that he is quite capable of doing for himself with proper advice and encouragement what he has long done for others for a miserable pittance.[5]

But even the reformers in the colonial office could not conceive of the lifeworlds birthed by bananas. While British botanist-cum-bureaucrats imagined fruits as a ripe market to absorb the derelict masses of former sugar estate workers, the advent of banana cultivation in Dominica ushered in a renaissance of peasant autonomy.

The transition of the green fig or "cooking banana" from an occasional feature of the Dominican diet to a staple provision exemplifies this renaissance for Trouillot. In the mid-twentieth century, the cooking of bananas—fried or, most often, boiled—put bananas to use in a fashion unthinkable for nineteenth-century liberals.[6] In this ordinary tradition of banana cultivation and cooking, a future beyond the vestiges of the plantation came into view.

By incorporating cash crops into everyday household use, Dominican peasants constituted an oddity in the history of capitalism. Peasants produced bananas for export; so, too, they consumed them daily. As simultaneously "a unit of production and a unit of consumption," the peasant labor process inhabited a value system distinct from that of waged work (Trouillot [1988] 2025: 154). As Trouillot observes, "Many Dominican growers like to imply that they are not in fact producing for the Geest transnational or the [Banana Growers Association], but are rather selling them some surplus of what some anthropologists would call their 'subsistence' production" ([1988] 2025: 158). When *Peasants and Capital*

5. J. Jones to D. Morris, CO 318/290, October 27, 1897, National Archives of the United Kingdom, Kew, 99.
6. Stephan Palmié reminds us accordingly of Cuban anthropologist Fernando Ortiz's likening of "social worlds to cooking pots in which heterogeneous ingredients—people, practices, modes of thought—are being stewed into each other in the hearth of history" (Palmié 2013: 29).

turns to the world of the transnational corporation, it reveals the other side of this hard-won independence.

To the World

The deception posed by the peasant labor process stems from its distance from the sites of its valorization in European markets. Trouillot ethnographically traces the itinerary of the peasant working day as the "activators" of this labor process embark on a pre-dawn passage from their homesteads to plots in the Bush:

> During the lone and long walk, principal laborers whose paths cross exchange greetings and best wishes for the day, but it is not the time for conversation. Most wear a jacket or a sweater; males wear a hat or a beret, females a hat or a cloth hairdress that protects them from the cold, but will also serve against the sun when, later in the day, the temperature rises by about fifteen degrees, as it does almost every day. One walks briskly through the mud: it has rained last night, if not the day before, and the sun rarely pierces through the trees strongly enough to dry the tracks. Though most peasants have become expert at making their way through the mud, the dark, and the occasional fog, the walk may take as long as one to two hours, because of the roughness of the terrain; there are so many gutters to cross, so many hills to climb, so many slopes through which one circles one's way down, so many other properties to avoid. ([1988] 2025: 245–48)

The work of Dominican peasants is not leisurely; it is hard. This early morning trek begins the ritual of work that includes weeding, fertilizer treatments, and the harvesting of provisions. But with hard work comes a measure of independence. Peasant work is not governed by hourly wages. It is not supervised by plantation overseers.[7] By virtue of bananas'

7. As Karla Slocum observes in her own ethnography of banana growers in St. Lucia, peasant cultivation often represented a conscious refusal of waged work: "Beyond conceptualizing freedom *against* the restrictive scheduling of work within urban businesses, growers understood freedom *with* its potential for social and economic security and advancement. They emphasized how, as banana growers, they had improved their social and economic lives by obtaining land on which to grow their fruit and then by working for themselves" (2006: 100).

incorporation into the daily nutritional intake of the household, there is a strong sense that activators make the trek for the immediate benefit of themselves and their extended family units, not merely the accumulation of petty capital.

However, the independence of the long journey into the Bush obscures another fact of peasant life in Dominica. Trouillot puts it bluntly, "Dominican yeomen and tenants are in fact working in their own gardens for a British-based transnational corporation" ([1988] 2025: 182). With the state-run Banana Growers Association (DBGA) operating as an intermediary, the bananas produced by freeholders and tenants are purchased by multinational Geest Industries for sale in the European market. As the sole buyer of Dominican banana exports, Geest fixes the price and dictates the terms of sale between peasants and the DBGA.

For this reason, peasants can hardly be said to be working for themselves or even for the Dominican state that extracts indirect taxes from the sale of their produce. They do not control the price at which their surplus bananas are sold. Meanwhile, the production of staple crops ensures the household nutritional intake necessary for the reproduction of peasant and proletarian labor power in Dominica. Bananas, in other words, are a peculiar commodity. They simultaneously protect producers against the volatility of international markets and insulate the corporation from the obligation to meet its employees' nutritional needs through wages or subsidies. As a corporate official said of peasant production of household staple crops during Trouillot's fieldwork in London, "We let them do it … It's cheaper" ([1988]) 2025: 189).

The independence of the peasantry is, at the same time, a boon to the multinational corporation. Trouillot meticulously leafs through the accounting books of Geest to demonstrate that its profits in the agricultural sector—fueled by the work of Dominican peasants—permit its other branches to place surplus capital at risk toward ventures in agricultural technology, management services, and computing. Far from a vestige of precapitalist societies or an obstacle to capitalist growth and innovation, peasants subsidize the growth of metropolitan capital one bunch of bananas at a time.

Dominican peasants are not disconnected from the world. They, like the enslaved and indentured workers of previous centuries, are essential to the accumulation of capital in the metropole. Yet, the alchemy that governs the exchange of bananas as they move from peasant plots to the DBGA to Geest and, finally, to British consumers obscures this entanglement. The obfuscation of this process is less disastrous for banana producers themselves—who maintain a spartan independence on the edges of this exchange—than it is for authors of an economic commonsense that considers the peasantry a drain on, rather than gift to, the post-independence course of national development in Dominica. At last, Trouillot turns to the banana day as a social drama through which relations between the village, the nation, and the world are articulated and can be made anew.

Banana Day Come

To what extent can banana days "be said to contribute to the awareness of surplus extraction as a national event?" (Trouillot n.d.a). The final section of *Peasants and Capital* sees Trouillot return to the question that animated his dissertation proposal nearly a decade earlier. Approximately twenty-four hours before "fig day," peasants are summoned by radio. In order to transport the harvest from the Bush to the boxing plant, all available hands are gathered to cut bunches of bananas. Large trucks or smaller pickups are dispatched. Those still in need of a courier negotiate with truck owners at the Four Road junction in Wesley. The bananas are inspected for quality by state-appointed selectors. Rejected bananas are held for household consumption or funneled into an informal trade brokered by "hucksters" with neighboring islands such as Guadeloupe.

In *Peasants and Capital*, Trouillot remains ambivalent toward the "awareness of surplus extraction as a national event." In his estimation, it is the "banana children" with whom the verdict on this question rests. Trouillot defines banana children as Dominicans who grew up in peasant households but left home to attend secondary school in the towns of Roseau and Portsmouth in the decade before independence in 1979. Throughout their education, they remain partially dependent on the peasant labor process. While pursuing secondary education in preparation for careers in private business or the civil service, banana children continue to receive weekly deliveries of provisions from their family plots. Their ascendance into a laboring class of postcolonial bureaucrats and functionaries is subsidized by the manual labor of food cultivation in the Bush.

However, even as the banana children acknowledge their partial dependence on peasant production, their transition from the village to the city is accompanied by a palpable scorn for agricultural work. Banana cultivation is considered "unworthy" of men and women who attended school outside of the village. Peasant production is chided as "just planting…fig" or "not really working" ([1988] 2025: 324). For Trouillot, the future of Dominica hinges on the banana children's recognition of the peasant labor process *as* work and an engine of national development. They will either champion the peasantry as the driving force behind their class mobility or tragically turn their backs on the peasantry as a vestige of a supposedly backward subsistence economy. The fate of the nation hangs in the balance.

As examples of what the anthropologist Brent Crosson calls "rural cosmopolitans" (2014: 21), banana children serve as crucial intermediaries between their home villages and the administrative centers of the new Dominican state. They traverse between patois and creole-speaking enclaves and the English lingua franca of national government and international commerce. As they prepared to take the reins of the Dominican state, they could draw on their upbringings to evangelize the potential of the peasantry and question the arrangements through which peasants are deprived of the surplus value their products realize on international markets. At the same time, they are endowed with skills that permit them to thrive independent of their peasant origins through posts in government or employment opportunities abroad.

Would the banana children invite their peasant guardians to join them in building the new state in Dominica? Or would they turn their backs on the peasantry in their pursuit of individual mobility within or beyond its shores? Trouillot does not allow himself to speculate. He does, however, underscore the urgency of this dilemma. The success of the Dominican state rests upon its capacity to repatriate a generation of banana children and lumpenized peasants into a labor process that birthed them. And Trouillot is alert to political economic developments that would soon imperil markets for Dominican bananas. In one of the final endnotes in *Peasants and Capital*, Trouillot sounds an alarm:

> [The] long-term downward trends in international prices will continue to afflict Dominica much more than it hurts most producing countries … Further, Geest is likely to deal with the Windwards in the very same way Britain dealt with its former colonies: having exhausted their resources for its purposes, it will increasingly turn to newer pastures. Last, no amount of wishful thinking on the part of Dominicans or promises from United States officials will give Windward bananas a share of the North American market, now dominated by the most powerful fruit-specialized transnationals in world history. ([1988] 2025: 372)

Here, a tacit subtext of *Peasants and Capital* is unveiled. At the moment of its publication, Dominica appeared destined for yet another crisis of production. The market for Dominican bananas would not survive the turn of the century unscathed. If metropolitan markets were certain to withdraw from Dominica, what would become of the peasants who sponsored the rise of the banana children as a professional and managerial class?

Rather than a quixotic reliance on the banana as an export commodity, Trouillot proposes a more modest program of food sufficiency guided by local production and substitution of imported foods. The success of such a program, he insists, will rest on the extent to which the expertise of the peasantry is integrated into the governance of the Dominican state. In their role as a "Trojan horse" between the peasantry and the state ([1988] 2025: 332), would the banana children exalt their peasant forebears as agents of an alternative path of development at the periphery of millennial capital? Where bananas once rescued Dominica after the decline of coffee and sugar, what would become of Dominica after it had outlasted its use to the banana multinational, Geest? While Geest safely parlayed its profits into lucrative business ventures in maritime shipping and logistics to secure a future after bananas, what would become of the Dominican peasantry when *banana day done*?

Banana Wars, First as Tragedy

During Trouillot's fieldwork in Dominica, European markets for bananas remained protected for traditional African, Caribbean, and Pacific (ACP) suppliers. Dominica reaped the benefits of preferential trade arrangements with the United Kingdom alongside Jamaica and other territories in the Windward Islands that were exempt from import duties levied on "dollar bananas" from non-Commonwealth suppliers. At the close of the twentieth century, preferential agreements for European Union (EU) banana imports came under pressure from US multinationals and Latin American banana-producing states to remove barriers to trade. Caribbean small farmers could hardly be expected to compete with the scale of Central and South American plantation growers in a free market.

The protections for ACP countries stemmed from the ethic espoused by the nineteenth-century colonial reformers who advocated for a fruit trade in Dominica nearly a century earlier. Protected markets for current and former British colonies remained sutured to values of imperial paternalism even after the transition to political independence for Commonwealth nations such as Dominica. From the perspective of the Caribbean, the moral justification for these arrangements rested on European governments' obligations toward their former colonies and overseas territories for historic injuries endured during and after the period of plantation slavery. Although the relationship between protected markets and reparations for slavery and colonization was never made explicit in the trade agreements between EU and ACP countries, this subtext pervaded dispatches between former colonies and the metropole.

In December 1989, mere months after the publication of *Peasants and Capital*, the Fourth Lomé Convention convened in Togo and reaffirmed EU commitments to traditional ACP producers. Article I of Protocol 5 in the Lomé IV agreement did not equivocate in its insistence that "no ACP State shall be placed, as regards access to its traditional markets and its advantages on those markets, in a less favourable situation than in the past or at present."[8] The enforcement of this provision, though, continued to trouble ACP countries as they entered the 1990s. Recently declassified communiqués between Caribbean heads-of-state and the United Kingdom reveal mounting anxieties over protected markets for ACP bananas. With the impending implementation of the European Single Market, Prime Ministers of the Windward Islands implored Downing Street to make good on its "firm statement of intent to protect the Banana Industry of the Caribbean after 1992."[9] In her reply dated April 30, 1990, UK Prime Minister Margaret Thatcher sprightly contended that she was "well aware of the crucial importance of banana exports to your economies" and pledged to "continue to fight hard to make sure you go on enjoying the preferential arrangements for bananas under the Lomé Convention."[10] In practice, the protections after 1992 amounted to a twenty percent tariff on non-ACP imports that could

8. *The Fourth ACP-EEC Convention of Lomé*, signed in Lomé, Togo, December 9, 1989.
9. Prime Ministers of the Commonwealth of Dominica, Grenada, St. Lucia, and St. Vincent and the Grenadines to Margaret Thatcher, Prime Minister of the United Kingdom, PREM 19/4067, April 2, 1990, National Archives of the United Kingdom, Kew.
10. Margaret Thatcher, Prime Minister of the United Kingdom to M. Eugenia Charles, Prime Minister of the Commonwealth of Dominica, April 30, 1990, National Archives of the United Kingdom, Kew.

hardly guarantee a secure market after the removal of trade barriers within the European Community.

In one of his last statements as Prime Minister of Jamaica, Michael Manley wrote to Thatcher's successor, John Major, with a renewed tenor of urgency:

> Over the last three or four years, representatives of our two Governments have had many discussions pertaining to the problems that bananas from Jamaica, the Windward Islands and other ACP countries would face as a result of the establishment of a [Single European Market]. There have similarly been discussions, at all levels, between representatives of your Government and those of the other Caribbean banana-producing countries, as well as between Caribbean and other European Government representatives.
>
> Each time, we came away from those meetings confident that the Government of the United Kingdom fully understood the problem and was committed to a resolution of the issue within the framework of the LOME Convention. However, recent developments have given rise to deep concerns and led to discussion of the situation today in the intersessional meeting of the Heads of Government of CARICOM.
>
> We now understand that persistent pressure from U.S. multinationals involved in the banana trade and who already control in excess of 85 per cent of the world banana market, outside of the EC, has led this attempt to apply a measure originally designed for temperate zone crops to bananas. Jamaica, the Windward Islands and other traditional ACP banana suppliers to the EC, have consistently pointed out, in discussions with Heads of Government, Ministers, Government officials and Commissioners of the EC, that the tariffication approach to the banana issue would be disastrous, not least because it would quickly destroy the Caribbean banana industry, and those of most other ACP producers.[11]

The crisis that Trouillot anticipated had come to pass. As the economist Anthony Payne observes, the first negative shock to the Dominican banana industry followed the adoption of the European Single Market in the period of 1992–1994. Banana production in Dominica fell from

11. Michael Manley, Prime Minister of Jamaica to John Major, Prime Minister of the United Kingdom, February 19, 1992, National Archives of the United Kingdom, Kew.

59,000 tons in 1992 to 43,000 tons in 1994. More pointedly, the export earnings from bananas fell at an even greater rate from EC$96 million in 1992 to EC$64 million in 1994 (Payne 2008: 319). The death knell arrived in the form of a World Trade Organisation (WTO) dispute orchestrated by the US multinational giant Chiquita and US President Bill Clinton. Challenging preferential markets for ACP bananas as "discriminatory" against dollar bananas produced predominantly on Chiquita plantations in Central America, Chiquita prevailed when the WTO Panel in May 1997 ruled in favor of the United States and its co-complainants Guatemala, Ecuador, Honduras, and Mexico. Caribbean banana-producing nations were among the greatest casualties of this "banana war" despite their exclusion from the WTO hearings. Between 1997 and 2001, banana production in Dominica declined further from 35,000 to 18,000 tons; export earnings declined from EC$45 million to EC$17 million over the same period.

The banana wars upended the peasant labor process and the social drama of the banana day that had captured Trouillot's attention in 1979. The ascendance of free market capitalism was disastrous for Dominica and the Windward Islands. At the WTO, the neoliberalism of late twentieth-century financiers landed a final blow against the liberalism of late nineteenth-century colonial reformers. However, while Caribbean heads-of-state decried the banana wars as a strike against their export and foreign exchange earnings, the greater disaster lay with the erosion of peasant livelihoods themselves.

As Trouillot underscored, bananas were not only important in their valorization as saleable commodities on international markets. Bananas served as a measure of protection against market fluctuations and fiscal crises for producers and their extended families. With the decline in the volumes of banana exports came a decline in the number of local banana growers and, in turn, the disappearance of a critical mass of agricultural expertise. The defeat of the banana wars was twofold. Revenues for the state and peasant producers dwindled. At the same time, the increasing dependence on imported food placed an undue burden on the working people of Dominica. The national food import bill rose nearly one hundred percent from US$10 million in 1990 to US$19.2 million in 1994. By 2005, the total had reached an exorbitant US$165 million (IICA 2007: 19). Rates of outmigration increased steadily after 1990. By 2020, fifty-two percent of all Dominican nationals lived abroad, with the largest populations of Dominican migrants residing (by order of total population) in the United States, the United Kingdom, and France (IOM 2023: 14). Today, migration remains a key driver of the national economy with annual remittances of greater than US$50 million reported from 2020–2022 representing approximately one-tenth of the Dominican GDP.[12]

The rise in outmigration and the skyrocketing food import bill dictated the shifting priorities of the Dominican state. Turning outward for solutions to the crisis, the Government of Dominica introduced a Citizenship by Investment program in 1993 that permits foreign nationals to receive citizenship in exchange for a minimum contribution of US$100,000 to the Dominica Economic Development Fund. Instead of a redoubled effort to promote the cultivation of staple crops for local consumption, the pursuit of alternative streams of foreign exchange earnings led several Dominican governments to pursue niche markets in ecotourism on the "Nature Island" and expand its role as a port of call for Caribbean cruise ships. Today, the expansion of the tourist sector is wagered on a new international airport currently under construction in the village of Wesley where Trouillot resided during his fieldwork more than forty years ago. Awarded to a Chinese construction firm, China Railway No. 5 Engineering Group, the location of the future runway and airport terminal are visible on either side of the road due north from Wesley. Anticipating this possible future in *Peasants and Capital*, Trouillot cautions against the tragic allure of looking only to the skies rather than the Bush as a fount of national development.

The sober reality of Dominica after the decline of bananas calls to mind the words of Trouillot's student, Yarimar Bonilla. Guided by her research on the neighboring island and French overseas department of Guadeloupe, Bonilla assesses the "contemporary political horizon [as] one characterized by a profound disenchantment with the modernist projects of decolonization, postcolonial sovereignty, and national revolution" (2015: 4). The caution issued by her mentor nearly three decades earlier anticipates the Caribbean's political present. When development programs seek desperately to attract foreign capital to the region and usher erstwhile peasants into waged work, they fall victim to the misguided assumption that a transition from peasant to proletarian livelihoods is indicative of progress.

---

12. The World Bank, "Personal remittances, received (current US$) – Dominica," https://data.worldbank.org/indicator/BX.TRF.PWKR.CD.DT?locations=DM. Accessed March 11, 2024.

On the contrary, the (Arthur) Lewis development model of "industrialization by invitation" that recruits multinational capital with the favorable conditions of tax holidays, currency devaluations, and low-wage workers has not absorbed those made redundant by the withdrawal of European markets for Caribbean bananas. Instead, they have joined the ranks of what Trouillot called the "lumpen peasantry," in which peasant livelihoods give way to unemployment, illicit economies, and the necessity to migrate in lockstep with a global reserve army of labor. In this respect, the decline of the Dominican peasantry reverberates in the countryside of Jamaica and the rural provinces of Haiti, where displaced small farmers descend on the urban centers of Kingston and Port-au-Prince. Where previously Trouillot reported that Dominican peasants weathered market crises with the assurance that "I can always eat my fig," unemployed urban dwellers do not enjoy this buffer against the perils of hunger.

After the failure of free market capitalism in the Caribbean, can the peasantry reconstitute itself? The conditions are not favorable. Decades of movement from the country to the city have severed generational cultivation practices and agricultural knowledge. To revive these practices would require a concerted, perhaps even evangelical effort to harness the practical knowledge carried forth by a resilient few. The growing intensity and frequency of climate disasters (including the devastation of Dominica by Hurricane Dean in 2007 and Hurricane Maria in 2017) are harsh reminders that no single Caribbean territory can embark on this journey alone.

The anthropologist Adom Philogene Heron is circumspect in his ethnographic account of Dominica after Hurricane Maria. This Category 5 storm ravaged the remaining smallholdings and provision plots on the island, exacerbating the food crisis triggered by a reliance on imports and prohibitive costs of foodstuffs for the majority of Dominicans who lived "hand to mouth" before the hurricane (Heron 2018: 123). In his view, the disappearance of the green fig (cooking banana) from local markets served as a visual reminder of the fury Hurricane Maria had wrought. But in this moment of despair, the green fig also surfaced as an icon of Dominican persistence in the wake of climate devastation. As Heron muses, "during my last week on the island, I recall an aunt's excited description of a man striding through the Roseau market proudly holding a stem of green bananas on his head: 'carrying that like a trophy, *wii*!'" (2018: 123). In a moment of uncertainty, perhaps the strongest argument in favor of the course of peasant-led development prescribed by Trouillot is the recognition that all alternative paths have been exhausted. To revise Trouillot with the help of Heron, the spark of a *re-reconstituted* peasantry will have to be lit by ordinary Caribbean people themselves. But now that banana day done, what will contribute to this awareness of the peasant labor process as a national tradition?

Banana Wars, Then as Farce

To read *Peasants and Capital* after the rise and fall of bananas in Dominica invites us to meditate on their possible renaissance. What are the futures of bananas and other staple crops in the Dominican countryside? Can the peasant labor process be reanimated toward novel programs of food sovereignty and direct democratic governance in the Caribbean?

Among the obstacles to this renaissance lies the commodity form of the banana itself. For metropolitan consumers, the banana is a quintessential fetishized commodity. As Trouillot observed in an unpublished paper delivered several years after the release of *Peasants and Capital*, fruit multinationals such as Chiquita labored to preserve the fetish of the banana as a tropical object of displaced metropolitan desire.[13] Much like the fictional corporate mascot of Chiquita Banana that played on sexualized tropes of the feminine body and the tropical alterity, Trouillot observes:

> We could note that Chiquita Brands has recently spent an inordinate amount of money to explore the U.S. housewife's preference for 7-inch long bananas. Corporate executives, mostly males, had previously assumed that "the bigger the better." Most bananas sold in the U.S. are about nine inch [*sic*] long. Apparently, the nine-inch preference was just an assumption; and Chiquita is now launching a campaign aiming at marketing the 7-inch long Chiquita-Junior. (Trouillot n.d.b)

---

13. As John Soluri observes in his historical ethnography of bananas in Honduras, "At the heart of the [United Fruit Company] campaign was an effort to inculcate consumers with the idea that not all bananas were the same. The Chiquita and Cabana brand names tried to re-define what consumers considered to be a quality banana by emphasizing features such as bunch symmetry, the fullness of individual bananas, and blemish-free peels that ripened uniformly" (Soluri 2005: 187).

Trouillot is alert to the sexual innuendo at play in this peculiar intersection of corporate marketing and plant genetics. But the banana is not overdetermined by its fetishized form. Bananas, when ripe, are sweet.[14] They are tasty and nutritious. Moreover, the predominant mode of consumption by metropolitan consumers encounters the banana as ready-at-hand. It can be peeled and consumed without additional cooking or preparation.

This combination of consumerist desire and gastronomic delight unexpectedly placed the banana at the center of social media debates over divergent visions of North Atlantic socialism. In July 2023, bananas inflamed debates on social media between "pro-growth" and "de-growth" models of socialist transformation. On Twitter, a modest claim by the critic Malcolm Harris that a socialist economy may mean "fewer bananas for American workers" prompted exasperated responses from online leftists, including "What are they going to do after expropriating Chiquita?"[15] Aside from the subtler dimensions of the disagreement between proponents of eco-modernism and de-growth, the preoccupation with the corporate form of Chiquita reveals an insidious perspective in which bananas are only intelligible as market commodities (and stores of exchange-value) and not as household provisions. While eco-modernists cheered the hypothetical expropriation of Chiquita to unmoor the banana from the dictates of multinational cartels, they shuddered at the suggestion that this could interrupt their enjoyment of exotic fruits.

Bananas in this vision of socialism are only significant when valorized *as* capital, but not when they are incorporated into a homegrown tradition of communal foodways. *Peasants and Capital*, conversely, asks us to engage Dominican peasants not simply as the laboring foundation of a North Atlantic socialism but as architects of a radical political horizon all their own. In the social media "banana wars" of 2023, the concept of the unripe "cooking banana" as a staple provision rather than a sweet indulgence remained unintelligible to the majority of its participants. Just as Dominican households put bananas to use in ways unforeseen by British colonial reformers, the socialist reformers of the

14. On the concept of sweetness and the commodity form, see Mintz 1985.

15. Malcolm Harris (@BigMeanInternet), "That means fewer bananas for American workers," X, July 17, 2023, https://x.com/BigMeanInternet/status/1681030410552197126?s=20; Guy Arizona (@guyofaz), "What are they going to do after," X, July 18, 2023, https://x.com/guyofaz/status/1681391135888146432?s=20.

twenty-first century could only behold the banana in its fetishized form. By extension, they could only imagine a socialist society founded on the equitable redistribution of tropical commodities to metropolitan palates rather than the cultivation and cooking practices of a Caribbean peasantry.

In their diagnosis of this Twitter firestorm, Anselm Kizza-Besigye (2023) reads this social media skirmish as a psychoanalytic drama motivated less by a genuine attachment to bananas as a feature of North Atlantic diets than an "anxiety around … losing the right to enjoy the products of capitalist exploitation from the periphery." This remains an unresolved drama in debates over the political future of the so-called metropole and periphery. Kizza-Besigye embodies the voice of a younger generation of intellectuals who have come of age after the dismantling of peasant livelihoods in ACP countries. Writing from the perspective of Uganda, Kizza-Besigye makes the stakes of their intervention plain: "If Ugandans have a social safety net, it is woven from banana fibers, and if there is a clear path to socialism, it will be lined with banana leaves." Trouillot would certainly concur.

Banana Day Done?

Today, Trouillot is revered as an anthropological theorist *par excellence*. He is celebrated for his musings on archives and historicity, colonialism and the culture concept, anthropology and the "savage slot." Lost in our celebrations, though, are the ordinary grounds from which this critique of the discipline took shape. In Dominica, Trouillot encountered a seemingly isolated corner of the world system that could only be understood through an inquiry into the colonial history of the West and a detour into the world of the multinational corporation. The turn to multisited ethnography (and with it the study of commodity chains, shipping and logistics infrastructures, and transnational migrant circuits) finds a crucial antecedent in the methodological toolkit developed by Trouillot for *Peasants and Capital*. Despite predating George Marcus's titular essay on the method of "multi-sited ethnography" (Marcus 1995) by more than a half decade, Trouillot is rarely credited as one of the progenitors of this approach. Nor is Trouillot cited by Marcus.

I rehearse this not only to declare that Trouillot arrived at this before Marcus, but to assess why and how his novel historical anthropology of the world system did not persist beyond the publication of *Peasants and*

Capital. If anything, the dictates of research funding in the social sciences have pushed anthropology toward a vulgar empiricism and fetish of the ethnographic present that Trouillot cautions against. An approach of this sort is ill-suited to the study of the Caribbean. The story of Dominica can hardly be told through a facile recourse to a Geertzian "native's point of view" (Geertz 1974). Dominica is not unchanging or monolithic. The cultures of the peasantry are intimately tied to transformations in the metropole and the arbitrary designs of colonial administrators. But they also represent the desires of Caribbean people to construct worlds that run contrary to these designs. Culture flourishes on the edges of the world economy.

In *Peasants and Capital*, Trouillot introduces his hallmark critique of ethnography that would resurface in his collection of essays, *Global Transformations* (2003). Troubling the disciplinary attachment to an "'ethnographic trinity' (one observer, one time, one place)" (Trouillot [1988] 2025: 21), he constructs a method befitting of the world Dominican peasants inhabit and make anew. Although many champion Trouillot as an anthropological theorist rather than ethnographer, his critique of a blinkered ethnographic presentism does not lay waste to long-term fieldwork as a methodological virtue. His concern is not with a native's point of view as the foundation of the ethnographic imagination, however. Instead, Trouillot deploys the "microlevel" analysis of ethnography to pursue an answer to the question: "Is there life beyond neocolonialism?" ([1988] 2025: 212).

Trouillot counters the chauvinism of those Marxist and world systems theorists who cannot see Dominica (or the Caribbean) beyond its domination by capital. To practice ethnography is to insist that motion does exist in the system, life can persist beyond neocolonialism, and the Caribbean is more than the vestigial remains of plantation capital condemned to a future of arrested development and climate extinction. The proliferation of what Sherry Ortner calls "dark anthropology"—accounts that emphasize the "harsh and brutal dimensions of human experience"—appear to be afflicted by the same pessimism that Trouillot strains against (Ortner 2016: 49). In truth, the crisis of Dominica after bananas resonates with the crises confronted elsewhere by climate refugees, migrant workers, and urban underclasses. Is there life beyond the bleak conditions of the present?

Dominican writer and critic Schuyler Esprit impresses upon us the necessity of forging lives beyond the present conjuncture in the Caribbean. We cannot afford to regard economic abandonment or climate extinction as a *fait accompli*. In an account that combines memoir with archival documents and ethnography with a Caribbean literary tradition, Esprit (2021) invokes her grandparents' generation as a paragon of the world that bananas made in Dominica, not simply a boom in agricultural exports but "a golden age of community accountability and sustainable living." If the conditions imposed by the WTO caused the banana children that followed this generation to seek opportunities elsewhere in tourism, service, and migration, then perhaps it is the banana children's children, like Esprit, who are best positioned to broker a revival.

Esprit channels the Bajan historian and poet Kamau Braithwaite in her insistence that we break from a vision of temporal progress that projects waged work and capital as the domain of futurity and peasant agriculture as a relic of the Caribbean past. Writing in the wake of Hurricane Maria, Esprit inverts this plot of pasts and futures when she suggests that the force of Maria and other climate disasters compels us to "move with and toward prior knowledges when the winds (literally) move us." Indeed, future prosperity may lie in a turn ostensibly backward toward the ideals of community accountability and sustainable cultivation. Just as Trouillot expressed skepticism toward historical materialist stages of development, this revival of prior knowledges cannot be romantic or absolute. Preferential markets for Caribbean bananas are unlikely to return. This sober reality demands that we imagine a political future for Dominica that is neither resigned to its inevitable subsumption by metropolitan capital nor quixotic toward small farmers as a remedy for the crises of climate and capital alike. In our recognition of peasant persistence in Dominica, though, we may dare to imagine a future beyond neocolonialism for the Caribbean and its fellow ACP countries.

Today, peasants are troubled by free markets, land grabs, paramilitaries, and state violence. But peasants do persist in smaller numbers. This calls into question their disappearance from the Caribbean public and intellectual spheres. Trouillot insists that even as they are displaced and deprived of their means of metabolic and household reproduction, the lumpen peasantry cannot simply be sacrificed at the altar of millennial capital and its netherworld of urban slums.[16] The danger of permitting

16. As Alyssa Paredes perceptively concludes from her fieldwork in the Philippines's Cotabo Province, "With industrial plantations in the Philippines and elsewhere purportedly beyond salvation, the ambit of political

Peasants and Capital to fall out of print lies in our willingness to permit the peasantries of today to fall out of our political consciousness. The pitfalls of structural adjustment programs aimed at the transition of peasant cultivators into proletarian workers have pointed many toward a revival of the agrarian question for a new century. This revival has sparked new generations of political actors who consider the peasant labor process vital to socialist transformations at the so-called peripheries of a capitalist world system (see Ajl 2021).

Trouillot's ethnography demonstrates that this unsettling of pasts and futures (and skepticism toward commonsense notions of development and progress) does not need to be dictated by intellectuals or experts. This philosophy is already immanent among cultivators themselves. Refusing to seek answers in the imagination of planners and consultants (the contemporary analogs to the nineteenth-century colonial administrators) Trouillot insists that we evangelize the tradition of Caribbean peasants to fashion lives that are not overdetermined by climate crisis or economies of abandonment. The disappearance of *Peasants and Capital* from print is symptomatic of the abandonment of the Dominican peasantry by multinational brokers and a Caribbean political class. It is symptomatic, too, of the currency (in the form of academic grants and professional appointments) afforded to sentimental accounts of subaltern brutality and wretchedness.[17] The republication of *Peasants and Capital*, then, is an occasion to reassess the past and future of Caribbean peasantries as inextricable from the pasts and futures of anthropology. If anthropology is to have a life beyond the present, it must insist that the Dominican peasantry and its compatriots on the peripheries of

---

possibility has only narrowed. The most utopic arguments imagine a post-plantation future, where industrial agriculture is brought down by incurable pathogens like FOC and gives way to other, more relational modes of living. However, in plantation zones around the world, it is apparent to local residents and ethnographers alike that where these zones are already in place, they are 'there to stay'" (Paredes 2023: 856). Indeed, any desire for peasant resurgence cannot be staked to an abstract utopianism but must necessarily engage scientists and collaborators alongside the designs of peasants themselves.

17. For a critique of ethnographic sentimentalism in contemporary anthropology, see Jobson 2020.

capital in the twenty-first century have a future beyond neocolonialism, too.[18]

References

Agard-Jones, Vanessa. 2013. "Bodies in the System." *Small Axe* 17 (3): 182–92.

Ajl, Max. 2021. "Does the Arab Region Have an Agrarian Question?" *Journal of Peasant Studies* 48 (5): 955–83.

Baker, Jessica Swanston. 2024. *Island Time: Speed and the Archipelago from St. Kitts and Nevis*. Chicago: University of Chicago Press.

Bonilla, Yarimar. 2015. *Non-Sovereign Futures: French Caribbean Politics in the Wake of Disenchantment*. Chicago: University of Chicago Press.

———. 2021. "Remembering the Songwriter: The Life and Legacies of Michel-Rolph Trouillot." In *Trouillot Remixed: The Michel-Rolph Trouillot Reader*, edited by Yarimar Bonilla, Greg Beckett, and Mayanthi Fernando, 163–72. Durham, NC: Duke University Press.

Bonilla, Yarimar, Greg Beckett, and Mayanthi Fernando, eds. 2021. *Trouillot Remixed: The Michel-Rolph Trouillot Reader*. Durham, NC: Duke University Press.

Crosson, J. Brent. 2014. "Own People: Race, 'Altered Solidarities,' and the Limits of Culture in Trinidad." *Small Axe* 18 (3): 18–34.

Esprit, Schuyler. 2021. "Heartland: A Love Letter to Fruit and Family|An almanac for Caribbean futures." *ArcGIS StoryMaps*, June 17, 2021. https://storymaps.arcgis.com/stories/d7e34a74695c4b54a55742e9e2d-5bf93. Accessed March 18, 2024.

Freeman, Carla. 2000. *High Tech and High Heels in the Global Economy: Women, Work, and Pink-Collar Identities in the Caribbean*. Durham, NC: Duke University Press.

Geertz, Clifford. 1974. "'From the Native's Point of View': On the Nature of Anthropological Understanding." *Bulletin of the American Academy of Arts and Sciences* 28 (1): 26–45.

Heron, Adom Philogene. 2018. "Surviving Maria from Dominica: Memory, Displacement and Bittersweet Beginnings." *Transforming Anthropology* 26 (2): 118–35.

18. For an elaboration of Trouillot's concept of Caribbean creolization as "culture on the edges," see Trouillot 2021c.

IICA (Inter-American Institute for Cooperation on Agriculture). 2007. *IICA's Contributions to Agriculture and the Development of Rural Communities in the Caribbean Region.* San Jose, Costa Rica: IICA.

IOM (International Organization for Migration) 2023. *Data Report: Trends in Caribbean Migration and Mobility.* San Jose, Costa Rica: IOM.

Jaffe, Rivke. 2024. *The Rule of Dons: Criminal Leaders and Political Authority in Urban Jamaica.* Durham, NC: Duke University Press.

Jobson, Ryan Cecil. 2020. "The Case for Letting Anthropology Burn: Sociocultural Anthropology in 2019." *American Anthropologist* 122 (2): 259–71.

———. 2023. "Facing the Flames: The Herskovitses, Trinidad, and the Anthropological Imagination." *American Ethnologist* 50 (3): 368–74.

Kivland, Chelsey L. 2020. *Street Sovereigns: Young Men and the Makeshift State in Urban Haiti.* Ithaca, NY: Cornell University Press.

Kizza-Besigye, Anselm. 2023. "Banana Republics." *Africa Is a Country*, September 11, 2023. https://africasacountry.com/2023/09/banana republics. Accessed March 11, 2024.

Lewis, Jovan Scott. 2020. *Scammer's Yard: The Crime of Black Repair in Jamaica.* Minneapolis: University of Minnesota Press.

Marcus, George E. 1995. "Ethnography in/of the World System: The Emergence of Multi-Sited Ethnography." *Annual Review of Anthropology* 24: 95–117.

Mintz, Sidney. 1985. *Sweetness and Power: The Place of Sugar in Modern History.* New York: Penguin.

Ortner, Sherry B. 2016. "Dark Anthropology and Its Others: Theory Since the Eighties." *Hau: Journal of Ethnographic Theory* 6 (1): 47–73.

Palmié, Stephan. 2013. *The Cooking of History: How Not to Study Afro-Cuban Religion.* Chicago: University of Chicago Press.

Paredes, Alyssa. 2023. "Experimental Science for the 'Bananapocalypse': Counter Politics in the Plantationocene." *Ethnos: Journal of Anthropology* 88 (4): 837–63.

Payne, Anthony. 2008. "After Bananas: The IMF and the Politics of Stabilisation and Diversification in Dominica." *Bulletin of Latin American Research* 27 (3): 317–32.

Price, Richard. 2022. *Inside/Outside: Adventures in Caribbean History and Anthropology.* Athens: University of Georgia Press.

Roseberry, William. 1988. "*Peasants and Capital: Dominica in the world economy* by Michel-Rolph Trouillot." *Nieuwe West-Indische Gids / New West Indian Guide* 62 (3/4): 165–67.

Slocum, Karla. 2006. *Free Trade and Freedom: Neoliberalism, Place, and Nation in the Caribbean*. Ann Arbor: University of Michigan Press.

Soluri, John. 2005. *Banana Cultures: Agriculture, Consumption, and Environmental Change in Honduras and the United States*. Austin: University of Texas Press.

Stocking, George W., Jr. 1995. "Delimiting Anthropology: Historical Reflections on the Boundaries of a Boundless Discipline." *Social Research* 62 (4): 933–66.

Thomas, Deborah A. 2004. *Modern Blackness: Nationalism, Globalization, and the Politics of Culture in Jamaica*. Durham, NC: Duke University Press.

———. 2011. *Exceptional Violence: Embodied Citizenship in Transnational Jamaica*. Durham, NC: Duke University Press.

Trouillot, Michel-Rolph. n.d.a. "Yeomanry and Nationhood: The Case of Dominica." Michel-Rolph Trouillot Papers, Hannah Holborn Gray Special Collections Research Center, The University of Chicago.

———. n.d.b. "Banana Wars: The Sweetness of Commodities." Michel-Rolph Trouillot Papers, Hannah Holborn Gray Special Collections Research Center, The University of Chicago.

———. 1977. *Ti difé boulé sou istoua Ayiti*. Brooklyn: Kolèksion Lakansièl.

———. (1988) 2025. *Peasants and Capital: Dominica in the World Economy*. Chicago: Hau Books. (Originally published by The Johns Hopkins University Press, Baltimore MD.)

———. 1990. *Haiti: State Against Nation, the Origins and Legacy of Duvalierism*. New York: Monthly Review Press.

———. 1995. *Silencing the Past: Power and the Production of History*. Boston: Beacon Press.

———. 2003. *Global Transformations: Anthropology and the Modern World*. New York: Palgrave Macmillan.

———. 2021a. "Anthropology and the Savage Slot: The Poetics and Politics of Otherness." In *Trouillot Remixed: The Michel-Rolph Trouillot Reader*, edited by Yarimar Bonilla, Greg Beckett, and Mayanthi Fernando, 54–84. Durham, NC: Duke University Press.

———. 2021b. "The Odd and the Ordinary: Haiti, the Caribbean, and the World." In *Trouillot Remixed: The Michel-Rolph Trouillot Reader*, edited by Yarimar Bonilla, Greg Beckett, and Mayanthi Fernando, 85–96. Durham, NC: Duke University Press.

———. 2021c. "Culture on the Edges: Creolization in the Plantation Context." In *Trouillot Remixed: The Michel-Rolph Trouillot Reader*, edited by Yarimar Bonilla, Greg Beckett, and Mayanthi Fernando, 194–214. Durham, NC: Duke University Press.

Wilson, Peter J. 1973. *Crab Antics: The Social Anthropology of English-Speaking Negro Societies of the Caribbean*. New Haven, CT: Yale University Press.

Preface and Acknowledgments

This book is about the cultivators of the Caribbean island of Dominica, the struggles that fashioned their past and the problems now shaping their future. There are many reasons for telling this story, the most important one being the near total neglect of Dominica by social scientists. Dominica is so unknown to the rest of the world that academics, journalists, or even diplomats confuse it with the Dominican Republic. This book is the first scholarly study to deal with the entire Dominican nation, past and present. Consequently, its findings are important. I hope that they will help break the silence that surrounds Dominica in particular and the Windward Islands in general.

This, indeed, is very much a Caribbean story. The Dominican experience remains unique, but it bears strong similarities to that of many neighboring territories of the Antilles and the Circum-Caribbean. The rise of post-plantation peasantries in that part of the world represents a sociohistorical phenomenon to which Western scholarship has not yet done full justice. This book tries to fill part of the lacuna. The relevance of this story goes far beyond the boundaries of the Caribbean itself, as I show in the first chapter.

This book resulted from a doctoral dissertation; in the process from proposal to thesis, and from thesis to this manuscript, I accumulated debts to many people and institutions. The Program in Atlantic History and Culture of the Johns Hopkins University funded my first summer fieldwork in Dominica, in June–August 1979. The longer fieldwork in Dominica (December 1980–December 1981) was assisted by grants both from the Inter-American Foundation and the Joint Committee on Latin America and the Caribbean of the Social Science Research

Council associated with the American Council of Learned Societies, with funds provided by the Ford Foundation, the Mellon Foundation, and the National Endowment for the Humanities. The fieldwork in England (January–May 1982) was assisted by a grant from the Inter-American Foundation. I wish to extend personal regards to Elizabeth Veatch, of the Inter-American Foundation: she was a most helpful fellowship officer. The Department of Extra-Mural Studies of the University of the West Indies, and its director, Professor Rex Nettleford, graciously extended institutional affiliation for my 1980–81 stay in Dominica. The Duke University Research Council provided support for the analysis of the data in chapter 8.

Write-up support for different versions of the manuscript came mainly from the Social Science Research Council, and the Department of Anthropology at Duke University. I did the final revisions during my residence at the National Humanities Center. I thank all three institutions, the Ford Foundation, which funded my fellowship at the National Humanities Center, and Debbie Benton Moore who typed the final version.

Many individuals helped during a process that lasted seven years. I am grateful to Hubert Charles, Roland Dejean, Edison C. James, Atherton Martin, Michael Murphy, Cornelia Williams, and Bernard Wiltshire, all from Dominica, for their assistance during my fieldwork. I also thank James Allister, Walston Allister, Angus Allord, Jacob Bony, Kent Brown, Frank Dunstan, Lincoln Robin, Andrew Shaw, and Kenneth Williams, all from Wesley. The contributions of the late Ernestine Allister and those of Agnes Allister, Roselyn Farrell, and Valda Hyppolite prevented some of the pitfalls of an exclusively male perspective. Leslie Africa and Osborne Richards provided an indigenous historical viewpoint that spanned four generations. Cecil Georges and the late Fred Henry were valuable field assistants. Fred impressed me with his knowledge of local and national history and prevented many errors of interpretation. With his death, I lost one of my most respected critics.

The field conferences of the Inter-American Foundation and exchanges with graduate students and faculty at the Johns Hopkins University and at Duke University also informed this book. David William Cohen, Christopher Chase-Dunn, Richard G. Fox, Ashraf Ghani, Sally Price, Carol A. Smith, Patricia Torres, Ronald Walters, and Brackette Williams commented on parts of the manuscript. Professor Martin Bronfenbrenner failed twice to convince me that the analysis in part 2 could be couched in terms of traditional economics. I thank him for trying so hard. Sidney W. Mintz and Richard Price, as teachers, as colleagues, and as friends, deserve special thanks. Professor Mintz was a demanding thesis director, yet one who allowed me to pursue my own intellectual development.

I saved for last the people about whom words will never be enough. Henderson Henry was a constant presence since 1979. This book is about his people; it is also about him. As one of the "banana children" I describe in this book, as a host, as a friend, he helped me find the difficult common ground between indigenous perception and academic discourse. The ethnographic chapters owe a lot to our long conversations in and out of the field. The entire book benefited from his comments. Czerny Brasuell also read numerous versions of the entire manuscript and kept me aware of the relevance of the issues in human terms. I cannot adequately thank her for her encouragement. Finally, Elizabeth Dunstan and her family allowed me to intrude into their lives: they were understanding companions and useful informants; their friendship remains priceless. My sons bore the burden of this book perhaps more than I did; I dedicate it to them.

PEASANTS AND CAPITAL

CHAPTER I

Peasants as Part-Economies

[Peasants] constitute part-societies with part-cultures.
—A. Kroeber, *Anthropology*

The wonder about "peasants" is their continuing existence. So many great minds have predicted their demise, so many revolutions promised their eradication. Still, they endure, however changed, however misplaced. Some social scientists, baffled by their incongruent presence, dismiss them with a stroke of the pen: peasants exist only in our imagination. What then explains the air of *déjà vu* which strikes the visitor from one village to the next in so many hills and valleys of at least three continents? One cannot reject the possibility of an illusion; but, if so, how is that illusion maintained?

Within the dominant historical perception of the West, the word *peasant* evokes a being of another age—indeed, one most typical of the Middle Ages—specimens of whom inexplicably survived the coming of civilization to the most backward areas of Europe. For most Westerners, then, peasants are just remnants of a premodern era. The presence of similar beings in Asia, Africa, and Latin America is integrated in that linear vision by the implication that these societies are still going through their equivalent of the "dark" ages.

To be sure, such linear vision is Eurocentric; yet ethnocentrism does not, by itself, invalidate that, indeed, peasants and peasantries present a puzzle to the modern world. The problem lies in the blatant contradiction between, on the one hand, the similarities among so-called peasants of all ages—however defined—and, on the other, the no less obvious trends of the world in which we live. Forms of production and commerce, political machines, ways of thinking and modes of daily behavior associated with capitalism over the past century and a half have now reached most portions of the globe. Some observers even suggest that this expansion is so systematic (despite the polarization it fosters) that one should approach the world as a capitalist network of dependencies, indeed, as a global system (Frank 1967; Wallerstein 1974). Such a perspective facilitates a holistic vision of contemporary world trends, but it also increases the immediate puzzle that the very existence of peasantries constitute. Why are peasants surviving? Is it only because they "fit in" the world? But if so, how? And if so, are all peasants integrated in their society and in the world at large in the exact same manner? Moreover, is it even legitimate to talk about peasants on a world scale? Is the word anything but a descriptive category within a Euro-American folk view? Given the context in which these questions emerged in the 1960s, and the rapidity with which they succeeded themselves in the seventies, it is not surprising that earlier definitions of peasantries—already questioned on their own terms—were challenged anew.

"Peasants" as a Category

Earlier definitional essays on the peasantry suffered from the superficial treatment of peasants by Western social scientists in the formative years of their respective disciplines (Mintz 1982). Out-of-context quotes of authorities (Kroeber 1948; Marx [1852] 1974) inevitably led to false starts; descriptive contrasts with "nonpeasants" led to imbroglios.[1] Thus, cultural definitions were, early on, greatly criticized or qualified (Mintz 1953). Likewise, doubts were raised about the validity of economic or political treatments based on Marx's historical study of France. In frustration, many writers dismissed the validity of the conceptual search (Dalton 1971; Moore 1972; Leeds 1977).

Still, the search continues; and there is hardly a recent monograph dealing with small-scale cultivators which does not add its share to the conceptual arsenal. For the sake of brevity, I note only four trends and their most important proponents. The first, which goes back to the Russian neopopulist Alexander Chayanov, views the idea of peasantry as fundamentally linked to a unit of production-consumption, the family farm, which is sole axis of a different economic structure (Chayanov 1966; Kerblay 1967, 1971; Thorner 1971; Harrison 1977). A second trend, best exemplified by the earlier work of T. Shanin (1971a, 1971b, 1972, 1973), tried rather to produce composite sketches of the peasantry, aimed at formulating a cross-cultural typification. Third, recycling Kroeber's idea of the peasantry as part-culture, others—most often anthropologists (e.g., Redfield 1956)—kept insisting on the originality of the peasantry as a distinct cultural tradition. I find the fourth trend most interesting despite its lacunae.[2]

As early as 1955, Eric Wolf proposed a reorientation of the theoretical search from analyses of contents to analyses of structures with the historically derived economic and sociopolitical relationships such structures included (1955: 452, 455). A little more than a decade later (1966), he underlined brilliantly the major empirical features to be accounted for by such a conceptualization. Unfortunately, Wolf did not combine his numerous breakthroughs; hence he avoided his most important (even though implicit) question: at what level of the socioeconomic structure can we conceptualize peasantries? A more explicit approach would have made clear that we must start not with glossarial definitions of the peasant "being," but with whatever process or processes that we can momentarily suspend, as it were, to discover the mechanisms of their "becoming."[3]

More recently, the debate over definitions of peasantries was rephrased in terms reminiscent of Wolf's (1955) initial question. Yet, in part because of the "discovery" in Western Europe, in the United States, and in India of Marx's *Grundrisse* (1973) and "Resultate" (Marx 1971, 1976), in part because of the widespread impact of Althusser and his associates' *Lire le Capital* (Althusser et al. 1973), that revival, in the seventies, was marked by an unnecessary intransigence about terminology.[4] The question as to what level of the socioeconomic structure best allows us to group peasantries was often answered a priori: either it is at the mode of production level, or it loses its significance. Dogmatism and empiricism ultimately produced similar responses, equally avoiding some of the complexities of the peasant question.[5]

The Peasant Labor Process

One of the ironies of empiricism is no doubt the way in which it can mask the obvious. Many conceptualizations of the peasantry seem to have failed not so much because they missed one or another factor among a probable set of empirical features, but rather because of the authors' conviction that they had to build a composite image that would fully and equally mirror all past, present, and future peasants, even if in so doing it would necessarily be equally removed from millions of real people. The goal here is more modest, and the epistemological assumptions much different. A conceptualization does not require a typification, let alone a typology. If the object of study is active—and I assume that human beings are—we can identify it through its performance in a manner akin to that of a physicist delineating a magnetic field or a biologist isolating a virus (Bhaskar 1979). Such a strategy more easily brings out the commonalities amid the field of differences that demarcate historical agents. Thus, on the one hand, we can agree with Mintz (1973), Bernstein (1977), or Harriss (1982) that the word *peasantry* is used quite too often to imply a homogenous people; but, on the other hand, we may not want to reject the idea that there is indeed an amalgam of similarities that practical knowledge or common sense registers inconsonantly.

The suggestion here is that most of the people usually covered at the first level of empirical categorization under the term *peasant* do indeed share a practice that remains their most obvious commonality; and that there is a working concept in the critical literature on political economy which could serve to isolate this practice. I try to elaborate on this concept, mindful that we are moving away from an essential peasant "being," but getting closer to a set of determinations of which that practice is the nexus, a *sine qua non* moment of their becoming.

The term *labor process* can first be grasped as a generalized notion that encompasses all human activity destined to produce useful objects (use-values). At such a level of generalization, the elementary factors of the labor process are human activity, that is, work itself, the object on which that work is performed, and the instruments used for this performance (Marx [1867] 1967, 1: 178). "The labor process, resolved as above in its elementary factors . . . is the necessary condition for effecting exchange of matter between Man and Nature; it is the everlasting Nature-imposed condition of human existence, and therefore is independent of every social phase of that existence, or rather, is common to every phase of it" (Marx 1967: 183–84).

But the universal necessity of organizing production only enhances the diversity of the actual practices which fulfill the universal need. If all human beings produce, they do not do so in the same manner, and the empirical conditions under which they produce encapsulate as many labor processes as we can distinguish specific types of work organization. Thus, we can speak of different labor processes, not only because we can empirically determine the factors involved in the production of one individual item but also because we can conceive of particular organizations of labor which recur with structural consistency. Often, indeed, the material and social conditions under which human labor is exerted are such that the processes they delineate constitute, through time, a social ensemble, regularly grouping specific laborers and means of work (Bettelheim 1976: 93–94).

Defined as such, a labor process implies specific instruments of work, regularly deployed on a particular object, in a particular unit of production, with a particular organization of the labor force, toward the production of particular products. We can apply the concept of different organizations of labor which historically reproduced themselves in different units of production, and identify, say, a manufactural labor process, a plantation labor process, or a peasant labor process. Tentatively then, we can define a peasant labor process as an institutionalized process through which a household performs agricultural labor on a unit over which it exerts a form of control that excludes similar groups, with instruments of work which it also controls in an exclusive manner and which generally represent less of an input than the labor itself.

The advantage of such a working definition is twofold. First, we isolate as much as possible the specific combination of productive forces which characterizes peasant units of production of different times and places. Second, and more important, we can also explore more systematically the various contexts within which this arrangement occurs without making an ideal peasant unit of production the fundamental category of our analysis. We could, ideally, study this arrangement in terms of its own laws of motion; but in actual historical analyses, we can also account for different social mixes. Indeed, we can look at situations in which an independent peasant unit of production does not exist as such but in which a peasant labor process occurs, say, on the margins of a plantation. Since we have not idealized a type, or even a role, we can more easily study different degrees of engagement in that labor process without having to shift definitions or build a never-ending list of universal subtypes. We can look at unfree people, migrants, wage earners, fishermen, and so on, partly engaged in that process for however short a time and under different economic umbrellas or systems.

Indeed, the major advantage of the concept of a peasant labor process set forth here consists in its being one with modest applications, one that, by definition, does not exhaust the conceptualization built around it, and necessarily calls attention to the larger socioeconomic and political networks in which are embedded the units it isolates. Yet, before giving full attention to that embedding, we can already sketch some of the social tendencies the work arrangement itself is likely to nurture.

The fundamental feature of the peasant work process is the overlap of the unit of production with a unit of consumption, an overlap that emphasizes the paramount importance of the domestic group for all people engaged in that type of work. The priority of living labor over labor embodied in the tools also reinforces the already crucial role of the domestic group. Thus we can suggest a tendency for all units engaged in that process to achieve, maintain, or restore a proper balance between the needs of the domestic group as a productive team and its consumption needs. Types of peasant families likely vary, at least in part, according to the contextual modalities of achieving that balance (Wolf 1966). Household composition often reflects a need for additional security by taking the form of variably organized extended families (Shenton and Lennihan 1981).

The paramount importance of the domestic group as a productive and consuming team and the preeminence of living labor over labor congealed or crystallized in technology suggest a complementary tendency to maintain and reinforce solidarity among the members. Conflicts do arise at times, threatening the fragile balance between production and consumption. So do sudden environmental changes, decisive in part because of the low input of technology. The inherent vulnerability of the production/consumption unit thus calls for insurance that can be normative as well as economic. Kinship, alliance, and patronage ties may, for instance, provide additional use-values or money when consumption levels cannot be maintained or extra labor when production falls. But they may also act to reinforce the cohesion of the domestic group by providing forums in which internal conflicts can be aired and defused. Finally, a relatively firm set of rules and obligations and their continuous reinforcement are likely to reduce, if not the chance of conflict, at least the ways in which particular conflicts can be solved.

A second general set of tendencies can be derived from the manifold importance of land in peasant activities. All human actions require portions of the surface of the earth as their spatial base; what distinguishes the peasant labor process is, first, its agricultural character. That seems obvious; but it is less obvious that, as a consequence, land is both object and instrument of labor in addition to being the place of work. Second, the preeminence of living labor enhances the importance of land among the instruments of production. That importance strongly differentiates, for instance, the peasant techniques from those of the capitalist farmer who generally relies much more on the dead labor embodied in tools. Third, the overlap between the production and consumption domains implies that the domestic group shares discrete portions of the earth's surface in both types of activities, even when the field is spatially distinguishable from the dwelling place. Ideally, in the peasant unit of production, the family that works together stays together. Land thus stands as a social identifier of those who participate in the work process and share the same dwelling area.

To be sure, many of the traits sketched here—and others that could be derived from the factors inherent in the work process—have been previously drawn in various forms in the literature on peasantries. Chayanov (1966, 1967), Redfield (1956), and Wolf (1966) have emphasized in various ways the production/consumption balance, the importance of land, the role of the domestic group, and the inherent vulnerability of the unit. The point here is not to claim any major empirical discoveries, but to suggest, on the one hand, that many of the sociocultural commonalities derive their impetus from the common work process and, on the other, that their specific modes of actualization vary according to the degrees and forms of engagement of a family in the labor process.

Thus, the disagreement with the marginalist or neopopulist approaches rests on our contention that no labor process can fully account for the social ensembles in which the units of production are embedded, that no society is a mere addition of enterprises. Likewise, this conceptualization differs from the moral economists' approach (e.g., Scott 1976) by emphasizing the practical basis of peasant behavior. Typically peasant motivations are not to be found in any pristine form in the real world, and can even be reversed under certain conditions. Thus, rather than claiming that the peasant "aims" at subsistence (Wolf 1955: 454) or "maximizes survival" (Wharton 1971: 70), we can suggest that the relative importance of living labor gives rise to a tendency to secure the reproduction of the domestic group before any expansion or renewal of the instruments of work. The argument is not simply one of terminology: in certain cases, a peasant family may well use the wages of one of its members to face its reproductive needs. With equal income, a capitalist farming family may very well cut down on "subsistence" as the only means of acquiring new inputs.

Durrenberg and Tannenbaum (1979: 59) correctly reassessed the Chayanov thesis on the production-consumption balance: "It is not the labor-consumer balance which determines the level of production. Instead, it is the intersection of the drudgery and utility curves. The utility curve varies with the consumer-worker ratio, cost of equipment, capital investment, cost of rented land, etc." The contention here is exactly that differences in the role of capital investment and cost of equipment as factors of the utility curve demarcate the peasant and the capitalist farmer at the level of the unit of production. These differences, in turn, suggest markedly distinct perceptions of the worker within each unit, hence different perceptions of the household of which he or she is a member.

Still, we cannot derive from the laws of motion of the labor process itself any peasant culture or tradition (Redfield 1960) that would recur, *mutatis mutandis*, in all peasant communities where units of the kind described here abound. As noted before, the concept of a peasant labor process, is, by itself, one of limited range; but its very limitations should allow us greater flexibility in historical analyses—a point to which I will return. What needs to be emphasized now is the manner in which those same limitations help us clarify the puzzle presented by the continuing existence of peasantries in a world economy dominated by capitalism.

Having proposed that the most basic commonalities among peasants are rooted in a particular labor process, we can, indeed, rephrase the question of a coexistence of peasantries and capitalism in more appropriate terms. How does that work process coexist with capitalism? By what mechanisms is it tied to capital?

To understand the implications of the question better, we need to emphasize that capital itself is not a thing, but a social relation of production (Marx 1976: 1982). That is, what distinguishes capitalism as a socioeconomic system is, essentially, a process of valorization by which the producer, through his or her labor, adds a value to a product that will eventually be reclaimed by the capitalist when this product, as a commodity, enters the sphere of circulation for which it was intended. Thus, the solution of the puzzle offered by the coexistence of peasants and capital requires not only that we abandon the Eurocentric view of peasants as atavisms but also that we qualify the common perception of capital as an accumulation of instruments and techniques. This done, the contradiction between tradition and modernity which has blurred our understanding of that coexistence disappears. We are dealing with a specific type of work and a larger ensemble of social relations characterized by the production and extraction of value; the challenge is to articulate those two levels. A prerequisite, then, is a delineation of the limits of the labor process itself.

The concept of a peasant labor process does not exhaust the conceptualization of peasantries built around it since it forcibly inherits some of the limits of the generalized notion. Marx (1967, 1: 184) called attention to these limits: "As the taste of the porridge does not tell you who grew the oats, no more does this simple labor process tell you of itself what are *the social conditions under which it is taking place*" (emphasis added). Both Pouillon (1976: 81) and Bettelheim (1976: 97) rightly insist that productive forces by themselves cannot generate specific relations of production. Dallemagne (1978: 94) emphasizes the determinant impact of social relations in the society at large on the organization of work: the labor process is only "the locus, not the cause of the exploitation." Wolf (1978) neatly distinguishes relations of work and social relations of production.

Thus, we should firmly reject M. Harrison's (1977: 322) contention that "the mode of production can be defined firstly as the labour process—forces of production, the relationship between the worker and the owner of the means of production, that between the worker and the product." This is both too much and too little. The labor process generates relations of work, of which the structural elements can be abstracted from the observation of daily activities within the unit of production. Yet such activities never fully reveal the nature of the surrounding context within which the unit functions. Thus, the labor process, as such, does not encapsulate the relations of production (Wolf 1978). In sharp contradistinction, the mode of production is not a simple abstraction of empirical realities. Its theoretical determination requires an analysis of relations involving ownership, work activities, surplus, and distribution. Observation of the labor process can lead us to formulate better questions about the social context within which labor is deployed; it cannot replace the examination of that context.

It appears then that a conceptualization of peasantries rooted in the concept of a peasant labor process forces us from the start to emphasize the structural relationships between peasants and the larger order to which Wolf (1966) called our attention. If the fundamental similarity among peasants is indeed a labor process, we know by definition that this process itself does not determine the character of the society in which it occurs, and that the people we come to call peasant might find their commonalities integrated in very different structures. Our conceptualization implies those similarities, but already foresees those differences. Our object of study turns out to be the society at large, or better, as Wolf perceived it, the nature of the links between peasants and nonpeasants, for the peasantry remains part-society, part-culture, and, not least, part-economy.

The peasantry is part-economy, especially in its relation to capital, primarily because the work process, which encapsulates its characteristics, does not exhaust the general process of production. The question of the coexistence of peasants and capital thus turns out to be, in theoretical terms, a matter of explaining how a type of work, atypical of the capitalist process of production, can be nonetheless a functional element of capitalism. It requires further probing of the capitalist process of production itself.

The capitalist process of production is the combination of two distinct processes: the work process itself and the process of valorization, one by which all commodities become commensurable in terms of the amount of abstract labor socially necessary to produce them (Marx 1967; Salama 1982). "But the labor process itself is no more than the instrument of the valorization process" (Marx 1976: 9910). The labor process, as material transformation, creates use-values; the valorization process, as a social transformation, produces the commensurability of the commodities.

Still, in the real world, both processes may be pursued, challenged, changed, or sustained by different social groups with a distinct past and distinct aims and values. History enters here, and it is possible that in specific circumstances some form of labor—especially one that historically preceded the emergence of the process of valorization—may contribute to the accumulation of capital without taking on the form of large-scale industrial production. The production process can be called capitalist inasmuch as its tendencies are determined by valorization. Yet the laborer may not be at the mercy of the capitalist to the same extent or in the same form as a full-scale proletarian wage earner. Such is the situation one can label "the formal subsumption of labour under capital" (Marx 1976: 1021).

Formal Subsumption and Simple Commodity Production

Marx, who coined the terms and emphasized the distinction between *formal* and *real* subsumption, saw the former as part of a continuum of "transitional subforms within the framework of capitalist production," a moment in the gradual takeover by capital of modes of labor developed before the emergence of capitalist relations (Marx 1976: 1019–22). At its highest stage, formal subsumption implied the monetization of all factors of production and the empirical dispossession of workers from all means of production (Chevalier 1983). Marx writes:

> The distinctive character of the *formal* subsumption of labour under capital appears at its sharpest if we compare it to the situation in which capital is to be found in certain specific, subordinate functions, but where it has not emerged as the direct purchaser of labour and as the immediate owner of the process of production, and where in consequence it has *not yet* succeeded in becoming the dominant force, capable of determining the form of society as a whole. In India, for example, the capital of the usurer advances raw material or tools, or even both, to the immediate producer in the form of money. . . . But here we have *not yet* reached the stage of the formal subsumption of labour under capital. (Marx 1976: 1023; *emphasis in original*)

And Marx goes on to say that though formal subsumption has *not yet* emerged also in the case of the domination of a labor process by merchants' capital, "the transition is more strongly marked here than in the case of the usurer" (Marx 1976: 1023).

More recently Banaji (1977: 1376) followed the letter of Marx's text to draw a distinction between *preformal* and *formal* subsumption of labor by capital. Preformal subsumption was to be viewed as one initial step in the long transition, roughly corresponding to the cases described above in which surplus value is produced and extracted but in which the capitalist is *not yet* the immediate owner of the work process.

As Harriss (1982: 291) points out, the argument—as couched by both Marx and Banaji—is eminently teleological. We now know better than to predict the immediate demise of all noncapitalist processes of work, and Harriss is right to criticize the conclusion, so often drawn from the "disguised proletarian formula," that "capitalism does prevent the development of capitalism, but only for a while" (Harriss 1982: 293).

However, neither the teleology nor the apparent paradox that it fosters is inherent in the formula itself. The real issue here is that of the integration of a type of work, not necessarily typical of capitalism, into a process of valorization that is, itself, the cornerstone of the capitalist system. In conceptualizing this integration or in examining the various and concrete forms it can take, one need not assume that capitalism has a will that manifests itself in historically specific contexts. Capitalism does nothing in the real world, but both capitalists and workers do have an impact—and presumably, a different one—on what exactly is being produced and how. An awareness of different levels of abstraction is crucial to bypass the teleological trap.

Differentiating various levels of abstraction also affects our understanding of capitalists' control over a particular work process. For example, it is important for us to know whether or not the material fact of exchange occurs in a particular society; but the explanatory power of this fact operates at a level of abstraction different from the global concept of "commodification." Similarly, the commensurability of all factors of production (that they can all be compared in terms of abstract labor) does not require the actual measurement of such factors as expressed in their exchange values. The exchange value of a commodity is only the expression of its value, just as its price is the monetary expression of its exchange value (Dallemagne 1978: 47–62). Marx (1967, 1: 94) writes: "It is not money that renders commodities commensurable. Just the contrary. It is because all commodities, as values, are realised human labour, and therefore, commensurable, that their values can be measured by one and the same special commodity, and the latter be converted into the common measure of their values, i.e., into money."

Thus, at the level at which the formal subsumption formula best imports, the material fact of exchange has less relevance than the commensurability realized through the process of commodification. In simpler terms, a material object does not need to change hands to become marketable, to be an integral part of a system of commodities. Nor does a laborer need to be in the job market for his labor power to be commodified (Chevalier 1983: 161). Hence, we can legitimately conceive the subsumption of a peasant labor process under a capitalist process of production without the empirical prerequisites of particular forms of exchange, particular forms of jural control, and so on. Theoretically, the economic process that typifies capitalism can be conceived as including the labor process that typifies peasants.

The integration of those who live and work as peasants in the sphere of valorization proceeds mainly from the exchangeability of the factors they use (including their labor) and the items they produce. However, that exchangeability does not fully realize itself in the marketplace: peasants do not necessarily buy everything they use, nor do they sell everything they produce. More important, they do not sell directly all of their labor power, though they may engage in wage-earning activities. In short, they do not depend exclusively on exchange, even though everything they own or acquire may be exchangeable.

The limited realization of that generalized potential for exchange is nowadays the fundamental guarantee of the survival of the peasant labor process in most of the Third World. Yet it creates a particular tension between use-value and exchange value which expresses itself through what Chevalier (1982: 118–119) calls "subsistence commodities." The existence of such items whose value is not realized in the marketplace, within an economy in which the worker remains, nevertheless and fundamentally, market dependent, is one of the most important characteristics of simple commodity production. Bernstein defines simple commodity production in the following terms:

> a form of production, the logic of which is subsistence in the broad sense of the simple reproduction of the producers and the unit of production (descriptively the household). . . . The needs of simple reproduction are satisfied, at least in part, through commodity relations: on one side, the production of commodities as means of exchange to acquire elements of necessary consumption, on the other side, the incorporation of commodities in the cycle of reproduction as items of productive consumption (e.g., tools, seeds, fertilizers), and individual consumption (e.g., food, clothing, building materials, kerosene, domestic utensils). (Bernstein 1981: 7)

There are obvious similarities between the simple commodity producer who emerges from this conceptualization and many contemporary cultivators engaged in what was defined as the peasant labor process (Friedman 1978, 1980; Chevalier 1982, 1983; C. Smith 1984a, 1984b). To the extent that one can speak of the formal subsumption of simple commodity production by capital, is it necessary to speak of a peasant labor process?

It has been said again and again (e.g., Ennew et al. 1977; Friedman 1980) that a definition of the peasantry can be achieved only through empirical generalizations and, as such, cannot have, in the discourse of political economy, the conceptual value of simple commodity production. Some writers come close to the assumption that contemporary peasants can be perceived, for all purposes, just as simple commodity producers (Bernstein 1980). What has not been considered is the possibility that there might be a need for *two* concepts, even though they overlap.

To start with, and to clear a misunderstanding, though the concept of peasantry has no theoretical status in political economy, the concept of labor process has a longstanding pedigree. More important, those of us who are concerned with the actual behavior of real individuals should regard with suspicion any conceptual scheme that starts at a level at which what people actually do does not really matter. It matters to simple commodity producers that they work on the land rather than on the sea, that they produce fruits rather than hats, that they can both sleep and work in the same room or not. It matters to them and probably to the economy.

The concept of simple commodity production operates at a level of abstraction different from that of the peasant labor process. The materiality of the factors actually used by the worker and the ways in which they are put to use are less important at that level than they are in the concept of labor process. Not all petty commodity producers are peasants; not all peasants are petty commodity producers. Further, not even all smallholders who produce commodities nowadays engage in a peasant work process. The juxtaposition of market dependence, mechanization, and state intervention within many national economies has contributed to shape the labor process on many European and North American small farms in such a way that the labor process differs from that of most Third World peasantries even though the owner-workers are, by any measure, simple commodity producers (Mollard 1977).

Hence, simple commodity production may include different labor processes: fishing or artisanal labor processes, or other agricultural work processes more technologically advanced than the peasant labor process (Wolf 1955; Firth 1966; C. Smith 1984a; Mollard 1977). The categories (peasant labor process and simple commodity production) may overlap in a discussion of the specific issue of formal subsumption, but if we lump them too precipitously we risk passing over important empirical differences between peasants and, say, fishermen and artisans or handicraft producers (e.g., Friedman 1980).

A sketchy comparison of fishing and farming as they occur in the Caribbean suggests that the material nature of the work involved and the perception of that materiality by the workers themselves may result in a different division of tasks within the family, and possibly, different notions of authority and different schemes of socialization. Though the fishermen in the South of Dominica (who are simple commodity producers) might be said to be integrated in the valorization process in terms similar to those by which the banana-producing peasants of the

Northeast enter into that same process, gender inequality, for instance, takes different shapes in the two contexts.

As a rule, women do not fish even in the so-called fishing villages, but in the banana-producing areas they participate in agricultural production. Yet this participation itself entails the possibility of female oppression in the workplace (the garden) in ways unknown to the wife of a fisherman. On the other hand, the fisherman's wife is likely to feel or be treated as more "dependent" upon her husband, and may try to obtain occasional cash by working as a seamstress. Now, the banana producer, the fisherman, and indeed the seamstress herself might all be thought of as petty commodity producers. But if we are concerned, as I think we should be, with the immediate and important impact of the work process on their lives, we cannot first approach it at the high level of abstraction implied in the concept of simple commodity production.

Finally, even when the peasant labor process is formally subsumed (as simple commodity production) under capitalist relations of production, its occurrence on the land, on the surface of the earth, sets it apart from all nonagricultural tasks. This observation, of course, raises the important issue of the role of rent in the process of valorization (Rey 1973; Vergopoulos 1974, 1978; Harvey 1982; Chevalier 1983). Land is both an instrument and an object of agricultural work. Further, it is characterized by its immobility and its relative scarcity both of which color actual phenomena of jural possession or dispossession and the perception of the parties involved. In few non-Western cultures can one equate the value attached to land with any other object monetarily equivalent. In the particular case of Dominica, one cannot clearly separate the fervor with which the peasants tried to maintain their status as simple commodity producers from the occurrence of production on pieces of land, the significance of which was not just monetary. Thus, though we should allow that the formal subsumption of a peasant labor process by capital often entails certain forms of subsumption of simple commodity production, it seems more precise to maintain the "labor process" terminology when discussing cultivators of the type with which this book is concerned. "Simple commodity production" is one notch closer to the general production process, one of the forms through which those engaged in the peasant labor process often enter the circuit of valorization.

Indeed, we cannot assume that the work process that typifies the peasantry is always integrated in the process of valorization in the exact same manner. That integration occurs through the social relations of production, namely, property relations, labor relations, as well as surplus relations or relations of distribution (Cliffe 1977), which are, themselves, products of a particular historical evolution. Moreover, in any society, such evolution is neither preordained nor unidirectional. In short, though the notion of subjugation of the peasant labor process is a theoretical construct, the study of the links through which a particular group of peasants comes to be integrated in a national society or in the world economy is always historically specific. It necessitates a procedure attuned to the theory, yet amenable to the particulars that this theory highlights in every case. Such a procedure, in turn, requires at least:

1. the identification of the particular historical conditions under which the group defined first engaged in the peasant labor process and maintained that engagement;
2. a study of the degrees and forms of that engagement, as determined by the relations of productions; that is, property and labor relations, as well as surplus relations or relations of distribution (Cliffe 1977); and
3. a determination of the means and degree of integration by which that three-pronged set of relations inserts the group within a process of valorization (Dallemagne 1978: 85), that is, a process of value circulation and, ultimately, of surplus-value production and capital accumulation (Marx 1976: 985–992).

   That integration in the process of valorization might, in turn, occur in varying degrees:

   a. through the direct sale of labor power by those otherwise engaged in the peasant work process (Mintz 1974b);
   b. through the indirect sale of labor power by way of usurers' or merchants' capital (Roseberry 1976, 1983; Banaji 1977; Shenton and Lennihan 1981);
   c. through the production of commodities produced outside of the peasant labor process, such as handicrafts (Wolf 1955; Smith 1984a);
   d. through taxation (Paul 1876; Tanzi 1976; Trouillot 1986a); and
   e. through the production within the peasant unit of commodities taken over directly by foreign or national capital, or by way of a simple commodity form.

Obviously, such mechanisms are not mutually exclusive (e.g., Trouillot 1980, 1986a) and serve as criteria of differentiation only in terms of their unequal importance. The priority of some mechanisms of integration probably affects the subsequent appearance and adjustment of others. Furthermore, the last three criteria imply an evaluation of the need of "outside capital" (Wolf 1955) to production. Also, though cases (b), (d), and (e) fit the model of formal subsumption of a labor process by capital, cases (a) and (c) suggest a slightly different form of symbiosis: the worker engaged in the peasant labor process enters the process of valorization not as a peasant, but as a participant within a different labor process. In case (a), the worker participates in the valorization process mainly as a proletarian. In case (c), the worker enters into valorization as a petty commodity producer but not as a cultivator.

Again, these various forms of integration often overlap in the real world, and only empirical studies can reveal the predominant conditions under which wage labor or handicraft production coexist with the peasant labor process or the preeminence of petty commodity production as the most effective linkage between peasants and capital. But the procedure for differentiating the peasantry from other social actors—and indeed for differentiating within the peasantry itself—must be applicable to particular historical contexts, and yet retain its logical consistency.

Levels, Scales and Units

Having couched the conceptualization in admittedly tentative form, we face the question of its relevance. On what grounds can such a conceptual construct be tested and refined? What should it add to our understanding of real peasants, their apparent resilience, their coexistence with capitalism?

It seems to me that any conceptualization of peasantries must face the question of its operational relevance in three distinguishable areas. It must be operational in

1. treating historical particulars outside of feudal Europe;
2. explaining the logic of the coexistence of peasantries and capitalism; and
3. enhancing our understanding of human agency within rural groups.

The treatment of particulars outside of Europe should test the conceptualization for cross-cultural and cross-historical validity and guard against popular perceptions of peasants in the West that may have been inherited from Eurocentric notions. With such a point of departure, one may more securely move to other areas.

A cross-cultural conceptualization of peasantries must also advance our theoretical understanding of the processes that support the existence of peasants in a world economy dominated by the laws of capitalist accumulation. Does that coexistence benefit capitalists in any way? What in the laws of motion of capital and the peasant labor process account for such a durable, even if peculiar, coexistence?

In that second area of relevance, while paying continuous attention to empirical materials and historical categories, we must be aware of a major shift in our level of abstraction. The new context should accommodate historical references, yet its boundaries are not historical. We are aiming at theoretical coherence in our treatment of peasantries, but the background, if not the measure of that coherence, is nothing but the structural coherence of capitalism itself. To the extent that we can build a structural case for the subsumption of a peasant labor process by capital, we will have pierced through the logic of a peasantry's coexistence with capitalism.

Yet the exposition of that logic will not necessarily exhaust the case of any peasantry, let alone that of the peasantry as such. To stop there, at best, might imply our agreement with the point of view that peasantries are but an occasional "form" of capitalist relations. At worst, it would suggest that peasant resilience is itself necessitated by capitalism for the benefit of greater accumulation. In short, our peasants would turn out to be undifferentiated puppets of capital.

Thus, third and finally, a cross-cultural conceptualization of peasants or peasantries should allow us to return to the direct study of human agency in contemporary rural settings, the area in which the theoretical corpus, sketched against prior historical particulars and refined in terms of structural coherence becomes fully operational. But how do we capture human agency without falling into the voluntarist argument that people are, ultimately, what they want to be? It is easy to notice that social agents observed individually or in small groups manifest diverse degrees and forms of consciousness, but is a mere empirical reduction of our field of observation enough to claim the irrelevance of structural constraints? It appears as if an empirical reduction of the field gives the observer at least a better chance to flesh out human agency, but we cannot assume so. Neither can we assess the actual cost of the procedure without a more systematic appraisal of the so-called microlevel, so dear to many anthropologists.

Few historians, sociologists, economists, or anthropologists can now dismiss the global relevance of capitalist expansion, yet many more are realizing that this admission itself remains insufficient in enhancing the actual quality of field research. In light of the impact of "dependency" and "world-system" theories on the social sciences, many empirical units easily treated by one observer seem now too artificially isolated on methodological grounds. Yet, at the same time, no single project will ever account for all the empirical particulars that could enhance our theoretical grasp of the rich complexity of humankind. Courageous attempts by at least one historian (Braudel 1967–79), one sociologist (Wallerstein 1974, 1980), one economist (Frank 1978), and one anthropologist (Wolf 1982) to combine empirical exhaustiveness and theoretical unification in a single work have met with unequally qualified success and verified the dilemma.

In light of that dilemma many scholars (including, for good reasons, quite a few anthropologists) are reformulating the question of the unit of analysis (last phrased in an uncompromising form by Wallerstein [1974]) in terms of the articulation of analytical levels. The trend seems to imply a new awareness of irreducible differences between orders of processes in the world to be studied and between discursive orders (Foucault 1972) in academia itself. I take the words *macrolevel* and *microlevel* as reflective of this awareness, not because the words themselves are new, but rather because those who now use them tend to insist on the necessity of bridging domains posed as irreducible. Indeed, whether couched in the historicist tradition, in terms of "local initiative and local response" (Mintz 1977), or in terms of an internal debate among "Marxists" (Tomich 1976; McLennon 1981), many new proposals underline the relevance of articulating "macro-" and "microlevels" (M. Silverman 1979; Friedman 1980; Kahn 1980; Trouillot 1982; Vincent 1982; Verdery 1983; C. Smith 1984a, 1984b).

Such a shift should be welcome for it forces us to turn to the interpenetration of processes of various kinds and extents rather than emphasizing the essence of the units to be studied and their empirical boundaries. The history of the ethnographic trinity (one observer, one time, one place), and the rise and demise of the concept of region in geography (Claval 1982; Stoddart 1981) suggest that the stress on empirical boundaries is, at best, the combined effect of the limits imposed by the temporary form of institutionalization of a discipline and the material possibilities of any single researcher.

From that viewpoint, the use of the term *microlevel* should not rekindle fading arguments about size or complexity. "Microlevel," as I see it, does not necessarily imply low complexity or small size of an empirical field.[6] Microlevel refers, rather, to the analysis itself. It is a property of the analysis in a manner akin to that in which the cartographic notion of scale refers to the map and not to the area. As large-scale maps often treat small territories, a microlevel analysis most likely projects a small empirical field, but one should not infer a methodological exclusivity from that preferred use.[7]

What change, then, does "microlevel" imply? The qualitative leap, as I see it, is a change in the terms of the analysis itself, an opening of its objects and strategies which enables it to deal more directly with various dimensions of human agency, especially individual agency.[8] The individual enters here as a bearer of social pressures, cognizant of some of these pressures, likely ignorant of others, but always able to influence the totality. The shift to a microlevel implies the acknowledgment of the individual's capacity to contribute to the historical process; to generate, so to speak, "more history" than the history of which he or she is the product. First, the individual may seek knowledge of hitherto unrecognized pressures, or ignore pressures hitherto uncovered, and act on that basis. More important, the individual exists only in society and, regardless of motives, his or her actions, combined with other results, produce unexpected, even unpredictable new trends (Giddens 1979, 1985). Finally, and most important, the individual's verbal and nonverbal behavior generates a residual of signification independent of his or her original intentions, irreducible indeed to the actual message. That residual can be interpreted, misinterpreted, or reinterpreted by others who may or may not act upon it. From that viewpoint, the individual always contributes to history, both voluntarily and involuntarily, and the microlevel appears to be the angle from which one most appropriately highlights those individual contributions (or partial sums thereof) to the historical process.

Yet, from that viewpoint also, the microlevel is a subordinate level of analysis, one that presupposes a hierarchy of structures (Godelier 1977) or a theory of "interdominance of fields" (Gronhaug 1979) and, most certainly, a gradation of intermixed processes as well as a methodological framework to grasp their articulation. This framework need not be the same in all instances. In our own case, given the overarching relevance of the valorization process, given the primordial mode of subsumption of the peasant labor process, how do we move from the societal pressures at large to the microlevel just defined? How do we delineate in time and in space the empirical settings best attuned to a microlevel analysis?

Historical Categories and Spatial Configurations

In a stimulating article on definitions of peasantries, Mintz (1973) suggested a reorientation of peasant studies toward the production of historically derived "middle-level" categories that would flesh out the historical diversity of peasant groups within a national society or a specific peripheral area like the Caribbean. Mintz has long demonstrated his powerful insight in deriving such subgroups from the Caribbean record (1961b, 1984), but little has been done since then to enable others to further systematically such categorization or even to repeat the feat in the Caribbean or elsewhere.

The conceptualization suggested in this work corroborates Mintz's own findings and leads to the methodology necessary to generate systematically the kind of historically derived categories that he both produced and called for. The repetition of this procedure within ever-decreasing historical boundaries produces increasingly smaller subgroups likely to be more limited in both chronological and spatial terms, and thus likely to be more manageable as units in an analysis carried to the microlevel.

Indeed, the first major advantage of this procedure may be its utility for producing or verifying long-range historical categories. Agrosocial groupings such as Mintz's "early yeomen," "proto-peasants," or "reconstituted peasantries" of the Caribbean can all be differentiated, first of all, according to the conditions under which they engaged in the peasant labor process and the subsequent degree of their engagement. The procedure thus expands our chronological, spatial, and social boundaries, since we can isolate, at that first level of differentiation, groups that spanned several centuries on a multinational base, some of whom do not even fit the traditional image of the peasant. As we will see later, the slaves who worked on their provision grounds, Mintz's "proto-peasants," did not engage in the peasant labor process in the same manner or to the same extent as the postslavery "reconstituted" peasantry. Property relations particularly ensured that the slaves' gardens were only appendages of larger units of production, the plantations. Yet one could also argue that the planters' emphasis on the plantation work process may have allowed the slaves a greater control of distribution than some of their free successors. Likewise, property and surplus relations generally imposed more stringent conditions on the postslavery groups than on the early yeoman.

More interestingly, in refining the procedure, one can also produce subgroups within those long-range historical categories themselves, differentiating in more detail, according to varied mechanisms of integration. Indeed, since our first criterion rests on the historical evolution of the peasant labor process, we can always reduce that historical base, so to speak, to produce categories of a smaller range by applying the procedure to ever smaller segments of population.[9] Increasingly detailed differentiation of the peasantry (in terms of the embedding of the labor process) brings us closer to bridging the gap between local particulars and world historical forces. On the one hand, we can produce categories manageable at the microlevel but, on the other, the smaller groups so produced have been identified primarily in terms of their integration within macrolevel processes.

The continuous reduction of the empirical field, which is likely to result from the repetition of the procedure of differentiation, departs from the arbitrary isolation of a village or community, as we see in chapters 2, 9, and 10. It stems from the historical ranking of the processes under study and the application of that hierarchy to the historically particular case at hand. The empirical units resulting from that exercise may very well be the same as those that could have been picked arbitrarily or intuitively. Yet, in many cases, the village or the community may be broken down in still smaller units and, at other times, the analysis may require the expansion of the area under study so as to encompass a much larger enclave that disregards administrative boundaries. Furthermore, as I hope to demonstrate later, in chapters 9 and 10, the deliberate shifting of the empirical boundaries by the researcher, on historical, socioeconomic, or cultural grounds, may produce at times a more viable unit, even if such a unit does not match perfectly preconceived notions of what a village or, for that matter, an enclave should be.

The Relevance of a Caribbean Case

To summarize the argument, I am suggesting here that if the word *peasant*, as such may be void of analytical validity, it reflects nevertheless a range of commonalities. These commonalities are not to be found in a common peasant essence, shared by individuals of different times and places. Rather, they spark from a labor process we can conceptualize. Since this labor process appears in markedly different sociohistorical settings, an understanding of particular peoples actually engaged in that process always requires an analysis of these settings. Since this work process also appears to be antithetical to the laws of capital accumulation, an understanding of the peoples currently engaged in this process also requires a formal explanation of the ways in which their production is integrated in the capitalist world economy. If the final aim is not so much the knowledge of the process itself but the understanding of real people in the field, the analysis must move down to the levels at which we can best observe human beings in their daily reality. In short, the suggestion is for a three-pronged approach that broadly corresponds to the discursive traditions and research techniques of history, political economy, and anthropology.

Needless to say, in any actual case study, the delineation of the theoretical contexts remains only a heuristic separation: the peasantry under observation can only be perceived from those three angles simultaneously. Further, the contexts themselves overlap at different points, as do the disciplinary traditions of history, political economy, and anthropology. The division of the case material in three parts—the nation, the world, and the village—corresponding to three different units of analysis reflects these three viewpoints, but also their imbrication. Results and conclusions achieved in one area are always provisional against the background of the other two. That three-pronged approach may seem less neat at times than a one-sided view, but the peasantry that, I hope, emerges from this procedure should be able to surprise us within the boundaries defined by its own history.

Such an approach may seem overly complicated because of the layers and circumvolutions it implies. Yet it did not originate in a theoretical exercise. It stems from a desire to account for the current existence of Caribbean peasantries in a way that would make sense not only of their choices but also of the conditions under which they made or continue to make such choices. The complexity of the Caribbean record does not leave many options: one can stick to prevalent theories and qualify the case to the point of irrelevance; or one can stick to the case and amend the theory. I choose to raise the theory to the level of reality. Thus to say that the case that follows demonstrates the conceptualization would be half dishonest and half tautological: the perception of one influenced the elaboration of the other, and vice versa.

The case is that of the Commonwealth of Dominica, an independent island-nation of the Lesser Antilles, on the eastern part of the Caribbean archipelago. It shows similarities with the other Windward Islands, Saint Lucia, Grenada, and Saint Vincent, or even some of the larger islands such as Haiti and Jamaica. Though its relevance is exceptional in many regards, this uniqueness itself stems from the ways in which Caribbean reality filtered through Dominican society. Dominica, then, is very much a Caribbean case; and it is worth indicating its significance as such.

The historical record suggests that the Caribbean does not easily fit the dominant vision of peasant survival. The preconquest Carib and Arawak populations do not come close to any general or specific notion of peasantries, the way some precolonial mainland groups might. In addition, European violence reached such proportions in the Antilles that the preconquest populations were virtually wiped out before the massive introduction of African slaves. Because of the systematicity of the Amerindian genocide in the region, whatever groups we may now describe as peasants reached there after the first European colonizers. The duration of plantation slavery and the military, economic, and political control exerted over the region by Spanish, British, French, Danish, and Dutch officials, merchants, and bankers suggest that the emergence and growth of peasantries occurred there only after the region was fully incorporated within the modern world economy. Caribbean peasantries, then, are peasantries who succeeded the penetration of the Antilles by the West. They depend principally upon plants and animals brought into the region in the course of that penetration. With such notable exceptions as maize, cotton, manioc, and sweet potatoes, the flora that sustain these peasantries have come not only from other regions but from other continents altogether, after the so-called discovery of the New World. Sugarcane and coffee, of course (Deerr 1949; Trouillot 1982; Mintz 1985), but also coconuts, rice, mangoes, breadfruit, most yams, bananas, and plantains exemplify the point (Mintz 1983). Caribbean peasantries are made up of populations whose very physical presence in the territories they now occupy came as a consequence of world capitalist development: the ancestors of today's peasants crossed the Atlantic under the supervision of merchant capitalists. What we have in Dominica and the rest of the Caribbean may thus be a unique historical record of peasantries emerging socially and physically after the penetration of a peripheral area by the West, an area in which no reference can be made to a past within the past—a sort of zero-degree peasant evolution within the sphere of Euro-American capitalism.

History, thus, challenges in various degrees and from different angles more sophisticated definitional approaches to "peasants" which reproduce, in part, the dominant linear perceptions. S. Silverman (1979) rightly suggests that the notion of a peasant tradition assumes a perpetuation of cognitive and behavioral patterns such that the final object of inquiry turns out to be the disruption of such patterns by outside forces.

But in the Caribbean, "tradition" in any given sense of the word succeeded modernity: the "peasant way of life" fully blossomed only upon the ruins of the plantations, amid the remains of the developed technology and the highly stratified social structure that King Sugar had fostered. Here, the disruption is our starting point. We cannot, for instance, make the now common reference to a destruction or even disintegration of the natural economy (Rey 1973; Bradby 1975; Bernstein 1979). To be sure, the concept of disruption has been questioned elsewhere both implicitly and explicitly, on primarily theoretical grounds (Kahn 1980; Chevalier 1983); but what we face in the Caribbean, after the Amerindian genocide, is an empirical record that renders any suggestion of an indigenous adaptation to capitalism blatantly questionable.

Likewise, this record limits the theoretical schemes that we can use to approach Caribbean peasants' involvement in international trade. The sheer weight of the evidence excludes, for instance, the neo-Smithian theory of a "vent for suplus production" which suggests that otherwise static agricultural economies found avenues for expansion in the unexpected opportunities offered by European trade. According to this model, modern peasantries, as we know them, would be otherwise closed economies marginally open to capitalist world trade (Myint 1958). But the history of the British, Dutch, French, or Spanish Antilles can hardly fit in such a deliberately benign vision. Again, the empirical weight of the Amerindian genocide, of the triangular trade, of the millions of tons of coffee and sugar produced during four centuries of slavery makes it impossible to suggest that Europe provided otherwise naive natives with some "vent" through which they funneled their otherwise useless "surplus" production. Indeed, and as we shall see later, the surplus category itself needs theoretical as well as empirical reevaluation. Suffice it to say here that Caribbean colonies did not enter into international trade through the accidental discovery of new opportunities. They were created *for* trade and surplus, according to the European mercantilist design. As I put it elsewhere: "From guests to hosts, from tools to buildings, from export crops to provisions and plantation to plantation, these were cloned societies, manufactured—as it seems—overnight for the sole benefit of capital" (Trouillot 1981: 38).

Theories that address the question of the emergence and resilience of Caribbean peasantries must take into account the initial violence through which the region itself was born. The peasantization of the Caribbean might then look less like a naive response to market incentives and more like a strategic barrier against other forms of forced integration in a world dominated by trade and profit.

The variety of situations under which peasantlike behavior occurred in the Caribbean and the time span covered by such occurrences (Mintz 1974a, 1978, 1979) also seriously undermine any conceptualization based on an empirical assemblage of economic or cultural qualifiers. If our approach to real peasants presents them as tokens of an ideal type, then what of the slaves who cultivated their provision grounds and sold part of their product in local markets? Even aside from the epistemological problems raised by such an approach, the category *peasant* becomes nonoperational, not because actual analysis would then require a potentially endless list of subdivisions (peasant-slaves, peasants-proletarians, etc.), but because in that context the first half of any such binomial would still not provide a basis for comparison, having no independent roots outside of the binomial itself.

The particular history of the Caribbean also calls into question the growing tendency to couch conceptualization of peasantries in terms of a precapitalist mode (or modes) of production. To be sure, the debate continues over whether any such mode of production to which peasants belonged can or will survive capitalism. But in the Caribbean, faced with the material impossibility of establishing an empirical connection with a preconquest past, we would be forced to suggest that capitalism had generated precapitalist modes of production. Such a theoretical leap seems dubious. At the very least, it requires careful probing.

In conclusion, the Caribbean record helps us emphasize the three major areas of inquiry underlined above:

1. Given that the record seems antithetic to the notion of a precapitalist mode of production, at what level of the socioeconomic structure can we start a conceptualization of peasantries?
2. If Caribbean peasantries could emerge and grow at times when the region was fully integrated in the capitalist world economy, what is the logic of that coexistence?
3. Since that logic—in view of what we know of both the Caribbean and capitalism—seems to suggest the overarching relevance of world historical processes, how does one move down from such macroprocesses to microlevel studies, and flesh out the continuing vitality of peasants as conscious human beings with a particular cultural heritage and with the power to modify that heritage itself?

Such are the difficulties and promises of any study of any Caribbean peasantry, no less so that of Dominica.

PART I

THE NATION

CHAPTER 2

Space: A Patchwork of Enclaves

And if the Indies are not where you are, I do not care! Indies you will be. West Indies, so that my dream will be fulfilled.
—Edouard Glissant, *Poèmes*

Somewhere between the first ventures of Henry the Navigator and the death of Pizarro, Western colonizers reaffirmed the magical power that names have to create social entities. A few lines on a map demarcating masses of land yet unseen by the conquerors created units that later seemed to take a life of their own. In the Caribbean itself, the task was even easier; the sea provided the natural boundaries. Not surprisingly, Christopher Columbus systematically named every island along his path, even those on which he did not land. On Sunday, 3 November 1493, he spotted a rugged land mass, and though, having found no convenient harbor, he could not set foot on it, he named it Dominica. But what, in fact, is Dominica, if not merely the land mass that Columbus spotted? Or rather, what makes it a legitimate unit of social analysis? Is it because Spain, France, and Britain ruled it, in turn, as a colony (Boromé 1972a, 1972b, 1972c)? Is it because, in 1978, an independent nation-state emerged from this colonial entity?

These questions are not rhetorical. Social scientists always inherit the colonizers' paths, just as the social sciences postdate the rise of the state in Europe itself. Power precedes scholarship: one engenders delineations, the other inscribes them. As followers of a certain kind, social scientists often take political entities as natural units of analysis.[1] Yet if one can safely assume that, as political entities, countries and colonies demonstrate some form of integration, there is no reason to presuppose that in each and every case that integration depends upon the same unchanged set of social factors. Thus though the names we inherit are likely to cover a sociohistorical reality, that reality itself always needs to be discovered anew.

The Dominica with which this book is concerned is an entity in the making, always to be discovered anew despite the dominant markers of its past. It is, at the same time, a patchwork of enclaves and a peripheral unit characterized by its role as a marginal banana producer for the world economy. Yet between the centrifugal trends, most perceptible in spatial terms, and the centripetal tendencies, spurred by a history of export-oriented agricultural production, the Dominican people continue to shape their future, and the peasant work process is one of the mechanisms through which they have learned to do so.

Dominica: The Spatial Dimension

To the visitor foolhardy enough to retrace in a small boat the path of the early Caribs, the island of Dominica surges suddenly from the sea, halfway through the Martinique Channel, like a sinking mountain resisting the pull of the depth. Behold a mass of dark green, a tropical iceberg of vegetation, almost in the middle of that arc where the Lesser Antilles delineate the Atlantic at the junction of two hemispheres. It first seems inaccessible, vulnerable only to the natural elements. That impression is reinforced as the visitor approaches, and suspects, rather than discovers, the central rain forest, with its multiple layers of vegetation which densely cover a succession of small peaks. On the leeward side of the central chain, the mountains descend toward the sea; but on the eastern or windward side, they end abruptly in precipitous cliffs. Here, nature seems to have provided us with a wonder and a challenge: for centuries, human beings have had to accommodate themselves within the marginal areas left between or around the steeps.

Crucial to the understanding of Dominican society, then, is its inability, as a sociospatial entity, to expand enough, either inward or outward, to encompass the whole island. Historical Dominica is but a narrow belt, at times scarcely a mile wide, which almost encircles the island, but is broken at points, especially on the eastern side, by the steepness of the mountains. The island itself is 29 miles long and 16 miles wide, the largest of the Lesser Antilles; but the figures of 289 or 305 square miles, often cited as its total area, are equally irrelevant. Most of that space is unoccupied. The propensity of Dominica's successive ethnic, religious, or political minorities (Caribs, Maroons, Rastafarians) to seek refuge in some remote mountain of the interior only verifies the remoteness of those mountains. Rural cultivators often manifested tendencies toward an inward expansion; but given their meager material means, the "flight to the mountains" often meant, at best, a two-mile retreat from the coastline. Probably fewer than 50 square miles of Dominican territory had ever been systematically used by humans for agriculture, habitation, or transport before the 1910s. Dominica entered the second half of this century with barely 25 square miles of land formally appropriated into private hands. In 1951, the total area under cultivation (including pasture land and land in fallow) was generally estimated at 30,000 acres, or about 47 square miles (Great Britain, Colonial Office, 1953). By my own estimate, this figure has not quite doubled during the last thirty-five years.

The ruggedness of the island long implied not only a restricted use of its total area but also, until recently, the isolation of its different clusters of population. For most governments, the conquest of the interior meant merely the building and maintenance of roads that would link, by land, opposite segments of the coastal belt. Such an enterprise, always heavily publicized, met with limited success. Up to the 1960s, boats and launches remained the major means of transport from one cluster to the next.

Overseas contacts were perhaps easier for the people of Roseau, the capital, and those of Portsmouth, the second major town. Today, Roseau and Portsmouth are still the only two ports capable of handling international shipping. Yet residents of at least three different enclaves at the northern and southern tips of the island sustained, quite independently, exchanges and communications with the neighboring islands of Guadeloupe and Martinique. Though Dominicans often left their native land, sometimes temporarily, and often for good, few people came to Dominica, and few of those ventured outside Portsmouth or Roseau. The advent of air transportation may have increased Dominica's relative isolation, given the difficulties of even finding a flat area suitable for the construction of an adequate airport. After World War II the government of nearby Saint Vincent operated a charter which landed twice a week in Souffrière in the South, whence passengers were taken by launch to Roseau. Small planes also landed at Portsmouth for a while, and, since the opening of the Melville Hall Airport in 1958, regular service by commercial carriers connects Dominica with Antigua, Guadeloupe, and Martinique when atmospheric conditions permit. But it takes two and a half hours to cross the few miles of serpentine road that link Melville Hall to Roseau by way of the Central Forest Reserve; and both Melville Hall and the tinier and more recent Canefield Airport are too small to handle even a middle-sized commerical jet.

Difficulty of access from one place to another within the island and the necessity of entering any cluster as if it were a different country reinforce the impression that Dominica possesses a wide variety of microclimates. To be sure, most of the island is subject to abundant rainfall (2,500 millimeters a year), and in almost every place—except for a small strip on the northwest coast—one should expect some precipitation two days out of three (MacPherson 1976). But the yearly averages conceal the specificity of miniature ecological niches. For instance, though the wettest season falls between July and October, daily patterns of rainfall, wind frequency, or wind direction accentuate differences between the leeward and windward sides of the coastal strip. Likewise, daily temperatures generally range from 78°F to 90°F and reach their national peak in July, but altitude or even mere proximity to the highlands determines actual variation within any small enclave. Daily changes can be extreme in the highlands, especially on the windward side, and one may feel the need for sweaters and blankets only five hours after walking bare-legged in the sun. At the same time, other enclaves might be facing their hottest night in weeks. Quite a few times, I have gone through the cold and foggy mountains of Bells in the wee hours only later to experience a sweltering afternoon in Roseau.

Clearly, then, the Dominican totality is as much an artifact as it is a creation of nature. Like the rest of the Caribbean, Dominica was meant to become a custom-made society, one that should have evolved, in space and in time, according to a mercantilist schedule attuned to the particular demands of European accumulation. That it was never so, that no Caribbean society ever fitted perfectly the master plans designed in London, Paris, Madrid, or Amsterdam should not surprise us. Yet in this case, one in which the environment itself so often impeded integration, we may want to keep in mind the original artifice: the imposed migration of ethnically heterogeneous Africans, the imposed integration of plants and animals carried over three centuries, and, no less, the imposed juxtaposition of languages and cultures. It is a vivid mark of its past history that the official language of Dominica is English whereas the majority of the population speaks a French-based Creole, the Lesser Antillean language common to Martinique, Guadeloupe, and Saint Lucia (and closely akin to Haitian). The preeminence of Roman Catholicism is also a legacy of the early colonization by France. Yet the Westminster-styled representative system and even the official name given to the country at the time of independence ("Commonwealth of Dominica") in 1978 display the political elite's desire to conform to British expectations, a desire understandably born of 173 years of continuous domination. Peasants work barefoot in the fields, fishermen engage the high sea to smuggle a few bottles of rum dearly bought from their cousins in Guadeloupe, while the Speaker of the House castigates "the Honourable Member for the Portsmouth Constituency" for having, once more, used the term *bourgeois* in the "Honourable House," despite previous warnings. Young men dream of lands they will never see, of work they will never do; schoolgirls face unwanted pregnancies while the Honourable Member reminds the Speaker that he was not using the term *bourgeois* but the term *bourgeoisistic* to refer to the tendencies of the ruling party.

The intent here is not to ridicule leaders of one of the few Third World nations whose rulers can claim at least as much legitimacy as those of any Western country. But those facts are on the record, and one needs to emphasize the apparent artificiality that national discourse can take in societies built only for the explicit benefit of others. In such a setting, statistical models designed for and verified against the reality of Western nation-states hide as much as they reveal. The unity of Dominica is not political nor is it occupational, at least in the sense that one has come to understand occupational categories in the West.

The Lessons of a Recent Census

The preliminary figures of the 1980 Census (still being processed at the time of this writing) estimate the total population of Dominica at 73,800 people. (Estimates for the year 1985 are as high as 83,000.) The youthfulness of that population is striking: 70 percent under 30; 54 percent under 20; 41 percent under 15. Nearly one-third of that population attends primary or secondary school full time. The second characteristic that the preliminary figures emphasize is a tripartite division of the population over fourteen. While 5,262 people fifteen years old and over worked for the government and some 7,500 worked for private employers in 1980, 7,758 people (19 percent of the population over fourteen) claimed to be self-employed. Most of them (5,515 people) worked in agriculture, and did so "without paid help." Fewer than 1,000 landowners used paid workers of any kind, and fewer than 1,500 workers perceive themselves (or are perceived) as full-time agricultural wage earners. Hence, grossly speaking, agricultural enterprises who used wage laborers employed an average of one to two workers per enterprise. To be sure, one would like to know the actual distribution behind those aggregate figures; and the figure of 1,000 landowners using paid labor is grossly exaggerated. But that is exactly the point: even if one stretches the census categories to the extreme, systematic engagements in agricultural *wage* labor do not involve more than 2,000 Dominicans, counting both employers and workers. The unity of Dominica is not that of its labor market. Rather, a clear division seems to emerge between Dominicans who work on land that they control, temporarily or definitively, as cash renters, sharecroppers, or yeoman owners, and those employed by the government or private enterprises outside agriculture. Still, between the people systematically working on the land, for themselves, and those firmly employed outside agriculture, there lies a multitude of some 18,155 Dominicans over fourteen who largely escape the census occupational categories. We have a better sense of them in the census results that indicate that about 4,627 people looked for work in the same year; but as is always the case with official figures, we can only guess at the thousands who did not even bother.

Two lessons emerge: on the one hand, an overall dependence upon the land, conveniently expressed by the Dominican national motto *Apré Bondyé Sé Latè* (After God Is the Land); on the other, an occupational fluidity, expressed by the respondents' reluctance to identify themselves in terms of a single and fixed category. Both points should be kept in mind throughout the rest of this chapter. They support my contention of Dominica's disjointedness, but also the argument about a unity shaped from the outside by the society's dependence on an export economy dominated by a succession of monocrops. To use a statistical metaphor, the "average" Dominican is torn by his or her dependence on the peasant labor process for food and cash income and his or her desire to engage in other activities.

Thus, the ambiguous treatment of occupational categories by the census is more reflective of reality than it is the measure of the ability of the census takers. At the time of my fieldwork there constantly appeared, in almost every village of Dominica, a category that any observer could quickly dispose of as marginal were it not of such an impressive size.

It is a huge and fluid group of people, somehow connected to the land through ties of kinship or alliance, but who as individuals do not own land. Most of them depend heavily on the peasant labor process for their daily survival, not so much because they systematically work on the land, but because they are tied to somebody who does, somebody whom they sometimes help. Their dream is quite often emigration, as long as their youth lasts. A government job for them is the second best choice, one that seems more "real," though it is as improbable in statistical terms as emigration itself. I have dubbed these individuals a "lumpen peasantry"; they people the pages that follow even when, for the purposes of presentation, I focus on the roles of the more constant producers on whom they depend.

The more constant producers are cultivators, the vast majority of whom engage in the peasant labor process on plots held in tenancy or in freehold. They plant and harvest diverse crops, the relevance of which may vary from one area to the next. However, coconuts, tubers (root crops), and bananas dominate the agricultural sector, both in terms of the number of cultivators engaged in their production and in terms of the gross volumes produced. Root crops can be sold for cash, but their general availability limits their value on the local market, and only a small portion of the national production is exported. In contrast, the volume of exported bananas exceeds by far that used locally. Since the early 1950s, bananas have been Dominica's leading export commodity. They remain so even though exports of coconut byproducts have increased dramatically, between 1982 and 1986, after this fieldwork was conducted.

Dominican peasants do not sell the bananas they produce on the open market. Rather, they deliver the harvest to a state agency, the Dominica Banana Growers Association (DBGA), which unilaterally sets the amount of cash that producers will receive for each pound of bananas delivered. The DBGA, in turn, delivers those bananas to a British-based multinational corporation, Geest Holdings Limited, which sells them in Europe, primarily in the United Kingdom.

I will return to the legal and economic ties that bind peasant producers with Geest and the DBGA especially in part 2, but two points need to be made right now. First, if occupational categories have any relevance to what people do, the most important occupational category in Dominica might be that of banana producer. Though the census data remain ambiguous, the DBGA files record by name more than ten thousand individuals on whose behalf bananas are delivered regularly throughout the nation. To be sure, important differences demarcate many of those individuals, and the analysis must address those differences. Still, we can propose a second generalization: the production of bananas and their subsequent appropriation by the DBGA and Geest constitute the most important mechanism integrating the Dominican peasantry in the sphere of valorization. The physical presence of that crop throughout the Dominican landscape already indicates the background against which we should look at Dominica's spatial dismemberment.

The West

The Dominican topograpy naturally divides the island into leeward and windward parts. Starting from the South, on the leeward side, one first meets the villages of Scotts Head and Souffrière which form a quite distinct unit. People there are integrated into the valorization process, not only through the occasional appropriation of their bananas by Geest and the DBGA, or through labor or rent transactions with citrus estate owners, but also through the sale of fish on the national market. These different paths to integration allow many fishermen-peasants of Souffrière and Scotts Head more room to maneuver despite patterns of indebtedness linked to their purchases of costly outboard motors. These are people as turned to foreign lands as they are to Roseau, Dominica's capital town (which is only a few miles from them), partly because of a long history of direct contact with Martinique. But neither the sale of fish nor that of goods acquired in Martinique can provide the cash necessary to maintain most families, and some individuals are still forced to work periodically on the citrus and lime estates that long dominated property relations in the area. The decline of the lime industry in the second half of this century has somehow weakened the estates, and has also cut down the source of income for many. Between 1970 and 1980, the population of the Saint Mark Parish, which comprises mainly Scotts Head and Souffrière, declined from 1,961 to 1,921 individuals. In short, though those who stayed may be more independent, independence itself has not been without social costs.

Fewer than five miles north of Souffrière, one enters the largest socio-spatial unit of Dominica, one that touches on three parishes (Saint Luke, Saint Paul, Saint George) to reach its highest demographic density and social complexity in the capital town of Roseau. From Pointe Michel in the South, to Mahaut in the North, the unit includes the coastal village of Loubière and the neo-urban area of Roseau (pop. 8,300) and its immediate dependencies, Canefield, Massacre, and Mahaut. It expands eastward, in the direction of the mountains, with four tentacles that link Roseau to Giraudel, Morne Prosper, Trafalgar, and Laudat. The total population of that enclave is now in excess of 27,000 people.

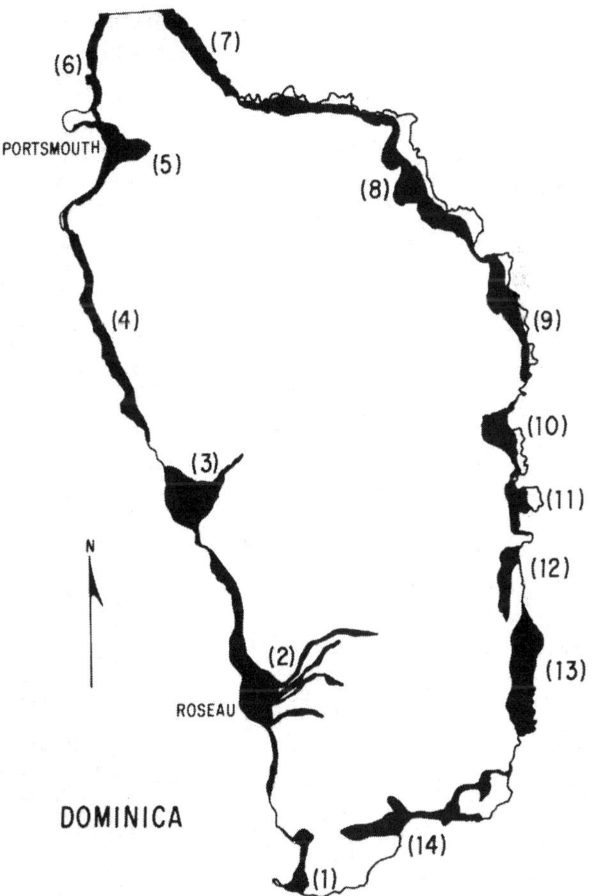

Map 2.1. A Nation of Enclaves.
The leeward side: (1) Scotts Head-Souffrière enclave, (2) Roseau and its dependencies, (3) Layou River enclave, (4) Colihaut Strip, (5) Portsmouth and its dependencies, (6) Tanetane-Capucine enclave. The windward side: (7) Vieille Case enclave, (8) La Soye District, (9) Carib Reserve, (10) Castle Bruce, (11) Saint Sauveur-Petite Souffrière, (12) Rosalie, (13) La Plaine–Pointe Mulâtre enclave, (14) Geneva and Grand Bay.

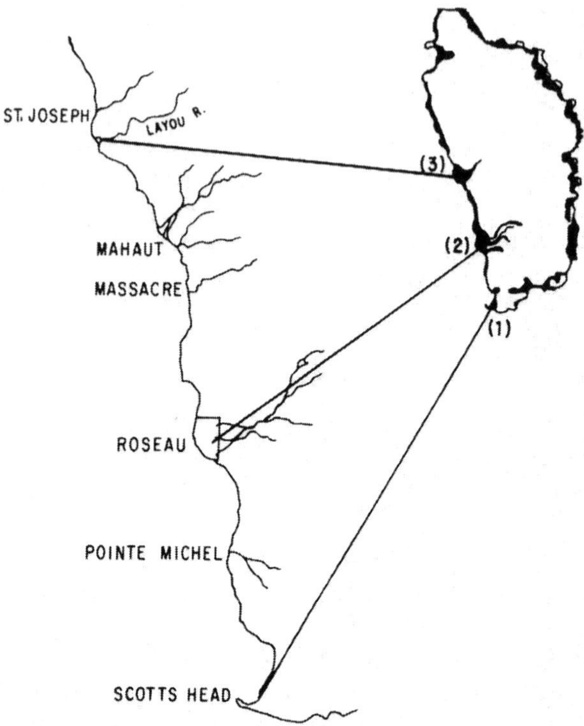

Map 2.2. The West: From Scotts Head to the Layou River.
(1) Scotts Head-Souffrière enclave, (2) Roseau and its dependencies, (3) Layou River enclave.

By and large, this is an area in which peasant control of the coastal lands, as freeholders or sharecroppers, never gained the momentum reached elsewhere in the island. Nowadays, many mechanisms of integration are at work in this large area, and one does not perceive among, say, Mahaut, Pointe Michel, or Giraudel, the similarities so obvious between Souffrière and Scotts Head, or, as we shall see later, Peineville and Vieille Case. From our vantage point, what first distinguishes those villages as components of the same socio-geographical area is rather the secondary role of bananas in the integration of people engaged in the peasant labor process. From Mahaut to Pointe Michel, the decline of limes and citruses (Dominica's prime exports in the first half of this century) brought a new dependency on Roseau. Even for those who hold a piece of land, easy access to town meant the possibility of wage labor, not

Table 2.1. Population Trends by Parish, 1970–1980

Parish	1970	1980	Percentage
Leeward			
St. Mark	1,961	1,921	– 2.03
St. Luke	1,633	1,503	– 7.96
St. George	19,470	20,501	+ 5.29
St. Paul	4,456	5,386	+ 20.87
St. Joseph	6,362	6,806	+ 6.97
St. Peter	1,701	1,601	– 5.87
St. John	5,226	5,412	+ 3.55
Windward			
St. Andrew	11,937	12,748	+ 6.79
St. David	6,707	7,337	+ 9.37
St. Patrick	10,075	9,780	– 3.12

Sources: *Dominica Statistical Digest*, 1978. Preliminary Results of 1980 Census, Dominica, Ministry of Finance, Statistical Division.

only on surrounding plantations, but also in commerce, agro-industrial plants, or private and public services. Population grew accordingly in the enclave, though it declined in Roseau by 16 percent between 1970 and 1980. The parish of Saint Paul, which comprises Mahaut and Massacre, registered the highest increase for that period (see Table 2.1).

These figures tend to confirm that many individuals otherwise attracted to what could perhaps pass for the only urban center of the island remain skeptical enough about sources of employment to maintain at least partial engagement in the peasant labor process. People hustle for cash, switching from one activity to the next, assessing dormant opportunities and creating new ones. However, they prefer to exercise their choice while based in an area close to town, but within which they can retract to be a peasant and have greater access to food without using cash. Accordingly, the range of occupational categories is greater here than anywhere else in Dominica, especially since the peasantry is not alone in its desire to occupy those lands that conveniently offer a combination of the rural and the urban. Old and newly cleared plots surrounding those villages are increasingly turned into residential neighborhoods for the well-to-do, Caribbean versions of suburbia duplicating patterns of urban extension that have already marked Jamaica, Puerto Rico, Trinidad, and

Haiti. "Mansions" (or, at least, what the folk perceive as such) spring up on the flanks of the hills, displacing (socially and, at times, physically) people who had long lived on the periphery between urban and rural life. At six in the morning, on any given day of the week, one may meet on the road children of poor families on their way to public school, neatly dressed in their only uniforms, a young adolescent running after three frantic cows, or a brand new Toyota speeding around the curves.

In the coastal villages of the Roseau enclave, the recent rise in the flow of cash, population shifts, and the ideological impact of the non-laborers' presence resulted in the creation of a lumpen peasantry torn between the security of the peasant unit and individual (or even individualistic) ventures into a world of commodities. Transistors and sweat suits abound in the area, but most villagers want to hold on to a piece of land through kinship or marriage ties, and still benefit from the greater flow of cash from wages or remittances.

The four tentacles leading respectively to Laudat, Trafalgar, Morne Prosper, and Giraudel do differ, in part, from the coastal dependencies of the capital town. By and large, they are the granaries (as well as the dormitories) of a certain elite. A particular ecology (higher altitude, twice greater rainfall) and a different history of contact with the town benefit small landowners who produce vegetables, root crops, fruits, or even meat and poultry which they sell in Roseau.[2] The security cushion that food production provides allowed social resentment to express itself in clearer terms within those villages (especially among the youth). Ideologies or religions that question the social order, such as Rastafarianism, found a more fertile ground in the Giraudel area than in the coastal villages. A young Rasta of Eggleston, near Giraudel, told me how he used the asset of a good secondary school education to find employment in Roseau. Yet he eventually lost the job on which he had learned to depend and returned to the village to work on the family farm and became a Rastafarian. He now loudly condemns "police brutality" and the "arrogance" of "Roseau people," among whom he counts some of his closest neighbors. Spurred by that kind of resentment Rastafarians kidnapped a prominent resident of the Giraudel area whom they dragged into the mountains of the interior and killed in February 1981 after the government had refused to engage in negotiations with them.

Less than two miles north of Mahaut, the area surrounding the Layou River distinguishes itself by probably the highest daily concentration of cash tenants and rural wage laborers in the island. In addition to estate work, many residents of the surrounding villages work in agro-industrial plants, notably a tobacco factory. Most bananas here come either from estate lands (where they are, at times, intercropped with coconuts) or from plots rented from absentee owners or richer peasants. Laborers are often exploited both by Geest (through the DBGA) and the estate owners. Still, in 1978, when the volume of exports reached its peak for the last decade, the boxing plants of Layou Park and Hillsborough processed 13.5 million pounds of bananas out of a national total of 86 million pounds. The population of the Saint Joseph Parish, which comprises that enclave, remains numerically stable (6,806 in 1980).

From the Mero River to Pointe Ronde, the long dry strip (less than 1,000 millimeters of rain a year) that runs along the littoral, encloses some of the oldest settlements of Dominica. At times, when goods and people moved primarily by sea, launches stopped regularly at Pointe Aronde, Colihaut, Salisbury, and Batalie, on their way to Portsmouth or Roseau, picking up the product of otherwise isolated estates. Now the motor road cuts through their lowlands, close to the seacoast, in the areas between the remaining fishing boats and the first houses, but isolation is no less.

Occasional wage labor on the declining estates or for the government (there is always some need to repair the roads), "subsistence" production, emigration or inland migration are among the many strategies devised on the ground; but strong mechanisms of integration are lacking. Not surprisingly, this is a choice area for government-sponsored, bilateral or "private" humanitarian projects; but increasingly, so are the northwest strips of many other Caribbean islands. The population of the enclave, which grossly overlaps the parish of Saint Peter (pop. 1,600), has declined steadily since at least the 1960s.

From the Picard Estate to the Cabrits, Portsmouth and its dependencies form an extremely complex enclave whose internal variations can barely be sketched in such an overview. The presence of a lumpen peasantry similar to that of Mahaut or Massacre is quite obvious there, but so is that of other subgroups engaged in the production of local foodstuffs. The recent opening of the Picard campus of a private medical school, attended exclusively by foreign students from North America or the Middle East, has raised prices (especially housing prices) in the area, but also contributed to greater cash fallouts than those from the suburbanites' presence in the Roseau dependencies. Integration in the valorization process through banana production is rarely exclusive in the various subparts of the greater Portsmouth area. Production of local food crops for the national market and for export to neighboring

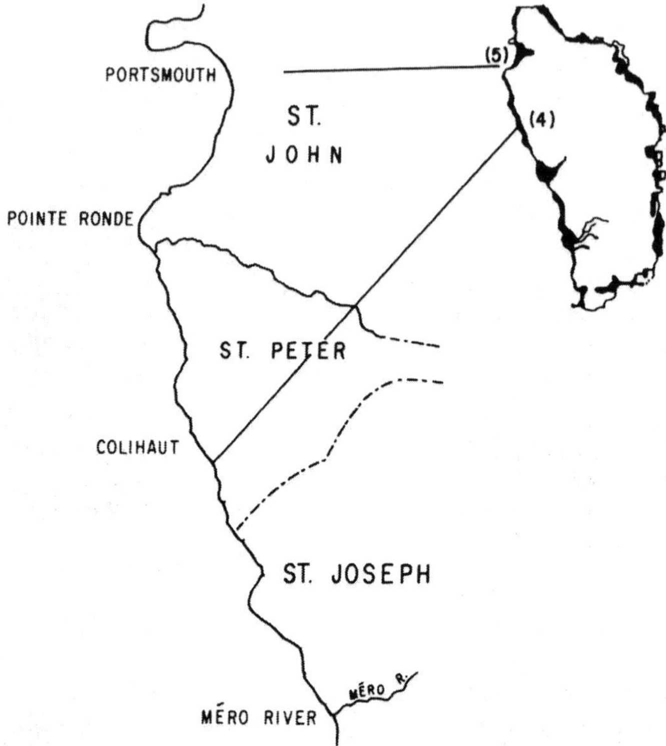

Map 2.3. The West: From Layou to Portsmouth.
(4) Colihaut Strip, (5) Portsmouth and its dependencies.

islands has always been high, and may have risen in the last decade. Indeed, Portsmouth (pop. 3,000) may have the highest density of professional hucksters in the island. A long history of independent contacts (by sea and, for a much shorter period, by air) reinforce the traders' independence.

The North

These descriptions lead to the conclusion that, from Scotts Head to the Cabrits, the rural dwellers' engagement in the peasant labor process varies from one enclave to the next and also within the same enclave. The leeward areas share various ideological, economic, and social mixes that seem to preclude exclusive engagement in the peasant labor process or often make primary engagement only a last resort. In other words, many people on that long leeward stretch are essentially agricultural producers, and among them many work primarily on land controlled by their family (as shareholders or freeholders, or cash tenants), but few tend to see the labor they perform on such land as an essential part of their definitions of themselves or as reflective of their aspirations. Participation in peasant work activities remains by and large in their perception, if not always in fact, a security cushion to fall back on in bad times, while seeking better prospects. What may surprise both the observer and the cultivators themselves is the permanence of their need for that cushion. They are not peasants in transition to another state or status, but, more consistently, peasants and something else, and that always varying "something else" provides at any given time the sense they have of themselves.

The most northern leeward enclave, which goes from Tanetane to Capucine, may thus be the only one on the leeward coast where the activities and the concerns of the people are primarily rooted in small-scale agriculture. Past the Cabrits, population density declines (I estimate the enclave's 1981 population at about 1,800 people), vegetation increases rapidly, and the villages remind one of the agglomerations in the interior or on the windward side. Significantly, density does not decrease as one gets farther from Portsmouth, but seems to respond to the dynamics of the enclave itself. Children of Capucine or Cocoyer go to the Clifton school which, in 1981, counted 240 students although the village population was around 400. Clifton villagers attend religious services in Capucine. Peasants in all villages cultivate plantains, root crops, cocoa, coffee, coconuts, and bananas, but the condition of the road has to a great extent hindered cultivation of bananas for the export market despite the proximity of the Portsmouth docks.

For many households fishing is an important activity, and villagers in Toucari, Clifton, and Capucine claim to be excellent seafarers. Contacts with Guadeloupe are frequent and often bypass the control of both French and Dominican governments. Not long ago, it was cheaper to bring into the areas goods such as sugar, flour, or rum directly from Guadeloupe than by way of Roseau. One feels Portsmouth's influence on the enclave, but it is closer to a "marginal area" than an internal periphery (C. Smith 1979).[3]

Capucine is the most northern agglomeration on the western coast of Dominica. Hence, our northward journey along that coast ends there, and we can now start a southward descent on the much more abrupt

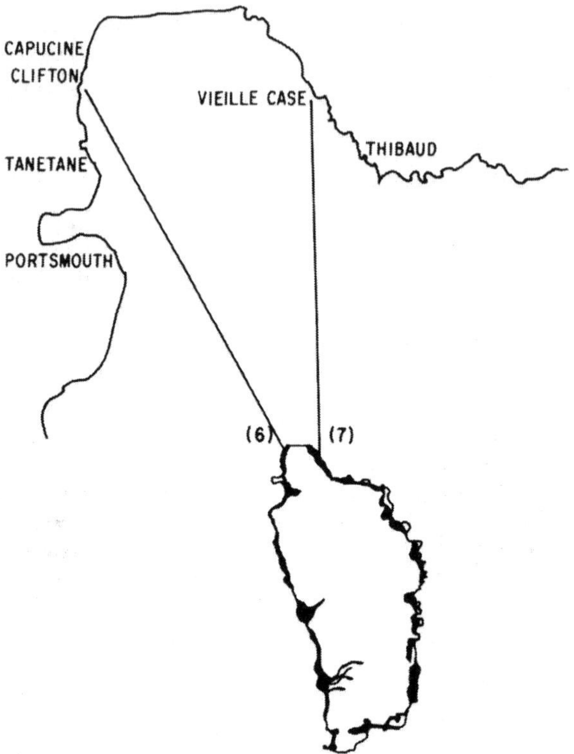

Map 2.4. The North.
(6) Tanetane-Capucine enclave, (7) Vieille Case enclave.

eastern or windward side. Such jumps are not so easy in real life, of course. One moves with various degrees of difficulty from one village to another on either side of the island, let alone from one side to the other. Indeed, the absence of direct contact between eastern and western enclaves epitomizes Dominica's dislocation.

Hence, though the straight distance between Capucine on the leeward side and Peineville on the windward is barely four miles, few people ever cross the island between those two points. The 2,826-foot Morneau Diables creates an impressive neutral border between the two coastal strips. Tracks and footpaths lead to the hinterland at the foot of the mountains, around the remnants of the Delaforde and La Source estates, but besides the difficulties barring a cross-country trip, there is not much incentive from either side to visit the other. Rather, Marie

Galante and Guadeloupe, which can be seen clearly from Vieille Case and Peineville, have been the main attraction for most yeomen on the windward side.

It is easy to emphasize unduly the French influence upon the northern strip of the Saint Andrew Parish. The spirit of independence that this enclave exudes stems partly from its contacts with neighboring French-speaking islands. The nearly unquestioned dominance of Roman Catholicism, the vitality of the Lesser Antillean Creole, the elaborate cult of the dead, all remind us, at times, of Guadeloupe, Martinique, or Haiti. But Vieille Case is as close to Guadeloupe as Scotts Head is to Martinique, and the nature of the contacts with the French territories rather than their frequency is what sustained the area's originality. Northern Saint Andrew offers, indeed, a nice example of the ways in which a historically particular integration in the valorization process underpins cultural differentiation.

To start with, this area is one of the few in Dominica in which peasants collect bananas rejected by the DBGA for sale outside of the country, establishing a tiny but independent alternative export circuit. But sweet cassava, sweet potatoes, and other ground provisions, and fruits, beans, peppers, and coffee, planted on the hills surrounding the villages, and sometimes intercropped with bananas, are likewise shipped out according to demand. Oral history confirms that the export of those commodities long preceded the rise of bananas. What we may have then in Saint Andrew North is a different history of integration. First, because of the enclave's isolation, the peasant labor process rests on firmer ground, that is, on property relations more secure from the yeomanry's viewpoint since at least the nineteenth-century decline of the coffee estates. Second, this typically peasant work process was itself integrated into a worldwide process of valorization in a manner independent, at least in part, of the rest of Dominica, through contacts with the French colonies. Third, and most important, those contacts included to a large extent the sale of commodities greatly appreciated in the neighboring territories, and were not limited to the mere acquisition by the Saint Andrew peasants of goods unavailable from Roseau or Portsmouth.[4] Today, banana production may be the most important mechanism of the Saint Andrew yeomanry in the valorization process. Yet peasants in the most northern part of the parish seem to have more maneuvering room than in almost all of the other enclaves of Dominica, and that independence stems from their early integration as independent traders.

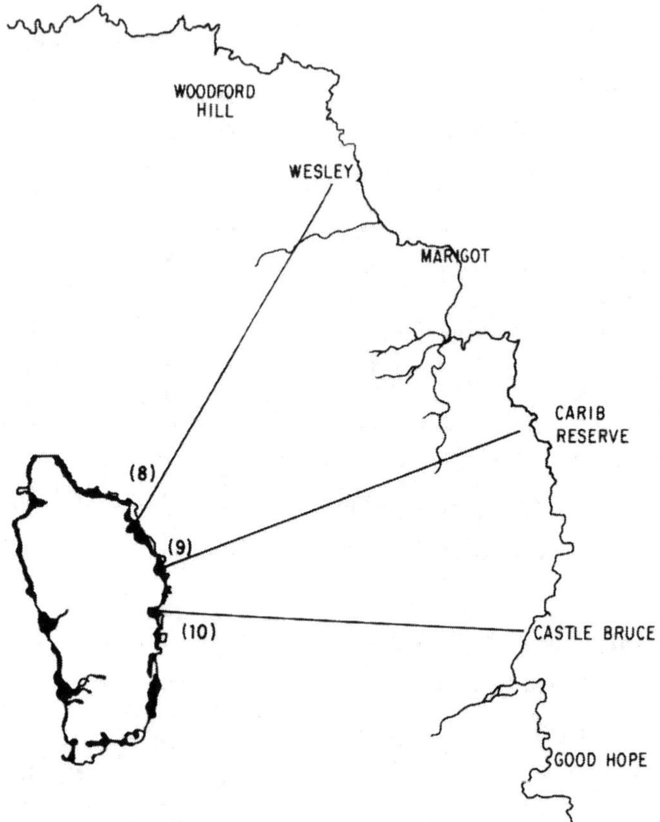

Map 2.5. The East: From Anse du Mai to Castle Bruce.
(8) La Soye District, (9) Carib Reserve area, (10) Castle Bruce.

Not surprisingly, Vieille Case's streets bear numerous signs of that independence. Handwritten posters remind villagers that the cleanliness of the area is a matter of communal pride. Likewise, though no one in the area would scorn a unilingual English speaker, villagers in the enclave show pride in their ability to speak *patois* (Lesser Antillean) with the least possible mixture of English words. Significant also, Protestantism has made relatively few inroads in the area. One could extend the list of examples; for instance, the tombstones of cemeteries standing out in the Dominican countryside vividly tell the long domination of a few connected families as well as the general relevance of family ties for all, including the humblest. It will be fruitful to keep those features in mind when we finally return to Saint Andrew South, the next geographical cluster on our southward journey along the windward coast, yet one that we will skip, for the time being, for the purposes of general exposition.

Saint David

South of Saint Andrew, in the parish of Saint David (pop. 7,300), is the next cluster of villages on the windward coast, the area commonly referred to as the Carib Reserve, though it extends farther than the actual territory left by the government to the remaining descendants of the indigenous people of Dominica. Ethnographies of the Caribs are accessible elsewhere though in dissertation form; suffice it to say, integration of the inhabitants of the reserve (most of whom are, at least in part, descendants of the early Caribs) occurred before the banana preeminence, through the sale of fish to non-Carib villages and the sale of handicrafts to visitors and tourists. Still, the increased and now overwhelming importance of banana production has been largely ignored by anthropologists despite its visibility. A well-known and active Carib Reserve banana boxing plant, run by the DBGA, collected 2,339,710 pounds of bananas in 1976, and more than 3½ million pounds in 1978. In 1979, it was among the nine most important buying points of the island; and it is perhaps significant that, in 1981, the Carib chief lived only a few yards away from it. From our viewpoint, the Carib Reserve fits into the banana-dominated part of the windward coast.

In sharp contrast with the treatment received by the Carib Reserve, scholars could not ignore the economic conflicts with the larger order on the issue of integration in the next enclave. Castle Bruce became a name in the Caribbean literature on social change because of the quite vocal desire of its estate workers to grasp what they perceived in the early 1970s as "a chance for a change" (A. Williams 1972). Indeed, in 1974, after some twenty months of strikes, protests, and negotiations, laborers of the Castle Bruce Estate, most of whom were residents of the adjacent village (pop. 2,000) of the same name, forced the government and the Caribbean Development Corporation, then owner of Castle Bruce, to lease them 153 acres of that estate to base a cooperative. A comprehensive study of *Rural Transformation Initiatives in Dominica* (Huggins et al. 1978) includes a fairly objective evaluation of that struggle and its aftermath. The laborers did not succeed in their early goals for a gradual disengagement from banana production despite much better odds than most Dominican peasants.[5]

The Southeast

The succession of villages which starts with Morpo, barely one mile south of Castle Bruce, and ends with Petite Souffrière (with Good Hope and Saint-Sauveur in the middle) may be thought of as a separate enclave, though one partly dependent upon Castle Bruce, if only because a few landless laborers migrated north in the best days of the Castle Bruce Estate. Fishermen from Saint-Sauveur sell a considerable amount

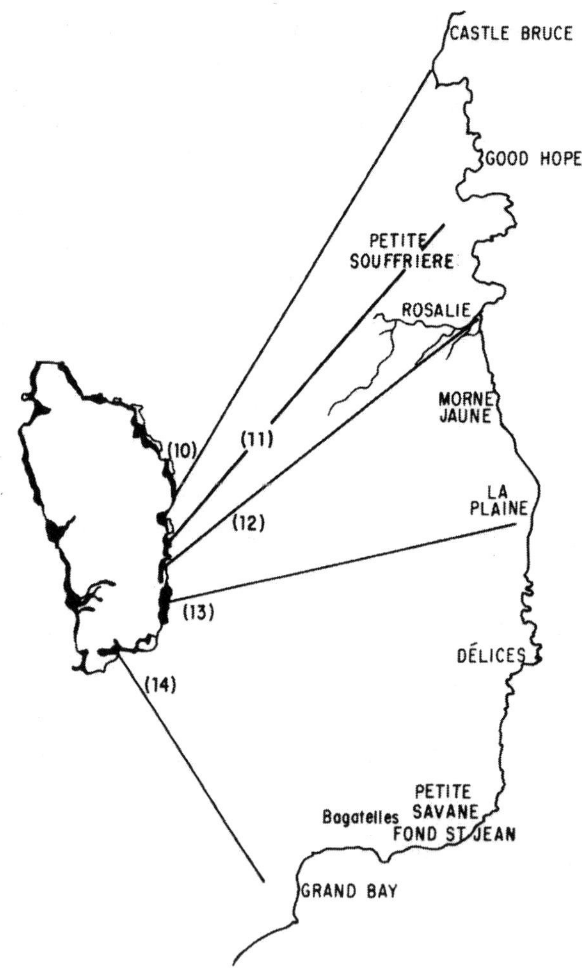

Map 2.6. The East: From Castle Bruce to Grand Bay.
(10) Castle Bruce, (11) Saint Sauveur–Petite Souffrière, (12) Rosalie River enclave, (13) La Plaine–Pointe Mulâtre enclave, (14) Geneva and Grand Bay.

of fish in both enclaves. Still, population density does not decrease in the second enclave in proportion to distance from Castle Bruce. Petite Souffrière, located at the very end of the road, is no less vibrant with life than Saint-Sauveur. Admittedly, it is a life that, in material terms at least, does not compare well with many other rural areas of Dominica. Difficulty of access adds to the problem of finding a viable productive base.[6]

Despite the isolation of the enclave banana production increased in 1980 and 1981. As other means of obtaining the necessary cash income dwindled because of market conditions and because of the devastation caused by two successive hurricanes, many people who had planted bananas only marginally up to then increased their engagement in banana production despite some immediate inconveniences. For instance, on "fig day," the day selected by the DBGA for banana collection, it is impossible to reach the capital, whether by truck or by jeep, as all vehicles carry bananas to the boxing plants.

Though the most southern house of Petite Souffrière may be less than a half mile from the Rosalie River, no motor road connects Rosalie to the villages to the north. Petite Souffrière lays at the far end of an impasse, and people there reach Roseau at best three times a week depending on the availability of transport. Reaching Rosalie, which is less than a mile away is a much more complicated affair if one uses public transportation. It requires an overnight stay in Roseau on the leeward coast, after which one crosses the island once more to return to the windward coast via the central road which circles Morne Trois Pitons. Some villagers do stop halfway, at the junction of the Castle Bruce and Rosalie roads, and try to catch the next transport in the opposite direction, but as one can imagine, the traveler has absolutely no control over the time of arrival if only because of the scarcity of motor vehicles in both areas. What was left of the old road between Petite Souffrière and Rosalie was totally impassable even with the sturdiest four-wheel-drive vehicles when I saw it in 1981; and residents of the area could not recall seeing anyone using it for years.

The lack of systematic communication between the two enclaves influences relations of production on the ground. The stretch that includes Rosalie, La Rivière Ciriques, Morne aux Frégates, and Morne Jaune is characterized, in part, by estate production and the relatively low proportion of small freeholders. Cash rent or sharecropping, notably on the Newfoundland, Rosalie, and O'Gowrie estates, was for a long time the only alternative available to most rural dwellers. Since at least the 1960s banana production has taken a much stronger foothold in that area than it ever did a couple of miles north, in Good Hope or Saint-Sauveur. Likewise, citrus production still lingers on rented plots.

Despite differences, the counterpoint between bananas and bayleaf is similar in the two enclaves. The coexistence of the two crops in both areas exemplifies the complex factors that influence mechanisms of integration on the ground. Peasants in both enclaves have long planted bayleaf on small plots they rented or held in freehold. To be sure, such involvement may have been greater in the first enclave. Yet in the early 1980s, in the aftermath of the devastation caused by Hurricane David, bayleaf producers in both areas increasingly shifted to banana production, whether or not such production was carried on land that they formally owned. The cost of starting banana production in a small field is lower than the initial capital required for bayleaf. Also, fertilizers are, at least in theory, available from the DBGA. More important perhaps, one can harvest the first bananas in a few months after planting and start collecting cash returns in less than a year.

Thus, quite a few economic reasons tend to support the decision of many peasants to change to bananas. But interestingly, some tenants and yeomen in both enclaves also expressed the opinion that, in sharp contrast with bayleaf, increased involvement in banana production, even on estate land, partly freed them from the domination of local "big men." The production of bay oil requires the local processing of the bayleaves, and the processing material is generally controlled by richer farmers, estate owners, or cooperatives which, according to some of my informants, do not provide equal access to all their nominal members. Individual producers are thus quite dependent upon a few personalities even though the bayleaf may be harvested on land they own. The owners of the boiling and processing machinery require a varying amount of the processed product or, more rarely, a fixed cash amount. The general poverty and difficulty for many laborers to acquire formal ownership reinforces patterns of indebtedness present at least since the days of limes and citruses. Moreover, favoritism and patronage muddle the "economic" transactions, and two informants claimed to have been denied access to a boiler though they were willing to pay for its use on the spot.

From the peasants' perspective, banana production, even on rented land, implies more rational and less demanding transactions, as long as the producer brings the product directly to the DBGA. Ironically, the same patterns of favoritism and patronage seem to reappear in different guises, as peasants depend on a few vehicle owners (often the same who control the bay oil machinery) to carry their bananas to the boxing plant. Only time will tell whether or not the peasantry of those two enclaves will not only substantially augment its income but also break some of its bonds through the increased involvement in banana production.

The tensions sustained by divergent mechanisms of integration are evident in the cluster of villages that includes La Plaine, Balisé, Boetica, Délices, and Pointe Mulâtre, even though property relations in the enclave have strongly favored the yeomanry's control of the units of production since the mid-nineteenth century. Indeed, even before the last spasms of the sugar economy, laborers gained access to small plots with a speed perhaps unmatched in the rest of Dominica. By 1893, the new small proprietors reacted violently to the defensive tactics, notably real property taxes, put forward by the nonlaboring classes. A visit by then Governor William Frederick Hayes Smith failed to appease them, and what is now commonly referred to as the "1893 La Plaine Uprising" ended with the death of four peasants shot by government troops.

Nowadays, as in the nineteenth century, peasants in La Plaine, Balisé, Boetica, Délices, Carib, Victoria, and Pointe Mulâtre continue to plant ground provisions as the villages expand spatially. Demographic and economic growth does not necessarily follow, though La Plaine had about 1,800 people in 1981. Rather, spatial expansion seems to provide new agricultural land, much needed in light of meager techniques, but the closing of a government-run local marketing depot has made the sale of ground provisions, usually the same kind the peasantry itself consumes, a much more difficult means of obtaining the necessary cash.

Likewise, in 1981 some peasants claimed that they were limiting their involvement in bayleaf production because they were forced by the government to sell bayleaf exclusively to what they perceived as an illegitimate cooperative and asserted that this restriction had strongly reduced their own bargaining power. The same patterns of indebtedness, patronage, and favoritism mentioned by bayleaf producers a few miles north seem to exist in this area, especially in Boetica and Délices, two villages more dependent on that particular crop. As exchanges of ground provisions against manufactured products from Martinique have decreased because of government crackdown on smugglers, the importance of banana production continues to rise. Relatively recent boxing plants in the area now handle much larger volumes of "fruits."

Thus, despite a markedly different past, the La Plaine-Pointe Mulâtre area offers some interesting similarities with the previously mentioned, more northern enclave. A more independent yeomanry seems to turn to banana production under the conditions dictated by the transnational, not so much to break bonds of clientele but rather to prevent their potential expansion in bayleaf production, and to compensate for the decline in the sale of ground provisions. Many villagers affirmed their readiness to return to intensive production of either bayleaf or ground provisions if conditions improved slightly in either market. An informant in Balisé repeatedly emphasized that bay oil "pays more" than bananas but that the cooperative's control limited the frequency of sales. "Bananas sell more often," and one needs the cash.

The South

If any passable motor road ran along the windward coast, one would cross Petite Savane less than five minutes after leaving the Pointe Mulâtre Estate. In fact, I had to reach Pointe Mulâtre itself on foot, and Petite Savane, about a mile south from the remnants of the old estate's machinery, is so isolated that one hesitates to place it within any enclave regardless of patterns of integration. I entered Petite Savane from the South on a different journey from the one that ended in Pointe Mulâtre, after going through the villages of Stowe, Fond Saint-Jean, and Bagatelle. In the last two-mentioned villages, patterns of integration duplicate those observed previously in Délices, but banana production has not provided an equally clear alternative, even in the aftermath of Hurricane David, partly because isolation impairs the safe and fast transport of the product from the field to the boxing plants and from boxing plant to the leeward docks. There are only two banana loading points in Dominica—one in Roseau, the other in Portsmouth—and both are on the leeward side. Nominally, Fond Saint-Jean, Fab, Pointe Carib, and Bagatelle form one administrative unit (for instance, they share the same Village Council) though Bagatelle stands on its own as an interior village that evolved around a declining estate. Likewise, Fond Saint-Jean, though a half mile south from Bagatelle and a half mile east from Stowe (in straight lines) stands by itself, at the bottom of an impasse, as its old French name suggests. Though poor in cash, Fond Saint-Jean villagers are excellent fishermen who regularly confront the harsh windward waves in rowboats or sailboats, and their protein consumption may be higher than that of most Dominicans. Fish is sold almost exclusively within the village.

Here, as in Petite Savane and Petite Souffrière, one should perhaps emphasize the cyclical breakdown of old or recent patterns of integration as much as the possible emergence of new ones. Such villages were formed by a reconstituted peasantry willingly rejecting a great participation in the national economy. New mechanisms of integration take a long time to establish themselves firmly and recede quite easily because of a complex combination of historical, ecological, and economic factors. More than Petite Savane and Petite Souffrière, Fond Saint-Jean is a good example of a village that hardly fits into any enclave, however defined.

After passing through the tortuous segment of motor road between Pointe Carib and Stowe, the traveler enters the last important enclave in this general survey of the Dominican coastal strip, one long dominated by the Stowe and Geneva estates and the populous village of Grand Bay. It is, in many ways, an area of great interest to the historian. The French town of "Grande Baye" proper grew on the site of the old Carib village of Berekua (or Berricoa). It was in that area that a free man of part African descent from Martinique, one Jeannot Rolle, tried to impose Christianity at gunpoint on the native Caribs. A few years later, the Jesuits established there one of the earliest and largest estates of Dominica, one that counted 194 slaves when it was recovered by creditors in 1765. Laborers of the Stowe, Geneva, and Bagatelle estates revolted during the so-called 1844 Census Riots, but, as we will see later, their employers reacted with ferocity. In the late nineteenth and early twentieth centuries, those estates were, in turn, acquired or supervised by some of the richest and most influential members of Dominica's "colored" elite (e.g., the Lockhart, Charles, and Fadelle families), some of whom later passed their properties to richer newcomers from the Middle East. In the 1970s, laborers of the area reacted once more to what they rightly perceived as oppression and burned down the Geneva Estate which was subsequently taken over by the government. In 1981, part of that estate was rented on a cash basis, mainly to Grand Bay residents.

Grand Bay itself is, by Dominican standards, a populous agglomeration with about 2,500 people in Berekua proper and at least as many in the greater Grand Bay area. It is a complex settlement, considered neither town nor village in its spatial morphology, in the services that it provides, in the activities of its residents. They include civil servants, petty entrepreneurs, agricultural tenants, but also a lumpen peasantry poorer in cash and culturally distinct from those of the Roseau dependencies. Rastafarianism thrives there as in Giraudel, but Grand Bay Rastas are, somehow, more mundane than those of the leeward highlands. Music is no less praised than in Mahaut, but young adults seem to appreciate local guitar players and singers performing on the street corner as much perhaps as the professionals packaged by the radio. Furthermore, radio reception is poor, whether one tries to listen to a foreign station or to the only Dominican one that effectively covers the other side of the island.

It would have taken much more fieldwork to rank precisely the mechanisms of integration of the peasant labor process in that region, but one suspects that a pattern may not be so strong in the Grand Bay area as in more uniform enclaves and that people tend to grab opportunities for cash as they appear. Occupational flexibility seems to characterize clusters in which the lumpen peasantry is strong. In 1981, the owner of one of the largest shops of Berekua confided to me and my native companions that he intended to close the shop fairly soon because the people could not afford the goods. And indeed, there, as in other shops throughout Dominica (in Souffrière, Castle Bruce, and La Plaine, for example), some of the goods had obviously been sitting on the shelves for quite a long time. Yet, to my knowledge, this particular shop was still operating at the time of this writing, a sign perhaps of the owner's inability to conceive of, or to reach, a more viable alternative, but from all indications business now is no better than it was in 1981. Not surpriingly, the parish of Saint Patrick which combines the Grand Bay and La Plaine areas lost population both in absolute and in relative terms between 1970 and 1980, after a spectacular rise in the 1950s and 1960s; and the new down trend continues. My preliminary comparison of the 1970 and 1980 census figures suggests that population under age fifty accounted for a substantial share of that loss; consequently emigration or migration rather than natural death probably caused the decline.

Conclusion

This tour of Dominica is not complete.[7] Yet it brings out a wealth of empirical similarities and differences and the opposing forces of division and integration. The detailed description of the island reveals a richness that exceeds by far what most people would expect in fewer than a hundred square miles inhabited by 73,800 people. Each enclave is markedly distinct; even within enclaves, the relative importance of certain crops, the degree of isolation, and the specific pattern of settlement accentuate differences. On a spatial dimension, Dominica is an island of scattered villages and uneven enclaves, not a given and unproblematic object of research and analysis. The immediately visible signs of dismemberment seem to outweigh the elements of unity. Here, space divides.

To be sure, recurrences cannot easily be dismissed even if the sum of the similarities falls way below the number of differences. The dominance of export-oriented banana production occurs often enough within enclaves or villages to allow some generalizations. Also, the predominance of small farms (three or fewer acres) is overwhelming.

Still, the unity of Dominica has to be looked for at a different level. The spatial description forces us to take a different vantage point, a historical perspective, to determine the mechanisms that account for the similarities observed. These mechanisms inhere not only in the succession of monocrops induced by French and British control over the island but also in the emergence and development of the peasant labor process, and the Dominican masses' nurturing of that process since the days of slavery. The two most pertinent generalizations about Dominica are that it is a banana-producing country and that it is a peasant country. They make sense only in historical terms.

CHAPTER 3

Time: An Island in the World Economy

Of my own belief in this story I shall say nothing.
—C. L. R. James, *La Divina Pastora*

But the business in which slaves are used is conducted by CAPITALISTS. *The method of production which they introduce has not arisen out of slavery but is grafted on to it.*
—Marx, *Theories of Surplus Value*

The most visible differences among the various enclaves and villages of Dominica have to do with the degree to which particular crops modify the landscape in and around them. Yet several of the crops that contribute to this local differentiation are not native to the island. Bananas, coffee, or bayleaf, to cite only three examples, did not originate in the Caribbean. Like most of the flora and fauna of the inhabited coastal belt, they were carried from elsewhere—often from faraway continents—by the same colonizers who brought to the Americas the ancestors of the Dominican people. In fact, the whole Dominican landscape testifies to a continuous intrusion by successive waves of colonizers, an intrusion that affected people, things, and animals according to plans made elsewhere. Though each wave left its own distinguishable mark, the domination itself was ceaseless. Many of the differences and variations that we saw earlier are in fact products of the same dynamics. They represent different moments of the same process. Here, time unites.

Crops tell the story of that intrusion perhaps better than many other markers because they also shed light on the rationale behind it. Beyond the adaptation and the reproduction of the various species and families that succeeded each other on these patches of land is the history of profit perpetuating itself. Thus the current preeminence of bananas among the export crops which compose the Dominican landscape is not only a spatial phenomenon. Time enters here first because this preeminence is relatively recent, second because it belongs to a series, the understanding of which carries us way beyond the natural boundaries of the island itself.

Indeed, only in 1953 did the export values of bananas surpass for the first time the total value of all citrus and citrus-derived products exported from Dominica. The growth started in the 1940s. Its pace was brisk, its momentum spectacular. By 1953, bananas represented 45 percent of all export values, establishing a supremacy that still exists today. That such dominance had been achieved by a plant cultivated for centuries by the Dominican masses without major visible consequences was perhaps surprising in the 1950s. But less so was monocrop dominance itself. Many times Dominicans had witnessed the rise and demise of particular productions: coffee, sugarcane, cocoa, limes, vanilla; and every new ascendance had been accompanied by subtle changes in social relations. The sudden dominance of bananas on the Dominican landscape thus represented both a break and a continuity. The historical unity of Dominica can first be grasped in this successive preeminence of diverse crops.

It might look presumptuous that I seem to seek the first unifying trends of Dominican society outside of the island itself. Yet no amount of wishful thinking will ever wash away the harsh reality of colonial domination. Those who fully bear the scars of that domination know better than to pretend that such scars do not exist. The history of the Caribbean, as we know it, starts with colonialism, and colonialism reinforced by genocide at that. People, crops, machines, political regimes, and economic goals themselves were imported. The system did reproduce itself; but it did so only within the two jaws of violence and profit. And profit, here, was the main rationale for violence. Any genuine effort to understand the formation of a Caribbean entity requires a framework that encompasses this background. It is in this light that this chapter emphasizes the colonial background of Dominican society and provides a viewpoint that balances the image of dismemberment presented earlier. To be sure, this new vantage point is also quite insufficient by itself if only because it implies some gross generalizations; but it makes no claim of empirical uniformity. Furthermore, understanding human agency requires placing actions within their structural limits. With those caveats in mind, I suggest that, first and foremost, the unity of Dominica is in its integration in the world economy, an integration best marked by the succession of crops that it exported.

Dominica's present position in the world economy was augured perhaps on that Sunday, 3 November 1493, when Christopher Columbus's crew first spotted the rugged island. Columbus dutifully named the island Dominica in honor of the day, thereby signifying its acquisition by the Spanish Crown. But having found no harbor on the windward coast, he pushed forward to the smaller island now called Marie-Galante (after Columbus's flagship the *Mariagalante*). Even tales of the abundance of gold in the Dominican rivers did not attract him later. From the admiral's viewpoint, the place was too large to be ignored, but its topography and the presence in its forests of the proud and fierce Caribs severally limited its usefulness.

Columbus's ambivalence was to be shared later—and in varying degrees—by successive Spanish, French, British, and North American officials. Dominica was important enough to be included in their economic and political schemes for the Caribbean, but their policies implied that, beyond this general inclusion, the island had only limited usefulness. Spanish ships often stopped there before or after cross-Atlantic voyages during the sixteenth century to take on wood and water; but Spanish immigrants made little effort to settle permanently (Boromé 1972a, 1972b). Thus, Dominica's real entry in the world economy did not occur before the middle of the seventeenth century. By then, says Joseph Boromé (1972a: 75), "France had planted her flag on Dominica (1635), made a treaty with the Indians (1640), sent in a missionary (1642), assumed proprietorship to the point of ordering (1643) that no strangers be permitted to settle there."

But even this was a false entry of a sort, barely more concrete than the inclusion of the island in the 1627 patent of the British Crown to the Earl of Carlisle. The Dominican landscape and the Caribs inhibited both French and British colonizers, as they had the Spanish before them. By 1660, Britain and France jointly agreed to abandon Dominica and Saint Vincent to the Caribs; and if both nations violated that treaty and many others thenceforward, it was perhaps more because world powers reserve the right to occupy other peoples' lands in order to prevent the imagined calamities that imminent conquest by a rival might bring than because of any major economic gains. To France, especially, effective control of

Dominica may have mattered much less than the prevention of a British presence in an island strategically situated between Guadeloupe and Martinique (Anonymous 1764).

From 1660 to 1805, according to which side the ambivalence tilted, a series of treaties and proclamations in turn affirmed or reiterated the policy of nonintervention or the right of occupation by one or another power, and an equally long series of military adventures (launched to enforce, test, or *de facto* annul these treaties) testified to the island's political and military vulnerability. The period of undisturbed British possession dates from 1805. To be sure, between 1660 and 1805, there were relatively long interludes of political "stability" and economic growth. The one that lasted from about 1730 to 1759 deserves particular attention, for it sets the stage for Dominica's first monocrop strategy.

Coffee

In the second quarter of the eighteenth century, the introduction of coffee in the Caribbean and the early interest French settlers and merchants showed in that crop may have contributed to a change in the attitudes of at least a few Frenchmen toward Dominica. As in Saint Domingue, though on a much smaller scale, coffee suddenly made valuable places that had hitherto been neglected. Coffee could adapt to the topography and even benefit from the abundant rainfall of the more accessible highlands. With its cultivation, Dominica modeled itself on the pattern of plantation slavery, and, engaging in the first of a series of monocrop ventures, made a more decisive reentry in the capitalist world economy.

From 1743 to 1753 the number of coffee trees nearly tripled. In the same decade, the number of slaves did triple and the number of white inhabitants doubled (Boromé 1972b). To be sure, in Caribbean terms, these figures only placed the whole of Dominica on the same scale as some of Saint Domingue's most productive parishes (Trouillot 1982). Moreover, on the local level, the production of other crops, notably cocoa, bananas, and ground provisions, in addition to logwood, also increased during that period. Yet in giving up Dominica at the Peace of Paris (1763), thereby ratifying the success of the last British invasion of 1759, France essentially ceded a coffee-producing island to Britain. Coffee production had grown from 684,700 trees in 1743 to 1,367,700 in 1749 and 1,585,400 in 1753 (Boromé 1972b: 97). In 1763, the year of the cession, total island production reached 1,690,360 pounds. Reconquest and occupation by the French (1778–84), restoration to Britain by the Treaty of Versailles (1783), two military attempts by French emissaries (1795, 1805) and the abrupt population movements that accompanied them affected agricultural production in many ways, but never altered the reliance on a monocrop economy. New British and Irish settlers did specialize in sugar production after 1763 but coffee's preeminence was seriously contested only after the likelihood of a new French invasion had dwindled to a remote possibility. A 1792 report lists fifty-two sugar estates in the island for a total acreage of 11,800 acres and even that number seems exaggerated (Prestoe 1875: 3, C.O. 74/33). At the time of the abolition of slavery in the British colonies, despite a two-decade decline, coffee production still contributed to about half of Dominica's export revenues, and net export quantities for 1833 amounted to 1,612,528 pounds (Table 3.1). Likewise, by the early 1830s, 45 percent of the slave labor force was still engaged in coffee production (Table 3.2) in striking contrast to the rest of the British Caribbean where coffee production had always been marginal, except in Berbice in the 1810s (Higman 1984: 68–70).

Table 3.1. Coffee Export Quantities, 1833–1896

Year	Pounds	Year	Pounds	Year	Pounds	Year	Pounds
1833	1,612,528	1849	48,446	1865	31,077	1881	8,118
1834	957,443	1850	65,899	1866	9,888	1882	12,843
1835	1,026,276	1851	59,470	1867	23,913	1883	8,048
1836	186,426	1852	69,426	1868	9,877	1884	1,081
1837	386,315	1853	60,512	1869	15,214	1885	3,691
1838	43,079	1854	14,382	1870	10,603	1886	3,900
1839	192,303	1855	24,243	1871	15,734	1887	8,908
1840	371,670	1856	44,830	1872	12,466	1888	9,591
1841	98,729	1857	25,228	1873	13,319	1889	13,645
1842	194,632	1858	9,288	1874	12,117	1890	16,478
1843	147,504	1859	24,394	1875	10,990	1891	7,420
1844	123,088	1860	18,056	1876	28,240	1892	22,020
1845	95,424	1861	19,940	1877	35,382	1893	8,890
1846	142,000	1862	12,034	1878	19,216	1894	14,264
1847	93,833	1863	20,508	1879	10,877	1895	19,020
1848	161,343	1864	20,556	1880	N.A.	1896	25,786

Sources: Prestoe, 1875; C.O. 74/33; *Dominica Almanac*, 1844; Naftel, 1898; ZHC1/6084

Table 3.2. Estimated Distribution of Slaves by Type of Activity in 1810, 1820, and 1830

	1810	1820	1830
Total number	19,000	16,550	14,700
Activity	%	%	%
Coffee	50.0	48.0	45.0
Sugar	30.0	33.0	35.0
Other agriculture	10.0	10.0	12.5
Cotton	0.5	–	–
Fishing & shipping	0.5	0.5	0.5
Urban	9.0	8.5	7.0

Source: Higman 1984: Table 3.8.

The preeminence of coffee distinguished Dominica from other British Caribbean colonies. To be sure, by the 1830s, the momentum was on the side of the new sugar planters, and Dominica came close to mimicking a "new sugar colony" (Higman 1984). Yet coffee still dominated the exports up to the 1840s, and just as it demarcated parishes and regions within colonies such as Saint Domingue and Jamaica (Trouillot 1982; Higman 1976) it made of Dominica a quite peculiar British colony. In the early 1800s, Dominica was the only British Caribbean possession in which a majority of the slaves cultivated coffee, and also the one with the lowest percentage of slaves working in sugar production (Table 3.2). This observation explains at least in part the spatial and occupational homogeneity of the slave population, both quite high by British Caribbean standards.

Sugar

The early preeminence of coffee only postponed the reign of sugarcane, that almost inevitable aspect of island history in the Caribbean. As mentioned before, in 1833 coffee exports amounted to 1,612,528 pounds, yet three years later, Dominica exported only 186,426 pounds (Table 3.1), a decline of 88 percent. Henceforth, large-scale production never recovered and, by 1873, the percent decrease for the forty-year period was as high as 99 percent. Sugar production, on the rise since the 1810s, reached new highs.

Many observers follow the analysis of Dr. John Imray (1848), a Scottish physician who settled on the island in the late 1830s and wrote extensively about Dominican flora, fauna, and agricultural production. They attribute the sharp decline of coffee to a blight (*Cemiostosa coffelum*) which reportedly destroyed most of the plantations (*Dominica Almanac* 1859, 1862; Great Britain Colonial Office, 1953: 48). Yet, as government botanist Henry Prestoe reported after an official tour of the island in the mid-1870s, the major causes of the coffee decline were of a socioeconomic nature. Prestoe noted that "the high price of sugar induced many coffee planters to root up their coffee and plant sugar-cane" (Prestoe 1875: 4, C.O. 74/33). By 1843, sugar exports exceeded 5 million pounds, exports of molasses reached 109,000 gallons, small figures in the larger Caribbean context yet quite significant for Dominica. Between 1853 and 1883, sugar, rum, and molasses together accounted for 85 percent of the total value of Dominican exports whereas the second most important crop, cocoa, contributed a mere 5 percent of such value. Coffee production reached record lows in the mid-1880s despite John Imray's efforts in the 1870s to promote the cultivation of Liberian and Cape Coast coffees immune to the Dominican blight. Dominica's changing plantocracy boldly and consciously entered into a new venture that would carry the monocrop strategy to extremes not achieved in the island's history until the twentieth-century banana boom.

The sudden shift to a sugar-based export strategy could not have been more ill-timed. The movement toward the removal of trade restrictions, which protected Caribbean sugar in England, had started a decade earlier and gained momentum in the 1830s. By 1849 the Navigation Acts disappeared from British Statute Books (Deerr 1949–50, 2:422–23). By 1854 all the protectionist barriers that shielded Caribbean sugar from free competition in the metropolitan market no longer applied, and by 1874 sugar from all over the world entered England free of duty (Deerr 1949–50, 2:431, 441, 443). Meanwhile the production of beet sugar, started in the 1750s, gained in magnitude, and the bounty system adopted by many European governments reduced the importance of sugarcane on the world market while expanding world sugar production. In the early 1840s sugarcane accounted for 95 percent of the capitalist world's sugar market; but between 1850 and 1940, 60 to 65 million tons of sugar were thrown on that market at prices below the cost of production and by 1884 sugarcane accounted for less than half of world production (Deerr 1949–50, 2:490, 504). Consequently, world prices fell sharply in the late 1840s (registering a 19 percent drop on the world market from 1846 to 1847) and even more drastically in the 1880s (registering a 31 percent drop from 1883 to 1884).

Prices of Dominican sugar were of course not immune to the international downward trend. They fell by more than 15 percent in the course of the years 1845–47 (Hamilton 1894: 84). Production decreased accordingly and by 1862 total Dominican output was no more than 2,000 tons. Net sugar exports in 1866 were lower than in the 1850s and early '60s, though variations in the units of measure and the increase of rum exports make it difficult to quantify the extent of the decrease in cultivation (Tables 3.3 and 3.4). Still, even the sixfold rise in rum export quantities from the 1840s to the late 1860s could not remedy the difficulties of the sugarcane monocrop strategy, for sugar byproducts themselves were not immune to the pricing crisis. Dominican molasses registered a 7.5 percent decrease from 1853–57 to 1858–62. Yearly production of sugar byproducts became erratic (Table 3.4).

Table 3.3. Quantities of Sugar Exports in 1852, 1862, and 1866

Size	1850	1862	1866
Hogsheads	4,043	3,192	3,010
Tiercces		849	744
Barrels		2,507	1,976
Bags		150	—

Sources: *Dominica Almanac*, 1852, 1864, 1868.

Table 3.4. Exports of Sugar and Sugar Byproducts, 1870–1874

	Sugar		Molasses		Rum	
Year	Cwt.	Value (in pounds)	Gallons	Value (in pounds)	Gallons	Value (in pounds)
1870	73,026	51,147	88,732	2,732	36,021	2,337
1871	66,219	46,356	94,015	1,921	40,615	2,545
1872	61,418	51,558	105,282	3,476	24,630	1,543
1873	69,300	51,927	95,613	2,081	16,282	1,140
1874	65,903	54,727	70,849	2,311	32,498	2,280

Source: Sugar Commission, 1898, Appendix C.

In retrospect, the last two decades of the nineteenth century give a measure of the miscalculations of the Dominican planters. By 1882 the price of molasses had declined by 12.5 percent from 1853–57 levels; and during that period the decrease for sugar was 29 percent; that of rum 31 percent. Rum export production, the first to fall irreversibly, decreased by 92 percent during the same period. Sugar production itself did not fall irrevocably until 1884–85. In that year, London market prices registered their sharpest decline in decades. In that same year also, the United States became Dominica's most important client by acquiring 96 percent (2,562 tons) of its meager sugar production.

However, access to the North American markets did not salvage the Dominican sugar industry. Neither did the erection of a centrifugal plant. Sugar exports to Canada started in 1893, but prices were lower than in Britain itself. Exports to the United Kingdom stopped in 1894 at a time when general prices in the metropolis had decreased by 42 to 45 percent from 1882 (Sugar Commission, 1897–98). Prices of Dominican sugar registered a substantial increase in the United States in 1895 and 1896, but such an incentive had come too late for the planters. Export quantities and values for sugar and cane byproducts to other territories never reached the level of exports to Britain alone in 1883 (Table 3.5). Indeed, the yearly export value of sugar and other cane products declined from 89.4 thousand pounds sterling in 1858–62 to 49.5 thousand in 1878–82 to 17.2 thousand in 1888–92 (Sugar Commission Report, 1897–98).

Consequently, sugar lost its primacy among the leading exports of the island. Its contribution declined from more than 94 percent of the total export value in the 1860s and 87 percent in the early '70s to 56 percent in

Table 3.5. Sugar Exports, 1883–1896 (in Tons)

Year	Raw Sugar	Centrifugal Sugar	Year	Raw Sugar	Centrifugal Sugar
1883	3,734	—	1890	2,314	—
1884	2,660	—	1891	1,636	—
1885	3,096	—	1892	2,216	—
1886	2,449	—	1893	1,352	122
1887	2,574	—	1894	1,050	170
1888	2,068	—	1895	735	110
1889	2,530	—	1896	610	229

Source: Sugar Commission, 1898, Appendix C.

Table 3.6. Value in Percentage of Major Export Commodities to Total Exports, 1882–1896

Year	Sugar	Cocoa	Limes	Year	Sugar	Cocoa	Limes
1882	72.13%	9.83%	8.19%	1890	43.90%	19.51%	24.39%
1883	72.41	13.79	8.62	1891	26.31	39.47	26.31
1884	68.29	14.63	9.75	1892	38.63	22.72	25.00
1885	70.83	16.66	8.33	1893	25.49	29.41	33.33
1886	56.26	27.08	10.41	1894	25.00	25.00	27.77
1887	48.88	23.25	20.93	1895	16.21	24.32	40.54
1888	50.00	23.80	19.04	1896	14.58	27.08	41.66
1889	44.44	26.66	22.22				

Sources: Sugar Commission, 1898; Appendix B, Watts 1927.

1886 and 26 percent in 1891 (Table 3.6). By 1896, export quantities were estimated at 845 tons, a decrease of 78.50 percent from 1882. By then, as the Royal Commission on West Indian sugar reported, there were only "two exclusively sugar estates in cultivation, and these, with part of [a] third, aggregating about 955 acres, [were] being worked as one property" (Sugar Commission Report, 1898b: 138). Not surprisingly, the proprietors did not reside in the colony. By the beginning of the twentieth century, Dominica started to import sugar for local consumption.

Thus the sugar-based economy had fared no better than its predecessor. In light of probable inflationary and demographic pressures, the material quality of life may have declined in the second half of the nineteenth century. As early as the 1850s, visitors did not fail to notice the dissolution (Davy 1854: 507) or the general stagnation. Charles William Day, who visited the island thrice in 1849 and 1850, says of Roseau, the capital: "The impress of extreme poverty is on everything in the place" (Day 1852: 174).

Local legislators tried to increase government revenues through additional taxes. Yet figures showing repeated excesses of revenues over expenditures, or even a generally favorable balance of trade after 1856, barely mask the deep-rooted problems of the sugar-based Dominican economy in the third quarter of the nineteenth century. First, the favorable yearly surpluses that they show are almost always too miniscule to bear any significance: revenues exceeded expenditures by eight pounds in 1877! Indeed, when looking at these figures, one cannot help but consider that, at the end of many of those years, an adroit manipulation may have, through a final touch, tilted the balance in the required direction (*Antigua Almanac*, 1852: 70; *Dominica Almanac*, 1859: 66–67; *Dominica Almanac*, 1862: 85–86; *Dominica Almanac*, 1864: 80–82; *Leeward Islands Almanac*, 1879: 170; Sugar Commission Report, 1898, Appendix C, part 9: 515–20).

Moreover, a diachronic comparison of those figures shows little overall continuous growth, but rather a seesaw motion. By 1864, the state was again on the verge of economic collapse. In that year, "the bankrupt state of the Treasury" contributed to the suspension of the militia, and public employees remained eight months, up to May 1865, without salaries. By then, additional taxes and duties, and the loan of 6,000 pounds currency had been raised in the hope of restoring the equilibrium of public finances (*Leeward Islands Almanac*, 1879: 163). Yet the story of migratory movements may even be more eloquent than the fiscal peripeteias of the mid-nineteenth century. Planters and laborers left Dominica en masse in search of better opportunities.

Cocoa

An examination of Dominica's economic history up to the early 1890s suggests that cocoa was the most likely crop to fill the void created by the demise of the sugarcane industry. Sustained commercial cultivation dated from the early period of uncontested French domination. From 1730 to 1759, the number of cocoa trees had jumped from 4,272 to 953,200 (Boromé 1972b: 97). The British takeover after the Peace of Paris does not seem to have stopped the growth: export production reached 20,000 pounds in 1765 (Goodridge 1972: 154), but fell during the peak period of the coffee preeminence.

Production picked up again during the 1840s, and cocoa partly helped to fill the void created by the decline of coffee: its value was second only to that of sugar and other cane products. Export quantities grew from 2,354 pounds in 1838 to 124,925 in 1858, and 342,935 in 1878 (Table 3.7). Cocoa contributed almost 6 percent of all export value from 1858 to 1882, a contribution that strongly increased in both absolute and relative terms as sugar's part of the total export value kept decreasing. Cocoa accounted for 4 percent of the export value in 1883, 23 percent in 1887; and in 1891, with an export production of 820,280 pounds valued at some £15,000, cocoa briefly became the leading Dominican export,

Table 3.7. Quantities of Cocoa Exports, 1838–1896

Year	Pounds	Year	Pounds	Year	Pounds	Year	Pounds
1838	2,354	1853	90,265	1868	171,980	1883	473,355
1839	7,470	1854	53,492	1869	225,922	1884	389,264
1840	7,830	1855	57,327	1870	135,439	1885	468,801
1841	4,171	1856	27,801	1871	202,433	1886	644,670
1842	19,264	1857	64,626	1872	204,773	1887	499,400
1843	[?]	1858	124,925	1873	186,688	1888	581,040
1844	11,648	1859	52,751	1874	189,782	1889	737,595
1845	24,752	1860	96,459	1875	194,498	1890	462,187
1846	12,988	1861	113,460	1876	336,151	1891	820,280
1847	29,473	1862	181,348	1877	367,146	1892	492,506
1848	37,221	1863	101,646	1878	342,935	1893	726,342
1849	27,589	1864	135,695	1879	411,704	1894	692,718
1850	29,475	1865	148,120	1880	428,871	1895	681,114
1851	34,315	1866	154,266	1881	757,866	1896	993,456
1852	70,283	1867	189,224	1882	382,490		

Sources: Prestoe, 1875; Naftel, 1898; Sugar Commission: 1897–98.

contributing in excess of 39 percent of the export trade (Table 3.6). Yet cocoa's supremacy died aborning: two years later, limes and lime byproducts took the lead among the exports, contributing 33.33 percent of all the values, and cocoa fell back to second place.

Limes

The pioneering of export-oriented lime cultivation in Dominica is usually attributed to the same Dr. John Imray who encouraged the cultivation of Liberian and Cape Coast coffee in the 1860s. The evidence rests solely on the testimony of Imray's successor, Dr. H. A. Nicholls, to the West India Sugar Commission (Sugar Commission Report, 1898b: 125; Watkins 1924: 39). But lime juice had been shipped out of Dominica at least since 1843, the first year of available records, with a feeble export of forty-three gallons. It is quite unlikely, then, that the earliest shipments were due to Imray's enterprise: he came to the island in 1832, and

Table 3.8. Early Exports of Lime Juice

Year	Gallons	Value in Pounds
1843	40	
1862	1,105	
1870	1,904	83
1871	3,593	170
1872	5,932	691
1873	7,317	738
1874	12,462	1,600

Sources: *Dominica Almanac*, 1844, 1864; Prestoe 1875.

lime trees take a decade to reach full bearing. Imray and other important estate owners, doubtful of sugarcane's success, probably turned to limes in the 1860s and 1870s, the very same period he proposed Liberian and Cape Coast coffee as an alternative export. Such timing would fit with the growth of production registered during the early 1870s (Table 3.8).

Market conditions were so favorable that by 1875 many lime estates were "yielding profits greatly superior to those arising from sugar cultivation" (Prestoe 1875: 19, C.O. 74/33). However, juice prices fell soon after, and the lime industry seemed doomed until the ever entrepreneurial Dr. Imray learned from Martinique the process of producing essential oil from the lime rind (Nicholls, Sugar Commission Report, 1898b).

The whole history of the Dominican lime industry suggests that its long survival rested as much on market incentives as on the planters' willingness and capacity to exploit to the utmost the botanical possibilities inherent in the plant. From 1843 to 1953 limes and lime juice were shipped out of Dominica in no less than eight different forms: raw and concentrated lime juice, essential oil of lime, otto of lime (the last two from the rind), pickled and fresh limes, citrate of lime, and citric acid proper. Such diversification makes it difficult to retrace now the evolution of production through standardized annual figures; but diversification sustained cultivation against numerous vicissitudes: hurricanes, blights, and a general fall in prices in the second half of the nineteenth century.

Limes and lime products were geared toward three specific groups for different uses. The British government used the juice as a beverage to prevent the spread of disease among soldiers and sailors; the calico printers of major British textile regions (Lancashire, Yorkshire) used the citric acid in their dying process; fresh fruits and especially concentrated juice entered into the composition of alcoholic drinks in the United States (D. Morris, Subsidiary Report in Sugar Commission Report, 1898a; Nicholls, Memorandum in Sugar Commission Report, 1898b; Wood 1922: 50–52; Watkins 1924: 223–24; Colonial Office 1954). Betting on the security of these markets, the local government and the Colonial Office encouraged new settlements: from 1890 to 1924 some five thousand acres of Crown land were acquired mainly by new planters (Watkins 1924: 185), and the Roseau Botanic Garden distributed hundreds of thousands of plants.

Values did not always rise in proportion to production, but still increased substantially. By 1891, the year cocoa led all Dominican exports, limes and lime products had steadily grown to contribute 26 percent of the export value. Two years later, lime products dominated all the exports and that preeminence did not end until 1953 (Tables 3.6; 3.9; 3.10). Indeed, by 1912 the trade with the United States had gained enough importance to justify the presence of a permanent agent of the New York firm that bought the bulk of Dominican fresh limes (Watkins 1924: 54). World War I, the devastation brought by the 1916 hurricane and the increasing competition from Sicilian lemon production did not much alter the planters' and the government's monocrop strategy even though they impeded production and sale. Between 1922 and 1928, lime products accounted for 80 percent of all Dominican export value (C. O. 152/410–55, 499). After 1925, though, the combined effect of red root and withertip diseases, Prohibition in the United States (1920–33) which curtailed drastically the use of limes in alcoholic beverages, and the Great Depression which affected all parts of the world economy threatened the lime preeminence.

In the late 1930s, coconuts and vanilla came to share increasingly substantial percentages of the export value, especially because a price boom in vanilla during World War II when supply routes from Asia to the Americas were cut off. However, in 1945, as production reached its peak, the world vanilla market collapsed. Coconuts did survive the restructuring of the international market for tropical commodities which followed World War II. The exports of copra, dried coconut meat from which oil is extracted, increased slowly but steadily from 1945 to 1965. Copra export value tripled during the 1950s (Table 3.10). But the spectacular increases of banana export value after the 1940s signaled, once more, the beginning of a new, uncontested preeminence. In the temporal dimension, the 1953 figures which crowned that new preeminence

Table 3.9. Value in Percentage of Lime Products to Total Exports, 1900–1924

Year	Lime Products (in Pounds)	Total Export Value (in Pounds)	%
1900	35,410	68,452	51.7
1901	34,670	66,892	52.0
1902	44,916	80,794	55.6
1903	23,156	69,384	34.2
1904	28,362	63,016	45.0
1905	38,660	78,035	49.7
1906	54,535	106,246	51.2
1907	76,237	124,294	61.3
1908	51,924	112,013	46.4
1909	54,248	102,339	53.0
1910	69,496	112,111	62.0
1911	72,661	124,678	58.3
1912	95,940	152,458	61.5
1913	142,082	190,701	74.5
1914	185,895	210,087	87.6
1915	174,404	218,466	79.8
1916	172,352	194,763	88.5
1917	204,899	220,241	93.1
1918	163,532	184,480	88.6
1919	196,401	246,833	79.5
1920	185,410	224,280	83.0
1921	176,808	201,535	87.8
1922	131,016	150,350	87.1
1923	88,863	114,112	74.4
1924	136,600	168,058	80.9

Source: Watts 1927.

represent both a break and a continuity. The sudden rise of bananas befits the image of a Dominica characterized by the monocrops it successively sold to the world. Yet, this is not the whole story. Neither the Dominica of scattered enclaves nor the Dominica of monocrops exists, as such, out

Table 3.10. Main Export Values (f.o.b. in $E.C., 000 omitted), 1950–1963

Year	Copra	Lime Products	Bananas
1950	147	662	558
1951	165	772	916
1952	230	1,469	1,168
1953	242	1,530	1,889
1954	276	692	2,485
1955	306	856	2,708
1956	254	652	3,793
1957	347	789	3,290
1958	295	1,723	3,718
1959	307	844	4,521
1960	437	878	4,126
1961	493	1,263	4,784
1962	430	1,498	4,875
1963	506	1,080	5,417

Sources: Great Britain Colonial Office, *Colonial Reports on Dominica*, 1950–65.

there. Neither the image of dismemberment nor the curves of the export figures encapsulate fully the Dominican totality. We need to superimpose these two images and bring together time and space. Only then can we discover the dimension marked by the structural constraints of space and time together, within which, yet despite which, people shape their lives.

Closer attention to the relations of space and time, for instance, reveals behind the linear succession of export monocrops what Robert Maguire (1975) calls an alternation of "coast and interior." Coffee, cocoa, and vanilla signified an inward expansion in the direction of the mountains, whereas limes and sugar were products of the outer edges of the coastal belt. Maguire's analysis is illuminating. Yet one suspects beyond the movement from interior to coast deeper mechanisms, incuding the plantocracy's propensity to resist the preeminence of any crop easily produced on peasant-held plots of the hinterland, and to acclaim and dearly to sustain any crop that fitted the plantation labor process better than it did a peasant one. Coffee, cocoa, and vanilla required little local processing. Coffee was grown by slaves, but in a plantation colony that then counted one of the highest ratios of freedmen in the British Caribbean (Higman 1984: 77; C.O. 71/55). Cocoa and vanilla were, by and large, peasant crops. The demise of coffee, the rise of sugarcane (despite an unfavorable world market), the repeated technological breakthroughs which revived the lime industry, all partly resulted from planters' efforts to control production. Coffee and especially cocoa and vanilla carried the hopes of the peasantry. Interestingly, coffee production regained importance during the decline of sugar (Table 3.7). Likewise, cocoa records were broken anew in terms of both export quantities and value in the early 1900s, that is, during the lime preeminence, to which they represented a peasant counterpoint. Thus the alternation of coast and interior crystallized different victories, different moments in the continuous struggle between opposed segments of the population to shape their lives as they best knew. The rise and demise of any commodity was not simply a mechanical response to market conditions, but the result of local actions and initiatives best understood in terms of that struggle.[1]

The stakes were numerous, of course. They varied not only according to race and class but also, at times, in terms of national origin, ethnic identification, perceived phenotype, and religious denomination. Categories that now seem clearcut to us were quite blurry, at times, for the people involved. But if we take as our guide the vast majority among the Dominican masses themselves a unifying trend seems to emerge. We recognize, on the one hand, the masses' propensity to secure a form of agricultural labor that would give them the largest immediate control over their labor power and the units on which they worked. Likewise, we identify in the opposite camp the nonproducing classes, anxious to maintain the plantation labor process they perceived as the warrant of their wealth and power, both before and after slavery. To be sure, the opposition between plantation and peasant work activities was not always the only issue in the Dominican class struggle. Yet even if it was never the most fundamental one, it was certainly, and for a long time, the empirical stake through which the fundamental issues were contested. As an outcome of that contest, the rise of bananas to export preeminence (Table 3.10) marks a key moment in Dominican history. It is the victory of a peasantry determined to control—in part, if not fully—the space on which it labored and the time it devoted to that work. The next chapters describe that struggle, which started even before the end of slavery.

CHAPTER 4

The Evolution of the Peasant Labor Process: The Past in the Present

Political struggle is enormously complex: in a certain sense, it can be compared to colonial wars or to old wars of conquest—in which the victorious army occupies, or proposes to occupy, permanently all or a part of the conquered territory. Then the defeated army is disarmed and dispersed, but the struggle continues on the terrain of politics and of military "preparation."

—A. Gramsci, *Prison Notebooks*

For if a man can make enough by cultivating his provision grounds to satisfy his wants, without labouring for hire of course he will prefer so doing.

—Lloyd to McPhail, 5 May 1839

The struggle of the Dominican masses before the rise of bananas among the export crops can be summarized as a series of concrete efforts to control land and labor. As monocrops succeeded one another, the organization of labor changed, sometimes at the same rhythm, often by a dynamism relatively independent from the dominant export of the day. Though trends in the world market influenced production and export, the concrete struggle over the control of the workplace, on the ground, always qualified the dominance of an export commodity. And that struggle involved, of course, much more than the production of the export crops so crucial to the colonizers. Once slavery ended and the threat of physical bondage disappeared, the Dominican cultivators sought control of the units of production, including those that did not produce for export.

Still, the emphasis here is less on the units of production (plantations, gardens, provision grounds) as such than on the economic and political mechanisms that yielded or impeded control over them, and the stakes such control implied. Second, and more important for now, the concept of a peasant labor process does not belong to the actual consciousness of past and present Dominican cultivators; rather, it is a tool by which I try to make sense of their actions and the responses their actions provoked in others. The concept requires a constant back-and-forth movement between the level of abstraction at which it operates and the existential reality of the actors themselves, a reality never fully recaptured by the analyst. The generalizations that follow must be read in that light. In what type of units did the peasant labor process occur? What was the legal status of the laborers? For what purposes were the crops produced? Answers to these questions help us delineate three domains.

The kind of unit within which the process obtained allows us to isolate a *spatial domain.* The status of the cultivators helps to isolate a *juridical domain.* The crops delineate a *commercial domain.* Of course, these domains overlapped in the real world. At times, the purpose changed while the units remained the same. At other times, the units changed while the ultimate goal of production remained essentially the same. Further, the relative importance of any one of these three domains influenced, at any time, the actual leverage the cultivators enjoyed in any of the two others. Under slavery, for instance, the fact of bondage clearly limited the cultivators' control of space and of the local market, even if not so much as one would at first tend to believe.

Each of these domains, in turn, included opposite poles; and whereas cultivators tended toward one pole, planters, merchants, and public officials usually aimed at its very opposite. In the spatial sphere, for instance, the peasant labor process operated both within and outside the estates. In fact, it first flourished within the estates at a time when it was cheaper for the planters to allow their slaves full control over the provision grounds from which these slaves gathered a substantial portion of their daily food. At that time, peasant-type activities remained under the shadow of the plantation labor process through which the major export commodities were produced. Obviously, the peasant work organization had different consequences later, in the spatial context of the small independent plots the laborers controlled in the latter part of the nineteenth century. Moreover, whereas nonproducers found it convenient to allow peasant work activities in the restricted space of the provision grounds, cultivators tried to expand that spatial domain so as to include the entire estate.

Likewise, the juridical domain also included two poles: coercion (especially under slavery) and civil equality. Here again, the process operated differently at the ends of the continuum: there was at the time of slavery what Mintz (1984) calls a "proto-peasantry"; and there was, of course, the independent yeomanry that slowly emerged after Emancipation. Here again, whereas the cultivators preferred freedom (however qualified), merchants, planters, and public officials tried by all means, even after the formal end of slavery, to maintain a juridical context that would restrict as much as possible the physical mobility and the political leverage of the laborers.

Finally, the peasant labor process tied into two separate commercial networks, one with a local destination known to the producers and one with a foreign goal. Here again, nonproducers and cultivators did not see eye to eye: merchants, planters, and officials tried to stop peasant-produced commodities from entering the foreign market. Thus, the issues were entwined, the fight was continuous, and the gains were often ephemeral. At any time, the relative weight of each of these classes or of factions within them implied a distinctive integration of the three different domains, hence a different historical context for a peasant-type control of land and labor.

Each section within this chapter broadly coincides with a particular conjunction of the three domains, a specific historical configuration of the peasant labor process. I first look at the emergence of the peasant forms of labor under slavery on the estates in the production of locally consumed provisions. I then turn to the evolution of those forms in the aftermath of slavery, first in the production of provisions, but also, and particularly, in the production of export commodities. Outside of estate boundaries, the peasant labor process first implanted itself in the production of provisions on Crown lands taken over by squatters. Finally, as more Dominicans acquired full property rights on small plots, an independent yeomanry used the peasant labor process in the production of provisions, and, as the twentieth century progressed, increasingly in the production of agricultural export commodities.

Table 4.1. Historical Configurations of the Peasant Labor Process

Cultivators by Periods	**Produce**	**Domains**		
		Spatial	**Juridical**	**Commercial**
Proto-peasants 1763–1838	Provisions	Estate grounds (marginal)	Slavery/apprenticeship	Local network
Maroons 1763–1838	Provisions	Crown lands	Slavery/rebellion	No network
Tenants 1838–1950	Export crops & provisions	Main estate grounds	Coercion	Local & international
Métayers 1838–ca. 1960	Provisions & export crops	Main estate grounds	Freedom/coercion	Local & international
Squatters 1838–ca. 1960	Provisions	Crown lands	Freedom/withdrawl	No network
Yeomen 1850s–present	Export crops Provisions	Individual or family grounds	Political & economic freedom	International & local network
Tenants 1950–present	Export crops	Estate plots	Political & economic freedom	International network

The progression is then more than a mere chronological one. Many of these configurations overlapped. The temporal dimension is not a unilinear sequence. Rather, the aim is to reveal, beyond the expansion of a form of labor organization, the thread that makes sense of the concrete actions of the Dominican people over time. The continuity I seek is that of the voice of these people if they could ever speak with one voice.

The Provision Grounds of Slavery

One of the most important and challenging aspects in the study of plantation slavery in the Americas is undoubtedly the question of the slaves' right to productive property. For if the slave himself was property, how did his or her access, however qualified, to productive property coexist with slavery? How did this coexistence modify not only his or her personal life but also the ideological and political context within which slavery itself was practiced? The manner in which the contradiction between slavery as a system and the existence of slaves' productive property originated and evolved within a particular society obviously bore heavy and immediate consequences for the economic, political, and cultural life of those who toiled under that system.

Now, more than a century after the total disappearance of slavery in the region, the existence of property rights—especially when they implied access to provision grounds and distribution of the products originating from such grounds—carries more than its obvious intellectual weight for students of the Caribbean. These grounds are at the core of the social genesis of many Caribbean nations; and for many peasants, the social and cultural significance vested in these lands under slavery has not lost its immediacy. How are we then to preserve this historical richness in a way that enlightens not only the understanding of slavery but also that of its continuities?

In his pioneering work on the rise and significance of the slave provision grounds, Mintz (1961, 1979, 1984) called the slaves who had access to such grounds on the plantation a "proto-peasantry," as I just mentioned. In a similar vein, Karasch (1979) has suggested the category "peasant-slaves" to define Brazilian slaves engaged in similar situations. Yet though such notions are powerful descriptive tools and valuable historical categories, they cannot provide a strong conceptual link between contemporary patterns of social reproduction and those of slavery. Mintz's own work provides similarly powerful categories bearing on other cases and periods, but the subject requires another level of conceptualization in order to avoid using a different, historically specific, tool for each and every set of circumstances.

The work of historian Tadeusz Lepkowski (1968–69) on Haiti proposes a focus on the "peasant breach in the slave mode of production." This is a promising approach, even if one questions the existence of a "slave mode of production," or the validity of what Alavi (1965) and Cardoso (1979) have called "colonial modes." However, Lepkowski does not reveal the nature of the peasant breach. At what level does peasant production introduce an anomaly within plantation slavery?

Building on Lepkowski, Cardoso himself (1979) identifies the peasant breach as a structure. He tests the comparative usefulness of the category through an analysis that touches different areas of the Americas: United States, Brazil, the Caribbean. Yet, the question of the socio-organizational level in which this structure fitted is left unanswered. It does not suffice to repeat after Lepkowski that the peasant-slave worked on lands that formed an integral part of a larger "organism of production." We must conceptualize the unit of production in terms of what we know of the empirical conditions of labor.

Economist Charles Bettelheim (1976) reminds us that any discrete unit of production brings together particular means of labor that workers activate through a specific work process. On the other hand, the record on Caribbean slave societies, such as Dominica, where slaves grew their own provisions, does not lead to generalizations about the use of time or the allocation of space for these provision grounds (Higman 1984: 204–5). At best, one can suggest that provision grounds generally appeared wherever plantation crops did not. And that itself, of course, varied from island to island and, sometimes, from year to year within the same estate. Likewise, the amount of labor time devoted to the provision grounds always depended on the requirements of the plantation crops. Obviously, one was not slave one day and peasant the next. Neither was one a slave only when stepping into that part of the plantation reserved for the export crops.

Thus, Caribbean labor organization was a curious hybrid indeed. The breach rested essentially on the juxtaposition of two different labor processes within the unit of production that was the plantation. Somewhere, on the ground, physical lines demarcated two types of work activities carried, essentially, by the same people. The provision grounds at times fell outside estate boundaries not because of the master's desire to create a different unit but because of the expansion of export-oriented production. Thus the spatial domain of the peasant labor process was always a remainder of the estate, and a varying one at that, the actual size of which was determined by a foreign logic. The metaphor of a breach is thus seductive in two ways. First, it reflects these empirical markers; second it carries also the connotation of a transgression. For though the plantation labor process, as exemplified in sugarcane production, obviously fits the organism, the peasant labor process appears to invade a unit of production certainly not designed for its accommodation. The conceptual difficulties faced by many scholars who studied the case stems from its inherent awkwardness.

The peasant breach consisted in the juxtaposition of two different labor processes within the same unit of production. But why did such a juxtaposition occur? What was the rationale behind this ungainly arrangement? Mintz (1979: 240) recalls that this apparently bizarre development "happened to suit the short-term goals of slaves and masters." What were these short-term goals? How important were they to slaves and masters? Why did the juxtaposition of two labor processes become such a viable short-term solution to the problems of feeding and clothing the labor force? Answers to these questions fall outside work activities. They pertain to the very rationale behind plantation slavery. It is essentially through the motives of the planters that we can understand

1. the factors that prohibited the use of the plantation as a coherent unit of food production,
2. the factors that prohibited the use of the plantation as an integrated unit of consumption, and
3. the factors that stimulated the acceptance of the slave family as a primary unit for the production and consumption of food items.

The major hindrance to the use of the plantation labor process in food production was, from the planters' viewpoint, the high cost of producing such food within the plantation economy. Such an enterprise would necessitate the systematic use of large quantities of unbroken land and the mass deployment of labor power otherwise available for the production of export commodities. It would require constant supervision, if not by the planters, at least by drivers and overseers. In short, such mass production of food would have diverted the planter from his primary goal: the production of export crops.

Of course, planters could have bought food in bulk instead of producing it on the estates. Some did so, and quite often, especially in the larger islands. Yet most reserved their cash for the purchase of specific items such as flour or salt cod which could not be obtained otherwise. The incentives against bulk purchase were twofold. First, prices were high, whether the food was imported or produced locally on specialized units. Second, large purchases involved cash exchange, and cash was then a rarity throughout the Caribbean. Even the commercialization of plantation crops involved little cash exchange. In short, buying food was not any more attractive to the planter than bulk production on the estates.

A third option would have been the direct exchange of plantation products for food in the local market, without actual cash changing hands. Yet it also presented major difficulties. In terms of the plantation's integration within the world economy, in terms of the planters' primary goal, such barter implied lesser profits than the sale of the same plantation crops on the international market. In short, it would also have been self-defeating.

Finally, owners and overseers may have made a political choice in deciding against any plantation-wide system of distribution. If they distributed the food themselves, if they controlled the local lines of supply or if they directly supervised production, they could easily bear the blame for the shortages that occurred. Moreover, such shortages would have been felt by the whole plantation at the same time, a fact that would increase their impact not only on the morale of the enslaved laborers but also on production itself. Thus bulk distribution tended to work against the primary goal of the unit almost as much as bulk production.

What emerges from this exploration is a major contradiction of New World slavery, especially as it occurred in the restricted space of the Antilles: the very same profit motives which made the plantation an ideal unit of production for the commodities aimed at the world market acted against its institutionalization as a coherent unit for the production or consumption of food by the enslaved labor force. Since all planters acted, in principle, according to the same general logic, any alternative that impinged on the mass production of export crops was to be rejected. Planters were not in the business of feeding slaves; their primary goal was profit. Edgar Thompson (1975: 255) says quite rightly: "In the business of running a plantation the feeding of [workers] and the feeding of livestock may be figured together and on the same level." Yet despite their claims to the contrary, white planters in the Caribbean could not but acknowledge that they were dealing with human beings, that their slaves could not figure exactly on the same level as their livestock. Thus to solve the economic dilemma, they relied on the very same humanity that they otherwise denied. They relinquished most of the responsibility for slave reproduction to the slaves themselves, in a way that no breeder has ever been able to do with livestock. In so doing, they protected their short-term goals, but they unknowingly set a trend that was to alter the character of many of these island societies. For the slaves were not livestock: they learned from the experience. They learned agricultural techniques; they learned economic practices; and, most of all, they learned the exercise of power that these practices entailed.

Other incentives to consider the slave family as a unit of production and consumption were not lacking; cultural traditions in both Europe and Africa regarded the family or the household as natural units of food consumption. The practice was attuned to the memories of many Africans and the paternalistic ideals of many European planters (Laborie 1798). From food sharing, the household turned into a consumption unit for necessities other than food and relieved planters of direct responsibility. In the instance of clothing, for example, family consumption freed owners from cash expenses much dreaded in the context of the plantation economy. As the slave family was allowed to sell some of its provisions, the burden of feeding and clothing the young and the disabled often shifted from owners to kin.

The extent to which these factors worked together in any particular situation depended primarily on the availability, within and outside the estates, of land that could shelter the peasant labor process in food production without reducing space reserved for plantation production. Steep or broken terrain, less fertile lands, forest lands, plots that, given the technology of the times or available capital, were not easily adaptable to plantation production, all were hospitable to the slave provision grounds. A mountainous topography, for instance, greatly favored the emergence and implantation of the provision grounds within the natural borders of any particular island. It is not by accident that the peasant labor process gained wider acceptance in Saint Domingue, Jamaica, Saint Vincent, or Dominica, say, than in Barbados, Antigua, or Saint Kitts.

In Dominica, land not readily adaptable to plantation production was available not only because of the broken and steepy terrain within and outside the estates but also because of low population density. Not surprisingly, then, despite the growth of coffee exports, peasant production of food had reached such proportions as to appall some observers. Masters boasted, no doubt with gross exaggeration, that each slave controlled at least half an acre of land (Higman 1984: 210). Thomas

Atwood, who resided in the island at the end of the eighteenth century, wrote:

> [The slaves] have there as much land as they chuse to cultivate for their own use, are capable of raising great quantities of all manner of ground provisions, garden stuff, and other things, with which they actually supply the markets on Sunday and some of them to a considerable extent.
>
> They likewise breed hogs, rabbits, fowls and other small stock for themselves; and many of them, who are careful in raising such provisions acquire a comfortable living, exclusive of what is allowed them by the owner. (Atwood 1791: 259)

Historian B. Higman (1984: 212) itemizes a long list of products from the slave provision grounds aimed primarily at the local market. It includes: "yams, plantains, bananas, cassada [sic] or manioc, eddoes, potatoes, ocoraes [okra], Indian corn, cale, pigeon pease, and several species of beans, and pine apples; and the higher grounds produce many kinds of European garden stuff, such as cabbages, carrots, turnips, beet root, lettuce, asparagus, artichoke, radish, cucumber, cellery, and herbs of all sorts, besides tropical fruits."

As the cost of living increased in the island, and as liberals in Europe pointed to the human cost of slavery or questioned its legitimacy, planters and the colonial government codified the customs that regulated the slave provision grounds. This formalization offered some ideological relief but more important, it relieved poorer planters from the obligation of feeding their slaves. Stipulated requirements varied (Higman 1984: 210), but the local legislature usually tried to prevent excessive neglect without cutting deeply into the profits of the majority of the planters. The last major piece of legislation regarding the slaves' provision grounds, "an Act to amend the laws relating to slaves" (C. O. 73/15, 376), dated 28 June 1831, reaffirmed in its first clause planters' responsibility to provide "sufficient clothing and food" to the slaves, including a pair of trousers to the males and a head wrapper or a cap, as well as a blanket every three years, and so on. These may not seem much, but many slave owners deemed themselves "too poor" to afford such expenses. The law allowed them to compensate for the lack of material goods by giving their slaves more independent labor time. Clause two of the same act read: "And be it enacted that Whereas there are many poor persons who are not able to produce the clothing required to be furnished to such slaves by the foregoing clause it shall be lawful for any such poor persons to grant to any of his or her slaves (being adult and capable of labour) in lieu of such clothing any number of days not less than twelve to be allowed to such slave consecutively of Saturdays and Sundays."

Clause five stated: "And be it enacted that every Proprietor, Renter, Attorney or Agent of any slave or slaves shall have the option of feeding them as directed in the first clause or alloting to them a sufficient portion of land for that purpose, not being less than half an acre for each individual slave and shall appropriate the Saturday in every week for the purpose of cultivating the same except during croptime" (C. O. 73/15, 376).

The law's careful setting of as many options as possible for the masters in a context in which cash was rare and purchased food was expensive underscores that the peasant labor process was allowed to flourish under slavery only insofar as it did not interfere with the main purpose of the estate. That purpose, the production of export commodities for profit, was carried exclusively through the plantation labor process, the working of which peasant-type activities were meant only to facilitate. Thus, the peasant breach did not constitute a new *mode of production* in the precise sense of this concept. It did not, in and of itself, lead to new relations of production, though it affected all three aspects of these relations: property relations, labor relations, and relations of distribution.

With regard to property relations, the sale of part of the produce—which specifically answered the problems of supplying necessities other than food—implied the slave's right not only to private property but also to private exchange. Yet the overarching property relations did not change inasmuch as the slave's control of any particular plot of land depended on the master's ownership of the estate. Moreover, the slave, though beneficiary of a right or control over his or her provisions which excluded the other slaves, remained the individual property of an individual master. In fact, the ownership of the slave class by the planter class remained the fundamental relation within the society even though some slaves did buy their freedom with the income accumulated from the sale of provisions produced on their grounds.

The subsumption of the peasant labor process also appears in labor relations: the independent use of the slave's labor time rested on the master's allocation of such time. The slave's major gain thus involved a limited right to private property and private exchange. From the slave's viewpoint, this right, in turn, had a beneficial impact on relations arising from the disposition of the product. The limited use of that property and the much less restricted use of the cash drawn from exchanges allowed the slave to deflect, even if marginally, the distribution of money and material goods, from the sharing of food or cash to the buying of his or her freedom. Such practices barely made a dent in plantation slavery itself, but they led to major consequences after the juridical change of 1838.

The War of Position

The 1834 Emancipation did not bring any sudden changes in the workers' conditions. The former slaves were bound to the same estates for a period of so-called Apprenticeship that lasted four years, but the Act for the Abolition of Slavery presented to the Assembly in April 1834 reiterated the owners' responsibility to furnish the labor force "with sufficiency of provision grounds." If food was not provided, the owner was to give the laborer "ground adequate, both in quality and quantity, for his or her support, and within a reasonable distance from his or her usual place of abode, under penalty not exceeding ten pounds for each offense" (C. O. 73/15, 403). At the end of Apprenticeship, however, on 1 August 1838, the laborers were formally endowed with the right to leave the estates, or, if they stayed, to negotiate labor relations. The various decisions they made contributed to a sudden expansion of the peasant labor process in Dominican society.

The laborers furthered the implementation of that process on the estates: (1) by keeping, when they stayed, the provision grounds of slavery; and (2) by trying to extend elements of a peasant work organization to the estate production of export commodities.

The most detailed evidence about the estates comes from the monthly reports of the stipendiary magistrates appointed to monitor the countryside immediately after the end of Apprenticeship. They were usually channeled by Governor Colebrooke to Lord Glenelg at the Colonial Office (ZHC1/1266). From the very beginning, they indicate that the laborers who remained on the estates did so on condition that they could keep their provision grounds. Indeed, commenting on those reports, the governor of the Leeward Islands stated in a dispatch of 20 November 1838 to the Colonial Office: "The peasantry thinks the land is theirs since they were secure on it in slavery" (ZHC1/1266, 167:405).

The right to the provision grounds was secured in just a few days. Stipendiary Magistrate William Lynch reported for August 1838: "Upon all plantations under profitable cultivation, the cottage and grounds are considered as part of the daily wages." Magistrate Howard Lloyds wrote in September about another district: "Cottages and gardens are allowed to laborers exclusive of their wages." By November, only in the parish of Saint Andrew were provision grounds not firmly guaranteed (ZHC1/1266, 158, 166, 167).

Current analyses notwithstanding, the officials of the time were quite aware that what they themselves were witnessing was nothing but the emergence of a peasantry. The governor himself uses the word *peasantry*, and both "peasant" and "peasantry" appear repeatedly in the field reports of the magistrates who covered the countryside. These witnesses could have been mistaken, of course. Yet I suspect that these words were used with cause. It seemed clear to planters and officials alike that the expansion of the peasant labor process in the postslavery context had far-reaching implications. Their words as well as their deeds, indeed the panic of many among them, reveal their awareness that the expansion of peasant work activities now threatened the relations of production at the core.

The planters' conscious class reaction is proof of this awareness. They bound together to put an end to a practice that they themselves, as individual profit seekers, had introduced mainly as a cost-cutting measure when slavery made them directly responsible for the reproduction of the labor force. The minutes of a meeting held by the major planters on 12 January 1839 reveal an unbreakable class solidarity on the issue of the provision grounds. Planters focused on these grounds because they anticipated that they would be the Trojan horse of the peasantry. They vehemently rejected "the mixing of wages and grounds" and insisted that laborers pay rent for their houses and grounds while receiving straight cash for their work. Indeed, some planters would have preferred paying relatively higher wages and charging rent to deducting such rent from wages, providing that neither party could terminate such an agreement without a twelve-month notice. The lieutenant governor and commander in chief commented that the proposals were sound but that peasants were not likely to enter such agreements. And indeed, they did not. They kept their provision grounds even during a work slowdown that they maintained over most of the island in the first months of 1839. Stipendiary Magistrate Lloyd reported on March 18: "[Some strikers] continue to occupy, as a matter of right, the houses and grounds which renders them independent of the owner of the soil" (ZHC1/1266, 177:442). In his inaugural speech of 19 April 1839 the newly appointed lieutenant governor deplored “the great indolence” of segments of the peasantry which illegally held “as if a matter of right their houses and grounds though they refuse to contribute any labor for the estates in return” (ZHC1/1266, 177:451).

The planters opposed the provision grounds at the end of Apprenticeship precisely because they foresaw the leverage that the continuing existence of such grounds would give the former slaves. History proved them right. The security of the provision grounds provided the laborers with a productive base from which to introduce the peasant labor process into the estate production of export commodities. They did not exert such pressures as a concerted group, however, but through the convergent effects of thousands of individual decisions.

I have studied some of those choices through the records of forty-one estates (twenty produced sugarcane and coffee, twelve sugarcane only, and nine coffee only) as reported by one William Lynch, stipendiary magistrate for the parishes of Saint George, Saint Luke, Saint Mark, and Saint Patrick South. Lynch’s observations were entered into a volume of the *Accounts and Papers* of the House of Commons (Session 5 February–27 August 1839) subtitled *Papers on the Conditions of the Labouring Population, West Indies* (PP, vol. 37, 1839, or PRO, ZHC1/1266) together with those of the other magistrates.

The unique feature of Lynch’s reports, as far as the Dominican countryside is concerned, is a combination of four lists summarizing labor conditions on more than fifty estates, all of which are mentioned by name. Yet since not all the data reappear with the same consistency on all four lists, and since some of those estates bore similar names, I reduced the list to forty-one estates. The primary evidence for each estate consists of:

1. the name of the estate and the dominant crop(s) it produced;
2. the number of apprenticed laborers on 31 July 1838, the last day of Apprenticeship;
3. the average number of laborers at work in the month of August 1838, the first month of “total” freedom;
4. the average number at work in September;
5. the conditions of work in September;
6. the average number at work in October;
7. the conditions of work in October;
8. the average number of laborers at work in November; and
9. the conditions of work during November (ZHC1/1266, 166, 167).

Between July 31 and December 1, those forty-one estates lost a total of 1,030 laborers, a decrease of 39 percent of their labor force of 2,634. The following conclusions are drawn from three different distributions of that decrease among the forty-one estates.

The first distribution seems to suggest that the nature of the crop cultivated on the estate did not make much difference to the former slaves. The labor force of sugar estates decreased 39 percent; the labor force of mixed estates declined 34 percent. Estates producing only coffee lost more, but most of the mixed estates were primarily coffee estates where sugar production remained marginal (Table 4.2).

The second distribution is more revealing. I put the estates into three categories according to their labor force on July 31: those with 20–50 laborers, with 51–100, and with more than 100. The relative decreases from July to November suggest that the laborers made a clear choice against the larger estates. The large estates' share of the total laboring population dropped from 47 percent to 40 percent, a net decrease of 49 percent on the large estates. Their average population dropped from 123 to 63 workers. All in all, 602 of the 1,030 laborers who deserted (58 percent) came from the largest estates. The mid-range estates did better: their share of the labor force increased from 29 percent in July to 32 percent in November. Thus, despite a net loss of 34 percent, their relative position improved. But the estates that best survived the laborers' flight were the small units with 20–50 workers. From July to November, their share increased from 24 percent to 29 percent, despite a net decrease of 27 percent of their population.

It seems then that the smaller the estate, the more successfully it could retain its labor force. That may be due to some positive correlation between size of estate and harshness of slave treatment under

Table 4.2. Distribution of the July–November Decrease according to Crops Cultivated

	Sugar, Coffee	Sugar	Coffee	Total
No. of estates	20	12	9	41
July labor force	875	1,245	514	2,634
% Share	33.21	47.26	19.51	100
Nov. labor force	575	756	273	1,604
% Share	35.84	47.13	17.01	100
Net decrease (%)	34.28	39.27	46.88	39.10

Table 4.3. Distribution of the July–November Decrease according to Size of Labor Force before Emancipation

	20–50 Laborers	**51–100 Laborers**	**101M Laborers**	**Total**
No. of estates	20	11	10	41
No. of laborers in July	630	769	1,235	2,634
Mean (by estate)	32	70	123	
% Share of July labor force	23.91	29.19	46.88	100
No. of laborers in Nov.	461	510	633	1,604
% Share of Nov. labor force	28.74	31.79	39.46	100
Net decrease (%)	26.82	33.68	48.74	39.10

plantation slavery. I have suggested elsewhere (Trouillot 1982) that the pressures of capitalist production on slaves' leisure and performance might rise with the size of the unit of production, as the requirements of the unit increasingly qualified allocations of time and space to the slaves. In the case of provision grounds, it is obvious that their existence depended heavily on the availability of time and space. The flight from the larger estates may be read as a statement about past treatment under slavery and Apprenticeship, but also as a commentary on the former slaves' desire to expand what we now call the peasant labor process (Table 4.3).

The third distribution groups the estates according to the conditions under which the former slaves performed in November. It shows that estates that relied on wage labor lost a greater proportion of their labor force. On the last day of Apprenticeship, July 31, they controlled 2,038 apprentices, that is, 77 percent of the population under study. In November, their share dropped to 68 percent of the remaining labor force, a net decrease of 47 percent. Of the 1,030 apprentices who fled for good, 953 (93 percent) came from wage-earning situations. Estates that simply asked for days of labor in exchange for use of the houses and grounds gained in relative terms despite a net decrease of 16 percent, as their share increased from 6 percent of the July labor force to 9 percent of the November labor force. Estates that allowed sharecropping gained the most. Their share increased from 17 percent of the July labor force to 24 percent of the November labor force, even though they registered a net decrease (Table 4.4).

Table 4.4. Distribution of the July–November Decrease according to Labor Conditions

	Wage, Labor	Labor-Rent	Sharecropping	Total
No. of laborers in July	2,038	160	436	2,634
% Share of July labor force	77.37	6.07	16.55	100
No. of laborers in Nov.	1,085	134	385	1,604
% Share of Nov. labor force	67.65	8.35	24.00	100
Net decrease (%)	46.75	16.25	11.69	39.10

The three distributions have so far considered crops, size, and working conditions as independent factors. Yet we cannot treat historical causality in a mechanical way; the reality, on the ground, must have been much more complex than any of these tables would imply. The relative decrease on any estate did not solely depend upon a single characteristic, or even upon a combination of features intrinsic to that estate. Not all ex-slaves returned to plantation labor. Moreover, not all those who returned went to the same estates where they had resided before Emancipation. Thus, for each and every laborer who returned, the decision implied not one but two evaluations, inherently linked in existential terms: whether or not to return to plantation labor and to which particular unit. The final decision itself was certainly made not only in terms of the characteristics of the estate (including its owner's behavior), but also on the basis of all the options available in a particular area (including the rejection of units otherwise accessible in simple terms of supply and demand).

One cannot measure statistically the interplay of all the options on the sole basis of Lynch's reports. Table 4.5 (which groups the forty-one estates under study according to the crops they produced and conditions of work in November) illustrates only some of the historical complexity behind the unilinear trends abstracted above. Here, the convergence of

Table 4.5. Crops and Labor Conditions in November 1838

	No. of Estates	Coffee	Sugar	Sugar/Coffee
Wage labor	24	4	12	8
Labor-rent	4	1	0	3
Sharecropping	13	4	0	9
Total	41	9	12	20

sugar production and wage labor is most noticeable and should help to modify the partial results of Table 4.2.

The rejection of wage labor and the preference for sharecropping are corroborated by two special groupings. The first special grouping comprises the thirteen worst cases of flight: the thirteen estates that lost more than 55 percent of their July labor force (Table 4.6). The second special grouping comprises seven estates which must have looked peculiar under the circumstances: the seven estates that gained laborers at a time when all the others were losing theirs (Table 4.7). Together, those groupings provide us a clearer picture of the alternatives perceived by the former slaves who returned to plantation labor. Which estates did they pick, and why? Which estates did they avoid as much as possible?

The first special grouping suggests that the former slaves avoided as much as possible estates that demanded wage labor. Ten of the thirteen worst cases of flight involved wage labor. Four of them (Goodwill, Aberdeen, Porée, and Providence) required the laborers to work five days a week, presumably with two free days to work on their own grounds. They lost from 58 to 66 percent of their labor force. Estates requiring more than five days of wage labor (Watton Haven, Morne Rouge, Bois Cutlet) tended to lose even more laborers. Three of the thirteen worst cases involved sharecropping, but the arrangements described here were not typical of sharecropping patterns. Champ Flor and La Tent estates, for instance, did not do well in the competition for labor. They allowed the laborers to share only one-third of the coffee, whereas several estates where offering as much as half of the production to the sharecroppers.

The former slaves could flee the estates that required wage labor, in part because they could obtain what they perceived as better conditions from other planters. Many planters reluctantly allowed their workers to share half of the produce; others required resident laborers to work on estate grounds for two or three days a week and to use the remaining days on their own plots. All the evidence points to the former slaves' preference for sharecropping and labor-rent arrangements. Indeed, six of the seven estates that ended up with more laborers in November 1838 than they had apprentices at the end of slavery involved sharecropping or labor rent.

Of the seven estates that gained laborers, one is a sugar estate, two are cofffee estates,and four are mixed estates (Table 4.7). None of them had more than sixty-two laborers in July, and most of them had fewer than that, the mean being forty-two. Of the seven, only the sugar estate relied exclusively on wage labor, and it registered the smallest increase: 1.85 percent, gaining one single laborer. A second used wage labor (five

Table 4.6. Estates with Extreme Losses

Estate	**Crop Cultivated**	**Labor Force July**	**Labor Force November**	**Decrease %**	**Conditions of Work November**
Goodwill	S[a]	158	66	58.22	wages (5 days)
Watton Haven	C[b]	88	31	64.77	wages
Mt. Prosper	SC	102	43	57.84	wages/labor-rent
Champ Flor	SC	27	11	59.25	1/3 of produce
Everton	C	46	18	60.86	wages
La Tent	C	35	13	62.85	1/3 of produce
Aberdeen	C	101	34	66.33	wages (5 days)
Porée	S	29	11	62.06	wages (5 days)
Union	C	110	19	82.72	wages
Campigny	SC	53	21	60.37	labor-rent (2 days), ½ of produce
Mrne Rouge	SC	75	24	68.00	wages
Bois Cutlet	SC	31	4	87.09	wages
Providence	S	140	48	65.71	wages (5 days)

[a] S = Sugar.
[b] C = Coffee.

Table 4.7. Estates Gaining Laborers

Estate	Crop	No. of Laborers in July	No. of Laborers in Nov.	% Increase	Conditions
New Providence	SC	62	65	4.83	labor-rent (2 days)
Castle Comfort	S	54	55	1.85	wages (5 days)
Durham	C	51	79	54.90	labor-rent (2 days), ½ of produce
Mt. Pleasant	SC	24	38	58.33	labor-rent (2 days), ½ of produce
Malgré Tout	C	38	51	34.21	½ of produce
Pt. Guignard	SC	37	43	27.02	labor-rent or wages
Deschaussez	SC	28	34	21.42	½ of produce
Total		294	365		
Average		42	52		

days a week) with other work arrangements for some laborers: house and grounds in exchange for two field days. One required just two days of unpaid labor from everyone. Two of the seven used sharecropping only, giving the laborers one-half the produce. But the most dramatic gains were made by the estates that allowed the laborers a choice between sharecropping and two unpaid working days. One registered a 55 percent increase, the other a 58 percent increase.

I have discussed these data and my conclusions elsewhere (Trouillot 1984). The main lessons of the exercise remain clear. First, a majority of the slaves abandoned the estates in the days immediately following the end of Apprenticeship. Second, many gradually returned. Third, and most important for the argument of this book, the combined distributions show that the former slaves who remained on the estates or returned to them had already made a clear choice against wage labor and in favor of sharecropping or labor-rent arrangements less than three months after the end of Apprenticeship. This preference would soon lead to the implementation of the peasant labor process in the production of export commodities on the estates themselves.

Capt. James B. Kingsbury, stipendiary magistrate for Saint Andrew, saw the first signs of that expansion. He reported on 18 August 1838, that is, just eleven days after the end of Apprenticeship: "On coffee estates, the laborers have generally contracted with the employers or proprietors to work for half the produce; some for a third" (ZHC1/1266, 161). Likewise, one month later, Stipendiary Magistrate Lynch reported with his usual acuity: "I am persuaded that field labour has not been so freely yielded for money wages, owning to an expectation on the part of the peasantry that many more of the owners of plantations will be compelled to give out their properties to be cultivated by them upon shares" (ZHC1/1266, 166:385). Magistrate Joseph Phillips, in turn, stared: "During the last month, the labourers on coffee and provisions estates nearly completed their agreements; bur few coffee planters can afford to give money for labour; several gangs have agreed to give labour for a portion of the produce, and others have given two and a half or three days labour for their house and gardens; on a few, the cultivation and manufacture of coffee is by task work" (ZHC1/1266, 166:394).

These dispositions of the laborers did not wither over time. Thc maintenance of provision grounds, labor rent, and sharecropping remained high on the unwritten agenda of the Dominican masses throughout the second part of the nineteenth century. Though the planters' power to impose labor conditions increased when sugar cultivation reached its climax, the impact of wage labor remained minimal on the national scale, and task work seemed to have prevailed (Naftel 1898: 19). A synopsis of the testimony of planter and politician William Davies to the West Indian Royal Commission in 1898 confirms the spread of labor-rent arrangements: "It has been customary for laborers on sugar estates to rent land or to have land allowed them free; the rent was paid in labor, for instance, a day's labor a month" (Sugar Commission Report, 1898b: 128).

Likewise C. O. Naftel, appointed by the Colonial Office to report on the agricultural capabilities of Dominica, wrote after a nine-week stay in the island: "The few labourers who live on the estates are generally tenants who pay a small rental for their gardens and work for the proprietor when required. On some estates, huts and small gardens are given to them for one day's work a week without pay" (Naftel 1898: 20).

The War of Maneuver

The struggle to maintain the provision grounds of slavery had all the qualities of a war of position. It was a mass struggle, with clearly defined camps and explicit objectives, and the comments of the field magistrates and the reactions of the planters reveal that both camps understood that any victory was likely to be decisive. The former slaves' strategic objective was to maintain control of the estate provision grounds, an objective quickly achieved. Yet, in and of itself, that victory meant only that the class struggle had reached a new plateau. As mentioned before, the control the peasant labor process yields to cultivators varies according to the relations of production within which this labor process is embedded; and the preceding analysis shows that the changes that immediately followed Emancipation did not affect the structural basis of these relations. Rather, the peasantry gained the ability to dictate the terms under which the ensuing battles would be fought. From this newly secured territory, the cultivators could then move toward new concessions.

Such moves were unequal, and for many reasons. First, no uncontested leadership had emerged from the battle over the provision grounds. In the immediate aftermath of slavery, that absence was not crucial. The issues were simpler. The struggle could be perceived as a common effort to maintain a right already verified by tradition. The cultivators felt attacked and responded in kind. In contrast, once these grounds were secured, the majority of the estate workers did not reach an explicit agreement about their next step. In the absence of a clear strategy, responses varied greatly and affected property, labor, and distribution relations differently.

In retrospect, though, the small wars of maneuver which punctuated relations between cultivators and nonproducers from the 1850s to the 1920s deeply affected labor relations by slowly eroding the resistance of the planters. By the late 1920s, they found themselves incapable of codifying such relations to their advantage. The peasantry's major victory in the series of raids beyond the trenches of the provision grounds was no doubt the widespread implantation of various forms of sharecropping. That practice furthered the development of the peasant labor process on the estates themselves. These sharecropping arrangements have been grouped in Dominica under the generic names of "Métayer," "Bais," "Beyiff," or "Share" system. Their impact varied with time and space, but the most prevalent variations were best summarized in a memorandum dated October 1, 1893, presented by District Magistrate G. R. Le Hunte to then Commissioner Robert Hamilton (Hamilton 1894: 109):

> There are usually two kinds of agreement, the first that the tenant shall cultivate the land, and plant it with permanent products, and that at the end of the stipulated time, deliver up possession to the proprietor, receiving compensation for the labour, &c. expanded by

> an estimated valuation of the coffee, cocoa, or other productive trees which have been planted by the tenant. The mode of assessment varies with local custom. While the trees are growing to maturity, the tenants cultivate the land with "catch" crops, yams, sweet potatoes, &c., commonly called "provisions." In the other class of cases of tenancy no time is stipulated for delivering up the land to the proprietor, and the tenant continues in occupation until required to give up possession, paying the proprietor one moiety of the produce of the land, whether permanent products or "catch" crops.

Though both Hamilton and Naftel emphasized the use of the Métayer system on coffee and cocoa estates, attorneys or proprietors of some of the most important sugar estates were also compelled to use forms of sharecropping along with wage labor. R. Chace (1983: 2) refers to the *Dominican* of 1842 to suggest that by that year "métayers and renters" produced about 20 percent of Dominica's sugar crop. In November 1877, the announcement in London of the sale of the 1,981-acre Rosalie Estate, which belonged to the powerful McLeod family, read: "Parts of the Estate are cultivated on the Métayer system and the Sale will be subject to the rights of the Métayer" (C.O. 441/3, 15). Indeed, some seventy acres of cane ready to be harvested for the 1878 crop were planted on the share system, and the official practice of the Incumbered Estates Commissioners was to notify the tenants before a final order for sale. Sharecroppers held the right to portions of the produce, varying from one-third to one-half of the actual crop in return for their labor. The proprietor provided not only the land, but the instruments of labor (Naftel 1898: 56; Sugar Commission Report, 1898a: 126).

All in all, it took the former slaves and their descendants a half century to implant firmly a peasant work organization in the production of export commodities on the estates themselves. Concessions were not easily gained and many cultivators suffered abuses and injustices of all sorts. Yet the continuous changes in labor conditions eventuated in a structural change at the level of the unit of production. By the 1870s, that unit had become the reverse image of the classic unit of plantation slavery. Indeed, whereas under plantation slavery provision gardens were mere marginal units attached to the plantation, in the latter part of the nineteenth century, the estate became a formal entity, the relevance of which was mainly juridical. The plantation labor process gradually ceased to be the dominant mode of work organization. The peasant garden of "catch" crops and provisions became the dominant unit of production. In short, the peasant labor process started to operate in the production of export commodities, even though property relations remained favorable to the planter class. Naftel's testimony on cocoa production makes the point:

> Even on the large estates there are seldom fields of any size, a plot of 20 acres being the exception. As a general rule, the size of the plot is regulated by the amounts of land opened by estate tenants as "provision" gardens, which are mostly about an acre or two in extent. When two or three gardens have been made contiguously, the proprietor sometimes joins them together by clearing the intervening bush or forest, and so makes a small field.

Moreover, cocoa trees "only receive attention when the tenant gives his vegetables a rough hoeing" (Naftel 1898: 34).

Despite such obvious gains by the cultivators in labor and distribution arrangements the peasant work organization of the nineteenth century may have rested on weaker socioeconomic foundations than the provision grounds of slavery. The contradiction between property relations on the one hand and labor and distribution relations on the other was obvious: planters owned the land, but sharecroppers could exploit the low supply of labor to impose distribution conditions more favorable to themselves. Moreover, the labor process hindered all chance of daily or weekly verification of labor performance, including productivity, by the formal owner. Thus, in comparison with slavery, cultivators' control over labor time and organization had tightened, but their individual grip on particular plots had loosened. Instruments and means of labor belonged to the planters; products of labor belonged to both, subject to planters' evaluation.

Such extensive control by the landowning class over property relations deflected the distribution of surplus even though distribution relations seemed favorable to the cultivators. The system was opened to illegalities: coercion, intimidation, expulsion on the planters' part; illegal occupation, voluntary decrease of productivity or reduction of labor time on the workers' part. A whole range of maneuvers must have been perceived as "fraud" by one side or the other. An equilibrium was hard to reach under such circumstances. The fragility of the context partly accounts for the temporary recessions or the numerous variations of the Métayer system and the continuous complaints of both owners and tenants.

Gains of the peasant labor process in the estate production of export commodities should not be evaluated, then, in terms of the amount of control exerted by individual tenants. Rather, the major change was in the nature of the struggle itself. While provision grounds remained secure, the front line of the struggle had reached the planters' territory, both figuratively and literally. The products in question were now export commodities, up to then planters' uncontested privilege. The locus of the contest was plantation land proper. That, for the workers, was a victory.

Planters reacted to this new defeat. For instance, many used the Métayer system for clearing forest or land lost to bush with the clear goal of evicting the tenants after improvement of the property, and then, perhaps, switching to lime cultivation with task labor, or accepting new tenants without proper compensation to the former occupants. One Jabez Bellot, planter and elected member of the Assembly testified that métayage was the "cheapest and quickest" way of cultivating cocoa; it allowed an early repossession of the improved property (Hamilton 1894, Appendix B, Abstract of Evidence: 27). Not surprisingly, soon after Bellot inherited his father's plantation, one of his tenants, African-born Fanny Firmin, stated in a petition to Commissioner Hamilton that she had been wrongfully evicted after holding and improving for thirty-eight years a plot on the Souffrière Estate, one of the properties of the Bellot family (Hamilton 1894: 107). Incapable of signing their names, Fanny and her son put their X marks at the bottom of the petition. It is most likely that many of the masses of illiterate tenants had previously refused to enter into written agreements because of the justified fear of the damage that such documents could inflict upon their freedom when drafted by profit-conscious planters. As the century drew to its close, written contracts became more common, but then, *planters* were more reluctant to sign (Hamilton 1894, Abstract of Evidence: 26, 39). One year before the Firmins' petition, Roman Catholic Father Lelièvre had witnessed in one parish the eviction of no fewer than sixty-five bailiffs (Sugar Commission Report, 1898b: 142).

As Thomas Cochrane reported to the Colonial Office, such injustices certainly impeded the full development of the Métayer system (C.O. 152/200). Yet many variations survived both the rise and demise of lime and the more recent preeminence of bananas on the export lists. At the time of this writer's fieldwork, between 1978 and 1982, labor arrangements directly descended from the old Métayer system obtained in banana production in various parts of the country: in the Rosalie Estate area, for instance, or in the Wesley area, on the Londonderry and Eden estates. The major impairment to sharecropping came not from planters' opposition but from other victories of the cultivators: the use of Crown lands by squatters and the growth of an independent yeomanry. As the former slaves and their descendants conquered access to habitable land outside of the estates, their need to reside on such estates diminished; and as they incorporated into their own gardens the production of exportable commodities, their reliance on estate labor also diminished.

Squatting on the Queen's Land

Historians had long surmised from travelers' accounts and reports of planters' complaints that the end of Apprenticeship brought a sudden decline in the size of the resident labor force on estates throughout the British Caribbean (Sewell 1861). Acknowledging a flight, most focused on its causes. Douglas Hall (1978) summarizes their conclusions, and one barely needs to modify his survey of the literature. For most writers, the end of Apprenticeship simply provided to the former slaves their first and long-awaited opportunity to flee the sites and the symbols of slavery (Farley 1964; Riviere 1972). Others, including Hall himself (1978), emphasized planters' attitudes against which the laborers reacted: the planters in essence chased away the laborers (e.g., Paget 1964). Finally, some pointed to the availability of alternatives to plantation labor (Mandle 1974; Mintz [1974] 1984, 1979).

Hall's article nicely sharpens the issues. Using the 1842 *Report of the Select Committee of the House of Commons on the West India Colonies*, Hall attempts to flesh out quantitatively (though not systematically) the extent of the flight in the whole British Caribbean. He also tries to assess whether that withdrawal "reflected an *intention* to withdraw" from the plantation economy altogether (Hall 1978: 7; emphasis added). Hall (1978: 23–24) concludes that planters' "attitudes led to the exodus" which was, however, affected by the former slaves' own ambivalence. They were torn, he suggests, between their hatred of the estates and their love for their homes and provision grounds located on those estates. The double emphasis is important and Marshall (1979), drawing from Hall, advances both conclusions; the very notion of a flight has become questionable, and understandably so. "Ex-slaves had more of an interest in improving their standard of living than seeking 'independence.' They believed, perhaps naively, they could improve their standard of living *on the estates*" (Marshall 1979: 246).

In Dominica, as we have seen, not all slaves shared such naiveté. If the sample of forty-one estates studied earlier in this chapter is representative, the immediate flight involved no less than 53 percent of the labor force, a decrease that was to stabilize at about 40 percent by the end of November. Thus, many former slaves made a clear decision against staying on the estates despite their legal right to do so. Indeed, until 1 December 1838, legislation forbade the expulsion of any former apprentice willing to keep his or her tenancy in exchange for three days' labor weekly (C.O. 73/16, 422). Yet the greatest number of flights occurred immediately after the end of Apprenticeship, in the months of August and September, exactly when the laborers had, at least formally, legal protection against eviction.

I have dealt elsewhere with some of the philosophical and methodological assumptions behind the "flight" debate (Trouillot 1984). Suffice it to say here that reasons why the free laborers would abandon the plantation on which they had been held in bondage should not be hard to imagine, even if we should not assume that, from an existential viewpoint, all slaves and laborers perceived "slavery" and "freedom" in the exact same manner. Marshall (1979: 246) suggests that "ties of sentiment and material interest" linked the former slaves to the estate provision grounds; and the suggestion should not be taken lightly. But in Dominica, there is little evidence to suggest that the cultivators associated particular plots to their general thirst for land. Rather, they were moved by the very idea of ownership to whichever plot could satisfy that thirst.

In his report for October 1848, Magistrate Lynch stated that those who agreed to work for wages tended to do so on plantations different from those on which they had been slaves, not only because they would earn more, but also because some had destroyed their old provision grounds in anger (ZHC1/1266, 167). Furthermore, inasmuch as planters favored wage agreements, their intransigent proposals tended to push the cultivators toward the occupation of nonestate land, if only as a security holding to fall back on in case of eviction from the estate. Magistrate James B. Kingsbury noted that, even when laborers agreed to work on the estates, their refusal to enter into permanent arrangements often stemmed from their hope that they would soon acquire their own plots. In the immediate aftermath of slavery, wages could not represent an overwhelming incentive to a population whose culture had not yet integrated the willful sale of its labor power as a fact of life. Many twentieth-century writers working on the British Caribbean attribute to the former slaves a trade-unionist interpretation of freedom characteristic of small segments of the North American or English working classes of our time. Magistrate Lynch, who observed the transition from apprenticeship to freedom, rightly wrote:

> The master during slavery, and employer subsequently, never contemplated the possibility of a labouring population becoming independent of them, whenever free. The peasant, however, is nearly so, because he had to supply his own wants whilst in a state of servitude, and received nothing more towards the support of himself and his family than six yards of oznaburgs, three yards of blanket, and a cap, if his master could give it, every 12 or 14 months and the privilege of cultivating as much or as little ground as he thought proper. (ZHC1/1266, 166:385)

In short, wages act as incentive for people who have learned to depend on them.

Both the negative recollections associated with particular estates (or the institution of slavery) and the potentially positive stimulus of wages must have been balanced against the laborers' desire to maintain provision grounds. As individuals, the former slaves thus faced a dilemma: to stay on the estate despite the repulsive memories, or to move away, even if such a move meant the loss of the provision grounds. The conflict was, of course, solved by each individual in light of his or her personal experience. But the drive for land was strong enough to lead great numbers of individuals into repeating elsewhere the experience of the provision grounds. After all, that experience was in their memories the only pleasant interlude in a miserable existence. In other words, most ex-slaves had little doubt about which type of work activities they preferred. In light of the planters' actions, the major issue for many laborers was the spatial domain in which the peasant labor process would operate, and as Mandle (1974) and Mintz (1984) argued, the possible choices increased with the availability of land outside of estate boundaries.

In Dominica, the amount of unoccupied land, the nature of the terrain, and the small proportion of whites multiplied the possibilities. The population sample studied earlier showed that 1,030 laborers (or 39 percent of the total) did not return to the plantations. Their choice of grounds affected the juridical and commercial domains; and the new configurations, in turn, provoked changes in labor, property, and distributive relations.

One such new configuration was the extension of squatting in the immediate aftermath of slavery. Only two months after the end of

Apprenticeship, Magistrate Kingsbury reported: "There appears to be an universal desire among the late emancipated laborers to possess land" (ZHC1/1266, 166:387). Such desire led many former slaves to occupy Crown and private lands for which they held no title, most notably along the coast, in the area commonly known as the "Three Chains."

When Great Britain took over Dominica after the Peace of 1763, it sent commissioners to the island to sell land to new settlers in the name of the Crown. At that time, in view of the probability of a French attack, a belt three chains wide, that is, three times sixty-six feet, measuring from the sea's high water mark and extending around the island, was reserved for the use of the Crown. The Crown intended to erect forts and batteries, but in the meantime, the proprietors whose purchases happened to adjoin the Three Chains would use the belt (*Dominica Almanac*, 1864: 55). After 1805, the threat of a French attack receded, and estate owners who had occupied parts of the Three Chains entered such lands in their formal transactions, often without prior clearance of a proper title. At the time of Emancipation, all around Dominica were large plots of unoccupied or insecurely held land, loosely controlled by estate owners. Many former slaves simply moved in:

> The abolition of slavery in 1834 and 1838 caused a large number of labourers who were unwilling to reside upon the places where they had been slaves, though content to cultivate them for wages to "rush like a torrent down upon the wake," and carrying posts and boards to the bays at night, houses were seen weekly rearing their trashy heads, irrespective of the law of meum and teum, as far as lands were concerned. Indeed, some people believed that the boon of freedom was incomplete, if not insecure, without a small piece of land being attached to it. (*Dominica Almanac*, 1864: 55–56)

The applications of the contiguous proprietors to the magistrates for the ejection of the squatters, as they were called, disclosed the infirmity of the proprietors' claims, since the process of legal ejectment proceeds not so much upon the absence of the supposed trespasser's title as upon the sufficiency of the would-be ejector's.

The government, of course, reacted forcefully against occupation and curtailed the 1844 disturbance—a wave of riots then thought to be provoked in part by evictions from the Three Chains and efforts to administer the first postslavery census. Commissioner Hamilton noted, fifty years later, that the repression was "severe" (Hamilton 1894: xii).

The administration also sided with the estate owners in many cases in which former laborers challenged their occupation of the Crown lands. Squatters on parts of the Three Chains contiguous to the Batalie Estate, locked in a confrontation with the estate owners, were forcibly moved by troops from the neighboring island of Antigua. Yet, as noted, the case for ejection was often hard to substantiate in court, since planters often lacked proper titles themselves. The legal imbroglio was not cleared up until February 1859, when the colonial secretary's office found a new rationale for ejection. The office argued that, since the period of contiguous proprietors' priority had long expired, preemption of the land by former slaves and their descendants had consequently expired with it. The same dispatch recommended that Three Chains' lands be sold under conditions similar to the selling of any other Crown lands, at the price fixed by the government, when sought by only one buyer, or to the highest bidder if there were more than one (*Dominica Almanac*, 1864: 66).

But the contest for the Three Chains had set many of the former slaves on a course that would not stop until their hunger for land was satisfied. If they could occupy what was purported to be the Queen's land on the shores they could equally occupy Her Majesty's land in the mountains. Occupation in the mountains was even easier since the necessary judiciary or military personnel to stop them was often lacking (ZHC1/1266, 161). Exactly six months after the June 1844 riots, Magistrate Joseph Phillips of the Saint John Parish underlined the need for resident magistrates to control the occupation of Crown lands of all sorts: Three Chains, town lands, and gardens, "all of which are built upon, and partially cultivated by hundreds of the peasantry, and, with very few exceptions, without the shadow of any right or title" (PP, 1845, vol. 31 [146]:39). It may have been more difficult to move against squatters in areas outside the Three Chains: the presence of a peasant family in the Dominican hinterland could go undetected for a long time if no estate owner had an immediate interest in the area. In contrast, squatters on the Three Chains sometimes worked on adjoining estates.

Still, whether on the shores or in the hinterland, unused or unoccupied lands provided many former laborers a haven to plant their roots. Between the 1840s and the 1870s, that is, during the time of the sugar preeminence, squatting practices increased in geometric proportions as the successful example of the most daring cultivators attracted the more hesitant ones. In July 1875, in his speech opening the Third Legislative Assembly, Governor Charles Monroe Eldridge noted continuing increases in the numbers of squatters (C.O. 74/33). In the same year,

Government Botanist Henry Prestoe (1875: 5) asserted that squatting was "one of the greatest evils the Colony now suffers from." Prestoe's description of the life of the squatter, with whom he also associates the garden holders, is worth quoting at length.

> The influence of the mode of life of the squatter and the garden holder, in a moral sense, is deplorable. The majority I have met with have relapsed under it to a state of semi-barbarism, especially about the hills in the north of the Island, where they have located themselves most distantly from civilizing agencies. Their houses are mere huts, not more than 6 ft. high at the top and inferior in all respects to the sheds which the Coolies in Trinidad put up to protect their cattle. The whole family of occupants appropriate the floor in company with, and in the same manner as, their more than half-starved dogs. The fire is made on the floor, and thus all within the hut is blackened by the smoke. The place of honour for the night seems to be a narrow blackened board. The stock of utensils consists of a round pot or pannikin, one or two broken calabashes, an old axe, cutlass or hoe, all looking too much like rejects from some other party better off. Here and there one sees a piece of damaged crockery, but more commonly an old rusty gun. (Prestoe 1875: 6)

Some people did prefer independence to a higher standard of living. Prestoe's arrogance comes, in part, from his lack of understanding that squatters lived in such conditions while work was available on sugar plantations. As is the case of some more recent observers, he seems appalled that some people did not respond to the supposedly universal stimulus of wages.

Squatters and hinterland garden holders mainly produced their own provisions, and became woodcutters to meet their few cash emergencies. In this way, they could live unmolested for years. Prestoe's tone notwithstanding, it is likely that some tenants or small owners in the villages were not faring better than the squatters. At any rate, despite proclamations to the contrary, the government itself could rarely enforce the laws against squatting.

Indeed, one major impediment to the prevention of squatting came not so much from the difficulty of identifying the squatter as from the impossibility of identifying all Crown lands. Since the middle of the century, the governor's discretionary control of the Crown Lands Fund had turned the fees collected from rentals or sales into a source of personal enrichment for high public officials, dimming chances of verification (PP, 1884, vol. 46; C. 3840,2:65). By 1894, Hamilton wrote: "There is no proper and complete record of Crown lands nor of private estate in the island. The Government have [*sic*] no means of knowing whether the lands on which many persons are living are their own private property, or whether they are the Property of the Crown" (Hamilton 1984: xxxi).

The absence or inaccuracy of records reduced the chances of detecting squatters who moved onto private lands abandoned by their proprietors, especially lands liable to be escheated (*Dominica Almanac*, 1879: 146). Squatters could work without threat of eviction long enough to save from the sale of their provisions and legalize their possession of the plots there or elsewhere. For if squatting did indeed allow the occupation of new territories, it also created wide disjunctures between the spatial and commercial domains of the peasant labor process. One suspects that even the most commercially minded squatters never gained full access to the local network and barely penetrated the export chain.

Squatting was thus an ephemeral configuration because of the limited security it provided for the peasant labor process, a fragility reflected in the dislocation of the different relations of production. Labor relations worked to the full advantage of the squatter who could dispose of his or her labor power at will, but only as long as possession, occupation, or use of the unit of production was not questioned. The social range within which the squatter could reap the benefit of this control over labor was limited. Property relations were unstable by definition, provoking, if not frequent moves, at least constant fear of interference by the state. Finally, because of the instability of property relations, relations of surplus and of distribution forced the squatter to remain close to the socially defined level of subsistence. Increased production, especially production geared to the market, could attract the authorities' attention to the squatter's presence. On the other hand, even a small decrease in a particular harvest could bring abject poverty.

Thus, for the rural toiler anxious to avoid familial if not personal disaster, for the planter anxious to obtain cheap labor, for the merchant anxious to profit from export, and the state official anxious to maintain an "order" beneficial to the metropolis, the many disequilibriums inherent in squatting were continuously troublesome. These actors tried to resolve the conflicts in very different ways. Ultimately though, law enforcement and planter pressure do not seem to have been the main factors in the decrease of squatting practices. The practice of occupying unused or contested land seems to have been abandoned by the majority of the cultivators themselves rather than curtailed by the nonproducing classes. The situation was inherently insecure for the producers, especially if they wanted to experiment with the production of the dearer export commodities. They slowly espoused the code of behavior typical of a rising yeomanry, increasingly respectful of the property rights that would guarantee their own survival and growth.

The Rise of the Peasantry

From the data based on Magistrate Lynch's reports of 1838, as we have seen earlier, 53 percent of the apprenticed laborers in Saint George, Saint Luke, and Saint Patrick South deserted the plantations within a few days of complete Emancipation. Though some 360 eventually returned (before the end of November), 1,030 did not. Many of the missing must have joined the growing number of squatters who took over private and Crown lands, including lands in the Three Chains. Yet Lynch himself provides us with another explanation for some of these absences. He wrote in his report for August 1838: "Lands fit for provisions being frequently on sale for at prices between 20s. and 30s. sterling per acre and so readily obtained for one moiety of produce from persons unable to enter into any other arrangement, a great portion of the labourers latterly attached to plantations, but now missing, have most probably overcome any difficulty to location elsewhere" (ZHCl/1266, 166: 385). Lynch's clue is precious. Some former apprentices did save enough from their occasional sales of provisions to acquire small plots, perhaps in association with friends, kin, or neighbors. However, most could not easily accumulate enough cash for such a transaction. Lynch's testimony is, therefore, important, since it introduces a type of arrangement that did not require any immediate cash disbursement and that could ease the passage to freeholder's status.

One would like to know, of course, if and how peasant proprietorship of land so obtained was finally registered. One would like to know also the role of the pre-Emancipation freedmen in these arrangements. Moreover, I suspect, from Lynch's brief description, that only a few of the less successful owners entered into such arrangements. Be that as it may, a particular form of sharecropping on small plots of provision land did allow a legal expansion of the peasant labor process outside the estates just a few days after the end of slavery. Possible paths to formal acquisition follow from this starting point. A. R. Lockhart did affirm in his *Précis of the Legislative History of Dominica* that many estate laborers in the thirties and forties used their savings to establish themselves as freeholders (Hamilton 1894: 48).

Not surprisingly, Hamilton dates the rise of the independent yeomanry to the immediate post-Emancipation period. As many estates fell after abolition, writes Hamilton, *"a class of peasant proprietors arose*, and they turned their attention mainly to the supply of what are called "provisions" in Dominica, that is, cassava, arrowroot, plantains, bananas, yams, &c." (1894: xiii; emphasis mine). Four years after Hamilton, Naftel made a similar statement, emphasizing that the process of emergence took only "a few years" (1898: 24).

As labor relations improved in favor of the sharecroppers in the 1850s and '60s, they increasingly bought plots of their own, hence deepening the social roots of the yeomanry. In his speech of January 21, 1862, Benoit Bellot, then Speaker of the Assembly, stated that many rural cultivators were still "daily and laudably exchanging the condition of daily labourers on the plantations for the position of Owners of land and shopkeepers" (C.O. 74/33). By 1872, the class of peasant proprietors acknowledged by both Hamilton and Naftel had solidified. While paying lip service to its entrepreneurship, President Alexander W. Moir made it responsible for a good half of the country's problems in his inaugural speech of 25 July 1872:

> At first sight, one cannot imagine how, with a population of over 27,000 inhabitants, so much of the island lies uncultivated, and so many natural resources remain undeveloped, and it is only when one discovers that the evil of the squatting system is unknown, and that the commendable and rapidly increasing *class of peasant proprietorship* is in existence that it is explained, how a general independence from the necessities to labour, with natural wants supplied cheaply, and without much exertion, enable the peasant to give, or to withhold, at his pleasure, that labour, without which capital is useless. (C.O. 74/33, Appendix to Minutes of the Legislative Assembly; emphasis mine)

The 1871 Census, published just one month before Moir's speech, had registered 718 "petty cultivators" in its long list of occupational categories. The number is no doubt significant though quite likely an underestimate: twenty years later the government recovered more than 1,500 properties for nonpayment of taxes (Hamilton 1894: xxiii). Then as now "fishermen," "carpenters," "masons," "hunters," "sawyers," or "hucksters," listed as independent census categories, also engaged in the production of provisions, if not export crops, on lands they or their immediate kin owned and controlled.

Purchases of small plots increased throughout the 1870s and '80s (PP, 1884, vol. 46, part 3, Dominica: 135–36), to such an extent that the provost marshall, Joseph Fadelle, pointed out to the Royal Sugar Commission of 1884, that seven-eighths of the cocoa and one-seventh of the sugar produced on the island originated from peasant lots (ibid., 147–49). Hamilton (1894: x) described "the bulk of the people" as "peasant proprietors." He estimated the existence of 1,119 properties worth less than twenty pounds, and 458 properties worth less than forty pounds. Not surprisingly, the number of estates had greatly declined by then, as well as the number of laborers on most estates.

Data from the 1891 Census on some of the estates first covered in 1838 by Stipendiary Magistrate Lynch confirm both the decline in the total number of estates and the size of their labor force. First, and most important, of the forty-one estates abstracted from Lynch's list of 1838, only twenty-eight appear in the comprehensive list of estates recorded in the 1891 Census. That fact itself is telling: as many as thirteen estates seem to have disappeared from the count. Among the twenty-eight that certainly survived by name, only three counted more laborers in 1891 than they had apprentices in July 1838, even though most had recovered from their record lows of August 1838. From July to November 1838, the twenty-eight estates had lost 42 percent of their labor force; now, fifty-three years later, and despite the much larger population, they had managed to reduce that loss to only 25 percent, and 518 laborers were still missing from the original count of July 1838.

The remainder of the census list shows that, despite regional variations, the relative shrinkage of the estates' labor force was a national phenomenon. Whereas 10,132 people still lived on estates, 10,904 lived in villages or "towns," exclusive of Roseau, the capital. As President Moir noted, a substantial number of the villagers could afford to live off the estates only because of the new independence they gained from land ownership. To be sure, variations affected by the general lack of communications within the island modified here and there the reality depicted by the census figures. The status of the cultivators hence varied from one parish to the next and sometimes within the same parish. Saint Patrick's southern part contained by itself two of the only three estates known to have gained laborers since the end of slavery. Villagers in Saint Patrick did not outnumber resident laborers as in other parishes. Saint Peter and Saint Luke were heavily peopled by the yeomanry. Saint Andrew encompassed two socially distinct enclaves: the estate-dominated South (the Woodford Hill, Wesley, Marigot area); and the yeomen-dominated North, around the village of Vieille Case.

However, the net decline in the total number of estates, the net and relative rise in the number of villages, villagers, and peasant proprietors were, by and large, national phenomena that continued unabatedly as Dominica entered the twentieth century. The correspondence between Administrator H. Hesketh Bell and the secretary of state for the colonies, shows, for instance, that despite Bell's efforts to attract large-scale investors from abroad, peasant purchases of land generally outweighed those of new plantation owners. From a total of 459 pounds collected from Crown land sales in 1903, "no less than 200 pounds was collected from peasants for small holdings" (C.O. 152/285). Among thirty buyers whose acreages are listed, only two purchased more than 100 acres. By 1907, Crown land sales for the half-year ending March 31 were up to 459 pounds, total contributions (new purchases, deposits, installments, etc.) had reached 838 pounds, but most individual disbursements were under 10 pounds (C.O. 152/299).

Not surprisingly, the 1911 Census registered the continuation of the relative decline in the number of estate laborers noted by the 1891 Census, though the island's population had increased by 26 percent since the former count. By contrast, the number of petty cultivators accounted for by the new census rose to 1,260. Yet again, that category did not pretend to include all those who were, at any time, engaged in agricultural labor on plots controlled by the yeomanry. If one adds a majority of the 725 fishermen and carpenters who were not Roseau residents, the actual number of petty cultivators immediately rises, approaching the probable reality of the time. Be that as it may, by 1927, Sir Francis Watts, another commissioner sent to report on the agricultural problems and possibilities of Dominica, acknowledged the presence of the yeomanry as one of the most "striking" features of Dominican society. He estimated the existence of 1,510 holdings distributed as follows:

Size of Holdings	*Number of Holdings*
over 100 acres	77
50–100 acres	99
under 50 acres	1,334
total	1,510

More specific figures showed that, in at least one district, 95 percent of the holdings "under 50 acres" were in fact plots measuring less than 25 acres. Watts (1927: 42) divided the district's 460 holdings under 50 acres as follows:

Size of Holdings	*Number of Holdings*
25–50 acres	23
2–25 acres	236
under 2 acres	201
total	460

Hence, by 1927, 44 percent of the holdings in Watts's sample district were under 2 acres, and only 5 percent were over 25 acres. The estates had virtually disappeared. Under the impetus of the cultivators, the peasant labor process had invaded practically every unit of production of the country.

CHAPTER 5

Factions and Strategies

The war of position requires major sacrifices from a majority of the population.

—A. Gramsci, *Prison Notebooks*

We only live to pay taxes.

—La Plaine peasant, 1893

Nonproducers in Dominica and officials in London observed neither idly nor passively the laborers' takeover of the units of production. Throughout the nineteenth century, the cultivators faced tactics designed to prevent, bypass, or co-opt the expansion of peasant forms of labor organization. Those tactics were designed, supported, or implemented by diverse groups within Dominican society who, at times, disagreed among themselves and, often, disagreed altogether with the long-term strategies and the immediate decisions imposed upon them by the Colonial Office. The ambivalence of one group, the post-Emancipation faction that later became known as the "Mulatto Ascendancy" and comprised mainly light-skinned descendants of the pre-Emancipation freedmen, epitomized the political instability of the entire society. Indeed, the "colored" elite of Dominica fitted awkwardly between the alliance of white planters and officials and the masses of cultivators both before and after slavery. Not surprisingly, mulattoes shifted positions and allegiances to suit their interests of the moment. Their history reveals, then, the variations of the forces in conflict and the gains at stake. In more than one way, the political rise of that colored elite paralleled the nonproducers' counterattack.

An Ambivalent "Middle Class"

A striking feature of Dominican slave society was the large proportion of people described as colored. The category was ambiguous, and perhaps intentionally so. It remains polyvalent today. At times it referred to slaves and free people alike; at other times, only to freedmen. Moreover, even when the legal status is obvious (as in postslavery contexts), one still does not know for sure which phenotypes the term covers. Nevertheless, the terminological ambivalence tainted nineteenth-century political practice to such an extent that the category became relevant in the concrete struggle for power.

By 1815, 2,666 people were classified as colored in Dominica, at a time when the colony counted only 1,123 whites and 18,862 slaves (C.O. 71/55). The proportion of colored slaves kept rising during the first half of the nineteenth century. By 1829–32, the colored accounted for 15.6 percent of all births among the slave population, with a peak of 32.9 percent in Roseau (Higman 1984: 152–53). Whatever complexion was actually covered by the category, it is quite likely that the large proportion of colored slaves helped to increase the proportion of colored freedmen, as slavery neared its end. Indeed, throughout the Caribbean, freedom usually "lightened" the perception of the same phenotype. Therefore, the high rates of manumission in Dominica tended to expand the purported size of the colored population. Manumission figures grew gradually from 1.8 percent of the slave population in 1808, to 2.2 percent in 1820, to 6.1 percent in 1834. The rate at which Dominica freed its slaves before the final abolition was second only to the Bahamas and Saint Lucia in the whole British Caribbean (Higman 1984: 381). Many of the manumitted slaves were females freed by their white or mulatto masters. Thus it is not surprising that females generally exceeded males among the "free colored," and that, by 1819, most free colored males were still under sixteen years of age (C.O. 71/55).

The uneven distribution of the category across legal, phenotypical, generational, and gender lines created a political ambivalence evident even before the end of slavery. At least some of the colored masters treated their slaves more severely than the white officials would allow (Hansard 1818, cited by Mathieson 1926: 97). Yet other freedmen had strong ties with the British antislavery movement. The colored were also divided along property lines: not all of them owned slaves or land. Although freedmen as a group represented more than two-thirds of the total free population, they owned only 22 percent of the slaves and controlled an even lower proportion of the export products. Many of the estate owners among them specialized in coffee, probably for the same reasons that *gens de couleur* did in Saint Domingue (Trouillot 1982): it required little capital and could easily be grown on the mountainous lands neglected by the more affluent white owners. Yet, at best, the free colored controlled only 19.1 percent of the coffee, 3 percent of the sugar, and 2.7 percent of the rum produced in the island in 1820 (Green 1976: 15). As in the rest of the British Caribbean, the vast majority were traders, craftsmen, or small landowners. What singularized them in Dominica was less their economic weight, albeit remarkable for the times, than their numbers.

Indeed, by the time of Apprenticeship, in 1834, colored, or nonwhites, constituted the bulk of the nonslave population. Further, most of the colored males, being neither estate owners nor laborers, fitted poorly within the plantation economy. They developed a penchant for politics. Motivations were not lacking: some genuinely wanted to express their compassion for the working masses, others their resentment of the whites who owned the best plantations or who acted as attorneys for the growing number of absentee proprietors. Many also understood that, given their civil status and their relative education in a country virtually without schools, their participation in public affairs could pave their way to wealth and security.

The British Colonial Office tried to contain such developments. Since 1771, Dominica had enjoyed separate government from the rest of the Leeward Islands, and by 1775, it was officially ruled by a governor, assisted by a nominated Council, and an elected House of Representatives, often judged unruly by metropolitan administrators. In 1833, three colored men used the new political and civil rights granted to freedmen throughout the region by the "Brown Privilege Bill" of 1831 to contend successfully for seats in the local House.

In 1833, partly to counteract that political gain, especially in light of the forthcoming Abolition, the British government put Dominica under the umbrella of a Leeward Islands governor based in Antigua, with only a lieutenant governor on the island itself. Still, in 1835, the freedmen managed to petition successfully against a census bill favored by the Colonial Office and already passed by the House on grounds that census taking would only succeed in "perpetuating the distinction between the whites and the coloured" (PP, 1845, 31: 31–32). Voting requirements then being the freehold of ten acres of land, or a leasehold worth twenty pounds a year in land, or twenty pounds a year in building, the freedmen sufficiently filled the lists of registered voters to control the House after the 1837 election. One of the white planters who witnessed this victory of the colored was to become later the chief executive of the island. Seven years after the elections, then President J. Laidlaw still could not swallow his anger:

> There was a general election of representatives, where these people were determined by a force of numbers, to place themselves in the ascendancy, by bringing into the Assembly a majority of their own class, and which was accomplished by the unlawful assemblage at the hustings of every black and coloured man capable of opposing a legitimate candidate or vote: the consequence was a total subversion of the election law, and their return secured. (PP, 1845, 31: 31)

Most whites shared Laidlaw's anger, even though they themselves did not earn their official positions any more legitimately than the freedmen. The attorney general at the time, William Blanc, also a white planter, had been nominated to the post despite his total lack of legal training. Yet he also could not contain his anger. He wrote to the governor: "The qualifications of candidates and voters are a perfect mockery. . . . The large proprietors, whose capital and industry maintain the credit and the public institutions of the country, are, by this subversion of the first principles of the constitution, virtually excluded from representation" (enclosed in Colebrooke to Glenelg, 16 August 1838; ZHC1/1266, 10).

By 1838, the earlier freedmen were more than ready to enlarge their political influence by including all nonwhites under their political umbrella. The ambiguity of the colored category predated their drive for power, and they adroitly tried to use that ambiguity to take advantage of the full demographic and electoral weight of the newly liberated laborers. The 1844 Census Riots proved them partly wrong, and demonstrated the complexity of factional politics in Dominica.

The actions taken by the laborers during the first week of June 1844, which came to be known later as the "1844 Census Riots," or "La Guerre Nègre," were rather benign (PP, 1845, vol. 31 [146]). As with many important historical events, their significance accrued through successive interpretations. Insofar as we can reconstitute the facts, the riots did not go beyond a series of walkouts, protests, and minor assaults against persons and property, which occurred in the early days of June as enumerators started to take a new census of the island population. The general climate was not one of calmness, of course, with some 1,500 protesters in the countryside. However, they did little more than threaten planters and officials (especially census enumerators). Historian Russell Chace suggests that they "wounded perhaps 10 to 12 enumerators, militiamen, and managers, none of them seriously" (Chace 1983: 6). One suspects that, without the repressive reaction of the planters and the government, the unrest might have quickly diminished. The immediate trigger of the unrest was no doubt the former slaves' belief that the "taking of names" was a prelude to the reestablishment of slavery.

The process of selection and interpretation which turned these incidents into the 1844 Riots or La Guerre Nègre and accounts for their importance started even before the unrest reached its peak. The chain reactions of journalists, planters, elected representatives, and nominated officials thus transformed the riots from what Schaff (1971) calls a "fact in history" to a "historical fact." Chace's paper provides the most systematic evaluation of the written record, and the specifics of the reaction: four dead, four wounded, and some three hundred cultivators jailed (Chace 1983). Ninety-four of the prisoners were tried, ninety of them convicted, including six who received death sentences. It is those trials, the diatribes that preceded them, the debates they provoked, and the conflicts and compromises they exposed that turned the unrest into an event of historical importance. They reveal the panic of the nonlaboring classes. Moreover, they suggest both the importance and the ambivalence of the rising colored elite.

Two trends appear clearly from the evidence gathered on La Guerre Nègre in the *Parliamentary Papers* (PP, 1845, vol. 31 [146]). First, most former slaves did not distinguish between colored and white owners. They attacked or, most often, threatened members of both groups. Second, the colored themselves wavered, at times absolving the laborers on grounds of ignorance, at other times calling for swift punishment; but in the end, despite their liberal rhetoric, they sided against the protesters. On June 12, immediately after the riots, the newspaper *Dominican*, then controlled by colored politician Charles Gordon Falconer, claimed: "The story of the Census Act being believed to be one for re-establishing slavery, is only a feint to cover a less honest motive": destruction or takeover of landed property. Three months later, the same paper loudly insisted: "There was no plot; no combination; no intention; as it has been attempted to be given forth to the world, on the [participants'] part, to subvert the constitution, and produce rebellion and revolution in the land" (*Dominican*, 25 September 1844).

At that time, some mulattoes occupied highly visible positions in the government; among them, notably James Garraway, by then a nominated member of the House; and Thomas William Rainey, an elected member, but also an appointed police magistrate. Both were to sit as judges on some of the trials following the riots. The prominent Bellot, Dupigny, and Lockhart families counted mulatto members as successful, economically and politically, as their white relatives. William Ellisonde, of Stowe Estate, testified, perhaps truthfully, that he had heard one of the "insurgents," African-born Rémy, telling another laborer that "all of the people of colour will weed our canes and that this country must be similar to St. Domingo," a reference to the Haitian Revolution (PP, 1845 31: 33). Laidlaw reported to his immediate superior, Antigua-based Sir Charles Augustus Fitzroy, that some of the rebels were "vociferating for the blood of the whites and the mulattoes."

The 1844 Riots indicated to the colored elite that not all the newly liberated laborers were willing to group uncritically along the established racial lines, and that some wanted to include in their considerations matters of class and color. Records of the investigation also suggest that matters of national origin, religious denomination, and length of stay in the island may have also created minor divisions among the white planters and officials. Yet the trials confirmed two major developments: first, the demographic weight of the newly liberated laborers, a political asset in a population quite difficult to contain physically in view of its spatial distribution and the rugged natural environment; second, the mulattoes' rise to hegemony in public affairs, a rise based in part on their demographic strength. Besides Judges Garraway and Rainey, seven colored persons (including *Dominican* editor G. C. Falconer) sat on the Grand Jury of sixteen members in the Special Court set up after the disturbances. Further, at least twelve in the initial list of petty jurors were colored. And the colored did flex their muscles during the laborers' trials, as well as during the questioning of planter-attorney Charles Leathem, a white immigrant who was accused of excessive brutality against the cultivators. Still, despite remonstrances to Leathem, the mulattoes generally sided with the institutional violence of the forces of "law and order."

Thus the white/black dichotomy presented by the earlier freedmen was not so pervasive throughout the nineteenth century as they wished it to be. The Mulatto Ascendancy was no more concerned about the laborers and the yeomen than the Colonial Office was concerned about European-born planters as such. They were only the most visible segments within the two most visible coalitions. At worst, the less powerful group in any coalition was always a pawn in the other's game; at best, alliances, even if genuine, were forced by circumstances.

Fragility stemmed from the differing material conditions of production for various members of those alliances. Those who occupied the top of the hierarchies of both racial camps had no direct interest in the actual organization of labor. The way in which production was organized, on the ground, mattered little to the Colonial Office or to the members of the ascendancy. The Colonial Office's objective was to maintain an order that would guarantee the British presence in the Caribbean and ultimately the unequal exchange between Britain and the sum of its colonies. Its priorities did not include the actual manner in which the surplus was transferred. The mulatto politicians dreamed of social status and economic wealth, and if accomplishing these goals implied being planters or estate attorneys so they would be. If, on the other hand, they could succeed without the encumbrance of running a plantation, so much the better. They had few qualms about ways and means.

In sharp contrast, the two groups most involved in production (the white estate owners or attorneys and the cultivators) kept the politics of production foremost among their concerns since their actual power came from their control of the labor process on the ground. We have already seen the cultivators' efforts to expand peasant forms of production and their reluctance to toil on another man's land. The European-born planters, or the white estate attorneys who in practice differed little from actual owners, had invested their money and relocated themselves only on the guarantee of their perpetual dominance of the plantations. Though many engaged in politics, though many belonged to the British Civil Service even before their coming to Dominica, their immediate interests were tied to particular plots of land, and it mattered to them how those were cultivated.

The diverse measures used to prevent, bypass, or co-opt the peasant labor process by way of state intervention in the processes of production and distribution reflected the divergences within the noncultivators. Those measures can be classified into three major categories: preventive tactics, defensive tactics, and co-optative tactics.

Preventive Measures: The Apprenticeship Formula

The measures taken to contain the existing estate labor force were of two kinds: those of a quasi-totalitarian nature, aimed at maintaining by force as many laborers as possible on the plantations, along the model perfected during Apprenticeship itself; and those that tried to contain that labor supply by reducing the economic options available to the former slaves. The latter measures were geared at limiting the laborers' access to (or gains from) productive resources, especially land. I call these measures *preventive tactics*, since those who tried to implement them meant to prevent the spread of the peasant labor process on or off the estates. Other measures tended to bypass the peasant labor process by supplementing the labor supply of the growing peasantry through immigration; some measures aimed to remedy the decrease of the labor supply on the estates through technical means. They were largely *defensive*, since they generally implied the suspicion, if not the belief, that the social and spatial extension of peasant forms of labor organization could not be stopped. Finally, I shall group under the label *co-optative tactics* the actions that tended not so much to prevent or limit the emergence and growth of a peasantry as to guarantee that the gains made by that peasantry within the units of production would not jeopardize the unequal exchange between England and its colony.

The first preventive measures were of a totalitarian nature. They stemmed from the belief, then shared by many European-born planters, mulatto politicians, and colonial officials in Dominica and England, that their gains implied the maintenance of the plantation labor process. Yet the availability of land outside of the estates indicated to many within all three groups that the physical containment of the laborers on the old units of production would not be an easy task. Acting on these beliefs, the governor and the lieutenant governor (on behalf of the Colonial Office), the Board of Council (on behalf of the European-born planters), and the House of Assembly (on behalf of some whites and most of the mulattoes) passed a series of laws to keep the laborers on the plantations through the threat (or the use) of institutional violence. In 1838, Antigua-based Governor Colebrooke had effectively warned the island government that, in view of the coming end of Apprenticeship, "a new system and entire code of laws are imperatively required to meet the incoming change" (ZHC1/1266, 10). Lieutenant Governor J. MacPhail delivered similar warnings in 1839.

In fact, the delivery of the local legislative package (spread over a period of thirteen years) had started before such warnings, and thus before the end of Apprenticeship itself. Besides the official granting of freedom, to be sure an important difference, there is no real marker in the legislative tradition between Apprenticeship itself and the period immediately following it. After all, the very Act for the Abolition of Slavery contained stiff penalties against laborers squatting on Crown lands or found "wandering" outside of their respective plantations. In the same vein, the full title of the final emancipatory act, the act that supposedly terminated coercion, read: "An Act terminating the Apprenticeship of the Proedial Labourers within this Island, on the first day of August 1838, to encourage settlements upon plantations, and to prevent persons squatting or establishing themselves upon lands for which they have no title."

Many other titles of acts, as they appear in the records of the House and Council from 1836 to 1838, are, by themselves, indicative of the totalitarian climate. One notes:

> An Act for subjecting offenders in certain cases to be punished by hard labour on the Tread Mill and for vesting the Provost Marshall with necessary powers for working such offenders and for making other necessary provisions relative thereto;
>
> An Act to make provision for the better administration of Justice in the Island of Dominica;
>
> An Act to repeal an act to establish a Company of Rangers of 1817 but establishing a Rural Police Force;
>
> An Act to enable the Justices in District Petty Sessions to appoint Rural Constables for this Island;
>
> An Act to establish a Police Force for the Island of Dominica, and the regulation thereof;
>
> An Act for the punishment of idle and disorderly persons, Rogues and Vagabonds, Incorrigible Rogues and other Vagrants in this Island;
>
> An Act to authorize Justices of the Peace in District Petty Sessions to dispossess and punish by summary process any person who hath taken or shall take possession of Lands, Tenements or premises, without right or title;
>
> An Act to Authorize Justices of the Peace to meet in Petty Sessions for the several parishes of this Island as included in Districts and to decide in such cases;
>
> An Act for the Punishment of Misdemeanors;
>
> An Act for consolidating and amending the laws relating to offenses against the person, Robbery, Burglary, Larceny, Forgery, Bigamy, Malicious Injuries to property and other offenses connected therewith;

An Act for the punishment of Tumults and Riotous Assemblies and for the more speedy and effectual punishing of the Rioters;

An Act to authorize Justices of the Peace in District Petty Sessions to dispossess or remove any person. (C.O. 73/15, 367–410)

Let no one believe that the stipulations did not carry the promises implicit in those titles. The act for the punishment of idle and disorderly persons defines as a "rogue" or "vagrant," and therefore, as a criminal "every person having in his or her possession any picklock, key, crow, jackbird, cutlass, etc., with intent to commit any felonious act . . . every suspected person or reputed thief frequenting any quay or wharf, or warehouse, near or" on his way to such. Purposefully nebulous, it gave right to "any person whatsoever to apprehend" the offenders. In fact, London sometimes felt compelled to tame some of these measures, and continuous revisions explain the return of some titles in subsequent sessions of the House.

Such measures were meant to be enforced at a time when near absolute political power in Dominica was concentrated in the hands of fewer than fifty men, all of whom, whether mulattoes or whites, whether merchants, planters, or professional politicians, were markedly different, socially and phenotypically, from the bulk of the population. Thus, the concentration of political and social power was not only high, but also quite conspicuous to those at the bottom. The spatial fragmentation of the island enhanced the visibility of the local lords within the enclaves they dominated. Official schedules had to accommodate the multiple occupations of that small elite. Attorney General Charles Lloyd, writing in March 1843, justified a bill presented the previous year and meant to change the dates of the Petty Sessions by saying that the presiding judges were "also Commissioners of Crown Lands, Visiting Justices, and Inspectors of Prisons." Three of them were "Members of the Legislature, and therefore Judges of the Superior Courts of Justice, consequently very much of the business of the country devolv[ed] around them" (C.O. 73/16, 466).

Quite fortunately for the masses, these few men did not see eye to eye even when their policies concurred. The very same sociospatial fragmentation that enhanced their individual power also cultivated conflicts among them. Moreover, the Dominican environment hindered their effective physical control of the whole island. Most of the windward side was accessible from the rest of the country only by boat; and heavy rains could occasion landslides, suddenly cutting one subregion off from the rest. Finally, and most important, the sheer availability of unoccupied land and the haven that the mountains of the interior offered to anyone brave enough to confront them meant that individual laborers could run away, at least temporarily, from physical punishment. Thus by 1855, the Apprenticeship formula was already obsolete for all practical purposes. The upper classes then concentrated their efforts on another variant of preventive tactics: economics would achieve what physical repression had not, with a little help, of course, from the legislators.

A Long List of Licenses

The master plan behind this variant came directly from the best that British political economy produced at the time. The Colonial Office laid out the strategy before the end of Apprenticeship. Secretary of State Lord Glenelg himself, in his Circular Dispatch of January 30, 1836, told all Caribbean governors:

> During slavery, labour could be compelled to go wherever it promised most benefit for the employer; under the new system, it will find its way wherever it promises most profit to the labourer. . . .
>
> Where there is land enough to yield an abundant subsistence to the population, in return from slight labour . . . labour would not be attracted to the cultivation of exportable produce until population began to press upon the means of subsistence. . . .
>
> The minimum price of land, therefore, should be high enough to leave a considerable portion of the population unable to buy it until they have saved some capital out of the wages of their industry, and at the same time low enough to encourage such savings by making the possession of land a reasonable object of ambition to all.

The secretary's instructions were very much in tune with the observations made then and later by writers such as Adam Smith, Herman Merivale, and especially Edward Gibbon Wakefield on colonization.[1] Yet in Dominica, at least, they were not easy to carry out. Wages were certainly not high enough to encourage savings; yet the decline of the estates had forced many planters to initiate various forms of sharecropping, and so lowered the price of private lands that freeholding had indeed become a "reasonable object of ambition to all." Most laborers were determined to acquire such land, however, without entering first into permanent contracts involving wage labor. As we have seen, they succeeded largely both in keeping the provision grounds and in securing land outside the estates.

Both Glenelg and Wakefield made it clear that the plan's ultimate goal was not so much to block the laborers' access to land as to induce laborers to toil on the estates. As soon as Dominican legislators realized that this tactic would not work, partly because they could not enforce it, they emphasized other means to achieve the same goal. They tried to force the peasantry into wage labor by raising the cost of other options available to the masses. The rationale was simple: if independent activities cost the cultivators too much, they would be forced back into estate labor even if they maintained their properties. Legislators did not hesitate to manipulate the tax schedules so that a number of properties, activities, and opportunites, otherwise accessible to the small elite, would become too costly for everybody else. Licenses were required for any economic endeavor or any movable or fixed property that could serve to free an individual from permanent labor on the estates. The Royal Commission on Public Revenues commented in 1883 that Dominica had the longest list of trade licenses in the British Caribbean (PP, 1884, 46:71–72). As early as 1839, retail goods licenses cost twenty-five pounds (C.O. 73/16, 426). The Rum Duty Act of 1866 made it impossible for most citizens to distill or sell alcoholic beverages, especially rum. At a time when male laborers were making about eight pence a day (females made less), an additional licensing fee of ten shillings increased the cost, already high, of operating a still. Even some of the small estate owners abandoned rum production. A retail liquor license cost five pounds in the country and twelve pounds in Roseau. Even some of the mulatto members of the House could not afford such licenses on their thirty pounds-per-annum salaries.

Not surprisingly, the list of licenses published by the official *Gazette* in the years 1865–68 (C.O. 75/1) indicate that only the cream of the elite could engage in such activities. Among the few licensees were William MacIntyre, planter, merchant, member of the House, with a retail license for his residence at the Wall House Estate and retail licenses for his estates of Goodwill, Sugar Loaf, Melville Hall, Macoucherie, Hillsborough, Clark Hall; Charles Leathem (the estate attorney accused of brutality during the 1844 Census Riots), by then a member of the House, with a retail and a still license for his residence at Harlington Cottage and still licenses for his estates of Hampstead, Eden, Woodford Hill, Londonderry, Hatton Garden; William Redhead, former acting lieutenant governor and member of the Assembly, with a still license for his estate of Charlotte Valley; Thomas Davies, member of the House, with still licenses on his estates of Belvedere and Porée; William Davies, later member of the House, with a still license for his estate of Bath; John Imray, M.D., later member of the House, with a still license on his estate of Batalie; Galvin Lucien Bellot, member of the House, with a still license on his estate of Check Hall; Benoit Bellot, former Speaker and still member of the House, with a retail license on his estate of Springfield; Thomas P. Trail, member of the House, with a retail license in Roseau; Joseph Garraway, member of the House, owner of Garraway and Company, with the only recorded wholesale license on the lists. Likewise, four planters and members of the House figured among the eleven individuals known to have held boat licenses in the year 1865: Joseph Bellot, Charles Beaurisseau, Charles Leathem, and James Garraway, the last for two boats. It goes without saying that any major movement from one part of the island to another, particularly as far as the windward and the North were concerned, depended on these individuals.

The better off among the small proprietors were clearly aware of the purposes of such licenses. Among the petitions presented at Wesley, in 1893, to Commissioner Hamilton, a letter from W. G. Marie, of Brookdale, claimed that an increase of the still license fee caused "irritation" among small proprietors who thought it was "enacted for the principal purpose of preventing them from having the advantage of using their stills for distillation of rum" (Hamilton 1894: 94).

The purpose of the licenses was not so much to extract surpluses from the peasantry or the small estate owners as to keep the former from engaging in activities that might increase their freedom from plantation labor and to prevent the latter from expanding their land. Another series of fiscal measures was meant to achieve two other goals: on the one hand, to prevent the expansion of the peasant labor process and, on the other, to siphon back to the government revenues from activities linked to that process. At the forefront of these tactics were the land and export taxes.

"We Only Live to Pay Taxes"

Even before the end of Apprenticeship, the schedule of export duties not only reflected the distribution of economic power in Dominican society but also reinforced the status quo. In 1836, the export duty on one hundred pounds of sugar was one shilling, compared to one shilling six pence for one hundred pounds of cocoa, two shillings for one hundred pounds of arrowroot, and three shillings for one hundred pounds of coffee. Obviously, the schedule worked to the advantage of British-born planters (most of whom were involved in sugarcane cultivation), and bore more heavily on the freedmen or the white planters of French origins involved in cocoa or coffee. Taxes on arrowroot were high, but in light of later increases, they reflect the negligible competition that small independent owners (mainly colored) could offer to the plantocracy, as long as the coercion of the laborers which originated with slavery remained in force.

The export taxes continued to reflect the differential power of diverse groups of planters until 1888. However, after 1838 they functioned primarily as a shield to prevent the products generated through the peasant labor process from reaching the custom houses and the wharves. Taxes stymied the commercialization of the typical peasant crops as soon as slavery ended. In 1839, taxes on one hundred pounds of arrowroot took the lead among the export duties, at the rate of six shillings. Taxes on coffee followed at four shillings six pence, those on cocoa at three shillings, and taxes on one hundred pounds of sugarcane were up to only one shilling six pence. Despite some rectification after Dominica was forced to join the Federation of the Leeward Islands in 1871, the schedules followed that pattern until 1888 when the export duties were abolished.

Yet if export duties did contribute to restrict the flow of plantains, arrowroot, "farine manioc" (manioc flour), or logwood produced by squatters, yeomen, or tenants, they nevertheless failed to curtail significantly the spatial expansion of the peasant labor process. The issue for the rising peasantry was as much social and political as it was economic. Many resigned themselves to ignore the export network, and restricted themselves to production for the household or the local market, a solution not entirely satisfactory to the Colonial Office which, at the time of federation, tended to see Dominica as potential supplier of cheap food to the more important sugar-producing Leeward Islands, especially Antigua.

Moreover, as much as such tactics hurt the masses, they also pressed upon many white and mulatto planters who could not afford exclusive commitment to sugar production. The list of 243 estates published in the *Dominica Almanac* of 1879 verifies the supremacy of sugarcane; but it also reveals a significant number of estates producing other commodities. Benoit Bellot, once Speaker of the Assembly, G. C. Falconer, long-time leader of the Mulatto Ascendancy, A. C. Potter, and other vocal politicians owned cocoa- or coffee-producing estates. Others, including members of the Garraway family, produced provisions for export. In the 1880s, Garraway & Company exported such provisions to a few other Caribbean islands. The duties somewhat limited the gains of such powerful men. Indeed, the planters' reliance on the export market paradoxically limited the impact of the export schedules on the peasantry: at the peak of Dominica's feeble sugar career, the high demand for provisions offered an alternative market to those engaged in the peasant labor process. After the sugar crisis, many more within the plantocracy joined or returned to the expanding group of cocoa or coffee planters. The legislators had less interest, then, in again raising taxes that fell on them and on their friends or allies as much as on the peasantry itself. By 1888, when it was clear to all that the world sugar market was collapsing (some would argue that it had collapsed by then) mulatto and white planters, local politicians and the Colonial Office were willing to admit the ineffectiveness of export duties in preventing the spatial and social expansion of the peasant labor process. In that year, export taxes were abolished.

This abolition was nevertheless a compromise, reluctantly accepted by colonial officials at the outcome of a heated debate on real estate taxes. In 1855, the government had imposed a Land and House Tax of 4 percent on the annual value of properties located in the towns and in the Three Chains. No taxation fell on estate owners as such. In 1886 though, following the recommendations of the commission on public revenues and expenditures, the governor provided the deciding vote to approve an annual land tax of one-half percent on the net value of all properties not covered by the Land and House Tax of 1855. Islandwide disturbances followed, encouraged if not led by the elected representatives, especially the mulattoes who had by then acquired enough land to dread any such taxation. Yet two years later, the Assembly voted to double the tax on houses and lots to 1 percent and quadrupled the land tax to 2 percent of net total value. The bill was pushed by the very same elected representatives who had previously opposed the lower tax because of the burden it would have brought on many small owners. At the same time, export taxes were abolished.

The replacement of the export duties by an islandwide land tax did not significantly affect government revenues. In the late 1850s, export duties and the old land and house tax together provided yearly some 1,700 pounds, then about 12 percent of all government revenues. In 1887, they still accounted for the same 12 percent of total revenues with payments reaching 1,896 pounds. After 1888, the higher land tax provided only a few hundred more pounds to the government, but since total revenues had increased, it generally accounted for the same 11 or 12 percent formerly covered by the export duties and the old tax on lots. The change shifted the burden from the planters to the peasants of providing those 1,900 or 2,000 pounds to the Treasury. Whereas export taxes fell only on exporters or producers of export commodities, the land tax applied to all owners whether or not their products reached any one of the two commercial networks. In fact, it bore most heavily on the small landowners with limited commercial involvement. Further, the abolition of the export duties—the official explanation for the sudden rise in real estate taxes—obviously relieved only those who had been paying it.

The Land Tax Act was inherently unfair; but several procedural irregularities which favored the planters made its enforcement even more unjust. Chief was the unfair evaluation of the small land holdings. The commissioners of valuation, allies of the planters or planters themselves, assessed the small plots at or above their market values while systematically lowering appraisals of estate lands. A few merchants and public officials acknowledged the existence of such practices and reported them to Commissioner Hamilton. So did many peasant proprietors. In Boetica they bluntly told the special commissioner: "The rich man's land is valued at about 5s. 6d., when ours, the small landowners' is not less than 5£" (Hamilton 1894: xxv). One La Plaine peasant testified: "We only live to pay taxes."

The land tax not only curtailed the acquisition of new lands by many potential yeomen but it also helped to recover lands already gained by the peasantry. Most illiterate owners of small holdings did not have the money, the knowledge, or the power required to contest or eventually modify, in court, such unfair appraisals. Hamilton himself estimated that in less than two years from 1892 the government seized as many as 1,700 to 1,800 properties for nonpayment of taxes (Hamilton 1894: xxiii).

The negative impact of the land tax on the peasantry was reinforced by better enforcement of the Road Tax Act of 1856. That act required a poll tax every four months from all persons aged sixteen to fifty at the rate of two shillings for males, and one shilling four pence for females. Consequently, the need for cash could have forced recently freed laborers to accept more casually the low wages on the plantations because of the list of licenses that curtailed alternative sources of cash. However, most took advantage of a provision that allowed them to substitute four days of labor every trimester. Over the years, that tax was modified to require up to six shillings or twelve days of labor from males and three shillings or six days of labor from females. The age range was extended. A new schedule based on property, and which did not take age into consideration, was introduced. It meant that a yeoman family wanting to escape the property-based road tax could not do so by transferring such property to one of the youngest or oldest members. Moreover, government agents pressed peasants to contribute cash payments instead of labor (Hamilton 1894: xxvii).

Laborers, dreading the prospect of thirty-six extra days of hard labor, avoided the tax through quite astute maneuvers: changes of names, of addresses, use of multiple identities, concealment of age, and so on. Small property owners could not so easily do the same: their families were necessarily less mobile, and their rights depended upon a clear legal identification. Yet their road tax was also based on property value. Thus, the registration of any garden or lot immediately put the owner and most members of his family within the reach of the law, as far as this tax was concerned. Proprietors of small holdings felt the pressure, and presented the grievance to visiting Commissioners Hamilton (1894) and Naftel (1898). Commenting on the combined effect of the land and road taxes and the horse license, W. G. Marie wrote in a petition presented to Hamilton in the name of many small property owners of Saint Andrew:

> Where the two latter (road and horse tax) pressed very much on them, especially when taken in conjunction with the first, is when they happen to be heads of young families, say in a case where the small proprietor has a family of five or six boys and girls, besides himself and his wife, from 16 years upwards. He has to contribute, besides his land tax, 6s. per annum for each of the male members of his family, and 3s. for each of the females; and should they, as is generally the case, happen to have two horses, very often more for the purpose of accumulating Creole dung for the use of their title cultivation than for the joy of riding, again they have to pay that heavily lately increased tax of 10s. for each horse. (Hamilton 1894: 43)

Thus the preventive tactics hampered the development of the peasant labor process, especially in the last quarter of the nineteenth century and the first two decades of the twentieth. The road and land taxes, taken in conjunction with the licensing laws, blocked many a peasant's access to formal ownership, and even resulted in the recovery of some land for potential use in plantation-type units of production. The availability of labor in the early 1900s encouraged Administrator H. Hesketh Bell to attract plantation owners back to Dominica. Bell felt confident enough to use such unusual means as paid announcements in the *London Times.*

That these strategies did not bring about the full reversion of the peasant labor process testifies to the determination and resilience of the peasantry, but does not at all imply inefficiency on the part of planters or colonial officials. The defeat of the planter class cannot be explained without reference to other Dominican particulars (including the natural environment and demography). One also needs to consider the international role of Britain and the specific context of the world capitalist economy during the thirty-year crisis between 1914 and 1945 which Giovanni Arrighi aptly called the "war of British succession." The international crisis affected Dominica in a manner markedly different from most of the West Indies partly because the defensive measures had not worked so well in nineteenth-century Dominica as they did elsewhere in the Caribbean.

The Defensive Tactics

Defensive tactics in the post-Emancipation Caribbean tended to bypass the peasant labor process by replacing directly or indirectly the labor power that the estates had lost. Foremost among these tactics were sponsored immigration of indentured laborers and technical improvement of the plantation labor process (Mintz 1979). In Dominica, the acquisition of some African laborers in 1838 clearly fell within an Antillean trend (ZHC1/1266). However, the earlier immigration was insignificant in terms of both numbers and duration.

Politicians and planters throughout the rest of the nineteenth century continued to suggest the immigration of indentured laborers. Speaker Benoit Bellot did so in his January 1862 speech (C.O. 73/33), and various commissioners who visited the island, especially in the latter part of the century, heard similar requests. The most detailed and formal plan for the acquisition of indentured laborers was put forward in 1909 by the Dominica Planters Association, then under the influence of a white South African–born estate owner, but it was rejected by Acting Administrator W. H. Potter and the Colonial Office. Suggestions were made in 1915 to import laborers from Barbados (C.O. 152/349).

The supplementation of labor power through immigration could not work so effectively in Dominica as it did elsewhere in the Caribbean—Trinidad or the Guianas, for instance—partly because of local deficiencies.

The island's topography had always limited its importation of slaves, and after Emancipation, emigration reduced the already small population. Residents left the island as early as 1839 (ZCH1/ 1266, 175), and many more left in the second half of the century, mostly males who went to search for work in Crab Island, the Guianas, or Venezuela (Hamilton 1894: 68; Naftel 1898: 19–20). Hamilton estimated that, in 1893, 7,000 native Dominicans were residing in Venezuela. To compensate for the lack of plantation laborers, Dominica needed more migrants than there had ever been peasants in its history. White planters and politicians did not object to such an influx, even though it would have totally changed the ethnic composition of the society; but they did clash on the issue of who was to pay for the enterprise. A memo of Attorney General Harris, dated 9 December 1909, stated that the political and economic "requirements of indentured labor are impossible to meet in Dominica." The administrator agreed, adding that the planters were not ready to finance fully an enterprise many of them favored, and that they could not even guarantee full employment to the eventual immigrants (C.O. 152/320).

The technical improvement of the plantation labor process also faced difficulties. The centrifugal sugar factory was quickly abandoned. Improvements in the methods of treating limes or manufacturing new lime derivatives never developed enough to replace significant numbers of workers. Thus, the two defensive tactics that worked quite well in other Caribbean territories, immigration and technical improvement, failed in Dominica, mainly because of the relative lack of capital and the broken topography. In light of that failure, nonproducers turned increasingly to co-optative tactics.

The Co-optative Tactics

The co-optative tactics did not affect the organization of labor within units of production but affected producers and nonproducers alike at the level of the social relations of production. They were aimed at integrating what remained, essentially, a peasant work process in such a manner that the fruit of the peasants' labor would benefit the state, the planters, local merchants, and, ultimately, North American and European capitalists. The first co-optative measures were included in diverse fiscal packages in the early nineteenth century.

Indirect taxation can be broadly characterized by a total disregard for the amount of an individual's income and the manner in which such income was acquired. As such, it does not affect processes of labor on the ground. In nineteenth-century Dominica, two forms of indirect taxation—import taxes and excise duties—were meant to channel to government a significant share of the money acquired by yeomen or estate tenants.

Though export taxes, the land tax, and various licenses were meant to limit the opportunities open to the peasantry, they did not constitute the major source of government revenues. By the 1830s, partly to draw upon the income of those already free, the government imposed import duties on all goods entering the island, except perhaps a traveler's personal effects. A generation later (July 1866), Lieutenant Governor James Robert Longden pointed out to the Assembly that import taxes were higher in Dominica than in any other British Caribbean or continental possession (C.O. 74/33). Analysis of revenue sources from 1852 to 1860 shows that before the tax package of 1855–56 import duties contributed from 50 to 60 percent of the government revenues. That share did not decrease substantially after 1856. From 1856 to 1860 import duties still represented more than 45 percent of such revenues. But during the 1870s, the accumulation of excise duties made these fees the second major source of government revenues. By 1882, excise duties accounted for 12 percent of these revenues, thus exceeding the sums collected from liquor licenses and land taxes (about 2 percent). However, import taxes still contributed as much as 37 percent of government revenues. Even after the major changes introduced in 1888, revenues from land taxes accounted for only 8 percent of the yearly totals. Import taxes still led (44 percent), and excise duties provided 13 percent of the government income. Excise duties were to reach their peak in 1893, providing 4,921 pounds, or 22 percent of the government income.

Thus, throughout the nineteenth century, though Dominican planters and politicians did not explicitly accept the possibility of the peasantry's victory on the crucial issue of the country's dominant labor process, the taxation system that they implemented implied the possibility of such a victory. Though some schedules within the various tax packages were meant to eliminate the peasantry's opportunities, the use of indirect taxation as the major source of government income suggests the legislators' knowledge that the laborers could find their way through or around the blockade. Indirect taxation insured that gains made by the laborers on or off the estates would eventually be recouped by the state and transferred to the dominant classes, and ultimately, to foreign-based merchants or industrial capitalists.

Yet three factors impeded the early integration of such a taxation system within a more coherent and explicit strategy that would systematically subsume the peasant labor process within capitalist relations. First, the passage from co-optative tactics—however extensive—to a co-optative *strategy* required a national consensus on the failure of plantation production. Diehard white immigrants would not easily admit to such a failure since that admission implied their own personal failure. Members of the mulatto elite—actual or would-be planters—were more likely to compromise only if they could find rewarding alternatives. Thus, many colonial officials saw viable management of Dominica in terms that implied the political conquest of the Mulatto Ascendancy.

The Conquest of the Mulatto Ascendancy

State politics in nineteenth-century Dominica were complicated by a chronic constitutional crisis. Official titles and positions changed repeatedly. The people who occupied those positions succeeded one another at an even faster pace. Between the constitutional changes and the changes in personnel, the relative power of the different branches of government also shifted, both because of the new rules and because of the new personalities crowding the political stage.

The bitter struggles of Dominican state politics started before the nineteenth century. In 1771, eight years after taking over Dominica, Britain gave Dominican planters the privilege of "separate government." The formula entailed the right of some property owners to elect some members of the local legislature. From then on, the fight between the executive and the legislative branches dominated the political scene. The composition of each of those branches varied. At times, the chief local executive was a governor who dealt directly with the Colonial Office. At other times, the chief executive was a lieutenant governor or a president who depended upon a superior in Antigua. Likewise, the legislative branch at times comprised only elected representatives; at others, some members of the Assembly were nominated by the Crown. Finally, a Board of Council with legislative prerogatives sometimes provided a buffer between the elected legislators and the chief executive with whom the board often sided.

Behind this constitutional quagmire was the constant antagonism between the representatives of the Crown, who tried to implement with varying conviction the policies of the Colonial Office, and the locally elected officials, who tried with varying selfishness to use state power for their own benefit. The antagonism predated the colored's participation in local politics, but it reached its apex with the emergence of the Mulatto Ascendancy (Boromé 1972d). For sixty years, from the time the colored took control of the House (1838) to the imposition of crown colony rule (1898), both sides vehemently protested against the other's repeated "abuses." Thus, even though the characters changed, the factions were clearly drawn: on the one hand, the "executive" (the cohort of Crown nominees usually led by the governor, including the Council); on the other, the "electives" (usually colored politicians elected by however dubious means).

Indeed, throughout the nineteenth century, the colored consistently used the techniques that first served them so well in the 1830s. They manipulated the lists of voters, the requirements for both voters and office holders, as well as their personal qualifications, in order to maintain control of the elected part of the legislature, if not control of the entire body. One common tactic (used also by their white opponents) was nominally to divide property belonging to any member of the clique in as many parts as possible to secure the eligibility of their cronies. The voters' list published by the official *Gazette* of 12 December 1866 shows Charles Lionné, Joseph F. Dupigny, Thomas P. Trail, Henry Ruse Elwin, Alexander Charles Potter, Charles Beaurisseau, each claiming "10 acres of land being part of Prince's Grove estate in the parish of St. John" (C.O. 71/5).

Propelled into power and effectively holding on to it by such tactics, the electives kept at bay the representatives of the Crown. In 1865, they were able to force the withdrawal of a bill introduced by the executive to make Dominica a crown colony. In 1871, however, despite their protests, the British Parliament and the Colonial Office imposed Dominica's inclusion in the newly created Federation of the Leeward Islands (C.O. 74/33; Hamilton 1894: 65–66). The colored still managed to maintain their say in the affairs of the state. In 1886, the executive lowered voting requirements, extending the electoral franchise to allow poorer members of the population to participate in the elections. The not-so-secret goal was to modify the composition of the electorate with the hope that new and different voters, not tied to the mulatto elite, would get rid of the most vocal members of the Mulatto Ascendancy and bring Dominica closer to Whitehall's control. The strategy failed. "All the electives had been returned except one, and his replacement shared their view" (Boromé 1972d: 127). The fight for the control of the local government continued, bitter and loud, as evidenced in the editorials of the *Dominican* and the *Colonist.* Yet, to the surprise of many, in July 1898, a new Assembly composed of six elected and six nominated members abrogated itself, and Dominica became a crown colony. To be sure, some of the earlier native leaders had retired or died by then; but many still pretended to hold high the banner of their independence from London. Moreover, the mass movements that many expected to follow the imposition of federation or the change to crown colony status did not occur.

The self-abrogation of the Assembly reveals how much the mulattoes' spirit of independence had changed between 1838 and 1898. Somewhere in that sixty-year span, they had lost their economic pretensions and kept only the brilliance of their rhetoric. As individuals and as a group, colored politicians were patiently and systematically allowed to mold new sources of income within the state apparatus. Because they now had economic alternatives, their original interest in the maintenance of the plantation system weakened. Further, participation in the Civil Service placed them in positions that widened the social and ideological gap between them and the laboring masses.

The executive allowed the native politicians to use the state as a substantial source of income, first by nominating them to salaried government positions, and second by engaging them or their allies as government contractors. Both tactics are demonstrated by the career of Charles Gordon Falconer, perhaps the most vocal of the mulatto politicians (Boromé 1972c). In 1865, Falconer was contracted as printer for the Assembly, and used the press of his newspaper, the *Dominican.* In 1868, he was nominated registrar general, a salaried government position. After federation was imposed, the executive made clear to the disgruntled politicians that they would find sources of income in government. In his message of February 24, 1874, Governor Henry Turner Irving stated: "As regard to the creation of a public career, I think that a Colony where, outside of the domain of agriculture and trade, there is no field for employment, except in the very narrow limits of the learned professions, the creation of a public service which shall take rank with those professions must be regarded as a great public good" (C.O. 74/33).

In 1893, the Dominica Grammar School opened in Roseau with the explicit aim of preparing Dominican boys for a public career. Now, almost a century later, most students of both sexes still state "getting a government job" as a major reason for attending the school. Many more adults and adolescents throughout the country identify a fundamental dividing line in Dominican society between civil servants and farmers, or government employees and peasants.

With the indulgence of the executive, colored politicians used their positions to perform various paid services for the government. Joseph Boromé (1972d) rightly points out that mulatto members of the Assembly systematically urged the passage of liberal laws to provide assistance to the poorest and most powerless in the society. Yet the programs so enacted used the services of these same politicians, their wives, their friends, or members of their families who, as government contractors, drew substantial profits from their seemingly benevolent participation. Records for the year 1866 reveal quite a few members of the Assembly in the lists of claimants to be paid for services provided to the government.

Dominica's tortuous topography and turbulent climate provided excuses for reckless spending. The Department of Public Works was, and remains, a primary area for public expenditures, but also a source of graft and political patronage. Famous mulatto politicians such as Falconer and Davies sat at various times on the Road Board, from which they gained substantial economic power. In the early 1890s, out of 29,000 pounds received from Great Britain for improvement of public roads, 10,000 was spent for imported materials and supplies; the rest was spent for local services. In the first decade of this century, the newly arrived white planters complained that the bad state of the roads was due to the abuses of native charlatans posing as genuine contractors (C.O. 152/327).

From 1898 to the 1978 Independence, Dominica's colored elite offered little opposition to economic policies designed in London. Their decline as an independent political force was due in part to demographic changes. Miscegenation had virtually stopped with the massive departures of European-born planters after the fall of sugar. The small size of the elite, who concentrated power in the nineteenth century, later hampered endogamous reproduction of an upper-class fragment clearly differentiated by color. As elsewhere in the Caribbean, terms such as "fair," "colored," or "light-skinned" came to refer to complexions increasingly closer to the dark end of the color continuum. And as those terms referred to darker complexions, the population they covered was also becoming more complex, more differentiated occupationally and economically than the colored elite of the 1860s. Terms such as "light-skinned" and "colored" still have political value in Dominica; but they do not refer anymore to a group of people united by their economic aspirations and their fierce resistance to Whitehall.

However, the trends in phenotypical variation should not blur the more important political conquest of the colored by the Colonial Office. The presidency of H. Hesketh Bell (1899–1905) exposes the nature of the compromise between the two camps. The mulattoes' approval of Bell's policies aimed at creating a new European-born plantocracy proves how much they had receded from claims of exclusive or even privileged control of the plantations. On the other hand, Bell's large public expenditures, increased employment in the state sector, and allegations of incompetence among the state's contractors give a measure of the local elite's new dependence on the redistribution of funds gathered through grants and loans by the colonial apparatus. Not surprisingly, the political heirs of the nineteenth-century Mulatto Ascendancy (though by no means an exclusively light-skinned group even by today's standards) were at the forefront of the local forces against full political independence in the 1970s. They repeatedly pointed to the eventual loss of grants, loans, and other privileges that colonial status implied. That, indeed, was a far cry from the position of their nineteenth-century forefathers. What had happened in between was the political conquest of the mulatto elite by the Colonial Office, the greater security of the colored in the local state machinery, and the development of the peasant labor process in export-oriented production.

CHAPTER 6

"I Can Always Eat My Fig"

"Traditions" which appear or claim to be old are often quite recent in origin and sometimes invented.
—Eric Hobsbawm, *The Invention of Tradition*

We boiled green bananas in an old iron pot and ate them with our fingers out of a calabash.
—Jean Rhys, *Wide Sargasso Sea*

The colored elite's propensity to turn to the state apparatus as their principal source of income, and their acceptance of the tighter control inherent in crown colony rule suggested an admission of defeat on two related counts. First, their new obedience implied their own inability to maintain (or even to restore significantly) the plantation economy without the help of the Crown appointees. Second, and more important, their near-total dependence on the colonial state apparatus for their own livelihood indicated their inability to formulate viable alternatives for the country as a whole. As parasites of the colonial state, they had gradually lost both the incentives and the right to intervene independently in debates on the process of production. Their retreat removed the sole local checkpoint to the executive since the end of slavery. It left room for a unified strategy aimed at limiting the expansion of the peasantry or at co-opting the peasants' control of the labor process.

The outcome was not predetermined, even if only because it required increased collaboration between metropolitan and local administration in designing a strategy that would appeal to all the nonlaboring classes. Further, the personality of the local administrator affected the formulation of strategy, especially if the metropolitan Colonial Office did not fully share his evaluation of local forces and possibilities. It is a measure of H. Hesketh Bell's character that, as chief administrator of the colony (1899–1905), he strove relentlessly to revive the plantation economy through an innovative strategy built around a massive influx of white planters. It is a measure of his acumen that he almost succeeded despite the reluctance of many at the Colonial Office. Yet it is a measure of the masses' resistance that this clever scheme was deployed in vain.

Bell's strategy rested on the opening of parts of the Dominican interior to provide hitherto unused land to new settlers willing to invest in citrus production at a time of rising international demand. The formula was not new: it proceeded from recommendations of Joseph Chamberlain's ministry to the British House of Commons to grant a financial package to Dominica in exchange for more direct Crown control over the local House. Bell could not have financed his projects without those funds. What singularizes Bell's application of the general formula is his systematic boldness, a public relations campaign designed to attract immigrants and overpower the mulatto politicians with little direct intervention from the Colonial Office. During the first decade of this century, Bell's various policies led to a revival of the plantation labor process, and many laborers returned, often as wage earners, to the estates. Exports of both cocoa and limes increased by plan. Bell successfully advertised abroad the benefits that Dominica offered to small investors willing to exercise patience. Planters came from neighboring islands, but also from parts of the empire as far away as Ceylon or South Africa. The 1911 Census shows 399 Europeans residing in the island, up from just 44 in 1891.

The ultimate failure of Bell's strategy seems at first to have been caused by unforeseeable natural and international circumstances, or the inability of his immediate successors. In 1916, a major hurricane devastated many of the lime plantations. Two years later, with the end of World War I, the demand for lime derivatives from the British Admiralty and War Office, Dominica's major European customers, dropped. Also in 1918, the United States government imposed an embargo on Dominican limes. By then, mulatto politicians, dissatisfied with crown colony rule, started a new campaign to return to an elected Assembly.

Yet the failure of the new policy rested also on a major miscalculation by planters and officials, especially Bell himself. Dominica had long been a single political entity; it was, most certainly, delineated by the sea, and could be seen as one geographical unit; yet in many ways, the topography and the lack of communication among the various parts of the island often turned parishes and villages into quite dissimilar economic patches. In 1900, Dominica was perhaps one nation (some would contest even that); it sheltered perhaps one culture (and that also is arguable); but it certainly was not a single labor market. The homogeneity Bell attributed to the Dominican labor supply was a miscalculation.

Long before the end of the war, new settlers repeatedly complained about the lack of internal communication which severely reduced their supply of laborers and forced them to pay what they thought to be prohibitively high wages (C.O. 152/327; C.O. 152/333). Bell did open a new road to the interior but without "feeder roads" from the villages it could not significantly ease the circulation of labor. Population density peaked, for instance, around Grand Bay and in the Marigot-Wesley-Woodford Hill area, but the supply of labor in these pockets did not imply an immediate flow to the new areas of increased demand accessible only from the capital town of Roseau. Roseau remained the revolving door through which anyone had to pass and was quite inaccessible for a Grand Bay or Wesley laborer. Further, the laborers' general preference for impermanent engagements meant that the number of cultivators looking for employment at any particular moment was, in fact, lower than the gross figures would imply.

Finally, one should not underestimate the cultural ties that united many landless laborers to the peasant labor process. Today, many still prefer to contribute labor on kin's or friends' properties for less remuneration than to work permanently on an estate. In the 1910s, the length of the trip to the interior lands precluded even weekly back-and-forth movements between the new estates and the coastal villages where most people resided. Implied was a clear choice between the security of existing social networks and the potential economic benefits of regular wages. Most Dominicans chose to stick with their culture. Welch (1968) pointed to the rural workers' strong preference, even in the 1960s, for a workplace easily accessible from home. Today, with a much more monetarized economy, rural dwellers still measure the incentives of manual wage labor in terms of the disruption that such activity would cause in their family life, and, at times, they dismiss possibilities of employment on that basis. Others, in great need of cash, may engage in such work outside of the village, experiment with the disruption for a few weeks, and then quickly abandon the job once their immediate needs have been satisfied. Many more must have taken that latter path in the early 1900s. With land prices staying as low as ten shillings an acre while wages continued to increase, it was fairly easy to engage in plantation work long enough to acquire a small plot (PP, 1907, 54:518; PP, 1919, 55:992). Most of the newly arrived white planters, unable to maintain a permanent labor force, quickly lost money. Expectations from Bell's extravagant advertising campaign inflated the dimensions of the failure. Dominica's reputation reached new lows. European planters returned to their native lands or went to seek fortunes elsewhere. Some may even have volunteered their services during the war in order to escape from the island and the debts they had accumulated. With the country on the brink of poverty, immediate solutions were needed.

Many observers had maintained, since the end of slavery, that the restoration of the plantation economy in Dominica was an impossible task; but this argument had often met resistance from planters in Dominica and politicians in Dominica and in England. In the post-Bell era, that resistance, wilted from a century of weariness, could not survive one more reevaluation. The white planters had left. The prestige of the local administration had disappeared with Bell's departure for Uganda. Native planters and politicians had been allowed by a succession of governors and administrators to mold a source of income that did not imply the survival of the estates. The Colonial Office could then move forcefully on proposals that had been incubating since the end of slavery and specifically implied the permanence of the peasant labor process. The new element was the certitude that the peasantry was there to stay and that export-oriented production would necessarily or even primarily develop on lands it controlled.

The policy shifts in Dominica were part of a larger trend of change in the attitude of British officials vis-à-vis all Caribbean peasantries. Richard Lodbell (1985) sees the report of the 1897 Royal Commission as pivotal to viewing the peasantries as an asset rather than a hindrance. He suggests three complementary, even if quite unequal, explanations: economic circumstances in Britain and in the Caribbean; personnel changes in the commissions investigating Caribbean territories; antiestablishment attitudes at the Colonial Office. I would certainly add the weakness of local planters and bureaucrats after 1880 and, especially, the resilience of the peasantry. For, in Dominica, at least, the official recognition of that peasantry as an economic and historical agent was begrudging. In the long struggle for the control of land and labor, it was a concession made to the cultivators, and a hefty one at that. But it was also a mixed blessing: colonial officials were not interested in the welfare of the peasantry as such, but in the sustenance of production. Hence, the recognition of the peasantry's resilience also meant a new awareness of the need to co-opt that peasantry. Since the previous generations of officials had not been able to destroy the peasant labor process, the issue now was how to best control it. The certitude that the peasantry was there to stay, the weakness of the local executive in the post-Bell era, as well as the obedience of the native elite allowed a fundamental change from the marginal co-optative tactics of the nineteenth century to a unified co-optative strategy.

From Tactics to Strategy

As early as 1838, Stipendiary Magistrate Phillips had concluded from his field observation that laborers should be encouraged to use part of their labor to cultivate exportable (staple) products instead of provisions for home consumption (ZHC1/1266). J. R. Longden's speech of 1865 exhorted the Assembly to help secure land to the peasantry for the cultivation of export commodities (C.O. 74/33). Governor Irving defended Dominica's forced participation in the 1871 Leeward Federation on the basis that it brought the opportunity to increase the sale of fruits and provisions to the neighboring sugar islands. Admittedly, most white and mulatto planters dreaded proposals of an export policy acknowledging the independence of the peasantry; but many politicans and merchants, some of whom were not white, hoped to benefit from the exportation of peasant crops. The Giraud, the Garraway, and the Fillan families certainly looked at such proposals with interest.

After the report of Government Botanist Prestoe (1875), proposals that implied the survival of the peasant labor process were often presented under the more general and less threatening heading of "diversification." After the obvious debacle of the estate-based economy in the 1890s, few of those who suggested the cultivation of a new crop ever specified that it was to be carried exclusively on the plantations (Hamilton 1894; Naftel 1898). In reviewing the prospects for various crops, Naftel rejected the cultivation of bay oil on the estates, but added with considerable foresight: "It would, however, be a remunerative cultivation for small peasant proprietors on hedges, walls or trees about their dwellings" (Naftel 1898: 38). In this context, the 1891 opening of the Botanic Station in Roseau takes new significance, an economic dimension that, as we are now discovering, was much the general rule in the British Empire (Brockway 1979). However strong was the desire to collect and classify rare or newly found native species of plants, the station functioned primarily as a distribution center and nursery for commercial species. At first, mostly planters used its services, but an increasing number of peasants were encouraged to purchase from it (Hamilton 1894; Naftel 1898). Likewise, the opening, in December 1900, of the Dominica Agricultural School helped the peasants master skills that they later used for their own purposes. Though the original object was to prepare "sons of peasants and small planters" as overseers or agricultural technicians of a kind for the estates (PP, 1907, 54:518), the practices and techniques mastered under the supervision of a Kew-trained instructor filtered back to the peasantry and contributed to the success of many small independent ventures.

General pronouncements in favor of diversification lasted at least until the report of Under Secretary of State for the Colonies E. L. F. Wood (1922). However, during the mid-1920s and the early 1930s, the failure on the local level of the recent white immigrants and the world crisis that culminated in the Great Depression forced the Colonial Office to intervene explicitly and systematically in favor of an export policy based on peasant production. The climate for such a move was particularly ripe in England itself after the publication of the report by the Imperial Committee on Marketing (1926–27).

In 1926 and 1927, the Imperial Committee on Marketing (PP, 1926–27, 13:799–836) had favorably reported on the prospects of a fruit trade between Britain and its overseas colonies. The stated goals included a manipulation of the British consumer in such a manner as to increase the demand for fruits produced in the colonies; research on the botany, cultivation, and conservation of fruits at leading universities such as Cambridge; and promotion of fruit cultivation and export in the dependencies themselves. The Dominican government happily followed its specific directives, and started, in 1926, the systematic promotion of fruit cultivation and exportation. It established the Government Fruit Packing Depot. It relentlessly tried to convince J. B. Charles, colored planter of Roseau, to sell Copt Hall Estate to establish a fruit farm despite conditions that the officials themselves deemed "harsh and unreasonable."

However, up to the 1930s, few experts expected a rapid and secure growth of the fruit trade. The 1928 hurricane had destroyed many coconut stands and many cocoa estates, and planters complained of the laborers' obvious efforts to take advantage of the situation (C.O. 152/410). To be sure, in a report dated 16 September 1928, H. Clark Powell did suggest that grapefruit could replace limes as Dominica's major export commodity. However, he emphasized that grapefruit cultivation would require a fair amount of capital and the maintenance of the estates (C.O. 152/410). The Empire Marketing Board was asked for help, but many in and around the Colonial Office had already rejected the very notion of the viability of plantation production in Dominica. The Colonial Fruit Grant Committee discussed Powell's proposals, stating that "the history of settlement in Dominica had not been encouraging," and that white planters with five thousand pounds sterling were not likely to establish themselves in such a place (C.O. 152/410).

It was in that same year, 1928, when all solutions seemed to lead to impasses, that the idea of more systematic reliance on the independence of the peasantry, put forward the previous year by a colonial envoy, Sir Francis Watts, looked its most attractive. Without daring to dismiss completely the plantation, Watts had suggested the creation of a Peasant Information Bureau, headed by a salaried "Peasant Adviser," who would systematically promote and supervise the cultivation of crops amenable to the peasant labor process. That bureau would also help the marketing of commodities so produced locally and overseas (Watts 1927: 43–47). Watts predicted that "considerable time would elapse before the advantages of [his] scheme became evident" (1927: 47), but one year later, the bureau was buzzing with activity. Under the tight control of Peasant Adviser J. C. MacIntyre, a Vegetables Growers Association was formed, and exportation of peasant-produced vegetables to North America started in 1929. However, the trade soon faced problems in the United States, up to then its major prospective market. The imposition of heavy duties by the United States government, the protected growth of North American vegetables, and the easier entry of Bermuda vegetables, more traditionally imported to the United States, together created a formidable barrier and shattered the hopes of Dominican producers and middlemen. Difficulty of entrance to the United States in turn hindered access to the Canadian market, Dominica's second prospect (C.O. 152/410; C.O. 152/411). Nevertheless, that limited experience convinced many officials of the general viability of Watts's proposals for a peasant-based export policy. The unsolved riddle was the choice of the crop.

Prior to Watts's proposals for Dominica, the Imperial Committee on Marketing had already drawn attention to the possibility of large-scale fruit production throughout the empire. It emphasized the marketing prospects of a selected number of fruits. The combined implementation of those related and quite compatible programs—one formulated specifically for the island, the second drawn at the level of the empire—was simply a matter of time. The Imperial Committee had insisted in its recommendations for the colonies on the regularity and continuity of supply (PP, 1926–27, 13:811). Pondering on Dominica's local problems, the Colonial Office itself underlined, in 1929, "firstly, the lack of capital, and secondly, the length of time which must elapse before the crops bring remunerative return" (C.O. 152/410). Thus, by the early 1930s, the most recent assessments of Dominica's situation in the British colonial empire indicated the necessity of finding a crop, most preferably a fruit, or one perceived as such, that (1) could be produced by independent yeomen, renters, or sharecroppers using the peasant labor process; (2) could be integrated in the overall colonial fruit scheme proposed by the Imperial Committee; (3) required little capital; and (4) required little time from planting to harvest. The crop that best fitted the bill was bananas. Despite the early reluctance of many officials, it was to become the product through which capitalism fully integrated and dominated the peasant labor process. Yet bananas' success did not depend only on the way it fitted colonial schemes. The Dominican environment, the botanical characteristics of the crop, a long history of the peasantry's acquaintance with its cultivation on their grounds, the Caribbean context, and, most important, the edibility of the product, and its easy integration in the cultivators' daily diet, all contributed to its rise as an export commodity. The success of bananas was, in part, the result of colonial schemes, but also belongs, in part, to the story of the peasantry's success.

A Long History of Acquaintance

The first bananas ever planted in Dominica were probably of the same Canary stock introduced by Spanish friars in Hispaniola in the early sixteenth century. Yet the figures quoted by Boromé (1972b) as evidence for the general increase of production in the 1730s and '40s most likely refer to plants of the "Gros Michel" variety, also known in Dominica as "Fig Laroz." Bananas (*Musa sapientum*) entered the slaves' diet, but never to an extent comparable to that of plantains (*Musa paradisiaca*). Likewise, small quantities of plantains were exported before the end of Apprenticeship, mostly to neighboring islands, and the government imposed export duties on plantains long before the first recorded banana exports of the 1850s. Thus, we take account of the few dozen bunches exported before the 1890s only to emphasize the history of banana cultivation as a contributing factor to the twentieth-century boom. Indeed, by the time the offices of the Banana Growers Association opened in Roseau, the Dominican masses had been accustomed to the cultivation of the plant on their own grounds for more than two hundred years. They were also accustomed to the daily consumption of its botanical twin—the plantain. They had witnessed and even contributed to, albeit irregularly, the limited exportation of both crops for almost a century.

Still, the first systematic proposal for large-scale export production was made at the end of the nineteenth century by a British-born medical officer and politician H. A. Alford Nicholls (1890). Enthused by the growth of Jamaican exports to the United States, Dr. Nicholls wanted to take advantage of the regular calls of the Quebec Steamship Company in Roseau to start what seemed to be a promising trade with the United States and Canada. His proposal was not followed and Jamaica remained until 1900 the only significant Caribbean exporter. Indeed, metropolitan attitudes toward banana production in the British Caribbean, especially in the Windward Islands, remained tied to the fortunes of the Jamaican banana industry until at least the 1950s.

The first recorded export of bananas from Jamaica was due to the actions of a certain Captain Bush who brought the fruit to Boston in 1866 (Beaver 1976: 32). From 1877 on, the Boston Fruit Company took the lead in the banana trade (a position it maintained long after it became the United Fruit Company in 1899). But a few months after the incorporation of the new company, Joseph Chamberlain, then British secretary of state for the colonies, learned that United Fruit was planning to start cultivation in Cuba on company-owned plantations. To sustain Jamaican production, Chamberlain subsidized the shipping firm of Elder Dempster, then controlled by magnate Alfred Jones, to start a trade between Jamaica and the United Kingdom. Jones had been involved in the banana trade betweeen the Canary Islands and the United Kingdom; but to carry out the West Indian venture he acquired, in 1901, its old competitor, the firm of Fyffes Hudson Company. Fyffes had brought the first commercial shipment of bananas to England in 1878.

The threat of large-scale production in Cuba by United Fruit never materialized because of problems unforeseen by United States planters; but Jones's creation, the new British firm of Elders and Fyffes, remained involved in the Caribbean banana trade despite its founder's neglect and the sudden indifference of the Colonial Office. One year later, in search of capital, Elders and Fyffes turned to the very company it had been created to challenge, namely, United Fruit itself. United Fruit quickly secured 45 percent of Fyffes' shares; by 1904 it owned half of the British company, and, by 1924–25, controlled 83 percent of its capital. Other North American interests controlled an additional 6 percent. Thus, less than a quarter of a century after Chamberlain had devised his scheme, no more than 11 percent of the company he helped to create was in British hands (Beaver 1976; Imperial Economic Committee 1926; Kepner and Soothill 1935).

Those developments worried the Imperial Economic Committee whose mandate was to counteract foreign, and especially North American, penetration of British markets. The committee thought the banana trade important enough to deserve one among eight special reports on specific fruits; and at the conclusion of its "Banana Report," it declared Elders and Fyffes' monopoly "undesirable" (Imperial Economic Committee 1926: 268). To limit the influence of the United States–owned firm, the committee proposed a multiphased scheme that aimed at guaranteeing (1) large-scale production of bananas in Trinidad, British Honduras, and British Guiana; (2) continuation of the already massive Jamaican production; and (3) marketing of all Caribbean production by a monopsonistic company based in Britain. In view of the difficulties barring immediate implementation of this scheme (the threat of diseases in Trinidad and British Guiana, for instance) immediate subsidies would first finance a "service based upon Jamaica, with St. Lucia and Grenada as complementary sources of supply" (Imperial Economic Committee 1926: 256). In short, Dominica was perceived as a last resort, a potential complement to Saint Lucian and Grenadian production, partly because the original banana scheme implied a plantation model. Not surprisingly, local and metropolitan officials did not pay much attention to an independent proposal by another fruit transporter, Swifts, who wanted to include Dominica in a Caribbean-wide plan to sell bananas to Europe (C.O. 152/398).

There are lessons here worth noting even if the ironies of the story are by no means unique. One wonders about the ultimate efficiency of a system in which the distribution of power allows a government to finance a commercial enterprise only to watch passively as it falls into the hands of the very competitors it was meant to oppose. One wonders even more when, half a century later, experts at the service of that same government uncritically offer the scheme on a much larger scale without even a mention of the first failure. One wonders, finally, about a system in which the inhabitants of neglected territories, such as Saint Lucia, Grenada, or Dominica, are heeded only as fallbacks in light of the importance conceded to another, neighboring colony. But the irony is, of course, that Saint Lucia, Grenada, and particularly Dominica became more dependent on banana production than the Colonial Office could have forecast; indeed, more dependent than Jamaica ever was.

Still, the Imperial Committee operated with a surprising degree of efficiency, at least in some specific areas. It rightly forecast the necessity of institutional control of fruit production under the guise of growers' representation in areas in which the peasant labor process obtained in the cultivation of exportable fruits. The strategy developed in the Main Fruit Report was applied to bananas. The committee wrote in its special banana report: "In the establishment of a shipping service, it would be most important for the shipping line to be able to negotiate with some representative body which was able to guarantee regularity and adequacy of supply. There is, moreover, the educational value of producers' organization in furthering the adoption of improved agricultural methods" (Imperial Economic Committee 1926: 264–65).

Of course, despite the somewhat polemical claims of Beckford (1967), the various Banana Growers associations of the Windward Islands and their more recent parent body, WINBAN (Windward Islands Banana Association), were no more representative of peasant growers than Jamaica's association or, for that matter, the other producers' organizations of the Windwards such as Saint Lucia's Coconut Growers Association, Grenada's Nutmeg Advisory Board, Saint Vincent's Cooperative Arrowroot Association, or Dominica's Fruit Committee. The British Colonial Office and its advisers never aimed at representativeness in pushing forward the creation of such bodies. The key point, rather, was the regularity and adequacy of supply which often necessitated a legal body able to engage in contractual activities of a formal nature in order to register, accept, and help implement, in the name of the people, monopsonies imposed from London. I will return, later, to the crucial role of the Dominica Banana Association, especially after 1952, but it may be worth noting now one more ironical twist that further qualifies the image of colonial omnipotence then cherished by metropolitan officials.

The Dominica Banana Association, the first of the Windwards, signed its first contract in the name of Dominican peasants, not with a British firm, but with the Canadian Banana Company Limited of Montreal, a subsidiary of the much dreaded United Fruit Company. In this contract, signed April 12, 1934, the newly formed association promised to deliver, and the Canadian firm agreed to buy, all exportable bananas of the Gros Michel variety grown in the island. Long before its 1939 expiration, the contract was extended to include a second five-year period, but World War II reduced naval movement in the area and, by the end of 1939, the association as well as the company faced serious difficulties. In 1940, supposedly for security reasons, the British government stopped all shipments of Caribbean bananas to the United Kingdom. A substantial part of Jamaican surplus production was then absorbed by the United States and Canada, thus making it harder for Windward fruits to gain a foothold in the North American market. Also, the difficulties of trans-Atlantic shipping during the war contributed to raising the price of vanilla in the United States, and indirectly impeded the growth of Dominican banana production. Peasants enjoyed the benefits of high returns for their vanilla, and vanilla remained Dominica's most important export until the end of the war. Still, banana production, which had seemed remote only sixteen years before, had taken a strong enough foothold in the island for London to provide an annual grant for its support.[1] Dominican banana cultivation continued under that subsidy, and exports doubled in the decade 1938 to 1948.

Yet the turning point was undoubtedly the establishment in June 1949 of Antilles Products Limited which signed a fifteen-year contract with the association, agreeing to purchase, and to sell in the United Kingdom, all exportable bananas of the Lacatan variety produced in the island. Moreover, the two British founders of the company, P. J. Foley and G.B. Band, started their own plantation on the Woodford Hill Estate on the northeastern part of the island. Woodford Hill forms an ecological unit with the neighboring estates of Eden, Londonderry, and Melville Hall. More important, these estates and the villages around them also constituted an economic enclave, and, in 1949, as often before, Eden, Londonderry, and Woodford Hill belonged to the same owner, in this case, one Captain V. Stebbings. My informants recall that at the death of "Stabin," his wife put the three properties up for sale. Thus, at about the same time that Foley and Band were acquiring the Woodford Hill Estate, two other newcomers, Dr. R. F. Armour, a West Indian physician educated at Chicago and Quebec and acting as medical offier in Portsmouth, and Frobelle Laville, took over Eden and Londonderry, respectively. Under the supervision of "Fole an' Bans" (as people in the area still refer to them), improved techniques of banana cultivation spread to the renovated estates as well as to the peasant gardens. Thus, by the time

Geest Industries took over the activities and the properties of Antilles Products (including the Woodford Hill Estate) systematic production for export had been going on for two years in that northeastern enclave.

The success of Antilles Products (and subsequently that of Geest) was also due, in part, to the intervention of the Colonial Office which prevented Fyffes from establishing over Windward production a monopsonistic control which would have secured its grip on Jamaica. In compensation, rhetoric notwithstanding (Beaver 1976), Fyffes was graciously allowed to take over the Cameroons. To be sure, one monopsony often equals another in the eyes of the producer, but the competition between Fyffes and Geest meant that the distribution of Windward fruits would not be totally dependent upon the real or imaginary importance of Jamaican production as perceived by London merchants.

No one can deny then that the world market at large and British colonial policy in particular greatly influenced the growth of banana production in Dominica. Yet the considerable evidence on the role of these external factors still leaves a set of unanswered questions. Merchant capitalists and metropolitan officials did nurture a demand for a whole range of tropical commodities, including many fruits. These policies were certainly not geared to bananas as such. What beyond the international incentives gave bananas a definite edge over other tropical commodities?

I will now return to Dominica's internal dynamics and emphasize the factors that favored the adoption of bananas as a staple commodity by the Dominican peasantry, readily admitting that similar forces may have been at work in Saint Lucia, Grenada, or Saint Vincent, although Dominica's early lead among the Windwards and Foley and Band's establishment in the Woodford Hill area suggest that conditions may have been more ripe in that island.

The Invention of a Tradition

People create their past in tones always renewed to better account for the present. That creation is never haphazard nor senseless, and it often reveals as much as the professional historian's own reconstruction. Most Dominicans nowadays would say that bananas, or "figs" (as they call them), have always occupied the preponderant place they now hold in the rural folk diet. Some would accompany that assertion with remarks about the nutritional value of the fruit. In her novel, *Wide Sargasso Sea*, quoted at the beginning of this chapter, Dominica-born Jean Rhys (who, incidentally, spent most of her life in Europe) pushes the legend of heavy banana consumption as far back as the days of slavery. Yet when forced to uncover systematically the factual past within their present, most men and women over fifty refer to a diet in which bananas were once much more of a fruit than a cooked staple; and the scanty written data tend to support that claim.

The same people are not lying in one case and telling the truth in the other. The legend of fig consumption is rather a good indication of the extent to which banana production fitted the practices and perceptions of the Dominican peasantry. Chances are that only a crop amenable to small-scale production could replace limes at the top of the export lists. Chances are that many such crops were equally acceptable to the Colonial Office and the local planners. What gave bananas the edge over so many possible alternatives, to the surprise, one might add, of local and metropolitan officials, was the extent to which it fitted the peasant tradition. To be sure, the first trials of the Vegetable Growers Association provided some crucial experience to future banana producers and exporters. Likewise, the five short years of vanilla's preeminence removed the last serious doubts about the feasibility of an export strategy based on a commodity produced primarily by the peasantry. That itself was a victory achieved over generations of planters and bureaucrats. Yet bananas crystallized that victory in a way that vanilla could not: it intrinsically tied mass production for the world market to household production.

The commercial production of bananas could be as easily adapted to the peasant work process as that of coffee, cocoa, or vanilla. In the Dominican context, banana production does not necessitate an economy of scale; and up to recently, medium-sized peasant farms competed well with the few remaining plantations. That success is partly due to environmental factors, especially since planting is the most important part of the production cycle (bananas require little postharvest processing aside from transportation). Temperature, rainfall, and the very steepness of the Dominican slopes all contributed to the development of the plant. Mean temperatures in Dominica fall close to the standard 80°F "considered optimal for both growth and yield" (C. N. Williams 1975: 29). Soil conditions vary greatly in the island but, because of their volcanic origins, many terrains provide, in varying amounts, some of the nutrients required for banana cultivation: nitrogen in the Middleham, Hampstead, or Melville Hall areas, potash in Moore Park and Blenheim, and so on. More important, bananas can flourish in a variety of soils, and the ultimate plant-water relations are often more important than specific nutrients. The root system is adventitious, and consequently does not reach deeply into the soil to draw water and nutrients. On the other hand, "there appears to be no developmental requirement for moisture stress for either flowering or ripening" (C. N. Williams 1975: 29). Rainfall and drainage (or a well-timed system of irrigation and drainage) then become crucial. In Dominica, the abundant rainfall largely compensates for the low moisture storage capacity of most soils, and the steepness of the slopes provides a natural drainage mechanism. By and large, bananas have as much water as they need, but never so much at one time as to be subject to major floods.

One can thus add the local environment as a major factor in the success story of bananas on Dominican peasant farms. The steepness of the terrain does not constitute the major impediment that it could otherwise have been; the units do not require irrigation; the size of the plots do not a priori prohibit their cultivation in bananas; and all those factors combined made possible the efficient adaptation of the crop by the peasantry. Productivity remains low, of course, because only minimum requirements are met in the labor process, and the "needs" of banana production could be increased *ad infinitum* for maximum technical efficiency. Still, the Dominican peasant, as a producer, could and can plant bananas with an efficiency hitherto unknown in the production of most other crops, and ecological factors contribute to this social adaptation. Yet an ecology is relevant only in human terms: properties of the natural world become advantageous only if people put them to use.

The banana preeminence is not a given of nature. Many commercial plants can be said to "fit" the Dominican environment, and some perhaps more so than bananas. Coffee is certainly a good candidate, and it can also be planted in small units. The success of cacao in face of the continuous opposition of the larger planters also suggests that the small farmers took advantage of a favorable ecological adaptation. Vanilla adapted quite well and preceded bananas among the export commodities produced on peasant farms. Yet the vanilla preeminence was short, drastically curtailed by the first market crisis. In contrast, bananas survived some sharp down trends in world prices, and production continued to expand throughout most of the low periods. What explains this relative resilience?

In general, commodities have no use-value for the one who produces them. Their use-value is realized when they are consumed by the buyer who acquires them. Yet the peasant labor process, even when embedded in a production process characterized by the circulation of commodities, usually stands as an exception to this rule. Peasants tend to produce commodities that have *some* use for them. This apparent incongruity within the system of distribution has less to do with the choices that the peasants make than with the agricultural nature of the labor process and its form of integration in the process of distribution. The unit is both a unit of production and a unit of consumption. Commodities produced within the peasant unit are not exhausted by their status as commodities. They are also something else, use-values, that is, what they appear to be in nature: vanilla, coffee, cocoa, bananas. And the peasant uses them as such. But this use itself is again limited by the nature of the crop and the set of social practices within which the producers operate. To put it simply, the optimum amount of vanilla, or cocoa, or coffee that any human being can consume is ultimately determined by nature. Below that natural and ever evasive threshold, the usual amounts consumed by particular peoples are determined by sociocultural choices.

In comparison to the other possible peasant crops of Dominica, bananas offered much higher consumption thresholds on both counts. These higher thresholds meant that the crop could be integrated in the peasant work process as well as, say vanilla or coffee, but reach a degree of consumptive integration that few other exports could enjoy. The crop fitted so well patterns of consumption that it could become a staple in the peasant diet. That fit, I suggest, was the crucial difference.

In Europe and North America, bananas are most often consumed as fruits, even though technically all *Musaceae* are herbs. But in some cultures (one thinks of the Caribbean, of course, but also India), bananas are also consumed in cooked forms, fried or boiled, just as plantains, their close relatives. It is primarily in their boiled form that bananas entered the daily diet of the Dominica peasants. The daily consumption of boiled bananas meant that the cultivation of the crop did not imply a split between commercially oriented production and production geared to the maintenance of the household. Rather, that cultivation remarkably brought together the divergent aspects of the peasant family: its role as a unit of production and as a unit of consumption. That convergence first stemmed, of course, from the botany of the plant and the economics of its commercialization, but the roles also merged at the cognitive sphere inasmuch as tenants and yeomen never felt that this new cultivation was imposed on them from the outside to fulfill the needs of a faraway market. Their prior acquaintance with varieties of the crop facilitated the cultural acceptance of its large-scale production. But moreover, mass production itself could be perceived as a continuation of the activities inherent in the maintenance of the provision grounds. Boiled bananas could join plantains and root crops as part of the principal meal of the day.

My informants disagree as to when boiled figs joined plantains and root crops in the family pot in the large numbers typical of the current diet in Dominica. Those who grew up in the 1950s claim that boiled figs "always" constituted a major part of their food. My own guess is that the passage from occasional food item to a daily boiled staple occurred during World War II or immediately after. At that time, yeomen and tenant farmers were increasing their participation in vanilla cultivation, and for the first time in Dominican history, the primary export of the island was by and large produced through the peasant labor process. The sudden increase of commercially oriented activity on grounds controlled by the family meant a reduction in the time alloted to food preparation. (Men, women, and children all contributed to vanilla production.) The time-consuming production of farine manioc, a preferred food item based on ground cassava, dropped drastically. Coincidentally, difficulties in maritime transport, which primarily affected the most delicate and fast ripening products, created huge surpluses of bananas, some of which was diverted to local consumption. A woman who worked as a cook on two different estates in the Wesley-Marigot area during the 1930s and '40s recalls dumping large quantities of green bananas in the huge pot in which she boiled the provisions brought by the daily laborers. A slight detail gives weight to her testimony: she had to mark all uncooked items with the distinctive sign or initials of individual workers so that they could identify their food at lunch time. Bananas were among both the softest and thinnest products in that pot, and required less boiling time than most other foods. Her dilemma was to mark every banana, deeply enough with the kitchen knife so that it was distinguishable at lunch time, but not so deeply that it would break while boiling! Difficulties multiplied as daily laborers brought increasing quantities of the fruit. The practice of boiling in one vessel all the laborers' provisions was abandoned with time, especially as estate wage labor gradually disappeared from the area; but the growth of the banana's importance in the daily diet had made its mark on the young girl.

The ease with which bananas could join provisions in the boiling pots allowed yeomen and sharecroppers a flexibility unmatched by any other export crops produced through the peasant labor process. Peasant households used relatively small amounts of cocoa, vanilla, grapefruit, or limes. Hence, at times, substantial parts of the harvest not absorbed by the local or export markets were discarded or left to rot. In contrast, one could greatly augment the proportion of bananas that entered the midday meal in order to accommodate a substantial part of the production not absorbed by the market. Moreover, as the practice spread to other segments of the population not primarily engaged in banana production, the local market for nonexportable green fruits expanded. And so probably did the market for ripe bananas which could still be consumed in raw form as fruits. Thus yeomen and tenants were more likely to take a minimal risk in starting or expanding their commercial production of the crop, since they felt that they could control excess quantities.

The disagreement among my informants over the time at which bananas turned into a major component of Dominicans' daily diet and the claim of so many among the older ones that everyone they know has been eating great quantities of boiled figs "since I know myself" also suggest an ideological ambiguity which may have facilitated, if not the adoption, at least the continuation of commercially oriented production. Many Dominican growers like to imply that they are not in fact producing for the Geest transnational or the association, but are rather selling them some surplus of what some anthropologists would call their "subsistence" production. Of course, they do not make the point in such terms, but rather by innuendo. In 1981, I raised a local politician's attention to the coming glut in the international market. He replied that members of the government, also anxious about the future of the market, were considering the possibility of slowly replacing bananas with essential oils, especially patchouli. A young peasant friend of mine interrupted the politician, and asserted that planting patchouli was "nonsense." "What will I do with that patchouli, if you don't buy it?" he asked. "I can always eat my fig." Of course, in no way could he and the eight members of his family absorb the product of the few acres of banana land that they controlled. But the point is, rather, that this young man had inherited the sense that banana production did not represent a venture qualitatively different from the tasks he and other members of his family performed essentially to maintain themselves. He and thousands of other Dominicans see the commercialization of those fruits as an operation quite similar in kind to the occasional sale of dasheens (*Colocasia ebculenta*) or tanias (*Xanthosoma saggiti folium*) which marked a good season. Bananas, often intercropped with roots, are eaten together with roots. From that viewpoint, the difference between banana and root crop sales is one of bulk and frequency. In the peasant tradition, commercial banana production does not represent a disruption any more than did the nineteenth-century exports of farine manioc. The co-optation of the peasant labor process through banana production could occur swiftly and, later, reach extreme proportions essentially because of the close identification of bananas with provisions, an identification rooted in the botany of the plant but also in patterns of production and consumption that Dominican rural cultivators had learned to cherish since the days of slavery.

To be sure, there are units of production in Dominica, today, which are still referred to as "estates," and contribute to the banana trade; but despite the character of land ownership of those units, tenants firmly control the labor process. Moreover, the bulk of the exports (about 75 percent) comes from the small farms whose numbers increased dramatically with the rise of bananas (Mourillon 1978). Between 1946 and 1961, the number of farms between one and five acres increased by 60 percent, and though the increase in acreage was less substantial, by 1961, 99 percent of the units of production were under one hundred acres, and 90 percent of those, in turn, were under ten acres (Yankey 1969: 29–32). By the late 1970s, DBGA records registered almost 10,000 independent growers; by 1981, 11,426, more than half of whom (6,426) were regularly bringing their bananas to the association.

Traditions are often recent inventions. Dominican cultivators have become massively involved in the production and consumption of a crop historically linked to the provision grounds of slavery. That involvement colors their vision of the past. In light of that past, banana preeminence appears as the final victory in the three-century-long struggle to make the peasant farm the dominant unit of the island by bringing the work process that typifies the peasantry into the production of Dominica's main export commodity. Here, production and consumption concur, and the past finally merges with the present.

Conclusion

The rise of bananas to preeminence among Dominican export commodities climaxed the struggle of rural cultivators to impose their preferred forms of land occupation and work organization. In the immediate aftermath of Emancipation, many established themselves off the plantations; some remained on the estates, retaining their provision grounds; and others managed to do both. By mid-nineteenth century, despite the diverse tactics of planters, merchants, and officials, the cultivators' individual decisions had the combined effect of crippling the plantation labor process. Though a substantial part of the major export commodities was still produced on estate land, by the 1880s the estate owners themselves had lost control of the work process. The inability of the colored elite to restore the plantation sector after the decline of sugar and their increased dependence upon the colonial state apparatus, in turn, reinforced the laborers' gains. The mulattoes' overemphasis on state politics implicitely acknowledged that the cultivators were to have the last word on the politics of production. Administrator Bell's strategy of attracting new planters and the growth of the lime industry, indirectly activated by the British Admiralty, slowed for a while the growth of the independent yeomanry. However, estate production did not survive unharmed the depression of the late 1920s. Efforts to revive the plantation labor process in lime production met with the laborers' indifference because the wages were unattractive in terms of the social costs they entailed. The spatial organization of the island and environmental conditions which reinforced the isolation of different enclaves greatly favored the cultivators' position. By 1927, Sir Francis Watts's report provided the first official acknowledgment that the descendants of the former slaves had won the battle for the control of the workplace in the production of export commodities, a struggle fiercely waged since the end of Apprenticeship.

Thus, though the preeminence of bananas came, in part, as a result of grand policies designed in London, the implementation of the combined strategies which favored that preeminence (Imperial Economic Committee 1927; Watts 1927) came as a consequence of the admitted defeat of British policy makers, local officials, and planters alike on the issue of control of the workplace. Moreover, the rise of bananas among the many crops proposed by the Colonial Office and pushed forward by local planners through the Peasant Bureau and various growers' associations came about, in great part, because tenants and yeomen saw in the large-scale commercialization of bananas only a mild disruption of the production and consumption patterns entailed by their control of the provision grounds. In terms of the immediate politics of production—a field best seized, in this case, from a historical perspective—that was a victory, and a major one indeed. However, that historical field in which the Dominican peasantry emerges as the dominant actor provides only one viewpoint, albeit an important one, to a complex reality. It cannot reveal all its dimensions. That same reality can be approached from a different viewpoint, with different—though by no means antithetic—conclusions.

PART II

THE WORLD

CHAPTER 7

Working for Capital

All that economic analysis can help to contribute is to remove some illusions and to help whoever is willing to look to see what their situation really is.

—Joan Robinson, *Aspects of Development and Underdevelopment*

Industry cannot last for more than a few weeks. Price to Grower already below cost of production.

—DBGA to Geest Industries, 1981

History has no logic, no predetermined outcome. It is carried out by human actors, not all of whom follow the same script. To make matters worse for the observer, some of those actors change the script in mid-course. Moreover, even when one can determine a continuity of actions and goals, substantial parts of the consequences remain unintended, gathering new meanings as scripts unfold, break or overlap, modifying one another through quid pro quos and improvisation. Finally, some of these unintended consequences may escape altogether the consciousness of many of the participants. Some consequences may belong to spheres of reality that the actors who start the chain or modify the course of a sequence are not immediately concerned with, discursively or practically. Others may simply fall outside the empirical field to which the actors have access. The actors' limited access to historical reality does not in any way diminish the intrinsic value of their knowledge. Rather their knowledgeability does not overlap each sequence of actions that their practice sets in motion or indirectly influences. Hence, one should welcome the current reappraisal of the subject by the social sciences, the ongoing "return of the actor" (Touraine 1984; Giddens 1979, 1985) from the vagaries of different kinds of structuralism. Still, the return to a viable notion of agency cannot be at the cost of finessing the structural constraints. If the subject is historical (and, in my view, the only subject worth attention is necessarily historical) then this very historicity sets limits, always reformulated, to the participant's knowledge and actions.

Hence, an investigation of a particular group of actors in the historical process can only produce a specific type of results. In many cases, such results may be enough for the task at hand. But this book requires more than we can see from the historical angle alone. The exploration of the temporal and spatial boundaries of Dominica and the emphasis on historical agency avoided the pitfall of approaching the peasantry as a function of capitalism, of discovering the main actors through their position within the system. But there remains more ground to cover.

First, since the bulk of the bananas produced by the peasantry is not consumed in Dominica, an investigation confined to the island entails obvious empirical limitations. Second, theoretically, the existence of a peasantry in a country fully incorporated in the capitalist world economy has become more puzzling. We now know more of the social tensions that accompanied this incorporation. The work organization that typifies this peasantry was imposed in the production of export commodities by the peasantry itself, and against the wishes of those who controlled Dominica's integration within the world economy. Planters, bureaucrats, and merchants alike perceived the growth of the peasant labor process as an incongruence, and recognized the peculiarity of the coexistence of peasants and capitalism. If noncultivators had it their way, the Dominican peasantry would not be what it is today. To explain fully the survival of that peasantry, we need to explore the mechanisms that integrate the peasant labor process within the world economy in spite of its relative incongruence. This chapter and the next expand upon the theoretical foundations put forth in the first chapter but tie them concretely to the case at hand. How is the Dominican peasantry integrated in the worldwide process of valorization? How much control do they have over that integration? Who benefits from that integration?

Some consequences of the historical sequence that ended with the peasantry's control over the labor process were immediately visible to the participants. Others are becoming more obvious to their descendants. Contemporary cultivators are aware, if not of the details of the sequence, at least, of its general progression. In most enclaves, a few estates went through a long period of agony; between the time I first went to Dominica, in 1979, and the time of this writing, I myself have been aware of the disappearance of a few more estates. Significantly, not one single Dominican peasant who expressed an opinion, voluntarily or at my request, relying on memory or on hearsay, looked with nostalgia at the days of plantation production. "Massa" days are gone, and Dominican cultivators are proud of this fact.

Yet some outgrowths of the historical sequence fall outside the immediate field of observation of Dominican cultivators, past and present. Others are empirically accessible yet are not necessarily tied to that sequence itself; and I will touch later on both types. More important for now is the need to note the limits within which the conquest of the labor process took place, for those limits also influenced the direction of change. The peasantry's victory fundamentally changed the exercise of power within the units of production, but it did not change Dominica's political and economic dependence upon Britain even after the 1978 Independence of the island. Nor did it change Britain's position in the interstate system. Finally, even though the politics of production had resulted in the downfall of the planter class, the politics of state control had not been modified to the advantage of the peasantry but to the advantage of the colored elite. The individuals who could have planted the seeds of a native planter class in the aftermath of slavery seized the opportunity to play a different role at the level of the state as a concession to both the peasantry and the colonists. However, their position yielded much institutional power on commercial relations to the outside, especially after the departure of the white immigrant planters.

Those commercial relations, Dominica's dependence, and Britain's position in the interstate system delineate a field beyond the peasantry's immediate reach. My approach to that field does not emphasize historicity, at least not in the manner of the preceding chapters. I do not deny that capitalists and government officials are historical actors but I take more pleasure in restoring for the record the inventiveness and the vitality of Caribbean cultivators past and present. Second, I suspect that individuality matters less within that expanded field. Third, and more important, even though history matters here, the material at hand lends itself to a satisfactory treatment with the tools of political economy and, to a lesser degree, economic anthropology. The political economy angle allows one to maintain the focus on the peasantry while enlarging the context.

Hence, our stage is now the world. Our time is not existential inasmuch as the motivations of the actors matter less on this plane than the consequences of actions. Our task is to determine the modalities under which the peasant labor process is incorporated in the capitalist world economy, and the consequences of that incorporation.

A caveat is in order here lest one misunderstands the thrust of the argument. We are now dealing with what we call "a structure of co-optation" but that structure represents only a moment of the historical process and provides a limited viewpoint of a complex reality. With this change in viewpoint, we shift to a different level of abstraction as well. There is no claim that this level of abstraction explains "more"; and I have tried to avoid metaphors that would suggest so. As noted before, our boundaries are no longer historical even though the empirical material remains particular and specific. Our "structure of co-optation" does not exist in the empirical world; it is not even an abstraction comparable to preceding historical categories such as the Mulatto Ascendancy. Historical references or empirical generalizations based on fieldwork enter here to flesh out an argument on the logic of the coexistence of a particular peasantry and capitalism. Empirical fact finding matters nevertheless. In the next chapter I will amplify in dollars and pounds the profits accumulated by Geest Holdings Limited, the Britain-based corporate group that distributes in Europe the bananas produced by thousands of Caribbean peasants, including those of Dominica. Still, the synchronic approach to the peculiar coexistence of peasants and capitalism aims at a theoretical coherence of which the measure is nothing but the structural coherence of capitalism itself as a global system. But that structural coherence, of course, is itself an abstract construct.

The major contention of this chapter is that the integration of the peasant labor process in the global process of valorization occurs in Dominica through the disguised sale of the labor power of the producers to the Geest transnational corporation. A detailed study of the transactions involving the Dominican producers, the DBGA, WINBAN, and Geest, reveals that the Dominican peasant does not engage in anything resembling a free exchange between seller and buyer. Instead, the conditions with which he deals make him more like a proletarian selling his labor power than a peasant selling a product. Yet, as peasant, the Dominican producer is engaged in a specific labor process; and my second contention is that this very engagement makes him potentially more vulnerable to capital. The "structural autonomy" (Archetti et al. n.d.) guaranteed by that labor process relieves the transnational of the necessity of paying labor power at its value, and may force the peasant producer to accept returns lower than the wages of proletarians. Other forms of surplus extraction add to that exploitation: an international transfer of value inherent in the "unequal exchange" between periphery and core in the world economy and a transfer of surplus labor within the confines of the Dominican economy. The continuing and apparently paradoxical coexistence of peasantries and capitalism finds its coherence in an acute exploitation which greatly contributes to capital accumulation on a world scale.

The Illusion of a Sale

One needs to eliminate a most important obstacle: the illusion that, somehow, Dominican peasants sell their bananas to the DBGA which, in turn, sells them to Geest. Those two sales never, in fact, occur, and the payment the peasant receives can only be in return for his labor power. To expose the illusion, we need to look at the legal framework within which the parties operate: the Banana Act of 1959 and the 1977 Banana Contract. The act, duly voted by the Dominican Legislature, confirmed the monopsony esablished by the government in 1949, first exerted by Antilles Products and later by Geest through the Dominica Banana Association. Section Three of the act creates a body corporate, the Dominican Banana Growers Association, entitled to "make contracts and to sue and be sued in this name; to acquire, hold and dispose of all kinds of property."

Section Two details the body's monopsony:

1. All bananas grown in the Colony and intended to be exported therefrom or intended to be used either wholly or partially as an ingredient in any manufactured product shall be delivered to the Association. . . .
2. No bananas intended for export shall be bought except by the Association or such person or persons as may be authorized by them under license. (Dominica 1963: 776)

One can already question the suggestion that a sale occurs under such circumstances. Can there be a sale without a market? Yet, for the Dominican peasant, there is no market other than the DBGA. The legal framework ties the DBGA to Geest as securely as it binds the peasant to the DBGA. Indeed, the 1977 Banana Contract builds on the foundation laid by the 1959 Act. The actors involved are, on the one hand, the DBGA and, on the other, Geest Industries Limited, Geest Industries (W.I. or West Indies) Limited interchangeably referred to as the company, and their common parent Geest Holdings Limited (which intervenes only to guarantee their performance). The marginal presence of the Windward Islands Banana Association (WINBAN) among the signatories is meant to guarantee the DBGA's performance. Thus, from the start, the peasants are left out of this agreement between corporate bodies, registered companies, and statutory boards, their case having been supposedly solved by the 1959 Act which forces them to deliver to the DBGA. Not only is their voice unheard, but their existence itself need not be acknowledged at the international level, except for a passing reference to "growers' rights" in the recitals of the contract.

The contract sets the margin of action for all parties. Significantly, John van Geest signed for Geest Holdings and both subsidiaries, an indication of the concentration of power at the top of the conglomerate. In sharp contrast, WINBAN does not represent the combined power of the Windward producers. Rather, its interventions only benefit the transnational. For instance, the Green Market Price, the fundamental item of the pricing system, is set in London by Geest "in consultation with WINBAN." Ideally, WINBAN's intervention should benefit the islands. In reality, its ineffectiveness provides Geest with a cover of legitimacy. WINBAN has only one official representative in England to verify Geest's complicated weekly computation and his office is not listed in the London phone book.[1]

The contract consequently distributes power among the parties. John van Geest's signature as representative of three among the five bodies involved evidently bears more weight than that of the two Dominicans representing the DBGA. But the terms of the contract also verify that inequality. For instance, the contract stipulates that the association shall deliver and that Geest will "accept delivery of and purchase from the Association all bananas of EXPORTABLE QUALITY" (DBGA et al. 1977: 2). However, such quality is never defined nor alluded to, even in Section Six subtitled "Acceptance." Yet Section Seven shields the company from most risks, and the final price to the association is that of "a ton of bananas of *exportable* quality which is *accepted* by the Company" (emphases added). The slip from "exportable" to "accepted" opens a large loophole; and without a definition of the first term, without stipulation of the conditions of acceptance, the DBGA simply functions as the local agent of the transnational. In short, the DBGA must deliver the bananas to Geest who may accept or reject them at will.

The examination of the legal framework thus reveals that within the structural boundaries set for the transactions, neither the peasants nor the DBGA have any control over the volume of bananas they deliver. Yet a sale would be taking place if, in either case, the party delivering the bananas had some bargaining power over the determination of the price of the product so delivered. In fact, quite the opposite is true. The pricing system totally restricts the DBGA's bargaining power vis-à-vis Geest, and, likewise, the peasants' power to discuss the price obtained from the DBGA. To understand the pricing system, we need to identify briefly the actors on the European scene.

Ideally, British banana importers sell the green fruits in bulk to "green handlers" or "ripeners" who prepare the bananas for wholesale distributors. Distributors, in turn, deliver nearly ripened bunches to fruit stores, street vendors, or supermarkets where the consumer buys them at retail prices. In reality, except for the consumer, any of those supposedly independent actors may be associated with the next one in the distributive process: importers ripen, green handlers may distribute, and wholesale distributors own stores. The real or imagined transaction between independent importers and green handlers is at the core of the pricing system.

The basic item in the pricing system is the Green Market Price (GMP), best described as the average wholesale price of green fruits projected a week ahead by Geest on the basis of its own information about the probable price of ripe bananas to be delivered to the distributors. As such, the GMP is a projection twice removed from reality: it is based on future supply and demand at the next lower level, a level of which the Caribbean associations have no knowledge. The basic payment to the Caribbean associations is nothing but whatever is left from the GMP after all deductions, and is computed by Geest. The DBGA is powerless in assessing the weekly GMP imposed by Geest, or in verifying the deductions made by Geest from that initial figure.

Though the DBGA has no access to the information on which Geest bases its GMP except through the sole representative of WINBAN, Geest is officially allowed to share its information with JAMCO (Jamaican Producers Marketing Company Limited), the third largest British importer. Given the oligopoly shared by Fyffes, Geest, and JAMCO (92 percent of the British market) and the history of government intervention in banana production and distribution in the British Commonwealth, the possibility remains that, beyond and above a degree of competition, the companies reach certain understandings on market shares or prices with the tacit approval of the British government. Moreover, through its own subsidiaries, Geest Holdings actually buys some 80 percent of the green fruits it handles as an importer (WINBAN 1980: 35). The possibilities for price fixing between branches of the same transnational are blatant. In short, the association has no previous knowledge of (and no way to verify) the original transactions at the root of the pricing system. More important, the deductions that Geest makes from the GMP to obtain the basic payment to the association involve a number of unverifiable transactions among Geest subsidiaries.

Geest groups its deductions according to the geographical areas in which the expense occurs, namely, the United Kingdom, the Caribbean (West Indies), and the Atlantic Ocean itself. The United Kingdom and West Indies expenses are divided into fixed and variable costs. In the United Kingdom, fixed costs are, in turn, classified into "discharging" and "distribution" expenses. Discharging costs include such items as the price of the British labor spent on the operation, the price of equipment, the cost of depreciation, costs and overhead for stores and offices. In most cases, Geest deducts 100 percent of such expenses from the price of the bananas. Geest does charge less than the total overhead cost of running its stores and offices to the GMP, but given the transnational's diversified activities it is impossible for the association to compute with any degree of accuracy the actual proportion, say, of heating oil or electricity, or security costs a specific office incurs because of its engagement in banana distribution. Distribution expenses likewise include the price of labor in the United Kingdom, and "establishment costs" which are, in fact, charged from the Geest Line (the shipping arm of Geest Holdings) to Geest Industries (the importer) for the latter's use of the line's facilities!

The variable expenses, reportedly met by Geest in the United Kingdom, fluctuate with the actual weight of particular shipments after an initial "shrinkage" (weight loss) deduction in that total weight. Such variable expenses include insurance, equipment, and installation costs, discharging and distribution expenses not met by the regular ("fixed") deductions. For instance, Geest subtracts from the GMP the overtime payments to British dockers when they are required to work irregular hours. It also collects from the GMP a bonus that it offers to the ripeners who are not linked to the Geest empire and who buy 20 percent of its imports.

In addition to the United Kingdom expenses (incurred mainly by Geest Industries and Geest Foods) and the Caribbean expenses (incurred by Geest W.I.) are the ocean charges of the Geest Line. They generally include 70 percent of all actual, previous, and future expenses necessary to insure the performance of the shipping company during a particular trip, down to the share of leave pay, health insurance, and retirement plan of the personnel. Once more, credits and charges among different branches of the Geest empire compound the difficulty of estimating the actual share of labor or capital allocated to banana handling during a specific trip. The Geest boats carry passengers as well as "exotica" from various Caribbean islands. Additional depreciation and financing charges make the final computation of the actual expenses of banana transportation during any single trip of a Geest Line boat an arduous task for even the most competent accountant.

The West Indian expenses form the first series of deductions made by Geest from the GMP to obtain the basic payment made to the association. Like the United Kingdom expenses, they are divided into fixed and variable costs. Credits and charges from one Geest-owned company to another baffled a team mandated by WINBAN to look into the transnational accounts. "Thus, in the West Indies, for example," states the team's report, "the Geest Headquarters Management and Facilities are employing services related to Geest Industries (W.I.) Ltd., Geest Industries Estates, Geest Industries Development, St. Lucia Distillers and Geest Line" (WINBAN 1980: 74). Further, even if one could specify the actual expenses incurred by each arm of the Geest empire because of its long involvement in the banana trade, even if one could itemize all the expenses of each specific shipment, one would then face the difficulty of breaking down those expenses among the four island associations according to their variable share of the market and their contribution to each shipment. In short, Geest's banana-related expenses accumulate and fluctate in ways that inherently escape measurement.

Yet, it is on the basis of those inherently variable and unverifiable expenses that the basic payment to the DBGA is derived from a Green Market Price that is itself an unverifiable projection. The subtraction of the United Kingdom and ocean charges from the Geest-projected GMP leads to a f.o.b. price in sterling ex post facto. Geest then converts that sterling price to Eastern Caribbean dollars (at its preferred rate), and deducts from the new amount its West Indian expenses. The remainder constitutes the price to the association.

Clearly both the legal framework and the pricing system deny the occurrence of a sale. Neither the association nor the peasants have any bargaining power in determining the conditions of each transaction, the volume involved, the quantity or quality of the accepted fruits. Neither group has any institutional channel to argue the GMP fixed by Geest or the deductions claimed by Geest on any particular shipment. Yet to reject fully the illusion of a sale, one needs perhaps to look at specific shipments and refer to direct observation to determine whether or not daily procedures may open a limited margin of action to the DBGA.

The Illusion of Local Control

Fieldwork at the headquarters of the Dominica Banana Growers Association, including two weeks of direct observation as well as examination of the DBGA's files, verified the contention based on analysis of the legal framework and pricing system, that no sale was taking place. On the contrary, the image of the association which emerged from this observation is that of a state agency acting as agent of a transnational corporation.

The limitations imposed on the DBGA by the rhythm of the banana trade were most perceptible during the fieldwork. Bananas are generally shipped on a weekly basis, though the precise interval may vary from five to ten days. The combination of speed and irregularity makes systematic verification of Geest' s figures by the DBGA totally impossible. The DBGA is simply not equipped for fast and precise accounting, even if it was to receive all the necessary figures from Geest and even if the sole WINBAN representative was regularly submitting reports to the association on the situation in London.

Further, the association is caught in a second cycle whose rhythm is even more rapid than that of Geest shipments: the payments to the peasant farmers. More than half of the DBGA staff deals directly or indirectly with the producers who daily visit the association's offices for payments, insurance, fertilizer allowance, and so on. An additional number of employees deal with bulk purchases of agricultural inputs to be distributed to the farmers, or to the diverse "buying plants" throughout the island. The few remaining at the upper ladder take care of general management. Because of the daily pressure little time is left to study Geest's figures which remain a remote concern.

More important, Geest itself does not act in ways typical of a buyer. On the contrary, it extends actual power beyond the limits set by the contract, and turns the pricing system into an instrument through which it dictates its conditions. Most often, the DBGA is first informed of the basic payment (i.e., its remainder) for a particular shipment and then receives the price schedule (the corresponding GMP and Geest's deductions) two or three days later. In practice, the price schedule often reaches DBGA management after the bananas have been loaded on the ships and taken by Geest for their cross-Atlantic journey. The following quote, from a letter of Geest's local representative to the DBGA chairman dated 6 November 1981, is typical of the character of exchanges between the two bodies: "Our Head Office in St. Lucia has advised that the price payable to your Association for bananas in respect of the above shipment is 38.778 Cents per lb. A Copy of the Price Schedule has already been posted to you by Head Office in St. Lucia." Since the "above shipment" was made the very same day, in no way could the association, even though it was sent the copy of the price schedule, question the basic payment. In fact, most of the bananas for this shipment had been cut, many had been delivered to the DBGA, and some had actually been loaded before the basic payment was known in Dominica. Further, the association's copy of the price schedule was stamped ten days later, on November 16, which suggests that it was received (or read) while the bananas were in or near England.

Similar conditions surround other shipments whose histories I have reconstituted from DBGA files. Moreover, in at least a few cases, the association learns not only of the price schedule, but of the basic payment itself (i.e., its final price) only after Geest takes possession of the bananas, which obviously cannot then be returned. A letter dated 26 October 1981 and stamped October 27 by the association's secretary, announced the price for a shipment on the Geest Bay that had been loaded four days before. Thus, the daily procedures reinforce Geest's unilateral power, and the bananas are actually shipped before any bargaining can occur, indeed before any possible intervention of the DBGA, short of a total withdrawal.

Ethnography also reveals that the peasants themselves are, in many ways, as limited in their transactions with the DBGA as the association is impotent vis-à-vis Geest's power. In fact, the actual practices that characterize, on the ground, the harvesting, collecting, boxing, and shipping of the bananas illustrate my contention that, through the DBGA, Geest actually enters into production.

The number of shipments ordered by Geest usually varies from forty-five to fifty in any given calendar year but, as noted before, the exact interval between any two shipments also varies and the loading date is rarely known in Dominica two days ahead. Moreover, though Geest is required by the contract to buy all bananas of "exportable quality," direct observation suggests that above and beyond the loophole inherent in that formulation, the transnational cannot possibly accommodate, at all times, the bulk of the Dominican production. The tonnage needed by Geest most likely varies, in part, according to conditions in the other Windward Islands, since Dominica is the most northern stop (and often the last one) on the way to England. It is also likely that bananas otherwise "acceptable" are not needed by the conglomerate during the winter, when demand generally decreases in Europe. Geest's load must reflect its needs and those needs are usually conveyed through the announcements of the DBGA regarding the "boxing" operations.

A "boxing plant" is best defined as any relay station that the DBGA designates as a collecting point of exportable bananas. Boxing plants are usually located between the field proper and the seaport warehouses. The bananas are washed and boxed there (hence the name) before being loaded on trucks which carry them to the coastal loading points of Portsmouth and Roseau. About forty-two boxing plants are now in operation, up from thirty-three in 1975. That increase (and the imprecision of the number) is due to the DBGA's recent decision to allow more estate owners and better-off farmers to select and pack their own bananas near the field or in the field itself. However, those "private boxing plants" process only a modest share of the national production. The vast majority of the peasant producers bring their fruits to association-owned plants, about twenty of which are spread on the outskirts of villages throughout the country. Those DBGA plants are permanent constructions, specifically built for banana collection, and are generally much larger, more stable, and more efficient than the private ones. Up to the early 1980s, they processed more than 90 percent of the exports. Through them the association exerts physical control over producer and product alike. Through them, and the association, Geest enters the production process on the ground in Dominica itself.

Peasants learn of "banana days" or "fig days" on the Dominica Broadcasting System (DBS), for a long time the only radio station in the island, though announcements may appear in the weekly *Chronicle*, the only regular newspaper during my fieldwork. On the announced day, and for the duration of their operations, the boxing plants designated by the DBGA are legally required to collect from the producers all bananas deemed exportable by the "selectors" working for the association. We will see later that this is not always the case, but my focus now is on two mechanisms by which the DBGA can, in fact, control the volume of bananas to fit Geest's expected needs for a particular shipment. First, the length of time during which any boxing plant is open is entirely up to DBGA management. Second, in extreme cases, some boxing plants might not open at all for the one or two days during which others are functioning at the times specified by the announcements. All in all, though particular peasants may decide on the amount of banana stems that they will carry to the selectors, though they may decide whether or not "to cut" (to harvest) during a particular week, the producers as a group have no immediate control over the volume of bananas actually collected by the DBGA.

The producers, as a group, are equally powerless in determining the type of fruit to be brought to the plants. The radio announcement usually specifies the characteristics required by the association: "light grade three-quarter fruit," "dwarf Cavendish will not be acceptable," or any other limitation to fit Geest's expectations. Likewise, the announcement states the price to be paid to the grower per pound of bananas selected by the association. In fact, this price is not paid at the plant; rather, the grower receives a receipt which can be exchanged for cash at DBGA headquarters in Roseau according to the rate stated at the time of delivery.

The Illusion of a Price

Ethnography thus further dispels the illusion of a sale between the DBGA and Geest or between the producers and the DBGA itself. Observations on the ground combined with our previous analysis of Geest's pricing system completely dispel the illusion of a price to the grower. Objections are similar to those raised regarding the basic price to the association. The "price to the grower" is a misnomer; for the DBGA pricing system reproduces that of Geest.

The DBGA derives its payments to the producers in a manner similar to that by which Geest figures its basic payment from the GMP. The association deducts from every basic payment whatever it judges to be its compensation for overhead and other expenses, and the remainder is the price to the grower. The only major difference between DBGA and

Geest procedures is that the growers are informed of the DBGA price a day or two *before* they deliver the bananas. At that time, the DBGA may or may not know what its own basic payment from Geest will be, but it has probably not yet received the Geest's price schedule. Admittedly, the association assumes some risk in announcing a price for which it has no justification. Still, in no way can peasants question that price. Their only short-term option would be not to cut bananas for a particular shipment, in which case they lose fruits which have reached maturity. Their long-term option is, of course, to abandon production altogether, a dreadful alternative until and unless they can be assured of another cash crop on such a regular basis. For the time being, they must accept the price and conditions imposed by the DBGA, just as the DBGA itself must accept the price and conditions set by Geest. However, the DBGA can likely recover previous losses by unilaterally lowering future payments to the peasants, but peasants themselves cannot recoup. Since there is no exchange, no bargaining occurs on price, quality, or quantity. Hence, the association is merely the governmental body through which the transnational obtains the peasantry's bananas without ever having to purchase them.

Indeed, the exposition of the legal framework, the analysis of the pricing system, and the observation of the contacts between the parties all lead to the conclusion that the bananas are handled as Geest's property *without Geest ever having to buy them.* The bananas are boxed, shipped, or discarded on Geest's orders. The DBGA can reject fruits from peasants only under the assumption that their quality would be unacceptable to Geest. There is no transfer of cash or acknowledgment of a quantified debt by Geest as the Geest boats take away the product. There are no prices, but rather the possibility of a remainder after Geest deducts its expenses. The order of operations characteristic of merchant capitalism (buy in order to sell) seems to have been reversed.

Indeed, having dispelled the illusion of any sale occurring in Dominica, we reach the logical conclusion that the first sale occurs in Britain, and involves Geest as a seller. The selling price between Geest and its British customers (green handlers or distributors) is fixed by principle before the so-called price to the association and long before the price to the producers. In fact, the price in London has to be fixed for the price to the association to become quantifiable. The exchange value of the commodity is ascertained in England, and nowhere else. The first real sale occurs there.

A further comment on the illusory character of the sales in Dominica: in theory, the basic payment to the association and the price to the grower could be zero or a negative number if Geest or the association expenses totaled more than the GMP. That, in fact, has happened in a similar scheme involving grapefruits, and some of my informants were totally appalled by a local association's request that *they*—the peasants—pay for fruits that *they* had "sold" weeks before and which had already been consumed by Englishmen.

The Illusion of Peasant Ownership

Having removed the illusion of any sale occurring in Dominica and, accordingly, the illusion of a price either to the DBGA or to the producer, we can now tackle the question: what, then, is paid to the peasants? One possible answer is that the price to the grower represents, in fact, the means of labor deployed under the peasant labor process. Yet if one agrees with Harvey's reading of Marx that "the transport industry is productive of value," and that "the bringing of the product to the market belongs to the productive process" (Marx quoted by Harvey 1982: 377), then the means of labor brought by the peasantry into that productive process (their tools and the land they control) corresponds to an infinitesimal share of the means of production. One figure will illustrate the point: records of Companies House in London describe the particulars of a 1982 mortgage of 4,903,618 pounds (sterling) held by Lloyds Bank on the merchant vessel *Geestport*, one of the Geest ships registered at the port of Boston. One need not even consider the value of the other three Geest ships, or of the facilities in Spalding, London, and the rest of the United Kingdom, to realize the discrepancy between Geest's and the peasants' shares of the actual means of production.

Moreover, beyond that comparison, one needs to establish an analytic distinction between the ownership of the means of labor (referring to elements entering a particular labor process, on the ground) and ownership of the means of production. To paraphrase Pouillon (1976: 81), the mere jural right of an individual to dispose of a specific material object has, in itself, little economic significance. As an economic concept, says Pouillon, the ownership of the means of production "does not appear as a [jural] right, but as the *power* to combine means of production and living labor to transform material nature into use-values, into products" (Pouillon 1976: 81; my emphasis, my translation). One should add that, under capitalism, the ownership of the means of production presents itself, concretely, as the power to combine such elements as necessary to produce commodities. As far as the bananas sold by Geest in Europe are concerned, Geest itself, rather than the Dominican peasants, holds the power necessary to combine such elements and activate the productive process.

Having dispelled the illusion of a sale in Dominica and qualified the importance of the peasants' ownership of the means of labor, we can now pierce another pernicious illusion, the illusion that, somehow, the bananas delivered to Geest might be a surplus produced by a peasantry otherwise meeting its needs through subsistence production.

The Illusion of Subsistence

In the literature on peasantries, anthropologists and economists tend to tie the notion of surplus to that of subsistence. To be sure, the determinant factor in that alleged correlation tends to vary from one discipline to the other (and sometimes from one author to another within the same discipline). However, such variations notwithstanding, the correlation itself tends to mask the terminological ambiguity of surplus. In lay language, "surplus" conveys the sense of an excess, an overplus, something more than what is needed, a denotation on which the American Heritage, the Webster, and the Funk and Wagnalls dictionaries fundamentally agree. This meaning passed into the professional literature with the connotation of"superfluous" (Merriam-Webster). Yet, and here lies the ambiguity, when used in a compound, as in surplus product, surplus labor, and so on, "surplus," in fact, denotes an appreciation, a subtraction rather than an overplus (except in the Marxist concept of surplus value in which it implies both).[2] In other words, there is no inherent denotation of an excess in those categories. Still, the connotation of an overplus has been carried over from lay language to the economic categories.

Thus, whereas anthropologists tend to view the observation of a surplus product or surplus labor as proof that consumption needs have been met, some economists tend to deny processes of surplus extraction on the basis of the precariousness of subsistence. Whereas anthropologists saw surplus and assumed subsistence, economists saw poverty and dismissed surplus. De Silva (1982: 450) rightly criticizes the contention that the peasantry is generally "incapable of producing a surplus." He writes: "This presumed relation between consumption levels and surpluses, if applied to the plantation sector, would lead to an obviously inadmissible conclusion, since the living standards of the labourers (the estate coolies!) are not markedly different from those of the peasants" (De Silva 1982: 81). Chevalier (1982: 117–18) rightly questions the use of sale ratios to determine peasants' capacity to live above certain levels of subsistence and/or their dependence on subsistence production. A peasant may sell 50 percent of his or her production and be less dependent on exchange for reproduction than one who sells only 40 percent of such production. The issue here is not that of cash use but that of dependence on exchange ability.

Equally interesting is De Silva's suggestion that economists' neglect of surplus extraction from the peasantry partially rests on the difficulty of submitting such extraction to accounting procedures. The point here is not to propose the means of such quantification—a task most certainly outside this writer's competence—but to suggest that, as a subsistence level cannot be deduced from the production of a surplus, so the production/extraction of such surplus cannot be inferred from an established level of poverty. Bagchi (1982: 167) calls for an analytical distinction between subsistence *sensu stricto* as observed in "tribal societies" by anthropologists such as Sahlins (1969, 1974) and the "last resort subsistence farming" of peripheral peasantries. Unfortunately, he does not pursue the implications of the distinction for a clarification of the concept itself.

The need for that clarification persists beyond the now faded debate between economist Harry Pearson and anthropologist Marvin Harris. Pearson (1957) criticizes the notion of surplus as "excess of goods," or "oversufficiency of means" on the grounds that the level of material subsistence in any society is inherently unmeasurable. Harris (1959), in turn, argues that Pearson is right for the wrong reasons. Harris also dismisses the notion of "surplus above subsistence," but suggests that the threshold of subsistence is quantifiable as "the amount of energy necessary to do nothing except what is biophysically necessary to satisfy the metabolic requirements of the population concerned" (Harris 1959: 189). Surplus is always an extraction, but, argues Harris (1959: 197), an extraction from "necessary rather than superfluous food supply."

Most nutritionists would agree with Harris on the possibility of determining exactly "what is biophysically necessary" for the energetic survival of a human population. But caloric intake is not the only measure of biophysical needs any more than the price of fuel is the whole cost of maintaining a car. Harris's emphasis on food masks other physical needs, such as the protection of the body against the environment. More important, the ethnographic evidence suggests that no society perceives or performs the productive tasks it sets for itself solely in terms of caloric requirements or protection against the environment. In other words, the subsistence level that is most quantifiable has quite a limited relevance to cross-cultural comparisons. Last and not least, if we can both conceive and measure a strict minimum level of physical requirements, we must also admit the logical and empirical possibility of an amount above that minimum. Necessity implies excess. Thus, Harris might have also been right for the wrong reasons: surplus is always extraction, but not inevitably drawn from a population living at subsistence level. The concept of surplus as extraction does not imply the concept of subsistence as necessary supply.

Indeed, in tributary societies, including feudal Europe, the subsistence level is imposed on the peasantry through noneconomic means from the outside: by the state, the landlords, or a combination of forces shaped by both. Surplus is extracted whether or not all segments of the population meet all their physical requirements. Marie-Antoinette's "let them eat cake" should remind us of upper-class indifference to those needs. Economist Joan Robinson insists that similar situations still prevail in many peripheral societies. In such cases, "there is no definite minimum below which the cultivators' consumption cannot fall" (Robinson 1979: 19).

Likewise, in societies in which rural cultivators are free, that is, in which they have acquired civil rights that guarantee their mobility and their power to engage in any form of economic relations as an alternative to starvation, the subsistence level can only be measured against the socially necessary cost of reproduction of the society at large. It is then conceivable that production within any familial unit engaged in the peasant labor process falls quite short of that socially determined threshold. It is even possible that large chunks of the peasantry, or, for that matter, the peasantry at large, do not meet those requirements even when a surplus product is extracted. Again, the difficulty of quantifying the threshold of subsistence should not mask the theoretical leap that the undue correlation between surplus and subsistence has maintained in the literature. The disappearance of nineteenth-century squatters in the mountains of Dominica may well be an example of the disintegration of a rural group unable to meet its reproductive needs despite partial involvement in the national market. Large chunks of Caribbean or Latin American peasantries (one thinks not only of Dominica, but also of Honduras, Nevis, or Haiti) may also fit the bill, as their rate of emigration, among other indicators, seems to suggest.

Yet disappearance, famine, and emigration are not the only possible outcomes. Peasants may join the ranks of the army or paramilitary forces, reinforcing the militarization of the state, or join the army of proletarians laboring in urban factories or rural plantations. More likely, though, as circumstances allow, they tend to combine inventiveness and conservatism by keeping their grounds, while engaged in parallel activities outside of the family unit. Quite often, part-time agricultural wage labor, sharecropping on additional land, domestic services in town or in the village complete the peasants' efforts to meet their reproductive needs. Those activities cannot be covered by the generic word *surplus*; in no way do they bring an excess of income to the peasant family. They are as necessary to its reproduction as the production of subsistence goods when the consumption needs of the household have surpassed its productive capacity. The same may be true of piece work at home, or of the production of agricultural commodities through the peasant labor process.

The Necessity of Banana Production

The suggestion that follows proceeds from the shattering of the above mentioned illusions: from the peasantry's viewpoint, the production of bananas to be sold by Geest as commodities on the world market by no means constitutes a surplus, if by "surplus" one means an excess. It stands as a necessity, equal to piece work at home and rural or urban wage labor. Throughout the nineteenth century, as household production fell increasingly below the necessary cost of reproduction, the rural laborers as yeomen or even as tenants gained increasing control over their labor power and the means of work. Yet the very extension of the peasant labor process implied a relative national self-sufficiency for locally grown food within various enclaves which, in turn, limited the profits from the sale of agricultural commodities within the island. Even today, opportunities for wage labor are sparse. The Civil Service, a legacy of the nineteenth-century co-optation of the Mulatto Ascendancy by the British Crown, remains the largest source of employment but one now drained of new promises and, at any rate, inaccessible to most of the peasantry. The necessity of maintenance and reproduction thus forces rural cultivators engaged in the peasant labor process to turn the assets they control (their means of work and their labor power) into the production of export commodities, especially bananas.

Yet, in the case of bananas, we have demonstrated the overarching control exerted by the transnational on the productive process and pointed to the low marginal value of the means of labor controlled by the peasantry. We have also demonstrated that the bananas are not sold. What then is paid to the producer if neither the price of the product nor the value of its means of labor? The only remaining possibility is that the "price to the producer" primarily covers the second item over which the peasants have some control: their labor power.

Through the subjugation of the peasant labor process, capital has turned Dominican yeomen and tenants into "proletarians working at home" (Amin and Vergopoulos 1974). Part of the peasants' labor power may still be engaged in the production of use-values for home consumption; part of it may be engaged in the production of commodities to be sold at the local market, but a substantial part of that labor power has no direct value for the peasant until and unless it enters into the productive process controlled by the transnational. Though that labor power has no value for its owner within the confines of Dominican society, it can be used by another party, the transnational, and, as any commodity, it acquires an exchange value through that exchange and because of that use. Dominican yeomen and tenants are in fact working in their own gardens for a British-based transnational corporation.

Unequal Retribution

How is surplus extracted under that system? To the extent that Dominican peasants are proletarians working at home, there is an inherent difference between the value of their labor power and the value of the bananas produced through the use of that labor power, the surplus value that characterizes capitalist production. That would be the case even if they were properly remunerated, even if both the labor power in Dominica and the bananas in England were exchanged at their actual value (Marx 1967; Salama 1982; Amin 1978; Dallemagne 1978). But if surplus value designates "the difference between the value of the labor power and the value of the product of labor actuated by that power" (Dallemagne 1978: 81),[3] the question as to how peasants actually reproduce themselves becomes crucial.

"The value of labour power is determined by the values of the necessaries of life habitually required by the average labourer" (Marx 1967, 1:519). Our "average" laborer is Dominican: his reproduction occurs within clearly defined natural and political boundaries, and "the necessaries habitually required" are those determined by a particular history and culture. Yet the bananas are sold on the international market, not only in Britain where Geest competes with Fyffes and Jamaican Producers, but also in other European countries reached by the Geest marketing empire. Geest's profits and rate of growth are measured against those prevalent in the world banana trade, and its survival depends on a constant reevaluation of its trade in the changing context of monopoly capitalism. That it cannot afford geographical or national boundaries is evident by its constant threat to purchase bananas produced elsewhere (a threat it does not hesitate to carry out when needed), its measures of diversification (investments in the transport industry or computer services), its ties with international capital (the Lloyds Bank mortgage is a case in point). Thus, whereas our peasant is Dominican in ways that he or she cannot escape, our capitalist and the bananas he controls are international.

The situation typified by the relative immobility of labor and the internationalization of capital and commodities has been defined as one that necessarily leads to "unequal exchange" (Emmanuel 1972). The terminological debate that followed the formalization of that theory (Amin 1973; Bettelheim 1972; De Janvry and Kramer 1979; Emmanuel et al. 1973) does not concern us here inasmuch as it does not undermine Emmanuel's fundamental contribution. If capital and commodities have become international, while human beings, as bearers of the labor power, remain confined within spaces naturally or politically delimited, the actual rate of surplus value varies from nation to nation, and possibly from region to region. In other words, both Geest and the United Kingdom gain from the production of bananas in Dominica, a society in which the "cost of living" is lower than in Britain. Transnational corporations act on the basis of this principle when they move their plants to Third World countries to assemble products that are then repatriated in industrialized societies. Governments in North America and Europe implicitly acknowledge the validity of the same principle when they allow or encourage such moves despite the temporary protest of organized labor in their respective countries. The difference between our case and that of "screwdriver industries"—and it is an important one—resides in Geest Industries' benefiting from the same "unequal exchange" without having moved any of its fixed capital to Dominica. Screwdriver industries or offshore light assemblies use the cheap labor available in peripheral societies to assemble foreign-made components for the benefit of transnationals and usually require fixed capital from a core country.

In the case of bananas, the characteristics of the trade in question, as well as the respective positions and roles of Geest and Dominica in that trade, reinforce the vulnerability usually associated with the theory of unequal exchange. Moreover, those characteristics also reinforce, from a different viewpoint, the vulnerability usually associated with the seller's position in discussions of "monopsonistic exploitation." It might be worth integrating here some elements of those different viewpoints to emphasize the ways in which the particulars of bananas in the world economy reinforce Dominica's vulnerability and, consequently, allow, at least in theory, for a much greater exploitation of the Dominican small producer.

Bananas have been, for at least the last twenty years, the most important "fresh fruit" in the world economy in terms of both volume and values (Valles 1968; Clairmonte 1977; Maillard 1969). Average world production grew from 34.5 billion pounds in 1948–49 to 58 billion in 1964–65. Between 1962–64 and 1965–67, to cite only one case, imports into Italy increased nearly 300 percent (Phillips 1973). While bananas grew in importance in the diet of Western Europeans, North Americans, Argentines, and Japanese, the tumultuous effects of that rising demand or, rather, the ramified interests that fostered that demand, in turn, changed the face of many peripheral nation states: notably Ecuador and Honduras in Latin America, but also Somalia in Africa, and, of course, Jamaica and thc Windwards in the Caribbean. The world rise of bananas also deeply affected the history of the Canary Islands, Cameroon, Panama, and Costa Rica, to name only a few. Yet though the impact necessarily varied from one periphery to the next, and from one importer to the next as well, the gauge against which it was measured differed qualitatively from core to periphery. Two figures might make the point: in the mid-1970s, though bananas indisputably led the world trade in fruit, the crop accounted for only 0.2 percent of the total world trade (Clairmonte 1977). At the same time, bananas accounted for more than 60 percent of Dominica's export values, down from 92 percent in 1968 (DBGA 1977; Chernick et al. 1978). In other words, while the world, as such, could live without bananas, Dominica itself was totally dependent upon that particular crop and remains largely so. In fact, most producing countries are more or less in similar situations of vulnerability (Clairmonte 1977; FAO 1980).

Second, and in sharp contrast to the producing countries' weakness, the major distributors share a striking oligopsony: United Brands (formerly United Fruit), Castle and Cook, and Del Monte control 70 percent of the world market (Clairmonte 1977). Third, the gap between the peripheries' weakness and the transnationals' power is increased by the direct political involvement of North American and European governments in the banana trade or issues directly related to it. Indeed, as we have seen in the case of the Colonial Office, partly because of the connections between banana production and railroad or shipping interests in Europe and in the United States, the transnationals' oligopsony in bananas and colonialist or imperialist interventions represent, from a historical viewpoint, correlative developments. Fourth, the Windwards' position among those already weak producers is one of extreme feebleness because of environmental conditions as well as technological nonadaptation. Fifth, as the member of the Windward group that is the most dependent on bananas, crippled by the inefficiency of WINBAN on such crucial issues as the GMP, Dominica has even less bargaining power than, say, Somalia or Cameroon. Finally, and not the least, Geest shares about 35 percent of the United Kingdom market. Though one suspects that undisclosed arrangements, combined with the history of colonial preferences that facilitated the entrance of Caribbean fruits in England, may have contributed to uphold its position, recent events suggest that it may be losing ground both in England and in the world market where it never has been a formidable competitor. Despite some guarantees given at the Lome Conference to the Windward producers, formal Independence, Britain's entrance in the European community, United Brands' growth, increasing purchases of Latin American (so-called dollar) fruit by Fyffes (United Brands' British subsidiary), all tend to suggest that Geest may need to make the best of a bad time while still possible. In concrete terms, it may need to use its own monopsony to the fullest, to extract more surplus from the Dominican producer.

Overexploitation

I have indicated two forms of surplus extraction, the first resulting from the sale of labor power, the second resulting from the reproduction of this labor power within a specific society while the products it generates are international. For the purposes of the demonstration, I have assumed that the price paid to the peasants actually covered their reproduction, that it could provide them "the necessaries of life habitually required" to survive in Dominican society. A third form of surplus extraction occurs, because the returns on the bananas fall lower than the necessary cost of reproduction in Dominica and because the peasants' engagement in the labor process now imposes on them the constant devaluation of their labor.

Dominican banana growers, yeomen as well as tenants, cover a significant part of their reproduction through the cultivation of provisions. They consume tanias, dasheens, plantains, indeed, bananas rejected by the association in the name of Geest. Some drink milk from their own cattle, and eventually eat the meat of the animals they raise. To be sure, this contribution to their consumption varies greatly within the island, and even within the same village. But the more this internal consumption occurs, the less the transnational needs to provide for the full reproduction of the labor force. The more an individual is engaged in a peasant-type production, the less the transnational covers the real price of his or her labor power.

The matter of conceptualizing the obvious contradiction of a labor power produced in Third World societies, outside of the laws of capital accumulation yet ultimately used by capitalism, has caught the attention not only of economists but also of historians, sociologists, and anthropologists. Yet an equally large body of literature has strived to explain the articulation of domestic (female) labor with capitalism in Western societies, generally building its arguments on the empirical and theoretical distinction between two types of activities (housework and wage labor) each of which generally rests on either side of the female/male divide and implics a different unit of production (J. Harrison 1973; Seccombe 1974; Gardiner 1976).

In the case of Dominca, as in many Third World countries in which a peasant-type production occurs, the spatial enmeshment of goods directly consumed by the productive unit and those which find their way to the capitalist market blurs such a neat distinction. Both types of production intertwine, especially with the practice of intercropping. Also, the elasticity of time allocation makes it difficult to distinguish neatly between labor time devoted to household goods and time devoted exclusively to the production of commodities. In short, market goods and household goods overlap in time and in space.

The case of domestic labor in the West is thus clearer, because one can easily conceptualize a situation in which (1) the housewife does not work for wages; (2) all her means of labor (from needles and pots to dishwashers and vacuum cleaners) are commodities; (3) her labor is directed at the reproduction of the labor power of an individual (say, an automobile or steel worker who does not perform any household work whatsoever) who works exclusively for capital.

Reviewing the theoretical literature on such cases, Himmelweit and Mohun (1977) forcefully state the conceptual alternatives one faces: either the law of value fully operates in the case of domestic labor, and one could then speak of surplus value, but all the housewife's products would be commodities (or, at least, in my view, "exchangeable"); or domestic labor yields utilities directly appropriated by the family, and one cannot then speak of surplus value, or even of a transfer of value. Himmelweit and Mohun opt for the second alternative; and, of course, with the possibilities so stated, there is hardly any other choice. Yet the authors fall short of conceptualizing what exactly is being transferred from the household to the factory.

Still, one need not discuss the possibility that the value category is applicable to household production in industrialized countries (since the housewife's means *and* objects of labor are all commodities) or the suggestion that domestic labor might be one more in an increasing list of "modes of production," to benefit from the way in which Himmelweit and Mohun sort out their categories. Given the possibilities they state, it seems, to this writer, at least, that only one category remains operational, that of labor itself.

More than a decade ago, anthropologist Pierre-Philippe Rey (1973, 1977) suggested a transfer of surplus labor from many Third World peasantries to capitalist centers, even though he first phrased it in terms of a transfer of "value" (1969), a position closer to that recently defended by Amin (1986). The digression on the issue of female domestic labor provides us with a clearer choice; it also questions the necessity of using the "mode of production" concept to analyze the transfer (Archetti 1978): each and every activity that produces use-values need not be understood as the manifestation of a non-or precapitalist mode.

In our particular case, in which some of the means of labor and the objects as well as the products of labor are directly used by the producers for their own survival and reproduction, one can use a process of elimination similar to that used by Himmelweit and Mohun despite the difficulty of separating, on the ground, the allocation of labor itself. The tanias, dasheens, plantains, sweet potatoes, and cassava manioc are planted, harvested, and consumed by the family as useful items, regardless of any occasional exchange value. Yet they enter into the reproduction of laborers who will ultimately produce bananas which are destined to be commodities, and would not have been planted otherwise. Thus, the labor embedded in them is transferred to the field characterized by the circulation of commodities and the accumulation of capital.[4] The difficulty of empirically isolating the two domains in terms of labor allocation should not blur the necessary theoretical distinction.

I have outlined the three major forms of surplus extraction from the gross mass of Dominican banana producers:

1. *surplus value* inherent in capitalist relations of production;
2. *transfer of value* because of the "unequal exchange" (Emmanuel 1972; Amin 1986) between Dominica, as a peripheral society, and European centers of the world system; and
3. *transfer of surplus labor* because, over and above the unequal exchange, the members of Dominican society who produce the bananas also directly produce a significant share of the goods they consume.

There are other forms of surplus extraction in Dominica. Most notable is the indirect taxation system hardly modified since the nineteenth century. That tax system and the processes of extraction of surplus value and surplus labor do set the context in which the other forms operate. They are the key elements in the entrenchment of the peasant labor process in a set of capitalist relations. An example is the virtual disappearance of ground rent, especially in its cash form. In 1978–82, plots of two acres were accessible to tenants for as low as twenty Eastern Caribbean dollars a year, even in some of the most productive banana districts. The elimination of cash rent implies the possibility for capital to extract a surplus not shared with a landed class (Rey 1973; Amin and Vergopoulos 1974; Harvey 1982). Most tenants now function in many ways as yeomen, though without the guarantee of legal ownership. Thus they are subject to the overexploitation experienced by the peasant proprietor.

The coexistence of peasants and capitalism owes much to the possibility in this case actualized—of capitalists' ultimately extracting, under diverse guises, more surplus from a peripheral peasantry than from proletarians at home and abroad. Corporate officials know as much. Even if they do not couch their analysis in those terms, their decisions speak for themselves. Often corporate behavior suggests that the issue is not whether or not but when to withdraw from agricultural production of crops that can be planted through the peasant labor process. Geest's case is telling.

In the mid-1970s, Geest management started a systematic withdrawal from banana production in Dominica and Saint Lucia. The Geest estates had fulfilled their two-pronged original function: to guarantee a minumum steady supply in the first twenty years of the enterprise and to serve as models for local cultivators. The 1978 statement of the chairman of the board hints at this past rationale: "We feel there is much to be gained by retaining [some] facilities to demonstrate to local growers the best practice to adopt to produce high quality bananas and at the same time obtaining optimum yields" (Chairman's Statement, 1978, Geest Holdings, C.R.O. 1068048).

In 1977–78, Geest tried to convince the government of Dominica (which had, incidentally, seized part of the Woodford Hill Estate supposedly to build an airport) to acquire the whole of Woodford Hill and the Bantridge and Portsmouth estates. The government wavered and finally declined, but Geest proceeded to sell as many plots as possible to local growers. By now, Geest has little if any land left in Dominica, and the Roseau Estate in Saint Lucia has been parceled to smallholders. Interestingly, Geest did not expect production to drop in the aftermath of those sales. The same statement quoted above mentions a new proposal to expand the carrying capacity of the Geest banana fleet. On the other hand, the chairman was somewhat laconic about the reasons why Geest was abandoning production: "These developments reflect our policy of leaving banana production so far as possible in the hands of local growers" (Chairman's Statement, 1978, Geest Holdings, C.R.O. 1068048).

One of my informants in England, a vice-president for another transnational involved in the banana trade, was much more direct. I had asked him why its own company had withdrawn from direct engagement in the labor process in another peripheral society. "We let them do it," he said. "It's cheaper."

CHAPTER 8

The Making of a Transnational

This story started somewhere else until I discovered it had two beginnings, so I had to tell you this one also.
—J. California Cooper, *A Piece of Mine*

Geest's strategy of keeping away from immediate control of the labor process on the ground proved to be profitable. During the thirty years it has been involved in the Caribbean banana industry, Geest grew continuously from its modest beginnings to become one of the most important close companies of the United Kingdom. In 1952, the year that Geest Industries picked up Antilles Products' banana contract with Dominica, its nominal capital was only 75,000 pounds. By 1981, profits alone exceeded a million pounds. Moreover, since 1972, Geest Industries itself has become part of a much larger conglomerate, Geest Holdings Limited, whose subsidiaries are involved in various types of activities from foodstuff distribution and agricultural engineering to computer services and leisure travel.

The main contention of this chapter is that the constant thread in the history of Geest's success is the profitability inherent in the informal control of peripheral peasant producers by capitalists operating from the centers of the world economy. The history of the Geest group offers two contrasting layers of appearances that must be dismissed in order to expose the brutal reality of the world-scale exploitation of Caribbean peasants. One is confronted at first with an enterprising family which seems to make the best of an expanding market. Then, as the figures grow and intertwine, as contacts expand, through loans, acquisitions, and new faces on various boards of directors, one discovers a complex and changing corporate structure, the intricacy of which discourages investigation. The analysis must go beyond those two images and deal with the question of the nature of Geest's profitability, the real momentum behind its expansion.

Peasant Labor, World Accumulation

First, one needs to document Geest's profitability itself, for the argument rests, in part, on the different ways in which that profitability materialized along the years. From 1935 to the present, profits did not accumulate at the same speed, nor were they always used in the same manner. One can distinguish roughly three periods of expansion and use of profits in the history of Geest:

1. the period of slow and steady growth that preceded Geest Industries' involvement with bananas (1935–52);
2. the twenty-year stretch (1952–72) during which increasing profits were essentially used to finance the expansion of the banana empire; and
3. the era following the 1972 creation of Geest Holdings Limited (the parent company of the Geest group), during which profits from the banana activities were used to finance diversification.

There is no need to dwell on the first period, briefly sketched below to provide a general background to Geest's post-1952 expansion. In the second period, Geest Industries' primary activity was the importation and distribution of Caribbean bananas in the United Kingdom. Given that extreme specialization, there is little else to explain the company's growth except its indirect control of the Windward Islands banana production. The third period is somewhat more interesting. It starts with the 1972 creation of Geest Holdings Limited, now the parent company of a multimillion dollar empire that comprises Geest Industries and numerous other enterprises. During that period, Geest increased the scope of its diversification schemes, but none of the other ventures initially matched the profitability of Geest's banana activities. Rather, the profits accumulated from bananas not only sustained the continuous growth of

Geest Industries but also financed the creation or acquisition of the new enterprises. These banana profits provided the company directors a solid basis from which to venture into new activities. Many of Geest Holdings branches were artificially kept afloat at the beginning by direct or indirect transfers from the banana industry. Thus, the proliferation of Geest subsidiaries, the survival of many of them in otherwise difficult times, can only be explained in light of the continuous profitability inherent in Geest's power to determine the price of the Caribbean cultivators' labor. In short, Caribbean peasants, including those of Dominica, subsidized not only the growth of Geest Industries but the making of the conglomerate itself and its continuing diversification.

The argument requires a change of perspective both from traditional approaches to peasant studies and from traditional corporate histories. The facts and figures used in this chapter come mainly from the records of the Companies Registration Office (C.R.O.) in London and interviews carried out in England with various individuals engaged in banana importation, marketing, and distribution. These sources seem far away from Dominican shores, but to show the ultimate consequences of the integration of the peasant labor process into a worldwide process of valorization research must be carried out in the arenas where the profits materialize. Studies of peasant exploitation too often stop at the political borders within which the peasantry toils, ending abruptly with the mere suggestion that such labor benefits somebody else elsewhere. Yet traces of the profitability of many transnationals' dealings with Third World peasantries exist in the West. To be sure, such records could be read differently, say, by a stockbroker or a market analyst. Further, in the case of close, or privately held, companies, such as those that comprise the Geest empire, detailed reports to stockholders are not easily accessible. By and large, public documents remain tortuous, even broken at times, but telling nevertheless if one asks the right questions. The research itself requires the shedding of a few illusions, of which the most important is what we might call the naturalness of profitability.

When I first heard of Geest in Dominica, the name was associated with the two brothers who founded Geest Industries, Jan and Leendert van Geest, and the success of the company itself—a success that many Dominicans are aware of—almost completely attributed to their ability to read correctly a naturally profitable situation. Indeed, the story of the Geest Group's financial success can be read, at first, like a popular novel extolling the virtues of laissez-faire entrepreneurship through the example of a closely knit family who just happened to be in the right place at the right time. The official C.R.O. records (more than 3,000 pages of annual returns, statements, and transaction reports from diverse Geest companies), show that such a version of the Geest story masks, in fact, a range of economic transactions requiring serious analysis.

However, it would be a mistake to treat the official records as unprocessed data with no inherent viewpoint of their own, an error systematically sustained by traditional corporate histories that present success as the combined result of acumen and luck. Data such as those available at the C.R.O. implicitly couch the trajectory of an enterprise as a series of transactions whose quantified outcomes happen to be positive or negative. The annual statements of accounts and the chairman's and directors' reports I consulted speak of turnover and profits, not of labor. From their viewpoint, it is as if the bananas fell from the sky. I, on the contrary, assume that labor creates wealth and that capitalists and financiers alike know this as well as I do, even if implicitly. Thus what first appears to be entrepreneurial acumen emerges from the description as implicit knowledge on the part of Geest and its financial backers of the structural inequalities that guaranteed their success. Investors who throw money about haphazardly simply do not survive. In the case of Geest, the expected profits materialized, and at a greater rate perhaps than anticipated. They are part of the record, couched in terms of growth rather than as results of Geest's control over the products and labor of the Caribbean peasantries. But, assuming that growth and profits must be generated, I take the continuous growth of both Geest Industries and its parent, Geest Holdings, as the key empirical evidence for the transfer of surplus theorized in the preceding chapter.

A Family Affair

The family saga version of Geest history, so common in Dominica, is partly sustained in England itself by the Geest family's half-century-long control of privately held, close companies, sheltered from public scrutiny. Jan van Geest and his late brother Leendert, two Dutch-born merchants, controlled the group for forty-five years as majority shareholders, directors, and one succeeded the other as chairman of the board of Geest Industries and its associated companies. In the background, one discovers their brother Marteen Johannes van Geest and, especially, their late father, Wailing van Geest, founding member of Wailing van Geest & Sons, a firm registered in Holland long before the creation of the British-based Geest Industries. In recent years, Leonard Wailing van Geest, son of Leendert, has emerged as a central figure, especially since he acceded to the chairmanship of Geest Holdings after his father's death in 1980.

In the early 1930s, both Jan and Leendert were partners in their father's firm, Wailing van Geest & Sons, then a modest enterprise based in Gravenzande, Holland, specializing in the cultivation and distribution of horticultural bulbs.[1] By 1935, Jan had crossed the North Sea to establish residence in Spalding, a little town in Lincolnshire, on the east coast of England. In December 1935, Jan incorporated Geest Horticultural Products, a private company with its registered office located in the coastal town of Boston, Lincolnshire. The nominal capital of 2,000 shares of one pound was divided among Jan, Leendert, and Marteen Johannes van Geest. Jan, listed as managing director, controlled 700 shares; Leendert and Marteen, both still residents of Gravenzande, held 650 shares each. The purpose of the new company was to produce and distribute "bulbs of all kinds, seeds, plants etc." (C.R.O. 308737).

The public records tell us very little of the first decade of Geest Horticultural Products. Though the firm survived, its nominal capital remained the same for fourteen years (C.R.O. 308737). One can suspect, at best, a small increase in profitability because of the general rise in prices of agricultural products during the war years. Be that as it may, the first turnabout in the fortune of the Geest brothers on the British side of the North Sea occurred in the late 1940s. In September 1949, the nominal capital jumped from 2,000 to 75,000 pounds, with Jan still holding the largest number of shares, and Leendert moving up to a close second. On December 31 of that same year Geest Horticultural Products changed its name to Geest Industries Limited.

The name change was not purely symbolic; nor was the anglicization of Jan and Leendert to John and Leonard, after Leonard's move to Spalding. These changes reflected the brothers' desire to take advantage of marketing and financing opportunities then available to them in England and augured a new emphasis on capitalization and continuous expansion. The special resolution of 16 August 1950 was explicit on this point: it was deemed "desirable to capitalise any part" of the reserve funds or profits of the company. Accordingly, Geest Industries bought a few agricultural ventures in England in the late 1940s and early 1950s.

Not all the properties acquired or controlled by the brothers in England were immediately integrated within Geest Industries or its forerunner, Geest Horticultural Products.[2] It seems that throughout the first decade of their activities in England the Geest brothers were not entirely sure of the direction of their operations and tried their hands at different things, even though horticulture remained their main concern, perhaps because it was a family tradition. Thus, in retrospect, the most crucial move was the 1952 takeover by Geest Industries of Antilles Products' banana contract with the Windward Islands.

The Roots of Expansion

Regardless of the immediate motivations of the Geest brothers, the move was well timed. In the aftermath of World War II, the state of the banana market in the United Kingdom signaled the possibility for a dramatic increase in imports from the Windward Islands. Chief among the factors that contributed to reshape the market were the difficulties encountered by importers of fruits produced in Jamaica and the Canary Islands. The Jamaican banana industry had been particularly affected by the war. Jamaican exports to England declined drastically and then came to a total halt because of shipping difficulties. After the war, wind damage and Panama disease (a fungus disease caused by *Fusarium cubense*) impeded a possible recovery, so that Jamaican exports to the United Kingdom for the year 1954 came to only 75 percent of the 1939 volume (Persaud 1967). At the same time, the general tendency toward increased protectionism in the fruit trade on the part of many European governments augured badly for the future of Canary Islands bananas in the British market. Duties on bananas from non-Commonwealth countries were expected to rise, as they did soon after the war and throughout the 1950s.[3] Thus the prospects were excellent for a rise in the Windward Islands contribution to the British market, and some observers still wonder about the reasons why Antilles Products sold out to Geest at a time when conservative estimates projected a tenfold rise in exports for the next few years (Caribbean Yearbook, 1950–54; Persaud 1967; Maillard 1969; Mourillon 1977).

In fact, the Windward Islands production grew even faster than many had predicted. Exports to the United Kingdom jumped from 34,300 long tons in 1956 to 170,000 in 1965 (Beckford 1967: 4). Moreover the Windwards' share of that market also increased dramatically from 7 percent to 45 percent in the same period mainly at the expense of non-Commonwealth countries (Persaud 1967; Maillard 1969). Caribbean producers undoubtedly benefited from that expansion, but in no way qualitatively or quantitatively comparable to Geest's benefits. From 1952 to the present, the story of Geest Industries is that of a series of spectacular increases in nominal capital, turnover, and profits, an expansion directly tied to the growth of the Windward production. Geest's control over that production guaranteed the immediate correlation between volume in the Caribbean and profits in England, at least for a time. Nominal capital grew from 100,000 pounds in 1953 to 500,000 in 1960, to one million in 1963, and three million pounds in 1965. Thirteen years after Geest started its banana marketing operations, the board was able to decide, at an extraordinary meeting of 2 April 1965, on the capitalization of 2.65 million pounds, most of which came from "the Profit and Loss Account of the Company." Ten years later, in 1975, annual profits alone had passed the one million pounds mark, and Geest Industries' turnover for the year was 57.85 millions. By 1980, both figures had nearly doubled: profits after taxation reached 1.97 million and turnover for the year was 103.91 million pounds.

Table 8.1 retraces almost a decade of that evolution by listing some of the numbers that evidence the continuous profitability of Geest's operations. The sums of yearly assets include all of the company's fixed and current assets, the ships, subsidiaries, investments, and debts of its parent company.[4] The striking fact about those figures, though, is the minor growth of assets, liabilities, and net capital compared to the fast

Table 8.1. Geest Industries: Capital and Profits after Taxation, 1972–1980 (in Millions of Sterling Pounds)

Year	Total Assets	Current Liabilities	Net Capital Employed	Turnover	Net Profit
1972	33.12	10.75	22.29	40	(1.—)
1973	30.79	6.96	23.77	47.87	.76
1974	28.96	6.15	21.99	49.31	.82
1975	29.72	8.27	21.45	57.85	1.34
1976	31.59	11.46	20.13	69.90	1.09
1977	28.93	9.61	19.31	73.94	1.50
1978	27.00	9.65	17.35	86.24	1.68
1979	24.70	9.27	15.43	87.90	2.32
1980	36.13	12.87	23.25	103.91	1.97

Source: Geest Industries Limited, Companies Registration Office; Statement of Accounts and Reports of Directors, 1972–81; C.R.O. 308737.

increase in the two right-hand columns, which reflect turnover and profits. The 1972 loss notwithstanding—a temporary setback because of a drought in the Caribbean and, most important, Geest's debts to finance its new fleet—net profits grew continuously during the 1970s to reach an all time high of 2.32 million pounds in 1979. Gross profits were much higher, at times, since the figures listed here were obtained after Geest's deductions of taxes and different charges which included varyingly depreciation, auditors' remuneration, hire of plant and equipment, bank and loan interests, pension fund contributions, and appreciable emoluments for the directors. In short, Geest Industries had become a quite profitable enterprise.

The Links to Finance Capital

Though profits were high, they were not always sufficient to finance the successive phases of expansion that would lead to higher returns. External financing was often needed, both before and after Geest' s involvement with bananas, but the Geest managers revealed themselves to be up to the task. Indeed, a textbook series of financing operations marks the Geest Industries' expansion: mortgages, charges, bank overdrafts, and setoff letters spiraling to eight million pounds of debts in December 1980. In the 1940s and '50s, the Geest brothers continually borrowed money to acquire properties in Lincolnshire, and they, in turn, were mortgaged or charged to finance expansion. Creditors included various Dutch and British companies, but the success of Geest financing was principally rooted in a privileged relationship with Lloyds Bank, a relationship that started in 1941 and continues today. It is mainly to Lloyds that the company turned in 1952 to finance its entry in the banana marketing operation after a consolidation of assets that included Geest Industries' acquisition of W. Groom (which had remained independent even with John van Geest as chairman of the board). In January 1952, Geest Industries mortgaged virtually every property the brothers and their associates held in Lincolnshire: a strip of land in Boston, a farm in Frampton, premises at Quadring and Spalding. Most of the charges incurred then were not fully satisfied until the 1970s.

The need for outside financing did not disappear after Geest's entry in the banana market. In the 1960s, while still indebted to Lloyds, Geest Industries moved to cut its use of chartered cargoes and acquire its own ships. New financing was needed. The Nederlandsche

Scheeps-hypotheekbank and the Ship Mortgage Finance Company, among others, financed the building of the vessels *Geestbay*, *Geestport*, *Geestcape*, and *Geesthaven*. The volume of bananas distributed by the company grew accordingly; and so did profits. By 1970, the company had done well enough in the banana trade to seek financing to construct new vessels again. Lloyds, this time, provided the mortgage on four new refrigerated vessels of 8,050 tons' capacity at a cost of twelve million pounds sterling each. Geest sold the old *Geestbay* and the *Geestport* at a profit, put two other ships into charter service, and used the remaining four as its "Atlantic fleet." Successive mortgages on the ships, bank overdrafts, and other charges continued to finance Geest's expansion well into the 1980s. All in all, more than twenty mortgage or charge agreements, most of them with Lloyds, punctuated Geest's capitalization from the 1960s to the present.

Yet, popular sagas notwithstanding, money does not produce money, and there is much more behind these arrangements than Lloyds's conviviality or Jan and Leendert's acumen. The accumulation of wealth requires human labor and usually not the labor of the wealthiest. To be sure, capitalists and financiers alike always take the risk of investment, but in this case the risk was minimal. It rested on the conviction of Geest Industries' directors that the fruits of the peasants' labor could be sold at a substantial profit for a period long enough to justify major investments, a conviction obviously shared by Lloyds and the other moneylenders. Those Dutch and British financiers contributed to Geest's capitalization only because they knew, within the accepted margins of error, that they would be able to cut their slices of the cake. And indeed, through interest payments on those loans, the financiers also benefited from the labor of the Caribbean peasants.

Yet it is part of the logic of capital accumulation that growth calls for more growth. At some point during the second phase of Geest Industries, the group of relatives and associates who controlled the company also realized that the European market for bananas would not always expand at the fabulous rates of the early days. It became clear to them that somewhere down the line the group's profits from bananas would exceed the sums that it could reinvest in bananas. To sustain growth in turnover and profits, it was necessary to engage in new ventures. The interesting difference, in terms of financing, is the extent to which the banana activities supported the creation or acquisition of these enterprises. On 25 August 1972, the Geest brothers created Geest Holdings Limited. Ten days later, the new company acquired the whole of Geest Industries.

John signed that agreement in the name of Geest Industries. Leonard represented the new parent company.

The Tentacles of Geest Holdings

If the proof of the pudding is in the eating, there is no better proof of the profitability of Geest's involvement in bananas than the extent to which that involvement itself sustained the other ventures of the parent company it helped to create. When Leonard van Geest succeeded his brother to the chairmanship of both Geest Holdings and Geest Industries in 1975, he acknowledged that the organization had "grown from its very small beginnings in 1935 to become one of the largest groups of private companies in the United Kingdom" (Reports and Accounts, 3 January 1976, C.R.O. 1068048). He also reaffirmed the need to invest elsewhere the profits accumulated so far.

> Our bananas and produce activities form by far the biggest part of our Organisation's operations, but with growth prospects in these areas being limited, our policy so far as Geest Industries Limited and its subsidiaries is [*sic*] concerned is to consolidate our banana and produce interests and to diversify into new business areas in which our distribution expertise and capability can be used to good effect. (Reports and Accounts, 3 January 1976, C.R.O. 1068048)

The diversification formula was two-pronged. First, it implied an expansion toward the marketing of a wider range of agricultural or food products, typified by the acquisition of Hortico International, one of Geest's most important competitors in the mail order bulb and nursery stock business, and the acquisition of Oval Eggs, a distributor of agricultural by-products. Second, within the larger corporate structure of the parent company, Geest Holdings Limited, the formula rested on the implicit wager that profits from Geest Industries as a whole would be substantial enough to subsidize, as it were, the other enterprises, especially during their first and most difficult years. In short, Geest's engagement in the banana industry was to finance diversification both within and outside agriculture.

That agenda, of course, was not presented in so many words; nor was it carried out so easily as it sounds. At any one time since the creation of Geest Holdings in 1972, its activities involved directly at least twenty affiliates. The full list of subsidiaries itself kept changing from both sales

Table 8.2. Geest Holdings Limited: Main Subsidiaries for the Years 1972–1973 and 1980

Original Companies, 1972–73	Companies Added between 1973 and 1980
Great Britain	
Geest Industries Ltd.[a]	Cambridge Computer Services Ltd.
Francis Nicholls Ltd.[a]	Celtic Catering and Marine Supplies Ltd.
W. E. Anderson Ltd.	G. H. Cooper Shipping & Supply
Eastern Computer Services Ltd.	Geest Horticultural Group Ltd.
Europa Horticultural Prod. Ltd.	Geest Mini Computer Systems Ltd.
Friendship Travel Centers Ltd.	Geest Motor Services Ltd.
Geest Transportation Ltd.	G. & Y. Cargo Ltd.
W. Groom Ltd.	Hortico International Ltd.
C. W. Lawrance Ltd.	Oval Eggs Ltd.
Geo. Massey & Sons Ltd.	Simons & Co. Ltd.
Southern Fruiterers Ltd.	Geest Industrial Group Ltd.
Spalding Bulb Co. Ltd.	K.U.S. Ltd.
Springwoods Ltd.	Midland Computing Center Ltd.
Stassen Ltd.	
Tomlin Brothers Ltd.	
West and Blake (Southend) Ltd.	
J. T. White & Sons Ltd.	
Saint Lucia	
Geest Industries (West Indies) Ltd.[a]	Geest Industries (Development) Ltd.
Geest Industries (Estates) Ltd.[a]	
Holland	
Hortico B.V.	
France	
Hortico S.A.	

[a] Companies that remained important throughout the period.
Sources: Geest Holdings Limited, Consolidated Accounts, 1972–80; Chairman's Statements, 1972–80; C.R.O. 1068048.

Table 8.3. Major Branches and Activities of Geest Holdings

Holdings	**Activities**
Geest Industries	Bananas, Produce
Geest Associates	Management services, computers
Geest Industrial Group	Agricultural equipment
Geest Horticultural Group	Horticulture

Source: Geest Holdings Limited, Reports of Director and Chairman's Statements, 1977–80; C.R.O. 1068048.

and acquisitions, and the relevance of the small companies fluctuated through the years.[5] Table 8.2 lists only the companies that most affected the returns of Geest Holdings during 1972 and 1980, the first and last year for which complete data were available at the time of my fieldwork. The differences between those two years testify to the continuing complexity of the enterprise.[6]

It is necessary to go beyond the complexity of Geest's corporate structure in order to underline the vital role of the banana activities in the rise and growth of the conglomerate. Table 8.3, a simplified sketch of Geest Holdings' organization, presents the conglomerate in terms of sectors of activities rather than in terms of registered companies. Based on the chairman's statements and directors' reports for Geest Holdings and its major branches, the table emphasizes four types of activities that Geest-controlled companies engaged in during the 1970s:

1. the production and distribution of bananas and produce mainly through Geest Industries and its subsidiaries;
2. the provision of management services and supplies, mainly through Geest Associates and its subsidiaries;
3. the production and distribution of agricultural leisure products, mainly through the Geest Horticultural Group; and
4. the production and distribution of light agricultural machinery through the Geest Industrial Group.[7]

None of these activities predates Geest's involvement in bananas except the production and distribution of agricultural bulbs by the original Geest Horticultural Products of 1935, the forerunner of Geest Industries. The groups themselves took shape only after the formation of Geest Holdings.[8]

Table 8.4. Geest Holdings Limited: Profits (or Losses) by Sector or Activity, 1976–1980 (in millions of sterling pounds)

	1976	1977	1978	1979	1980
Bananas & produce	.40	1.56	2.25	3.18	3.85
Engineering	.34	.25	(.25)	(.28)	(.09)
Computers	.21	.06	.07	.23	.27
Total[a]	1.10	1.95	2.11	3.18	4.20

[a]Total includes miscellaneous sectors.

Source: Geest Holdings Limited, Reports of Directors and Chairman's Statements, 1977–80; C.R.O. 1068048.

Second, and more important, despite this ongoing diversification, the bulk of the profits of the conglomerate still come from its banana activities. Table 8.4, based on the directors' reports for Geest Holdings, documents the share of the three main sectors (bananas and produce, light engineering, and computer services) in the total profits of the conglomerate from 1976 to 1980. It reveals a disproportionate contribution of the bananas and produce sector to the financial health of Geest Holdings. Despite meager returns for the year 1976, that sector provided almost 90 percent of the global profits accumulated during the five-year period, to wit: 11.2 million pounds of a 12.5 million total (Table 8.4). Since bananas constitute by far the most important commodity within the so-called bananas and produce sector, they remained the backbone of the Geest empire long after its diversification.[9]

My third and most important point about the growth of Geest Holdings has to do with the implications of the first two. Both the chronological development summarized above the relative importance of different types of activities within the conglomerate show that Geest's involvement in the Caribbean banana industry subsidized its growth and diversification in England. The support came to the subsidiaries in two ways: first, in the form of payments for services rendered by them to the branches involved in banana transportation and distribution; second, in the form of shared assets, or assets transferred within the conglomerate.

Interestingly, the organization of the data available in the public records does not allow the quantification of those two forms of support. Payments for services rendered by fellow subsidiaries are not itemized in the annual reports of the diverse affiliates, nor do they enter in Geest Holdings' final turnover figures. Thus, for instance, the WINBAN report states laconically that the computer arm of the Geest empire "provides computer services to the Geest Organisation (*we understand*) at a competitive price." (WINBAN 1980: 13; emphasis added) Yet no one outside of Geest's senior management can know, for sure, the exact amount of the profits the computer branches gain from banana-related activities. Likewise, the United Kingdom expenses deducted from the banana prices include the cost of handling equipment obtained from the Geest Industrial Group (WINBAN 1980).

Still, we need not know the exact figures involved in order to expose the mechanism at work here. In light of the history of these companies, in light of their relative importance within the organization, we can conclude that they perform those services at a profit.[10] And we know already that the costs of such services are deducted from the Green Market Price and passed to the Caribbean associations which, in turn, pass them on to the peasants. The conclusion is unavoidable: the labor of the Caribbean peasants subsidized, in a measure (yet) unquantifiable, the growth of the various branches of the Geest empire which performed services deducted from the Green Market Price.

The contribution of Caribbean peasants to Geest Holdings' growth and diversification in the form of direct and indirect transfer of assets between companies within the conglomerate is no less certain. Yet this form of subsidy is also impossible to quantify, given the organization of the available data. The annual reports of each subsidiary note the aggregate cash value of assets received or disposed of, but give neither the sources nor the targets of these transfers.[11] The prior processing of the data makes it impossible to determine the net cash value of the transfers over time, let alone the exact contribution of any single subsidiary to the aggregate sums transferred to another subsidiary by the holding company. Still, as soon as one puts aside the quest for an exact quantification and uses the evidence to find out which sectors benefited from these transfers, it appears clearly that the group companies that headed the nonbanana sectors benefited disproportionately from transfers of assets within the conglomerate.

The Geest Horticultural Group (the company that headed Geest's horticultural sector) clearly drew more out of the conglomerate than it returned. Its total profits during its first seven years of operation were about a half million pounds, a meager figure, indeed, when compared with Geest Industries' yearly average of 1.5 million pounds of profit for the same period. At the same time, the group maintained huge debts to the holding company or to other fellow subsidiaries amounting to almost two million pounds in 1978. Clearly then, Geest's horticultural ventures were dependent upon assets accumulated elsewhere within the conglomerate even after the purchase of Hortico International.

Similarly, the accounts of Geest Associates reveal that the conglomerate artificially sustained another important nonbanana sector that would not have survived on its own. Geest Associates never became a viable subgroup within its first nine years of activity, even though some of its own subsidiaries performed quite well. In 1974 (two years after its creation), Geest Associates registered a dismal profit of 762 pounds after taxation. The situation worsened in 1976, and Geest Associates, as a group, registered a loss of 57,212 pounds before taxation. Yet it was still able to expand and acquire Cambridge Computer Services in 1977, a major step in its attempt to "meet the rapidly increasing demand for complete mini-computer systems" (Chairman's Statement, 1977, C.R.O. 1068048). The ability to expand despite the losses rested undoubtedly on the fact that, in 1976, the bulk of the group's current liabilities (939,537 of 1.2 million pounds) was in the form of debts to the holding company or other subsidiaries within the conglomerate. In 1977, losses grew to 113,894 pounds, current liabilities amounted to 794,601 pounds, 502,965 of which were due to other companies within the group (Geest Associates, Statements of Accounts and Directors' Reports, 1976–77; C.R.O. 1060806).

Likewise, the severe recession that hit the market for agricultural equipment in the mid-1970s struck a major blow to the pretensions of the newly created Geest Industrial Group. The best year during that decade was 1974, when profits reached 201,572 pounds. But in that same year, current liabilities exceeded current assets by 59,188 pounds. The bulk of those liabilities (1,202,566 out of 1,795,840 pounds) was in the form of debts to other branches within the conglomerate, in addition to amounts received as group relief (Geest Industrial Group, Statements of Accounts and Directors' Reports, 1971–80; C.R.O. 257425). Yet senior management, convinced that it would survive the down trends, held onto the agricultural engineering sector. It survived long enough indeed to secure advantageous contracts for trailers for Tanzania and disk harrows for Turkey in 1979.

Thus all the three second-level companies that headed the three major nonbanana sectors were kept alive until at least the late 1970s by assets transferred from the conglomerate. Since the conglomerate itself comprises only four major sectors, it does not take much mathematics to conclude that the bulk of the net assets transferred came from the bananas and produce sector. Hence, not only can one suggest that Geest relied on bananas to finance its initial steps toward diversification, but one can also conclude that profits from the banana operations sustained the three other groups during almost a decade. Peasants from Saint Lucia, Saint Vincent, Grenada, and Dominica can be said to have subsidized Geest's move into agricultural engineering and computer services. Their labor, in part, financed the acquisition of Cambridge Computers and the sales of machinery to Turkey and Tanzania. If the final measure of the profitability of an enterprise is in what it allows its owners to do, Geest's co-optation of the peasant labor process in the Caribbean revealed itself to be quite profitable, indeed, on the world scale.

Conclusion

The concept of labor process pertains to production only in the limited sense of the transformation of nature that occurs within the observable boundaries of specific units: farms, factories, plantations, and so on. But the struggles that social agents engage in to achieve control over that process occur both within and outside those boundaries, and their results vary accordingly. Production implies much more than work activities: it entails a hierarchical set of social and economic relations that provide the context and shape the finality of work. Thus, we should distinguish between the immediate control of the labor process and the general control of production. The first is confined to the units of production and results mainly from the struggles that occur there, what Burawoy (1984) has called the "politics of production." The second does not necessarily derive from struggles within the units but shapes decisively the results of those struggles.

The general control of production entails an indirect control of the labor process regardless of the immediate politics of production. The social agents who share or contribute to that type of control need not set foot within a farm, a plantation, or a factory to exercise their domination. They need not own the units as such: they may be bureaucrats, financiers, merchants, or entrepreneurs residing in faraway lands. The key to their power resides in their ability to influence the mechanisms through which a particular type of work (and the units within which it is carried on) is integrated within the general process of production. Though those integrative mechanisms are economic, the means by which they are imposed are not exclusively so. In fact, they are quite often political in the strictest sense, and entail legalistic maneuvering as well as military maneuvers. The state enters here with its monopoly on violence, its ability to tax citizens differently, its power to allocate expenditures according to the priorities of those who control it. And at the periphery of the world economy, colonialism and neocolonialism provide the context within which the politics of the state take place.

Within that analytical framework, the current coexistence of the Dominican peasantry and world capitalism appears as the result of a dual evolution. On the one hand, Dominican cultivators were largely victorious in their struggle to control the units of production by imposing the labor process that best encapsulates that control. They gnawed at the plantation regimen with such conviction and persistence that planters, merchants, and bureaucrats all admitted defeat on those grounds. On the other hand, local and metropolitan bureaucrats guided the integration of the peasant labor process imposed by the cultivators into a national and worldwide process of valorization.

That integration itself does not devalue the concrete and historic gains achieved by the peasantry: cultivators who remember the days of the lime plantations have no second thought on that point. But the particular form of that integration into the world economy does ensure that the fruits of the labor performed within the peasant units ultimately benefit capitalists based in the metropolis. It also ensures a higher cost of reproduction for the peasantry itself, paid in the labor embodied in the bananas and in the cash it spends for the commodities that it does not produce. Thus, as it stands, the integration of the peasant labor process into the worldwide process of valorization generates an inherent inequality. That inequality expresses itself in the capitalists' power to impose the conditions under which the peasants can exercise their control of the labor process, but it is also revealed, more crudely perhaps, in the sheer magnitude of the profits they accumulate.

PART III

THE VILLAGE

CHAPTER 9

Wesley Ville La Soye

Most people don't know that: there was never a Wesley.
—Fred Henry, native village historian; interview with the author, 1981

Lasoye should be specially represented . . . on the grounds of having peculiarities special to itself, which are as follows: soil, product, language, custom, habits and religion.
—Petition of the inhabitants of Wesley, 13 December 1893

Once revealed, the harsh realities of neocolonialism take such grand dimensions that little else seems to matter. Is there a relevance to ethnography?

Many anthropologists choose to avoid this question, and the reality behind it. After all, the more powerless their subjects, the more their studies could be taxed as irrelevant. Thus a number of ethnographers, worried at losing their own importance, bury themselves in their traditional descriptions, taking the position of the mole, that what they do not see does not exist. Yet, as they often return to the "field," they are forced to admit with every trip that the peoples whom they once saw as culturally untamed have become more like them, more "Western," more "modern," and usually much poorer.

The growing attention to matters of world political economy within anthropology has not yet reconciled the relevance of microlevel descriptions with the reality of international domination. In many studies couched in terms of political economy, especially those with a Marxist bent, Third World peoples appear doomed or dumb in spite of the undying sympathy of the authors and their wishful visions of a revolutionary future. In the meantime, ethnography remains entrenched in its dilemma, with moles and visionaries unaware of the assumptions they share about both the nature of the world and the nature of knowledge (Trouillot 1985b). And domination goes on its peaceful way, somewhere, out there.

Yet the question that ethnography must face is quite simple even though its answers are not: Is there life beyond neocolonialism? Can we make sense of what dominated peoples say and do in their daily lives without keeping silent about their forced integration in the international order and yet without reducing their lives to the fact of that integration? Somehow, the knowledge that Geest's payroll of nineteen million pounds sterling was, in 1979, six times more than the total revenues of the government of Dominica is not enough to make us understand the peasants of Dominica. Even our discovery of the mechanisms by which this imbalance is achieved (chapters 7 and 8) enlightened only one aspect of those peasants' reality. What else is there to know? Is there more to the existence of Dominican peasants than their subordination to Geest Holdings? Or rather, given the importance of that dependence, is there anything else that matters?

The question is necessarily political and some of its ramifications lead far beyond the bounds of academic debates. But it is also both an epistemological and a methodological issue. It has to do with our perceptions of what constitutes knowledge about the social world, the procedures we use to produce that knowledge, and the relationships we want or fail to recognize between our changing knowledge of that world and its ongoing transformations. My own position is one of intellectual modesty. I readily concede that no single viewpoint can fully account for all aspects of social reality, in part because I believe that a discourse can never reach the limits of the practice of which it speaks. Thus I assume that ethnography, as a specific discourse, has different limitations than both history and political economy. I also assume that it has different truths to reveal.

However, the nature of the knowledge that ethnography should reveal is still undefined. This imprecision stems, in part, from the very richness of human life observed on the ground. Further, ethnography has traditionally portrayed itself as a discourse that does not need definite methodological or empirical boundaries.

Levels and Units Revisited

Thirty years ago, anthropologist Raymond Firth (1961 [1957]), who had, himself, contributed greatly to setting the standards of modern ethnography in his *We, the Tikopia* (Firth 1936), gently reminded other anthropologists that the actual isolation of their empirical objects of study was only "relative." Since then, it has become a cliché to repeat that anthropologists traditionally sundered their "villages," or "communities" from the wider networks of which they were parts. Yet a cursory appraisal of the other disciplines that deal with humankind suggests that the neglect of wider networks was not the posture of anthropology alone. Polar oppositions in the social sciences and the humanities (literate/illiterate, developed/underdeveloped, urban/rural, modern/backward, historic/prehistoric) all connote isolations that blur not only the extent but also the nature of the encounter between the West and the rest of humankind. All suggest dichotomies of one sort or another, clear-cut empirical boundaries that reproduce themselves within and across nations.

Anthropology helped to legitimize most of those dichotomies, but it did not create them all. In fact, as far as peasant studies are concerned, anthropologists inherited the rural/urban distinction and only later did some of them become its ardent proponents (Benet 1963; Newby 1978; S. Silverman 1979). More important, the crucial matter of the methodological underpinnings behind the definition of any unit of analysis remains controversial in most disciplines. The issue even gains in importance as specialized practitioners seek to integrate in their research the results achieved in other disciplines (LeRoy Ladurie 1969; Braudel 1967–79; Wallerstein 1974–80; Tilly 1981; Wolf 1982).

But anthropology has not merely been a scapegoat. First, it reproduced in extreme forms, and, at times, enhanced under diverse guises, many functionalist or structuralist assumptions common to the social sciences (Murphy 1971). Second, anthropology complicated further the proper identification of the units of social analysis by its refusal to assess the epistemological roots of ethnography. Ethnography can rightly be considered as anthropology's most powerful addition to the pool of techniques used in the social sciences, a vital tool of microlevel analyses. Yet ethnography evolved and spread as a recognized practice two steps ahead, so to speak, of its methodological evaluation (Harris 1968; Malinowski 1967; Webster 1983; Trouillot 1985b). In other words, its practical contribution outdistanced its "capture" as an "appropriate domain" within academic discourse (Thornton 1983).

In such a discursive context, practitioners came to see what I call the "ethnographic trilogy" (one observer, one time, one place) as a methodological necessity, with careers hanging upon the proper performance of this ritual. The practical restrictions suffered by ethnographers at the beginning of the century were forgotten, and fieldwork material often came to exclude, as if by principle, most empirical data out of the immediate reach of a single observer. Thus, more perhaps than other disciplines, anthropology blurred the necessary distinction between research technique and methodology (Schaff 1976), and took its units of analysis for granted.[1]

This methodological disarray produced at least two unfortunate results. First, it led to the wrong emphasis about the relevance of ethnography as a research technique: it related that relevance to the small size of the empirical field rather than to a distinct viewpoint, thus compounding the confusion between microlevel and small scale. Yet, if the microlevel is the one at which individuals with their histories and their historical perceptions are best perceived, ethnography remains an essential part of the discursive tradition that deals effectively with that level.

Second, and paradoxically, despite the emphasis on the small size of the empirical field, little effort was made to set precise boundaries on methodological grounds. Boundaries usually fell wherever they seemed most obvious to the observer.[2] Not surprisingly, villages and communities emerged from this exercise as unequivocal units of analysis. As prominent an anthropologist as Robert Redfield could write: "The small community is another of these prevailing and conspicuous forms in which humanity obviously comes to our notice"; one that can be known "directly, and even without much effort to analyze or classify" (Redfield 1960: 1, 157).

We now know better, of course. A world-historical perspective teaches us that empires, countries, regions, are fabrications of a kind, that communities are created just like company or university towns even though through different processes. The ethnographic discourse must reflect that historical process: it needs to pay more attention to the past and present transformations that continue to shape the reality of the population clusters we often take for obvious and fixed entities.

Part 3 of this book deals primarily with what seems to be an obvious entity: the village of Wesley. Its overarching argument is that Wesley is multidimensional, socially and spatially, in part because it has been shaped substantially by its integration in the nation and in the world. To be sure, the entire Dominican totality must be understood in a world-historical perspective. However, the description of the enclaves in chapter 2 already indicated that the whole differs from the sum of the parts, and that the national impact of Dominica's integration was felt differently by various subgroups within the countryside. The in-depth observation of a single village allows us to explore the range of these variations.

Yet we cannot take that village as a given entity, despite its unique name, its "independent" Village Council, and its 2,800 inhabitants who clearly define themselves as "Wesley people." Rather, we will keep on redefining the entity itself, as the description goes along. Hence, history remains relevant within this ethnographic approach: Wesley had to *become* Wesley and its past transformations continue to contribute to its present identity. Political economy remains no less relevant: Wesley, like most Dominican villages, can be perceived as part of a particular enclave, identifiable in terms of the specific mechanisms that historically integrated its rural workers into the process of valorization (chapter 2). But here I will further insist that not only the boundaries of the enclave changed over time, but even the boundaries between the village and the enclave shifted and continue to shift.

This chapter summarizes the transformations that led to the nineteenth-century creation of the enclave of Saint Andrew South, and the concurrent emergence, within that enclave, of a residential unit referred to as Wesley, or Wesley Ville La Soye by many contemporaries. It emphasizes the sociocultural features that demarcated the area from the rest of Dominica and continue to bear on its present character: the return to the past provides the background against which the ethnography (chapters 10 and 11) projects Wesley as a nexus of ongoing transformations spurred by the encounter of local, national, and global trends. The village, so conceived, is not a microcosm of the society but a particular configuration in time and space of the processes that affect the nation. It is a "conjuncture" (Harriss 1982), an empirical moment in which those processes merge concretely within the daily existence of specific historical actors.

From La Soye to Wesley

The history of the villages that cling to the northeast coast of Dominica, from Anse du May to Marigot, overlaps only in part with that of the parish of Saint Andrew, of which they form the largest and most southern division. Saint Andrew South (sometimes referred to as the La Soye

District) is clearly distinguishable from the most northern part of the parish (see chapter 2). Its population clusters share a common history within the larger Dominican past and a common form of integration within the national economy.

Nowadays, the most salient marker of the Saint Andrew South enclave is the overwhelming presence of bananas. To be sure, bananas generally dominated the occupied part of the Dominican landscape. Yet a drive or a walk on the roads and tracks that skirt around the villages of Wesley, Marigot, or Woodford Hill suggests that this predominance may reach a peak in those areas despite the conspicuous presence of coconuts in many fields. After just a few days' observation, one is also struck by cultural differences: the La Soye District houses the largest number of Protestants in Dominica; and many of its inhabitants are native English speakers or bilingual speakers of English and an English-based Creole ("Kòkòy") notable in Woodford Hill, Wesley, and Marigot. Further observation reveals that the large volume of banana production is coupled in that enclave with considerable control of the labor process by the cultivators.[3] By and large, since the mid-1970s, Saint Andrew South has been, in Dominican terms, a cluster of "rich" villages, occupied by prosperous and independent peasants.

The independence of that peasantry is, in fact, as recent as the autonomy of the agglomerations. Every village of the enclave only recently exchanged its reliance on its neighbors for a more direct integration in the national economy. In that process, each gained or lost territory, social, and political or economic networks, and in redefining itself as a village, consequently modified the whole enclave. Moreover, the rise of these villages followed (or, at times, intersected) islandwide economic trends, themselves characterized by the rise and fall of particular export crops and of the work regimen through which those crops were produced. Thus, in many ways, the history of these villages is also the history of the estates that surrounded them, the history of the crops they produced, as well as the history of the peasantry's struggle to affect relations of production at the level that it best controls, that of the labor process. From 1749 to the present, the names La Soye, Lasoye, La Soie, or Lasoie have interchangeably been used to designate different empirical realities: a few square miles of coastal land, the southern part of the Saint Andrew Parish, the whole parish itself, the village of Wesley, or the village and the cultivated areas surrounding it. The ambiguity likely started with the formation of the colonial French militia when Dominica was divided into eight military districts whose boundaries the militia officers barely knew.

By then, a few Frenchmen had settled around a tiny head of land on the northeast coast, which they referred to as Pointe La Soye. So was created the Quartier de La Soye, a military and administrative entity with no specific empirical referent except a tiny stretch of almost useless coastal land. Significantly, only two assistant adjutants headed the La Soye militia; most other districts counted at least one captain, one lieutenant, and one sublieutenant (Boromé 1972b).

La Soye did not prosper much under French control. Or rather, Pointe La Soye itself did not, though northern Saint Andrew (the Peineville-Thibault-Vieille Case enclave described in chapter 2, then a part of the La Soye District) was, since the early eighteenth century, a significant producer of coffee and cocoa. In the meantime, an equally small number of French people had settled a few miles south of Pointe La Soye, around a river and a bay that the native Caribs used to call Pagua and that the new colonizers gallicized into Marigot. In 1765, two years after the British took official control of Dominica, Governor Robert Melville issued from Grenada a proclamation aimed at changing place names in Dominica, Saint Vincent, Grenada, and Tobago. The Quartier de La Soye was renamed Saint Andrew Parish. Most of the British names, except those given to the parishes, did not survive. Saint Andrew South itself was still referred to as the Quartier de La Soye well into the nineteenth century.

The survival of the French name stems in part from the lack of interest of the earlier British settlers in that isolated region; they preferred the more accessible parishes on the leeward coast. A general account of Saint Andrew South for the year 1821 lists twenty-three slave owners, only seven of whom had more than ten slaves (Table 9.1). Names and patronymics on the list suggest that the enclave did not witness the concentration of French-owned coffee estates, with ten to twenty slaves each, which characterized the northern part of Saint Andrew. Here, the dominance was British; the major crop, I suspect, sugar. But it was a dominance that rested mainly on the disproportionate size of three or four properties.[4] The predominance of planters of British origin and the large size of the labor force on a few major properties distinguished Saint Andrew South from the rest of the parish, and, perhaps, from the rest of Dominica. Further, these features reached their peak in the subarea delineated in the North by the Woodford Hill Estate and, in the South by the Melville Hall Estate. The emergence was then dual: the core plantation area that comprised the Woodford Hill, Eden, Londonderry, and Melville Hall estates—the area I call Plantation Wesley—started to be

Table 9.1. Slave Owning in Saint Andrew South in 1821

Owners	Number of Slaves	Owners	Number of Slaves
Aberdeen, Robert	68	Hughes & Casey	18
Burton, Joseph	11	Lowell, Langford	263
Burton, Rebecca	9	Melville, John M.	151
Burton, Monimia	6	Noble, Edward L.	3
Burton, Sarah	1	Powell, T., & Josias	79
Burton, Elisa	1	Sablone, Charlotte	8
Burton, William	5	Simpson, O., & children	10
Burton, Joseph	2	Trial, M.	3
Burton, R. & others	5	Warner, Major	197
Bedereaux, J., heirs	4	Waddington, Ann	2
Brumant, Jean C.	8	Waddington, heirs	3
Hughes, Michael	1		

Sources: *Dominica Almanac*, 1823, 1821 Census.

distinguishable from the enclave at the same time that the enclave was becoming distinguishable from the rest of Dominica.

Thenceforth, the disproportionate role of the large estates remained a constant in the history of the enclave, but until the 1860s each plantation more or less independently reached the outside world, and La Soye was then perceived primarily as an administrative (and ecologically isolated) subpart of the Saint Andrew Parish. Further homogenization occurred in the 1860s when most of its estates fell under the control of planter-attorney Charles Leathem. Though the different properties were worked as separate units, Leathem's control unified their integration in the national economy and their impact on the then emerging villages. And since his most important properties within Saint Andrew South were concentrated in Plantation Wesley, the impact of that area on the rest of the enclave grew accordingly.[5]

The Leathem era was a decade of land consolidation and high productivity in Saint Andrew, during which the estates gained land and reaffirmed their control of the cultivators. The impact of that decade remains crucial in defining both the enclave and Plantation Wesley. It is a sign of that impact that long after Leathem's death two or more of the estates surrounding Wesley would often be controlled by the same owner and most would produce the same crop. In fact, one can argue that Leathem lost power in Saint Andrew only because the forces that worked against the consolidation of the estates had received an invaluable push from outside the enclave: Leathem's final defeat in the 1865 election for the La Soye seat was orchestrated by his archenemy Charles Gordon Falconer, leader of the Mulatto Ascendancy. Leathem contested the qualifications of the victor, won the right to new elections, and lost again.[6]

Leathem's electoral defeat was possible in part because of outsiders' influence but in part also because of the rising yeomanry's access to alternative resources that could be used to challenge planter power in the La Soye District. Those resources were not, at first and primarily, of an economic nature. Rather, formal education constituted the most obvious asset of those who wanted to provide an alternative direction to the enclave. Indeed, by the middle of the nineteenth century, the La Soye District looked like a bastion of formal education in rural Dominica. Five years before Leathem lost his seat, one out of four school-age children in the area went to school, by far the highest ratio of enrollment in the Dominican countryside.

The key to this outstanding record of school attendance is rather simple: La Soye children went to school partly because they performed better. And they performed better essentially because they understood English (then and still the language of instruction) far better than most Dominicans. That peculiarity itself stems from La Soye's history which gives the enclave a unique cultural configuration within Dominican society. La Soye is an economic entity, but it is also a distinct subculture.

Wesleyan Wesley

Professional historians, linguists, and anthropologists have yet to explain the origins of the cultural traits that distinguish Saint Andrew South from the rest of Dominica, especially the extremely high number of Protestants and the equally high number of native English speakers. Most Dominicans are Catholics. Most rural dwellers speak and understand a French-based Creole (Lesser Antillean), despite their varying abilities to speak or understand English in prescribed circumstances. In Wesley, Marigot, and Woodford Hill, however, many villagers have no competence at all in the French-based Creole. Rather, some of the young adults and many of those over fifty speak an English-based Creole that they refer to as "Kòkòy," a language in its own terms, not spoken in the rest of the island. In Wesley itself, some of the elders (especially males over sixty-five) speak only the most basilectal forms of Kòkòy (forms farther away from standard English) though they usually understand simple sentences in English. Monolingual competence in basilectal Kòkòy is less characteristic of Woodford Hill and of Marigot. Likewise, the proportion of practicing Protestants declines in both Woodford Hill and Marigot, though it increases again in the more northern villages of Dos d'Ane and Anse du May. One suspects that the village of Wesley and the estates immediately surrounding it were the center from which English, Kòkòy, and Protestantism spread unevenly to the rest of the La Soye District.

Two historical versions account for the district's cultural traits. The first is implicit, uneven, and incomplete, but can be pieced together from official documents. It emphasizes the religious distinction of the area and records scholastic achievement; but here, language seems to follow religion, and the records, at least those I have consulted, do not deal with the question of the ultimate origins of these cultural traits.

The second version is that of oral history, and is much fuller and more explicit despite its variations. Its first undisputed fact is that of a specific La Soye-bound migration. When asked about the factors that explain the linguistic and religious originality of their area, most Wesley people immediately point out that their ancestors, in sharp contrast with other Dominican villagers, came from a neighboring, English-controlled island. The date of that migration, the exact sequence of events, the name of the island of origin, the social, cultural, or phenotypical features that distinguished this population from the rest of Dominica vary with the narrator. Yet more often than not, according to the oral tradition, the ancestors of Wesley's peasants were brought from Antigua by the (unidentified) owners of the Melville Hall Estate. They were primarily English or Kòkòy speakers, and transmitted their language or languages to their descendants.[7]

Oral and written traditions reveal different emphases. Wesley people emphasize a single migratory move and the linguistic differentiation it implied as the fundamental markers of their past. The written records I pieced together, on the other hand, gave early attention to religious differentiation. They emphasize linguistic distinctiveness as a later development closely linked to an exceptional advance in formal education, but they remain silent on the original migration itself.

I personally believe that oral history does a better job here than the written record. I agree with the emphasis on a discrete migration: there is no other way to explain the cultural originality. But the quantitative trends emphasized by the official record may help locate the move more precisely.[8] More likely than not, the English/Kòkòy-speaking immigrants were slaves of a Methodist persuasion who came to Dominica between 1787 and 1807.[9] In a report dated 1 October 1838, Capt. James B. Kingsbury, stipendiary magistrate for Saint Andrew, states: "In the Lasoye quarter of my district there is a commodious Wesleyan Chapel, always well attended by the labourers" (ZHC1/1266). And since at least 1848 a resident Wesleyan preacher was permanently based at La Soye.

The most important effect of the Wesleyan presence was its impact on the formal education of the villagers. The instruction was modest but for a long time it remained the folk's only alternative to illiteracy and their major means of consolidating the assets inherent in their greater familiarity with the English language. The Methodists' impact as educators boosted their prestige, and Methodism came to symbolize all the cultural pecularities of the area, even though the actual proportion of avowed Methodists declined. Oral history, then, quite rightly emphasizes language as the most important variable in the chain reaction: the students' linguistic ability led to the Methodists' success which, in turn, led to the association of the area with Methodism, even though the religious impact of Methodism itself declined.[10]

In 1859, that is, within the time span of the long decline of Methodism, the recently opened "Wesley Ville La Soye" Methodist school boasted the third largest enrollment of the island, with eighty-six pupils studying under the supervision of the Reverend O. P. Castor. In 1870, the Wesleyans opened their second school in the district on the Hampstead Estate, and five years later, they moved the older school farther south, to Melville Hall, thus closing in on the enclave from both extremities. Attendance rose in both institutions and, in the third quarter of the century, average attendance at Melville Hall was second only to the Roseau Central School for Boys *(Dominica Almanac*, 1861, 1862, 1864, 1875; C.O. 74/33).[11]

The 1878 opening of a Roman Catholic school by Father Brancherau may account for the decrease of Wesleyan worshipers in the district between 1871 and 1881. (All indications are that the number of Catholics grew significantly after 1878 until the mid-1950s.) Yet the alternative had come too late to diminish the Methodists' clout and the reputation of the Wesley Ville La Soye School. By 1875, the agglomeration located between the Melville Hall and Woodford Hill estates was already being referred to as the village of Wesley. In a report entered on 22 July 1875 in the Minutes of the Dominica House of Assembly, School Inspector Watt commented on the exceptional advances of the Wesleyan schools, including that of La Soye: "The *village of Wesley* and the Melville Hall estate contain a rising generation whose educational wants are supplied by the Lasoye school alone" (C.O. 74/33; emphasis added). In 1884, Provost Marshal Joseph Fadelle, who both as official interpreter and as inspector of the schools had monitored for years the linguistic and educational situation in the island, testified to the Royal Commission on Expenditures: "At the exception of the Lasoye district where the Protestant element preponderates, and where the school is a Wesleyan one, go to any plantation and count 50 labourers, men, women, and young boys and girls, at work in the field and factory, and there the great probability is that you will not find one that can read" (PP, 1884, vol. 46; C. 3840 2: 142). It is interesting that Fadelle speaks of a Protestant predominance. He had access to the figures that indicated the opposite: he helped to compile them. Besides being a school inspector, he had acted as registrar of the island. Yet for him, La Soye was Wesleyan. Wesleyans came to typify the agglomeration in the eyes of villagers and outsiders alike primarily because they provided a formal education that was seen to distinguish the enclave from the rest of Dominica. The combination of Methodist preeminence and widespread literacy, although strongly qualified in fact, came to symbolize the cultural identity of the enclave. Residents of the area delineated by the estates of Woodford Hill in the South, Melville Hall in the North, Eden in the East, and Londonderry in the West had been at the center of both the linguistic and the religious diffusion. They became the main proponents of the perception of the enclave as an English-speaking bastion of Methodism. As Wesley people, they epitomized the differences through which the whole La Soye District came to identify itself and, in so doing, they also consolidated their own identity.[12] Sometime in the 1860s, Pointe La Soye became Wesley, a village associated with fluency in English and high-level literacy despite the more complex reality and a village associated with Methodism, a generation after the majority of its population had stopped being Wesleyan.[13]

The Emergence of the First Yeomanry

The death of "Sugar King" Charles Leathem on 8 August 1867 precipitated a decline in the fortunes of the estates that surrounded the rising village of Wesley: Melville Hall, Eden, Londonderry, and Woodford Hill. The last three properties, directly controlled by Leathem, suffered the most.[14] Three major units then totaling a nominal acreage in excess of three thousand acres, and representing more than half of the plantation lands of Dominica's most viable sugar district, suddenly fell into near total neglect. Not surprisingly, the relative independence of the residential agglomeration that they surrounded increased. The residents strengthened their sense of belonging to a unit no longer an appendage of the plantation lands in part because of the cultural developments described earlier.

By 1891, the population of Wesley had grown in excess of 450 residents. In contrast, the total population of the two estates immediately surrounding the village (Eden and Londonderry) had declined to 52 residents, not all of whom were laborers. Woodford Hill Estate (northwest of Eden) and Melville Hall (south of Londonderry), in turn counted together 257 residents (Table 9.2).[15] By 1893, when Special Commissioner Robert Hamilton picked Wesley as one of the eight centers at which he held hearings on the general conditions of Dominica, a discrete community had emerged among the ashes of Plantation Wesley. A new social force had affirmed its rights: a yeomanry strongly rooted in the peasant

Table 9.2. Population and Houses of the Saint Andrew South Estates, 1891

	Families			Number of	Population by Sex		
Estates	**4R**[a]	**5R**[b]	**Total**	**Houses**	**M**	**F**	**Total**
Blenheim	89	4	19	19	44	49	93
Eden	35	–	12	12	7	18	35
Hampstead	203	10	42	44	110	103	213
Hatton Garden	18	–	6	6	11	7	18
Hodges	14	–	2	1	9	5	14
Londonderry	12	5	4	4	9	8	17
Marigot	184	–	46	46	77	107	184
Melville Hall	99	8	30	30	51	56	107
Moore Park	111	–	22	22	49	62	111
Woodford Hill	150	–	50	50	76	74	150

[a] 4R = number of persons living in houses with four rooms or less.
[b] 5R = number of persons living in houses with five rooms or more.
Source: 1891 Census.

labor process yet quite anxious to participate in the national economy on terms it meant to dictate.

The petitions, letters, memoranda, and oral testimonies volunteered to Hamilton (1894: 39–40, 93–7) at the Wesley Dispensary on 13 December 1893 flesh out the changes that occurred in Saint Andrew after the 1870s. First the list of witnesses documents the visibility of a small but growing yeomanry. Only two planters testified in person, compared to five small holders.[16] At the very least, some forty small proprietors directly contributed to Hamilton's inquiry through their endorsements of diverse documents. Since the participants were all adult males, and since the vast majority of Wesley's population was composed of children, it is likely that the small proprietors represented a substantial proportion of the adult population.[17]

More important than numbers at the time of Hamilton's visit were the signs of exceptional vitality of the La Soye yeomanry. Testimonies and memoranda document the multiplicity of its endeavors. Residents had become accustomed to a minimum cash flow during the Leathem era, and they may have felt the need to implement new strategies to procure similar amounts after the decline of the plantation labor process. The grievances and claims presented by the peasants were collective demands, substantiated by typical cases, rather than individual complaints. They particularly show the peasantry's collective awareness of the imbalances inherent in the taxation system erected in the 1850s, described in chapter 3.[18]

The small proprietors did not limit themselves to such issues as taxes, government inverventions, and regulations about which they felt compelled to react. They also emphasized formal education, internal transport and communication, centralized sugarcane processing, and electoral representativity, matters that reveal a systematic identification of the mechanisms necessary to their continuing social and economic rise. Such positive projections countervene the ideological limitations that moral economists tend to impose on the yeomanry whom they fossilize as an essentially reactive force (e.g., Scott 1976). In 1893, the Wesley peasantry was not simply reacting: its grievances and claims show the small proprietors turned to the future rather than the past. Gone were the days of the "sugar kings"; and the new planters who moved in the area, James Colin McIntyre (of Hampstead) or William Davies (of Melville Hall), never hoped to exert the social domination that characterized a John Melville, a Charles Leathem, or a William McIntyre before them. These were, simply, different times.

Facing the Crisis

Though the days of sugar kings were gone, the La Soye yeomanry did not immediately achieve its goal of sharing the export market with the planters. As mentioned before, its own rise was partly due to the decline of sugarcane. Yet sugarcane itself was replaced by limes, and the transition did not exactly benefit the yeomanry. First, it occurred slowly. Second, the commercial production of the new crop required technical and economic assets far beyond the reach of most Dominican peasants. The very fact that lime trees took about seven years to bear was enough to discourage most small proprietors. Hence the stronger the yeomanry in a particular area, the more it was hit by the transition. Boundaries within enclaves shifted accordingly.

The postsugar stagnation and the rise of limes to preeminence among the national exports continued to differentiate the Wesley area from the rest of Saint Andrew South. By 1891 the center of export-oriented production in southern Saint Andrew was shifting to the north-central area that comprises the villages of Bense, Anse du May, Dos d'Ane, and the Blenheim, Moore Park, and Hampstead estates. The population of those three estates largely surpassed that of the units immediately surrounding Wesley (Londonderry and Eden), and even Woodford Hill and Melville Hall did not match Hampstead's 213 residents (Table 9.2). Banking on this labor force, planter James Colin McIntyre turned the Hampstead area into a prime supplier for the international firms that established large-scale lime production and export in Dominica at the turn of the century (Rowntree & Company, L. Rose & Company). The northern part of La Soye was drawn increasingly toward Portsmouth where L. Rose owned the lime-producing Picard Estate. To this date, the old Saint Andrew South remains divided between the Wesley-Woodford Hill-Marigot area and the Blenheim, Moore Park, Hampstead area, which still leans toward Portsmouth despite the strong similarities that tie it to the enclave.

In the 1880s, as Hampstead, Blenheim, and Moore Park started on the particular course that turned them into a citrus-dominated area until at least the 1960s, Marigot and Wesley fell under the dominance of mulatto planter and politician William Davies, Jr.[19] Davies was one of the few investors in Dominica to admit the rise of the yeomanry and face the consequences of that acceptance. In political terms, this recognition implied the need to court a larger and more independent electorate. In economic terms, it meant a symbiosis of villages and estates in which the villages would function as permanent sources of occasional labor to agro-industrial units relying increasingly on fixed capital.[20]

Davies's eventual failure was due, in part, to the speed at which he moved, his fascination with sugar, and a lack of money capital resulting from his compulsion to invest too much too soon. One suspects, though, that his political opponents capitalized on Davies's well-known arrogance. First, they successfully blocked two of his projects: the construction of improved shipping facilities at Marigot and, especially, the building of a railroad which was to cut diagonally across Dominica and link La Soye to the leeward side (C.O. 152/200; C.O. 152/213). That defeat, in turn, limited the political returns from Davies's contributions to the infrastructure of the district, and the mulattoes lost the legislative seat for Saint Andrew South.[21] The political center of La Soye shifted from the Wesley area to the north-central part of the enclave, furthering the differentiation noted earlier.

Davies did not fail in all of his ventures, and his modest successes reshaped boundaries within the enclave almost as much as his defeats. Though his grandiose plans to link the whole of La Soye to the rest of Dominica fell through, he managed to increase substantially contacts between his own estate of Melville Hall and the capital town of Roseau. As a result, two distinct trends set in. On the one hand, the Marigot-Wesley-Woodford Hill area as a whole became increasingly differentiated from Blenheim-Moore Park and Hampstead. On the other hand, within the first group, Melville Hall and Marigot were being drawn increasingly toward Roseau in a manner independent from Wesley and Woodford Hill. In short, not two, but three, recognizable subareas started to emerge within La Soye, though the one that comprised Wesley itself resulted largely from the increasing differentiation of the two others between which it fell.[22] The southern tip of La Soye experienced a semblance of revitalization whereas Eden and Londonderry withered.[23]

In the early 1900s, a group of British newcomers (mostly retired officers) tried to revitalize Plantation Wesley. Together, they held a total of 2,750 acres left from the disintegration and reconstitution of Eden, Londonderry, and Woodford Hill. Yet the confidential survey of G. A. Jones (MS, 1916), written in the aftermath of the hurricane that cost Davies's life, and the more general report of Watkin (1924) suggest that their success was quite modest. Both productivity and actual acreage under cultivation remained low, especially if compared to the more northern estates of La Soye like Blenheim or Hampstead (Table 9.3).

Table 9.3. Acreage and Lime Production of the Estates in Saint Andrew South, 1916

Estate	Total Acreage	Acres in Limes	Lime Production (in Barrels)
Woodford Hill	1,123		
Eden	525	150	10,000
Londonderry	1,098		
Melville Hall	1,383	40	5,000
Hatton Garden	300	50	4,000
Concord	253	—	Less than 1,000
Blenheim	1,151	70	10,000
Hampstead	697	—	10,000

Sources: G. Jones 1916 (MS); Watkins 1924.

Thus, Plantation Wesley experienced the postsugar crisis more dramatically than the rest of the La Soye enclave. Its distinctiveness, which had reached its peaks in the Leathem days, resurfaced, by default as it were, during the 1890–1940 crisis, not so much because of its own internal development but because of the divergent evolution of the southern and northern thirds of the district between which it fell. It remained for a long time the most isolated part of the La Soye Quarter. Whereas limes replaced sugar in the northern estates, whereas limes and coconuts shared preeminence in the more southern units, they never really filled the void left by King Sugar in the central Wesley area. Partly because of that very weakness, banana production was to find one of its most fertile niches in Wesley.

The Formation of the Banana Belt

Indeed, this conjunction of factors may not explain Foley and Band's personal decision to purchase Woodford Hill and establish there the first banana estate of Dominica, but it does suggest that both the speed and the modality of the rise of bananas to preeminence were strongly influenced by the character of the Wesley area. In fact, that third of the La Soye District had an impact not only on the whole enclave but ultimately on the national economy, confirming, once more, the necessity of including diverse layers of "local response" (Mintz 1977; Trouillot 1982) in analyses otherwise sensitive to world historical forces.

First, the pronounced weakness of limes in that part of the enclave explains, in part, the willingness of the owners whose estates bordered on Woodford Hill to follow the steps of Foley and Band and allow or encourage banana production on their own estates. Second, the owners of both Londonderry and Eden were themselves newcomers who, like Foley and Band, had bought from Mrs. Violet Stebbings, the widow of the last of the British officers who had succeeded themselves in the area. Third, the relationship between estate and village (redefined since Davies's days) and the limited yet noticeable impact of coconut production meant that the owners could carry the experiment with little or no risk. Informants confirm that bananas were first planted by sharecroppers on uncultivated parts of the estates (often cleared by the tenants) in a pattern reminiscent of Naftel's description of Davies's Melville Hall. As the owners' newly planted coconuts matured around the bananas, tenants were quickly evicted. The coconuts themselves required little labor and wage workers were used essentially to weed once in a great while the fields of mature coconuts. Most often, underpaid children and women picked the fallen fruits, and a few laborers worked in the "copra house."

The production of bananas on a sharecropping basis did not disappear completely around Wesley until the late 1970s. On the other hand, it never gained a strong foothold either, even in the early days, in part because of the estate owners' greater interest in coconut production. But that interest itself was due to the planters' inability to control labor. The villagers had no incentive to return to the sharecropping system. Prior to bananas, they had sold their export-oriented commodities to estate owners primarily for two reasons. First, both sugarcane and limes required postharvest processing that they could not carry out. Second, the estate owners had exclusive links to the merchant houses and greater access to the means of transportation. Thus, even an independent producer often had no choice but to bring his cane, his citruses, or even his cocoa to an estate owner.

The vanilla interlude itself did not improve significantly the peasants' position. It provided them with a cash crop in which the estate owners were not interested, but which the peasants themselves could not easily channel outside the area. Vanilla was planted primarily on mountainous Crown lands, and the producers did not have to share their harvest with an owner. However, "green" vanilla was not very profitable, and vanilla curing could take up to three or four months. Further, vanilla, like cocoa, was bought primarily by exporters based in town, and peasants had to devise the means of transportation.

Bananas suddenly removed all these obstacles. First, individual banana producers could initially sell their fruits in the very same condition and on the very same day they were harvested, simply wrapping them in their very leaves or, later, in foam pads provided by the association. Peasants paid transportation fees to Portsmouth (twelve cents a bunch in the early days), but since they were all cutting on the same day, access to a vehicle was fairly guaranteed. (The association itself made sure that enough trucks covered the area.) More important, the fruits were delivered to the representatives of a national body which did not care to determine the actual property from which the bananas came.

These factors were pivotal in the estate owners' decision to decrease the acreage of estate land sharecropped in bananas. In no way could they control the exact quantity harvested and determine their share (usually a third) with precision: the pace of the cutting itself was too fast, the number of tenants and the total number of bunches too great. Further, they could not enforce their rights on the product as easily as they could when the harvest (sugarcane, or limes) was delivered directly to them. Disgruntled, estate owners returned to coconuts, relying increasingly on the scheme I described earlier: renting the land at a nominal fee (simply to maintain their legal right of ownership), but intercropping their coconuts with the bananas so as to benefit from the labor and the inputs of the tenants.

Wesley people were aware of the rationale behind the scheme, and those who still worked on parts of Londonderry or Eden at the time of my fieldwork clearly attributed it to the "wicked" ways of the owners. Yet many tenants of the 1950s and '60s saw the arrangement as a chance for a change. Labor was the factor that they best controlled, and they exercised full right on its product for an undetermined period of time. The challenge was to increase labor to such an extent that however short the time they occupied a plot, they would benefit enough from it to make it worth their while. Many saw this challenge as a race between human labor and nature itself. The more they could produce and sell acceptable bananas before the natural growth of the coconuts evicted them from a particular plot within the estate, the sooner they could accumulate enough cash to buy their own land. They welcomed the challenge, moving from one part of Eden to the next, from Eden to Londonderry, saving two crops, losing the next, one eye always on the coconuts. The most audacious squatted on Crown lands in the mountains, which they later purchased from the government. Many supplemented their income with wages from Melville Hall and Woodford Hill where they learned improved techniques which they transmitted to their kin. As years went by, they discovered that the race was longer than most anticipated: estate owners "gave them notice," prices fell unexpectedly, hurricanes and diseases destroyed their plants. Some found out, to their surprise, that their course was not against nature alone. Yet they held on. By the time my fieldwork started, in 1979, all signs indicated that they were winning the race.

CHAPTER 10

"Neither Here nor There": The Ethnography of Mediation

Houses constructed of old Coca-Cola signs, a cuisine littered with canned corned beef and imported Spanish olives, ritual shot through with the cross and the palm leaf, languages seemingly pasted together with "ungrammatical" Indo-European usages, all observed within the reach of radio and television—these are not the things anthropologists' dreams are made of.
—Sidney W. Mintz, Foreword, *Afro-American Anthropology*

I never knew there is a Coke in these parts.
—Ama Tata Aidoo, *Dilemma of a Ghost*

Claude Lévi-Strauss wrote in his influential *Structural Anthropology* (1963: 285): "Ethnography and history differ from social anthropology and sociology, inasmuch as the former two aim at gathering data, while the latter two deal with models constructed from these data." From my viewpoint the division is not so precise. As an ethnographic construct, Wesley cannot preexist our discovery. It is a product of both observation and analysis, for observation always requires a preclassification: one who sees everything does not see "any" thing. There is no such thing as "unprocessed data": *facts* always come down to us with a first layer of significance. Observers necessarily manipulate their object: the "census taker" is always, in part, a censor (Benveniste 1969: 143 ff.). But if so, if prior categories are, to a certain extent, unavoidable, we might as well bring them to the forefront instead of bending unconsciously under their influence. In the long run, both the analysis and the description might benefit from the observer's awareness of the terms under which observation occurs.

In describing Wesley I want to emphasize its integration in a larger socioeconomic order. Yet the processes by which this integration occurs are not necessarily observable as such in the empirical world. Some are more blatant than others. Some just cannot be perceived from within the village. Yet all leave concrete signs of their occurrence. Indeed, there exists today, throughout the world, billions of objects and living beings whose very presence testifies to the links between the apparently remote place where they are found and the rest of the world. Part of the ethnographic enterprise is to identify them as signs of that encounter. I call "empirical elements of mediation" these observable links (things, people, events, practices, aspects of reality) that tie the rural groups engaged in the peasant labor process among themselves to other rural groups, to urban classes, and to other areas of the world economy. They are our easiest point of entry into the field of mediation.

M. Silverman (1979: 482) rightly argues that mediation links not only societal levels but also competing subgroups within the countryside and, in so doing, affects the "dynamic of economic differentiation." She draws on the history of Rajgahr, Guyana, to demonstrate the multifold roles of mediators in faction and class formation. But agents of mediation are not always at the front stage, and "primordial loyalties" (Alavi 1973) do not always coalesce on the political scene. Thus, if, following Silverman, we suggest that mediation turns out to be a sum of unequal and contradictory processes, we should further insist that its various elements, and their differential relevance, are neither self-evident nor predictable. Mediation, as such, does not have a logic: individual mediating processes may lead to dead ends, and mediation as an empirical field is full of holes and broken lines.

Two factors explain this disorder. First, though studies of mediation have emphasized formal economic or political ties (e.g., patronage, clientele), the actual liaisons from which individual mediating processes eventuate may belong to any sphere of human activity, or overlap different arenas of social life. For instance, a particular marriage or christening may reinforce economic or political arrangements, but it remains in its own right a marriage or a christening. Second, not all the events that may constitute individual mediating processes are the results or products of conscious and rationale decisions. Many come as unintended results of routine actions in which people might engage without any transactional aim. In short, there is more to mediation than the traditional mediators of the anthropological literature; and the inconsistencies inherent in certain rapports place them out of reach of traditional network analysis.

The field of mediation, understood in such broad terms, is then, by definition, empirical, and we penetrate it by way of the discovery of the empirical elements of mediation. Such elements, characterized by their function at particular moments (rather than by their functional nature) can be spatially fixed or mobile. Mobile elements of mediation can be, in turn, material (*instruments of mediation*) or human (*agents of mediation*).[1]

Spatially fixed elements of mediation are "set objects," that is, things that rarely (if ever) move; yet they bring together, in or around them, peoples of different kinds. First among those fixed objects are the economic "relay points" (Girault 1981) of distribution and circulation. In Wesley, there are about nineteen shops of varying importance which offer rural dwellers products manufactured outside the village and most often outside the country altogether. Yet the most important economic relay point is located at the southern edge of Wesley and relatively far from any residential area. It is the Londonderry Boxing Plant to which the Wesley people weekly deliver their bananas to the DBGA, and to which I will turn later. Many other spatially fixed elements of mediation are located in "Residential Wesley" itself. Seven chapels serve to bring Wesley peasants into weekly encounters with ministers from town or from foreign lands and fellow church members from Woodford Hill or Marigot. The health and police stations and the post office also function as spatially fixed elements of mediation.

The mobile elements of mediation are more difficult to pin down because of their great number. It may be useful to list a few, simply to underline the empirical richness of the field, the extent to which thousands of small objects repeatedly verify the encounter between the peasantry and the larger order. The commodities that Wesley peasants buy from the local shops are obvious parts of that encounter: milk, candles, matches, salt, kerosene, flour, canned food, and, topping the list, sugar and oil. Yet the weekly newspaper brought from town or from Marigot, the vehicles that regularly carry Wesley people to Roseau three days a week, the "Juicy truck" which delivers soft drinks to the shops, the remittances coming from family members in England, Guadeloupe, or the United States also serve to bring Wesley peasants in contact with the larger order. Radio programs also function as elements of mediation. The Dominica Broadcasting System (DBS), Antilles Radio, FR3 Guadeloupe bring to the Wesley people news of faraway lands and songs produced in other cultures. As mentioned before, Wesley people do not speak a French-based Creole. Yet through the programs broadcast by those stations, Wesley youngsters become familiar with the songs of Tabou Combo, a Haitian band based in New York. Adults' and adolescents' views of the world are shaped by people as far away as the London-based broadcasters of the BBC World Service, and the average Wesley high school student knows much more about Asia, Africa, or even Europe than his or her North American counterpart.

Those objects themselves are mobile elements inasmuch as they are moved by human beings, the ultimate mediators. Matches become commodities because people buy them. Airwaves become sounds because people listen to them; and sounds turn into news broadcasts only because they are meaningful. Behind the thousands of objects that sustain the encounter between the peasantry and the world at large stand hundreds of people who can be directly observed activating the movement of those objects. Together with other individuals, they contribute to link societal levels: they are "agents of mediation." The term is not restricted to the mediators favored by the anthropological literature. Dallas (1982: 75) says quite rightly that "in effect, all members of a given society are connectors." To be sure, many agents of mediation may consciously partake of transactional aims (Barth 1963); and political leaders, brokers, middlemen, hucksters, shopkeepers do function more visibly and more systematically in the global mediating process. Their preponderant role in articulating group relations should be emphasized especially since the tools for analyzing such preponderance have been increasingly refined (e.g., M. Silverman 1979, 1981; Soiffer and Howe 1982). But a whole range of other people who may not systematically function as brokers or middlemen may, because of their occupation, contribute to the invasion of the village: teachers, police and health officers, truck drivers, missionaries, hikers, campers, or, indeed, anthropologists. In cases in which the preponderance of traditional mediators is low, the presence of the occasional mediators might strongly affect the cultural or political balance. They may also, at other times, unintentionally contribute to the erosion of the traditional mediators' power. Other people provide empirical linkages among the peasants themselves with various degrees of systematicity: owners of rum shops, organizers of cockfights and domino contests, local choir leaders, "disco" owners or village calypsonians.

Agents of mediation operate within a context that is not only social but spatial. We see them acting and moving only because of the fixed background created by the set objects: buildings, grounds, fields, and roads. Those fixed elements of mediation help us define what many geographers would call a relative space. As Gatrell (1983: 4) suggests, "Any relation defined on a set object creates a space." In that sense, identifying the buildings, the grounds, and the fields within and around which Wesley people move helps us set the various spatial configurations of the village. Within each of these configurations, we should be able to see, in turn, the relative importance of various mediating processes.

Spatial Configurations: Central Wesley

Contemporary Wesley first appears to the observer as a succession of houses densely packed on both sides of the road from the Melville Hall Airport to Portsmouth, just after the Londonderry Boxing Plant. For most Wesley villagers, though, that mile-long stretch is only the Main Road, the southern part of which they commonly refer to as Eden Road. They view it as important, but in no way does it encompass or typify the sociospatial entity in which they live. Mixing native perception with an independent spatial analysis, we consider that stretch as the backbone of a centripetal area defined here as Central Wesley, the center of a particular mix of mediating relations.

The prominent physical feature of Central Wesley is not a building, or even a group of buildings, but rather a whole intersection strategically located on top of a hill, about a half mile from the most southern houses. Wesley people refer to it as the "Four Road." It is here that Wesley intersects with Dominica both physically and figuratively. It is here, in the wide open space in front of the police station, that politicians from town hold their rallies. It is here that one stands the best chance to catch a transport southward to the airport, Marigot, or Roseau or, inversely, to Portsmouth. It is here also that Wesley meets itself daily.

There are no buildings at the Four Road proper, except the police station, in front of which a few female street vendors usually sit in the early morning or in the late afternoon, offering to the village bread, "sweets," or, more rarely, fruits gathered from different parts. With their back against the station entrance, they almost face the post office. To their right is Church Street, which leads to the Roman Catholic Church and the Catholic-run preschool. The intersection on their left leads to the

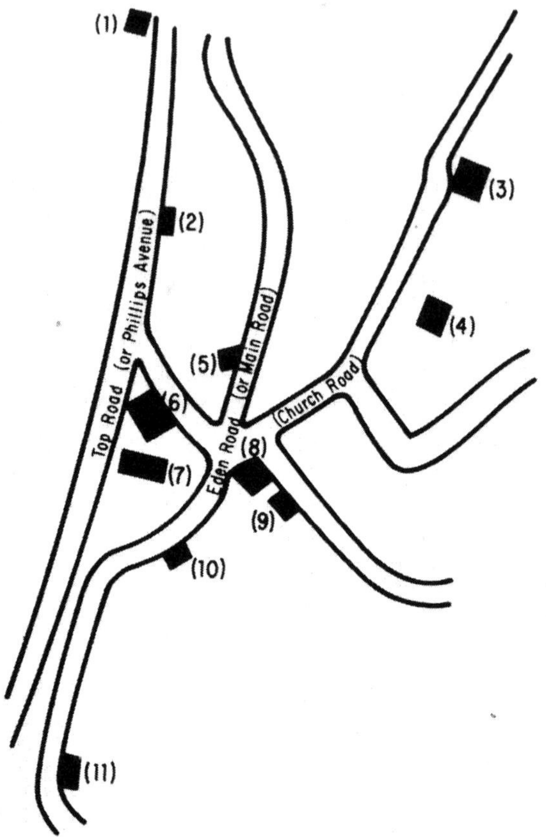

Map 10.1. Central Wesley.
(1) Seventh Day Adventist Church (school), (2) Christian Union Mission Church (school), (3) Roman Catholic Preschool, (4) Roman Catholic Church, (5) Post Office, (6) Methodist Church, (7) Wesley Elementary School, (8) Police Station, (9) Pentecostal Church, (10) Baptist Church, (11) Old Post Office.

Methodist Church and the Wesley Elementary School. Though not at the intersection per se, both churches dominate the corner from the top of their respective hills, both higher than the Four Road itself. On the down slopes from both churches are their respective cemeteries. Past the Methodist cemetery, one enters Top Road, the second major artery of Central Wesley, the location of the Christian Union Mission Church and the Seventh Day Adventist Church.

Empirically then, we can describe Central Wesley as a triangle roughly delineated by the Seventh Day Adventist Church (on the northwest), the Roman Catholic school (on the northeast), and the old post office (on the south). In addition to about one hundred households, that triangle includes four schools, seven churches of different denominations, the police station, the post office, the Village Council office, two cemeteries, and the most important shops and bakeries of Wesley (Map 10.1).

Many processes of mediation intertwine within Central Wesley. A substantial part of the peasants' income is siphoned through the shops concentrated within that triangle, from which they are channeled to town merchants and, ultimately, to industrialized countries. Fourteen of Wesley's nineteen shops are in Central Wesley, many of them on the Main Road. One is more likely to find in the larger Main Road shops items missing in the smaller shops: canned corned beef from Argentina, canned fish from Japan, canned milk from the Netherlands, powdered chocolate from Trinidad, frozen chicken from the United States, or scented candles from Europe. The absence of a staple item (e.g., sugar from Guyana or flour from the United States) on any of the shelves usually implies a villagewide, if not a nationwide, shortage.

Central Wesley is not only a place of economic mediation. Domino players from diverse areas meet at the police station or in the rum shops of the triangle. Likewise, three afternoons a week, tens of villagers of different ages gather at the post office to collect their households' mail, picking up their letters one by one, as the clerk reads aloud the names on the envelopes. It is here that children learn the formal names of their neighbors, even though they may never use them. It is here one concretely senses the presence of Uncle Joe from England, brother Trevor from the States, Ma Bernice from Guadeloupe. The various expressions of surprise, happiness, disappointment, anger, or expectation that this litany of names provokes on many faces tell more vividly than any analysis Wesley's connections to the rest of the world.

Hence, the heart of Wesley, its most visible and most frequented subpart, is a space defined by a number of fixed objects, buildings, grounds and roads, which all testify to the village's integration in the larger world. Those fixed elements of mediation speak of religious, economic, cultural, and emotional connections with faraway places. An afternoon at the post office tells us of the emotional cost but also of the economic rewards of recent migrations. The police station reminds us of the power of the Dominican state. The churches verify the penetration of ideologies and belief systems introduced and constantly reinforced from the outside. The physical size of these elements, their relative durability, their immobility, the impression of permanence they convey, their very concentration on and around the hills, in short, the many ways in which they physically dominate the village are spatial metaphors of the imposition of the world they represent.

We are quite far, then, from the image of an inward bucolic "little community." Central Wesley plays a two-sided role in defining the village. It functions as a centrifugal force, Wesley's window to the outside; yet it also has a centripetal character. More important, ethnography reveals that those two aspects are moments of the same dialectical movement: Central Wesley unites the village in part because it divides it and reshapes it in terms of its relations with the outside. Its fixed elements of mediation do bring together every week a large number of Wesley people. Yet each of those buildings or grounds unites the villagers in the name of a rationale that is not a local one. Women go to the shops to buy imported groceries or pay their bills, and they meet one another in the process of doing so. Men gather at these same shops to play dominos in the evening, but partly because the drinks (also imported from town or from abroad) are accessible in those places.[2] Likewise the post office brings together people who might not otherwise have met each other that particular afternoon; but their primary reason for being there is the very absence of those who have left to join the larger world. One politely greets strangers and friends while standing at the Four Road at the wee hours waiting for the next public transport to Roseau; but the reason for being there is obviously not the conviviality, however warm it might be.

Similarly, church members congregate in locales that are defined according to variations in beliefs and rituals codified elsewhere. One might join the Pentecostal Church or the Baptist Church because a kin is a member; one might even go to a specific service because a friend or a neighbor is going; but the customary right to penetrate any one of those temples and participate as a full member of the congregation in its regular activities is bestowed, at least in part, by one's tacit acceptance of belonging to a worldwide fraternity of believers. Likewise, even though people go to funerals for reasons quite remote from religious affinities, the burial grounds themselves are markers of differences that originate from the outside: Catholics, Methodists, and, since the last few years, Seventh Day Adventists have their own cemeteries. The largest gathering I have ever seen in Wesley was a political rally held at the Four Road by a Roseau politician. The unity of Wesley as a village is shaped at Central Wesley, yet Central Wesley itself is shaped, in part, from the outside.

The central triangle is the area in which Wesley takes its own measure and that of its residents, and status and prestige can be built or destroyed. Those who go to church and those who do not, those who drive to town or to Portsmouth, those who buy frozen chicken parts, those who receive remittances from abroad, those who go to school, those who dress well for weddings and funerals, all pass through that area, judging one another and being judged, in turn, against the entire village. The spatial conjunction of activities not only ties the peasantry to the larger order but also links rural dwellers differentiated by income, religion, sex, age, status, and, indeed, place of residence. It gives Central Wesley its crucial importance in our conceptualization of the village. The physical centralization brought about by the intermingling of mediating processes confirms the unity of Wesley as a single sociospatial entity. It is that centralization on and around the Four Road which pulls together the diverse residential blocks scattered around the Eden and Londonderry estates. It is that centralization which allows us today to see Wesley as one village. Wesley people meet themselves at the heart of Wesley primarily because here is where they meet the rest of the world. It is only as a center of mediation, as the point of encounter of Wesley's most outward spatial elements, that Central Wesley becomes the locus of Residential Wesley's unity.

Spatial Configurations: Residential Wesley

The difference between Central Wesley and Residential Wesley is not simply a matter of size. From an empirical viewpoint, the area I call Residential Wesley includes all the private dwellings of Central Wesley. Viewed from above (Map 10.2), it looks like an open hand of which Central Wesley would be the thumb. The roads to Priest's Gutter, Bottom Wesley, and the Baptiste-Walker's Rest line stand as the longest fingers of that open hand. Mopo, Hill, and Poor Man's Corner are at the junctions of the fingers.

All but two of the major arteries which tie those subparts to Central Wesley are dirt roads upon which motor vehicles move with varying degrees of difficulty. The vast majority of Wesley houses spring up along those dirt streets, often in a dense succession, with their backs against the hills. Smaller tracks circle around the houses. They often lead to modest backyards with occasional fruit trees, or they may stretch through the slopes and intermingle with the almost indiscernible paths villagers take on their way to the faraway gardens. Most houses are made of local or

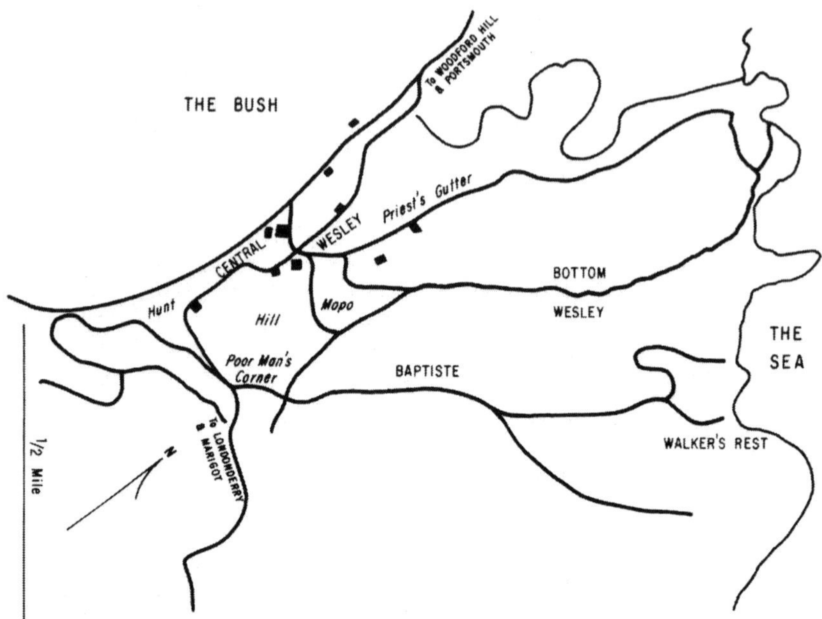

Map 10.2. Residential Wesley.

(more recently) imported wood boards, and many stand three to four feet above ground, supported by wood piles of unequal length which compensate for the unevenness of the terrain. In this eastern region of frequent rainfall, these *pilotri* not only support the house, but also serve to elevate and protect residences from the ever-present threat of flooding. Roofs are usually made of imported shingles or of galvanized aluminum.

The houses of Residential Wesley lodge some 2,800 people divided in about 570 households. These figures place Wesley among the five most populous villages of Dominica. The close succession of houses along Wesley's main arteries (except in the Walker's Rest area) and the constant presence of individuals at the front windows, on the porches, or in the streets reinforce the impression of high density. Yet a 1979 house-to-house survey of 456 of Wesley households (comprising 2,136 individuals or more than 75 percent of the village population) reveals that household size is not so large as one might think.[3] Only 24 of those 456 households have more than nine individuals (Table 10.1). Rather, more than half of the population is concentrated in households of one to seven individuals. About 33 percent of Wesley's total population lives in households of one to five individuals. In fact, statistically speaking, the leading type

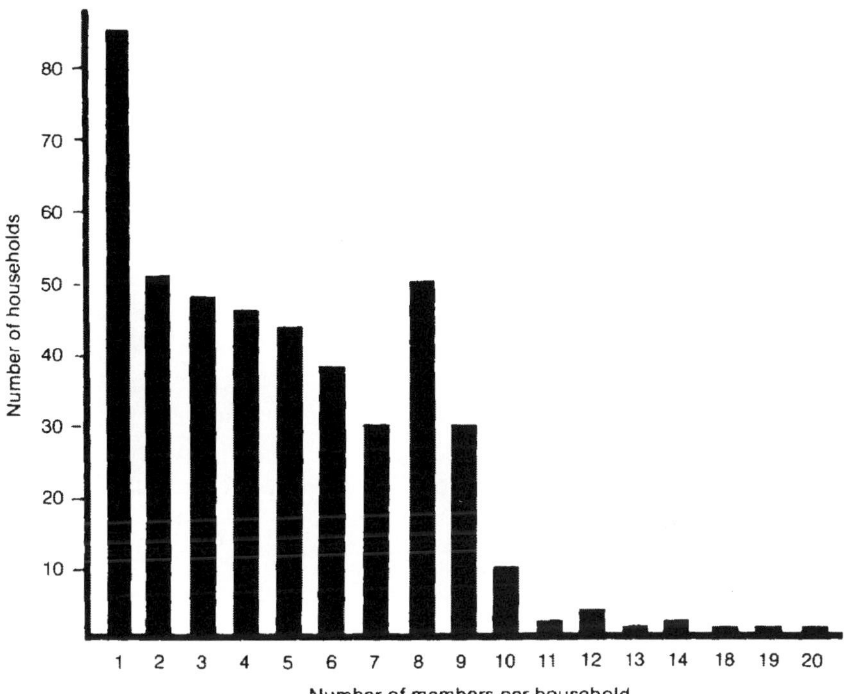

Figure 10.1. Wesley: Population of 456 Households, 1979
Source: Based on data provided by H. Henderson Henry.

of household has a single member. The eighty-six individuals who lived by themselves in 1979 represented only 4 percent of the population surveyed, but 19 percent of the households.

Table 10.1 suggests that small-sized households are not an aberration: statistical frequency systematically declines as household size increases. The noticeable exception is that of the group of 51 households with eight members each. They represent 11 percent of the total households but account for 408 people, that is, 19 percent of the population studied. Hence, I use them as the cutoff point. Yet even though this breakdown indicates more people living in eight-member households than in any other category, the first generalization remains true: most Wesley households comprise one to seven individuals (in that order), and the majority of Wesley people live in households of such sizes.

One needs, then, to balance the initial sense of overcrowding with an awareness of the relative isolation and atomization of Wesley's population, especially since the various subparts of Residential Wesley manifest little social autonomy. Baptiste, Priest's Gutter, and Mopo are centrifugal patches with little internal unity. They relate to one another, as fingers on the same hand, but only by virtue of being dependent upon the same center. No religious organization has established a chapel at Baptiste or Bottom Wesley, and none is likely to do so soon. No priest or minister lives at Priest's Gutter. No political party has held a meeting at Walker's Rest. No major shopkeeper has established a business at Hunt (though in more recent years Hunt has tended to be perceived as a natural extension of Central Wesley). The social and economic exchanges that mark these various subareas and link them to one another differ then in nature from those relations that link them to the administrative, religious, or economic centers on and around the Four Road. One may come from Mopo to attend a wedding at the Methodist Church, but if the groom is from Baptiste, the reception will likely be held there, and friends and kin will follow the couple from Central Wesley to Baptiste for this less official part of the event. Likewise, one may walk from Bottom Wesley to the Walker's Rest area (or vice-versa) to visit an old aunt and bring her some provisions. However, the farther one is from the Four Road, the fewer the commodities worth the walk between any two residential subareas.

Thus, in contrast to Central Wesley where the village meets itself and intersects with the nation and the world, Residential Wesley counts few fixed elements of mediation. The houses themselves function as such, of course, but in quite limited ways. Visits from neighbors are rather rare, especially when compared to visits from friends or relatives coming from other parts of the village. Ties are rarely established on the sole basis of proximity, and the reserved cordiality of Wesley, Marigot, and Woodford Hill villagers differs from the more jovial welcomes of those they call, somewhat pejoratively, *patois* people. This is not to say that warmth and cooperation do not tie residents of different subareas and that one should not expect a neighbor's help and support in an emergency. Rather, in the absence of residential blocks grouping close kin into continguous households, as in the case of the old Haitian *lakou* (Bastien 1985) for instance, primordial loyalties produce a spatiality that does not privilege residential proximity. Wesley people do not live on the land they farm, and traditions that have maintained the indivisibility of some agricultural plots ("family land") do not extend to places of residence. Thus neighbors are neither kin nor friends, at least not necessarily so. When questioned about the infrequent exchange with his or her neighbors, an informant may answer, somewhat out of patience: "Me tell you me na tek on dis people, non."

One is quite far, then, from the idyllic image of the "little community" depicted in the traditional anthropological literature. Not that such a loss should be viewed with nostalgia. To be sure, the atomization and the competition among peasant units brought about by the extensive production of bananas have recently cut short some traditions of cooperation; and Wesley people admit that much. Yet one wonders how close reality ever was to the little community image. Moreover, it is the lack of cohesion of each residential subarea that verifies, in part, the global unity of Wesley as a village. The lack of autonomy of those areas is both a cause and an indication that the people from Hunt, Hill, Poor Man's Corner, Mopo, Priest's Gutter, Walker's Rest, and Eden Road share the same social pool from which to build their most immediate relations. Kin, friends, and enemies are spread throughout those sections, and the hundreds of individual ties across the fluctuating boundaries of the residential subareas thread the spatiality of Wesley as a village. Those centrifugal patches constitute the counterpart of the centrality typified by the Four Road. They mediate among people equally engaged in the same labor process and equally integrated in national structures.

The Bush

There may be not more than ten houses west of the area demarcated by Hunt and the Top Road, but Wesley expands the most in that direction. In search of a land base for their production, Wesley people established for themselves, between the Woodford Hill and Londonderry estates, a dependent territory which expands westward, sometimes as far as three miles inland. It is an area in which they have invested heavily, not only their meager capital, but also their labor, their emotions, and their aspirations. They consider that territory as their prime conquest, the prize of so many battles against nature and also against the estates. They talk about it with a mixture of pride and uneasiness, often with the implicit suggestion that one has not seen all their worth until one hears about "my little piece, way way up in the mountains." Yet despite the parcelization that the existence of so many "little pieces" suggests, the atomization that so many independent histories verify, the physical dismemberment of the territory itself into tens of gutters and hundreds of hills, Wesley people see it as a unified space, the "Bush."

We may define the Bush as the area to which Wesley people carried the peasant labor process with the expansion of banana production. It does not belong to a cognitive map of Wesley village, and not just because it is not used for residence. One suspects that by projecting it as a distinct entity, though closely related to the village, Wesley people keep alive the history of its conquest. I try to respect that view, yet at the same time I seek to integrate the Bush into the study of Wesley's different spatialities by insisting on the relations to which it gives a spatial base.

The Bush is the domain par excellence of the peasant labor process. Squatters first established control over mountainous parcels that they severed from the forest with the explicit aim of bypassing the estates and carrying their preferred organization of labor elsewhere. They passed the feeling and, at times, the security of possession on to their descendants. "My father had a piece of Crown land in the mountains," says one among several informants who saw no apparent conflict between the Crown's formal ownership and their parents' actual control of the parcels. "In the old days, people planted provisions up there," says another. A third adds, more to the point perhaps, "I have title for this piece, now."

Indeed, since the 1950s, many squatters throughout Dominica took the opportunity of the government's new land policy to purchase at low cost Crown plots that they had occupied undisturbed for some time (Yankey 1969). Some of my Wesley informants recall that the actual purchase price of their plots was not much higher than the surveying fees. A 1971–72 survey, admittedly based on a small sample, suggests that almost 21 percent of the cultivators in the Londonderry area held land that they had purchased from the government by then (Baker 1975: 9). Many of those Crown lands stand on steep slopes. Most are hard to reach despite the recent proliferation of tracks and feeder roads, and a significant number are not fully utilized even by local standards. Still, both the number and the proportion of owners who now hold titles for land bought from the government have certainly increased considerably since the early 1970s.

So has the proportion of yeomen who purchased from individuals, a proportion already estimated at 33 percent of the banana cultivators in the Londonderry District in the early 1970s (Baker 1975: 9). The yeomen acquired some lands from estate owners in the intervals between the successes of the major estate crops, especially after the respective falls of sugarcane and limes, as the 1915 map of the Londonderry Estate indicates (Map 10.3). However, the vast majority of purchases postdate the preeminence of bananas. They came as a direct result of the increasing control of the labor process by cultivators engaged in banana production on estate lands, when estate owners decided to turn to speculation. Many peasants reluctantly accepted the inflated prices, essentially because estate lands are much more accessible from the village and generally closer to main roads than most Crown lands, and access, as we will see, remains a crucial factor in peasant production of bananas. Further, by the late sixties, the best Crown lands had already been bought.

The effect of the more recent purchases on Wesley's spatial configurations was to enlarge the uncontested domain of the peasant labor process and to bring the Bush closer to the village itself. Indeed, high or low, inherited or recently cleared, the plots share the distinction of having been tailored or reshaped explicitly for the peasant labor process, and nearly half of them have never been worked in any other way. As mediation with the larger order characterizes Central Wesley, and mediation within the peasantry characterizes Residential Wesley, the near unmitigated presence of the peasant labor process seems to typify the Bush.

The absence of mediators is a physical one in the predawn hours when the earliest peasant workers go into their fields. The predawn segment of the working day belongs to a particular household member, the activator of the labor process, the person who continuously sets that process in motion and who is also—in the case of Wesley—the principal laborer. That worker is usually a male between thirty and sixty years of age and is distinguishable from the rest of the household not so much by status as by the essential fact of being the one who devotes the most labor to the family plot. As activator of the peasant labor process, the principal laborer plans the use of the field in such a manner that bananas can be harvested throughout the year.

Occasionally some household members called upon for specific tasks accompany that worker, but most often the principal laborer goes to the Bush alone, especially if the principal laborer is a male head of household and the father of young children living at home with both parents. The children probably go to school, and in any case, one does not expect them to wake up at four or five in the morning to get ready for the long walk to the mountains. Their mother or stepmother stays with them: she will prepare breakfast and wake them up, often in that order.

During the lone and long walk, principal laborers whose paths cross exchange greetings and best wishes for the day, but it is not the time for conversation. Most wear a jacket or a sweater; males wear a hat or a beret, females a hat or a cloth hairdress that protects them from the cold, but

Following page: **Map 10.3.** Peasant Purchases of Plots from the Londonderry Estate, 1915.

ST ANDREW
DOMINICA
THE SEA
74
73
EDEN ESTATE
GOUNARA GUT
BURTON
From Eden
"FELICITE"
NOTE
This plan is a copy of plan attached to my certificate of title with the addition of the remainder of LOT 71 and also LOT 75 shown by dotted red lines
NOTE
A 42 Acres
B 1 Acre
C 50 Acres
D 15
E 40
F ½ Acre
George Harry
Jacob Burnett
Joseph Valmont
Cemetery
LONDONDERRY ESTATE

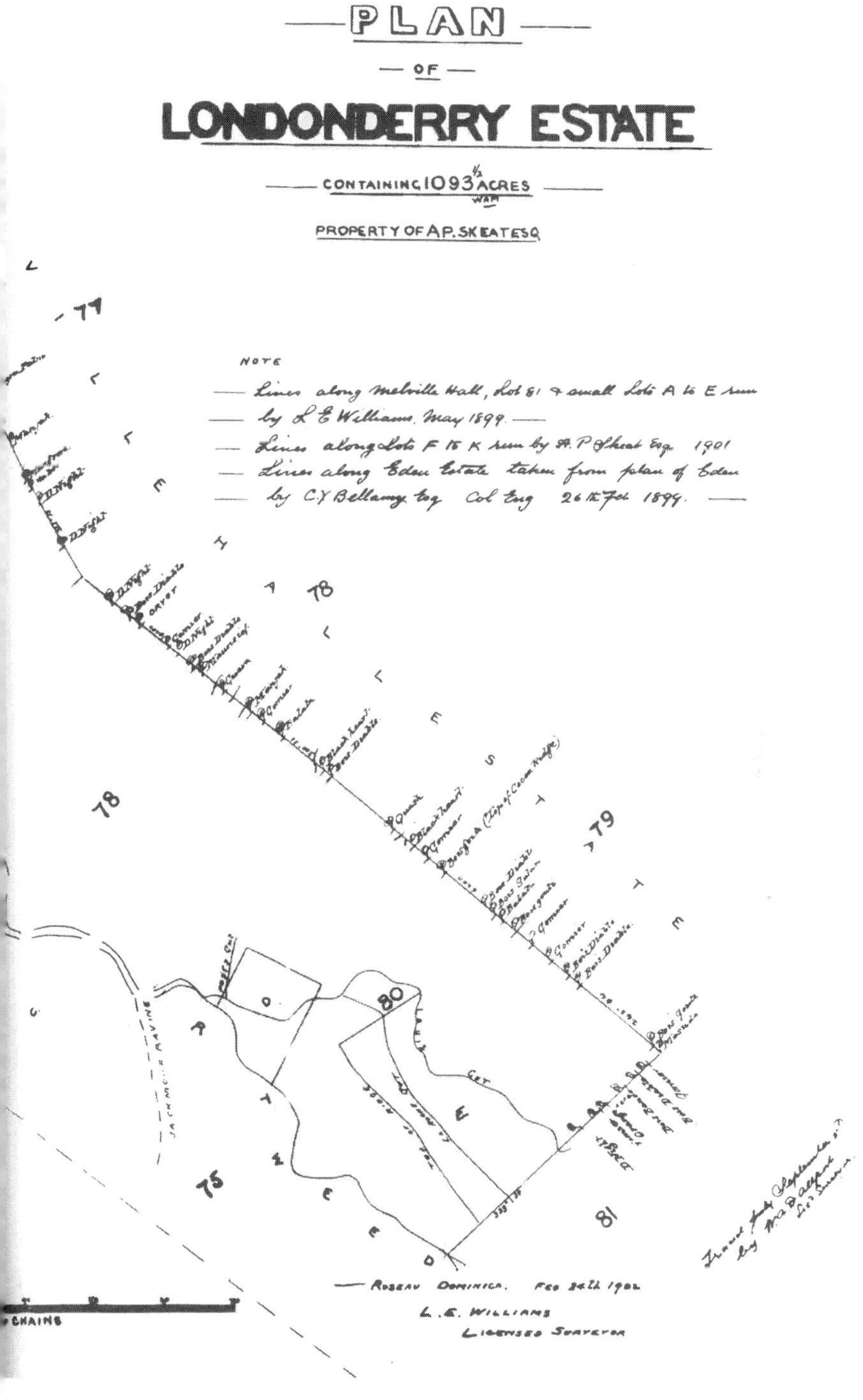

OF

LONDONDERRY ESTATE

CONTAINING 1093½ ACRES

PROPERTY OF A.P. SKEATE ESQ.

NOTE

— Lines along Melville Hall, Lot 81 & small Lots A to E run by L E Williams May 1899 —

— Lines along Lots F to K run by A. P Skeat Esq. 1901

— Lines along Eden Estate taken from plan of Eden by C.Y Bellamy Esq Col Eng 26th Feb 1899. —

— Roseau Dominica. Feb 24th 1902

L. E. Williams

Licensed Surveyor

CHAINS

will also serve against the sun when, later in the day, the temperature rises by about fifteen degrees, as it does almost every day. One walks briskly through the mud: it has rained last night, if not the day before, and the sun rarely pierces through the trees strongly enough to dry the tracks. Though most peasants have become expert at making their way through the mud, the dark, and the occasional fog, the walk may take as long as one to two hours, because of the roughness of the terrain; there are so many gutters to cross, so many hills to climb, so many slopes through which one circles one's way down, so many other properties to avoid.

However long the walk, the principal laborer reaches the plot before the sun fully rises, and immediately starts the task at hand: weeding, spreading fertilizers brought to the field days before, or deflowering some grown bunches. If he is a male head of household, his wife or his children may join him a few hours later, bringing him breakfast. If single and male, the principal laborer eats alone the food prepared by a female parent; women generally prepare their own "tea." Work resumes soon after, until perhaps the early afternoon, at which point some laborers may go back to the village for lunch with the rest of the household or may be joined by additional household members who share the most arduous tasks or help carry back to the house provisions for consumption or coconut meat that will be dried and sold in town.

Household members provide help without reluctance, when they are called on, and, in turn, expect to contribute to quite specific tasks. The rhythm at which they provide that help depends much on the way in which the principal laborer activates the peasant labor process. Cycles and requirements vary according to the conditions of the field, the state of the adjoining provision grounds, the presence of secondary crops like coconuts or grapefruit, and so on. Throughout the year, each minor cycle might require additional labor. Digging and planting a new portion of bananas is such an instance. On the other hand, the activator of the work process must also take into account the availability of household labor which tends to rise in the afternoon and in the summer months. Finally, the experienced laborer also considers daily and seasonal variations in the environment: for instance, many tend to plant bananas "when the moon is going up." Root crops, on the other hand, especially yams, are planted "when the moon is going down." Thus the successful principal laborer must exercise extensive managerial skills, accounting for labor availability, consumption needs, as well as environmental conditions in order to decide on the spatial division that best fits the plot and to organize the work cycle for each division.

Variations around this typical pattern abound, of course. It is only a generalization useful to suggest recurrent practices. Most principal laborers go to their gardens five to six days a week, and each working day lasts from six to nine hours. The state of the various portions also influences the length and intensity of the work periods, though less than it affects the participation of the rest of the household. After the initial planting of a new portion comes a low-key period during which the young bananas require more care and skill than sheer energy. Then, relatives and friends might enter the field only to help harvest bananas on another portion or uproot some provisions. In the nine-to-twelve-month period during which the newest portion reaches maturity, the principal laborer performs most of the routine tasks: fertilizing, weeding, deflowering, or hand-spraying of insecticides. Yet, on a typical plot of two acres, by necessity the oldest planted portion is ready to be planted anew, and a second one might be next in line for digging, long before the newest bananas reach their harvest point. Thus there is almost always a portion of the banana acreage that requires extra labor within any two-week period. Likewise, the coconuts planted around the field or the provision grounds of the most tired portions impose their own secondary cycles which may be at odds with those of the various banana parts, and family members might be called upon accordingly.

Still, despite the sudden increases in the number of laborers provoked by these cycles, despite the fairly continuous presence of family members that several cycles may require throughout a particular week, farming is perceived as a lone activity by Wesley people. The principal laborer controls his or her field in direct and unique relationship with the Bush. His or her perseverance and foresight, the investment of personal attributes in the field, and, of course, the extent of individual authority can mean the difference between success and failure, and in turn affect the whole household. In some cases the status of the principal laborer does not automatically grant authority over the other workers. Single women hiring occasional help, nephews or grandchildren activating the labor process on a kin's land fit such cases. Yet because of the necessity of maintaining a balance between production and consumption, between cash and provision crops, the whole household tends to uphold the principal laborer's authority, once the individual's responsibility has been established. The work process is always a household concern rather than an individual one.

I have elaborated upon the principal laborer in part to emphasize the roots of the feeling, shared by most Wesley people, that the encounter with the Bush is a one-to-one battle. One suspects that, in the context of the fight against the estate owners, the solitude of the principal laborer expresses a mixture of pride and humility common to many pioneers. Many Wesley people express these feelings when they talk about "my little piece in the mountains." From their point of view, the Bush is part of their daily life as conquered territory and, in that sense at least, is part of Wesley.

Londonderry and the Greater Wesley

A student of the elements of mediation may include, within a sketch of Wesley's space, places that do not seem enclosed within the residential boundaries of the village. The Bush is such a space. So are the Londonderry, Eden, Melville Hall, and Woodford Hill estates (though few Wesley people still work at Melville Hall or Woodford Hill).[4] In trying to conceive Wesley as a set of overlapping spatial configurations within which people and things move on a routine basis, we discover that the boundaries of the village penetrate way into what is, or what was until recently, plantation land. Some Wesley people occasionally work on Eden, and a significant minority still hold plots in what remains of the Londonderry Estate. Melville Hall still constitutes an attraction, partly because the government uses a small portion of it for various agricultural experiments. Further, the remainder comprises the Melville Hall Airport, for a long time the only airport of Dominica and a substantial source of income for Wesley people (firemen, air traffic controllers), not so much because of the number of individuals it employs, but rather because of the size of their paychecks. Those areas create a different spatial configuration which I call the Greater Wesley (Map 10.4).

Two spatially fixed elements of mediation further increase the importance of the Greater Wesley area. One is a building originally used as part of an agricultural station; it now houses the only secondary school of the northeast. The second is an open structure, essentially a roof supported by posts, under which stand some fixed scales and some basins of masonry. The bareness of that structure and its often desolate appearance should not deceive us. It is the Londonderry Boxing Plant, the most important element of mediation in our ethnography of the village, even though it is located outside Residential Wesley. It becomes alive about twice a week, on "fig days," when Wesley peasants deliver their bananas to the DBGA.

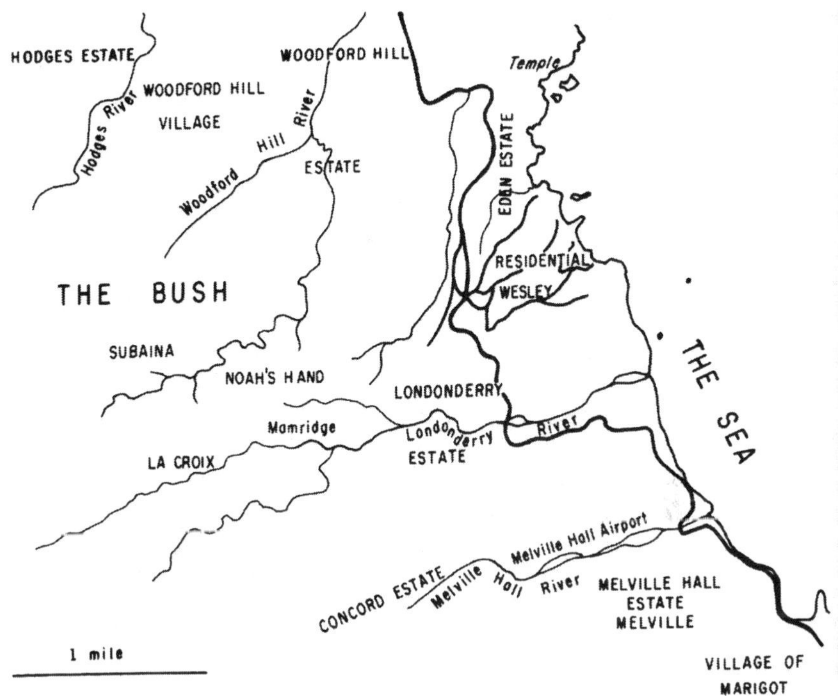

Map 10.4. The Greater Wesley Area.

I have mentioned before that the differential importance of diverse elements of mediation can sometimes be perceived at critical moments of mediation, that is, periods when diverse individual mediating processes coalesce and agents of mediation are more likely to appear up front. Political rallies are such obvious moments, and they do occur occasionally in Wesley. Weddings and religious ceremonies also encapsulate diverse mediating processes. Yet in Wesley the most important ones are the banana days (or fig days) which regularly force the villagers into an encounter with one another as well as into an integration within the world economy. We need to stop for a while at this meta-event: at no other time does Wesley reveal so much of itself.

Wesley villagers consider Londonderry the most important boxing plant of Dominica and official documents support that contention. Figures from the DBGA files show that Londonderry repeatedly held the record among Dominican boxing plants for the volume of bananas it collected during the 1970s and the early 1980s. It reached its peak in the late 1970s, collecting 7,040,040 pounds of bananas in 1976, 5,321,115 in

1977, and 7,465,725 in 1978. Figures for 1979 and 1980 reflect the sudden drop in export quantities caused by hurricanes David and Allen. The association and Geest authorized the boxing plants of the Roseau area to resume activities soon after the hurricanes, and kept Londonderry closed. In spite of that longer period of inactivity, Londonderry never ranked lower than third in the early 1980s.[5]

Londonderry is not the only boxing plant to which Wesley people bring their bananas. In 1981, I estimated fifteen private and public boxing plants of all sizes in the Wesley area. They process in any good year eleven million pounds of bananas produced by the peasantry. It is within the space they define that Wesley peasants relinquish the product of their labor, that processes of surplus extraction become material. The emphasis here is on Londonderry simply because it is to this particular boxing plant that most Wesley people carry their bananas. Every week, between two hundred and three hundred producers find their way to Londonderry and deliver to the representatives of the association loads of bananas which may reach a total as high as 275,000 pounds. The volume handled at Constant Spring and Vauxhall is much less, though a boxing plant recently opened in the Bush itself is slowly gaining momentum.

News of the opening of Londonderry and Constant Spring for reception of bananas, originally broadcast on DBS Radio, quickly spreads through Wesley by word of mouth. Less than two hours after the announcement, most of the producers know that the association has "called for fig." The official announcement usually comes late, often eighteen to twenty-four hours before the opening of the plants. It specifies two consecutive days during which the association will accept bananas at a particular boxing plant, and the opening hours for each day. The precise schedule varies according to the association's sense of the day and time at which the Geest boats must reach and leave the Portsmouth docks. From 1979 to 1982, Londonderry itself was most often scheduled to function from 7 A.M. to 3 P.M. for two consecutive days, but actual collection continues sometimes beyond the scheduled closing time (especially on the second day) partly because of local pressure, partly because of Londonderry's national importance.

The specification of the days and hours during which Londonderry accepts bananas for a particular week sets in motion a range of activities which require precise timing on the part of the peasants. In theory, the association accepts only bananas that have been cut on the same day they are delivered. In practice, some producers cut late on the preceding day, but they run the risk of having their bananas rejected: the pace of the ripening process increases immediately after cutting, and most peasants can tell from looking at the cut, the fruits, or the stems if the cutting occurred more than twenty-four hours before. Moreover, since the actual announcement comes about twenty-four hours before the opening of the plant, and since the actual days and hours of collection are hard to guess, one stands to lose more by cutting early than one would gain from an early delivery.

Timing is thus essential because of the way in which labor and transportation requirements, hard to meet on their own terms, must fit within DBGA procedures and, ultimately, within Geest's schedule. Given that the bananas must be cut on the day specified for delivery, more than one worker is usually needed to harvest even a small portion of a plot. The bunches must be cut from the trees, wrapped in banana leaves, and carried by hand to the outer limits of the plot. From there, they are placed into the vehicle, usually a pickup truck or a jeep, that will carry them to Londonderry. Few Wesley residents own a motor vehicle, and many households need outside help to harvest their bananas in the limited time allowed by the DBGA schedule. Cutting thus implies an effort to reach for limited resources in a time span controlled from the outside. Moreover, the competition for labor and services involves, theoretically, all producers: exportable bananas must be delivered within those two days; they are, by and large, useless to their producers if cut before or after the time specified for a particular week.

Wesley peasants reduce the externally imposed competition through a customary schedule according to which individual producers tend to deliver most if not all of their fruits during one of the four fig days usually available during a fortnight cycle. Even though the boxing plant usually opens for two days every week, most producers tend to harvest fortnightly, and many use only one of the two consecutive days. This informally accepted schedule makes competition manageable: roughly half of the producers compete weekly for the limited resources, and closer to one-quarter compete actively for labor and services on any single fig day.[6]

Variations within the general pattern based on the needs and desires of particular producers, not to mention their unequal possibilities, abound. Some peasants clearly prefer to use the first of the two days. Producers who control two or three plots tend to cut from only one at a time; but the few who control more than three plots tend to be successful enough to have easy access to a motor vehicle and use both days. Producers with more than three acres in bananas using only the labor available in the household may cut weekly or, alternatively, may use the two fig days of a single week. So do producers who control more than ten planted acres even though they may hire labor. Small peasants who unexpectedly see a great number of their fruits rejected at the plant may return with new bunches on the next day. Still, the aggregate effect of the major patterns is one of reduced competition.

Competition becomes manageable, but it still requires much planning and physical effort. Hence, producers prefer to plan an early delivery, whichever fig day they pick. Early delivery also avoids a long stay at Londonderry: on a crowded day, one can spend up to three hours from the time the bananas reach the plant to the time they are actually selected and registered by DBGA representatives. With another three hours to secure the vehicle, harvest the bananas, load them carefully to avoid bruises, and drive to Londonderry, the whole process may easily exhaust the entire day. Hence, an earlier start is a guarantee against the disastrous effects of any sudden delay. Further, many peasants believe that the selectors are more lenient in the morning and reject a smaller proportion of the harvest. Systematic observation of more than twenty operating days at Londonderry and four days at Constant Spring by this writer (in 1979 and 1981) suggest that the actual increase in the proportion of bananas rejected in the afternoon is negligible. Selectors react differently. Some admit that, as the day goes by, they become more concerned about the growing piles of rejects that will go to waste and are willing to accept more bananas than before. Others admit that the bunches brought by a latecomer are evaluated in light of fruits rejected earlier in the day. Moreover, as we will see later and as most selectors admit, the status, the behavior, and the personality of the producer all influence selection.

Still, most peasants try to go to sleep early on the eve of the fig day they choose to use, even if they do not plan to be at Londonderry in the early morning. A few may linger at the rum shop, celebrating somehow in advance their expected income (even though they will not receive the actual cash payment before at least a week); but the vast majority do not hesitate to break a conversation, a visit, or a domino game with the explanatory announcement that "tomorrow is fig."

On fig day itself, the entire village wakes up earlier than usual. Many peasants who do not plan to harvest their own field will nevertheless help a friend or a kin to do so and prepare themselves to work. Others who intend to reach the boxing plant in the latter part of the day still rise early, if only to take quick care of matters that stand between them and the expected time of delivery. From about 4:30 A.M.—that is, at least two and a half hours before the opening of the boxing plants—an unusually large number of people walk the streets of Wesley. Those who have already secured the use of a vehicle gather the friends and relatives who will help them harvest. Yet given the short notice, many are still seeking a transport to carry their fruits to Londonderry. They may stand at the Four Road, waiting for an acquaintance to pass, and inquire if he and his vehicle are available. Or they may walk to someone's house to obtain an early commitment. They use multiple strategies to coax the owner-driver into giving them precedence over competitors, and that initial search may be seen as the event that sets in motion a range of conflicting processes of mediation. They may remind the vehicle owner of a service rendered in the recent past or of a kinship link rarely acknowledged. At no time do Wesley people call each ocher "kòz" (cousin) more frequently than during a fig day.[7]

Indeed, the actual manner in which a family's fruits reach Londonderry both reveals and reinforces ties among and across rural subgroups. The vehicle used might belong to a distant cousin, and the fees for its use vary in light of reciprocal obligations; it might be hired from a richer peasant, a civil servant, or a shopkeeper, and its owner-driver paid by the bunch. But vehicles are in such demand on fig day and road conditions are so bad that many peasants may informally contact a second driver as a protection against unpredictable circumstances. Vehicles are never lent without a driver from the owner's household, and only one shopkeeper regularly employs a part-time driver. Thus, a producer also estimates the chances of reaching the boxing plant on time in terms of the availability of a driver from the owner's household. In turn, the order in which a driver decides to meet individual requests may reveal his social priorities. Regular clients and close kin take precedence over occasional customers or, at least, are guaranteed to reach the boxing plants on time. Yet, partly because roughly one-fourth of the producers intend to cut on a given fig day, most demands are met one way or the other. A busy driver who rejects a request is likely to suggest another vehicle to the customer whom he cannot serve. Likewise, producers most often address their requests to owner-drivers who are most likely to serve them.

Thus, rather than the skill in cutting and harvesting, it is the efficiency with which one's bananas are brought to the boxing plant that serves as measure of social standing. The belief that cutting early is better may have come from the practice that most "big men" do deliver their bananas earlier because they own a vehicle or can easily gain priority of use. Independent female producers must fight harder, against odds, in that race for the reaffirmation of prestige. Often they must secure kin, friends, or task workers to help harvest the bunches and load the vehicle. Further, women do not drive. Poorer peasants may be ridiculed if they carry their bunches on their head, as some are at times forced to do, or if they use an animal—a less likely option, and one even more prone to ridicule.

The fig day as a moment of mediation reveals the vehicle owner as one of the most crucial and most interesting links between the Wesley peasantry and the larger order. Vehicle owners are important because of the amount of surplus they transfer to nonproducers in town and abroad. Further, this transfer is additional to the surplus siphoned to Geest by the DBGA and its agents. In fact, it occurs, chronologically, slightly before the transfer involved in the sale of the bananas. Finally, vehicle owners have few economic gains to show for their activities as agents of mediation. Even though their monetary gains and losses fluctuate much less than those of the DBGA, partly because the terms of their engagement with the peasants are relatively stable, their net profit is quite small. Rather, what the vehicle owners gain the most from their role as agents of mediation on fig day is prestige or rather what Peter Wilson (1973) calls "reputation."

Yet the vehicle owners' gross returns are not negligible. The charges they impose on their fellow villagers are substantial, and they continue to rise. Producers paid forty cents (Eastern Caribbean [E.C.] dollars) a stem in 1979 and sixty cents in 1981–82, figures that have increased since then. Prices quoted to close kin and "best customers" were around fifty to fifty-five cents in the latter period. Producers claim to pay transportation fees one or two weeks later after they cash their vouchers at the DBGA office in Roseau or at the end of the next fig day at Londonderry itself. Some carry the debt much longer and a few manage to escape payment at times, especially if the vehicle owner is a close friend or relative who forgives the debt. Occasionally, an owner-driver might suggest or agree to forgive part of the debt if most of the producer's bananas are rejected, and the driver was there to witness the fact. Much less often, a producer ends up owing more to the driver than the cash value of his voucher. Still, despite those variations, in any two-day cycle some two hundred peasants who do not own a vehicle bring an average of twenty-five bunches to the plant for a round total of about five thousand stems. This represents a potential transfer of $2,750 E.C. a week from the peasant producers to the vehicle owners at 1980 prices.

Further, this transfer occurs in principle before the selection of the "exportable" bananas by the association, a fact quite detrimental to the peasant producer. Let us suppose that a typical peasant brings twenty-five bunches of bananas to the plant for a total of 875 pounds. He owes the owner-driver $13.75 regardless of the proportion of those bananas accepted by the selector. Let us also suppose that one-third of his bananas joins the pile of rejects. The peasant receives a voucher for $111.15 for 585 pounds of bananas (at the 1979–81 prices). Our peasant has lost at delivery 12 percent of the income expected from the bananas. Now, if the vehicle owner helps six such peasants in the same day, he will collect $82.50 for that single day. Since vehicle owners try to lend their services for both consecutive fig days within a week, while peasants usually cut only one day, at the end of the week, the vehicle owner has gained $165 against the peasant's $115. The following week the vehicle owner accumulates a similar amount whereas the peasant is most likely to skip a harvest, and the discrepancy in net income looms larger. By the end of a four-week month, the vehicle owner has gained $660 against the peasant's $230. This discrepancy has increased since I carried out my fieldwork. Banana prices went down, but the price of transportation jumped to $1.25 E.C. a bunch in 1984.[8]

However, the bulk of the moneys collected for the transportation of the bananas to the boxing plant does not remain in the rural areas. A substantial part of it contributes to the payments on the vehicles themselves, most of which are small pickups, purchased at exorbitant prices ($20,000 E.C. and more in 1979), financed at high interest rates (20 percent or more) with productive land used sometimes as collateral. Some of it covers the gasoline used to run the pickups. During the time of my fieldwork, gasoline prices stabilized around $6 per imperial gallon in town, and $7 to $7.25 in the rural areas, and the purchase of gasoline by Wesley drivers significantly contributed to the importers' profits. Likewise, most vehicle owners belong to the minority of Wesley households that use electricity. Their houses are generally supplied with tap water, for which they pay an annual fee. Thus, though one can argue that vehicle owners do benefit from their weekly activity as owner-drivers, and do enjoy a higher material standard of living than most Wesley residents, they function mainly as collectors of surplus for nonproducers in town and abroad.

Not surprisingly, vehicle owners themselves are not always richer than their clients of the day. Most are heavily indebted; others are civil servants with better credit, but not necessarily much greater income than their customers. For them also, the stakes can be measured in terms of both cash returns and prestige. They often boast about the number of people who asked them for help; and they also take pride in making as many trips as possible to Londonderry, for maleness is also measured by the efficiency with which one goes through the muddy terrain without damaging the bananas.

In an area in which most adults over thirty remember the name of the first "big men" to own a truck, driving a vehicle inherently brings social prestige. For instance, young males successfully utilize this role in courtship. More important, although the owners are paid for transporting the bananas, drivers and producers alike tend to think of the activity as implying some kind of favor on the owner's part. A partial explanation may be that not all drivers received payments in cash in the early days. Also, until the late 1970s, transportation prices fluctuated more widely than they do now. Vehicle owners, in turn, continue to enjoy small favors but also yield greater social and political influence than agricultural producers who may not possess a means of transport yet may be earning similar net incomes.

Though this additional political clout may reveal itself only at times of crisis (as it did in the summer of 1979 during the nationwide protest against the government of Patrick John) or during election campaigns (as in 1980), the vehicle owners' social prestige is evident at different moments during a banana day. Many producers accompany the driver on various trips, in part to secure their turn, in part to enjoy the ride, or sometimes for the sole benefit of being seen on a transport. At Londonderry itself, drivers are at the center of many of the small groups which form and break in front of the selecting area throughout the day. They may monopolize conversation and receive or direct attention in a critical moment, that is, at a time when ties are being reinforced, broken, or established.

Checking the Scene at Londonderry

Up to eight hundred people may pass through Londonderry in the course of a single fig day, some delivering bananas, some accompanying a friend or a relative, some selling food or drinks, some collecting money for bananas delivered the week before, others—mostly adolescent males—just checking the scene. The most permanent actors, some twenty to twenty-five people temporarily working for the DBGA occupy center stage, under the roof of the boxing shed, the open structure where the bananas go through their first processing. At the eastern edge of that structure, yet still under the roof, stand the selectors who evaluate the bananas, accept or reject parts of a producer's harvest, supposedly according to criteria passed on by Geest to the DBGA. In fact, former selectors especially tend to agree that they rarely know or understand all the variables on which they should base their judgment. They all can determine whether the bananas have been harvested more than twenty-four hours before selection. Yet beyond this, for lack of better training, their evaluation of the green bananas does not differ much from that of any North American or European customer examining ripe fruits in a supermarket: size and the absence of bruises matter more than anything else. Once the selector has cut away the rejects from the rest of the bunch, he removes the accepted fruits from the stem. Then, one of the recorders sitting in the back writes down on the producer's voucher the weight of the accepted bananas.

After selection, the accepted bananas are washed in the basins, then boxed. They emerge from under the roof at the opposite end of the selectors, to be loaded on trucks which carry them to the Longhouse depot in Portsmouth. Female workers generally handle the washing and boxing, male workers exclusively load the trucks, but selectors may be of both sexes. The participation of those workers as agents of mediation brings out the DBGA penetration of Wesley's daily life. Many of those workers are Wesley or Marigot residents, temporarily employed by the association. They do not share the benefits or the security of employment enjoyed by most civil servants, the DBGA higher brass, or even a lower-level DBGA employee working in town. Most of them acquire their part-time job through patronage. Yet though their actual on-the-job performance may be looked at as yielding little prestige, their very presence under the roof testifies to their connections in town or in the village. Among the adolescents shouting jokes at the truck loaders from the yard may be a youngster who has unsuccessfully tried to get that temporary loading job himself, another who boasts that he was offered the job and declined it, and a third who is likely to be loading the truck himself three or four weeks later to the genuine surprise of his peers.

In contrast to loading and boxing, the position of the selector and that of the recorder carry some inherent prestige. They testify to more important connections. Employment as a recorder also speaks of one's ability to read and write, and recorders have occasionally acted as ad hoc supervisors. Indeed, the recorder's position is the most stable and the most prestigious one below that of boxing plant supervisor. Recorders are generally women who obtain the job through patronage.

The selector's job is also perceived as a more permanent occupation though it does not entail security of employment. Further, the selectors' physical position at the end of the shed, next to the DBGA scales, brings them into a direct encounter with fellow villagers. Even if temporary, the physical and social demarcation between them and the producers who wait in the yard and never fully penetrate under the roof, even to hang their bananas on the crow bar where they are examined, is obvious. Thus, occasional employment as a selector may well improve a peasant's standing and bring the friendship or, more often, the wrath of fellow villagers. Yet any selector, in turn, evaluates the bananas according to the grower who brings them.

The proportion of rejects that a particular grower is forced to accept is then a reverse measure of his or her social standing and acumen. Many producers actually choose their selectors carefully, picking the line in which they will stand, factoring in their degree of acquaintance with the selector, his or her reputation, the length of the line, and so on. Once that selection is made, the producer "seasons" himself with the selector by verbal communication with the selector or with onlookers, or with body language, trying to influence the coming evaluation of his harvest. "I look at them straight in the eyes," says one. Others claim that the selectors know from the producers' looks and postures the ones who "don't take nonsense" from them.

Obviously, trends emerge in the weekly repetition of the encounter. A more prominent grower is likely to see a greater proportion of his bananas accepted by any selector. On a few occasions, I have observed the person bringing the bananas calling the selector's attention to the name of the actual registered grower. Likewise, male adults tend to receive fewer rejects than women of similar age. Within both sexes, people between twenty-five and fifty years of age tend to obtain better results than, say, adolescents or very old producers. Not surprisingly, even though anyone can deliver the bananas in the name of a grower, growers who are physically unable to reach the boxing plant themselves try to give their harvest to the trusted kin most likely to influence the transaction positively. Likewise, age, sex, physical strength, and a whole range of other individual characteristics further modify member differentiation within a particular household in determining the one who is given the responsibility of taking the bananas to the boxing plant. All are aware that idiosyncrasies, including the personality of both selectors and producers, come into play at the moment of selection. In any given year, the returns of an outspoken peasant ("bold, but not too bold," said one informant) are likely to surpass those of a more quiet individual of the same sex and age with similar technical and economic resources. Peasant families as well as individual growers bet on personal attributes.

Moreover, the biweekly display of social influence and personal character occurs in front of a relatively large audience, and many Wesley residents feel that Londonderry is the place where a banana-growing family's worth is best gauged, since anyone can measure the amount of a sale. It is not unusual to hear "X is not playing big, but he sells more figs than Y," or X is "going down these days" or "making it now." Many villagers comment that the proliferation of private boxing by individual growers in the early 1980s prevents them from finding out "who is big for true." Moreover, as the successful repetition of the encounter with the selectors may lead to economic improvement for a particular grower, so the biweekly verification of one's "bigness" may turn into a self-fulfilling prophecy, guaranteeing favors (credit at a shop, help in transportation, etc.) which might have not otherwise been granted. Those favors, in turn, enhance social prestige.

The public evaluation or confirmation of social and economic worth continues at Londonderry even after the last banana truck has left for Portsmouth. As noted before, most producers harvest every two weeks. Yet on the week that they do not cut, many still come to Londonderry in the late afternoon or early evening to cash their vouchers from the past weeks. Association representatives bring the cash from town and publicly call the grower in whose name bananas have been delivered two weeks before. At each call, a grower (or trusted kin) breaks from the group, presents the voucher, signs (or marks) the payment book, and collects the appropriate amount.

Clearly, the DBGA representatives function here as economic agents of mediation. They also force upon the community a public assessment of its members. Though amounts are not revealed publicly, the cash passes from the representatives to the growers in front of a large audience which has become quite adept, after weeks of repetition, at determining broadly the range of the amount involved. Further, the regular presence of a particular family member at times of payment may be as significant an indication of his or her role within that family as his or her presence at the time of fruit collection.

The third and last important operation at Londonderry is the reclaiming of the rejects. Fruits not accepted by the selectors may be carried back by the producers who brought them, or by passersby who simply pick them up from the ground. Rejects may be used for home consumption, or may be sold to hucksters who regularly trade in town or in other islands nearby. Various processes of mediation are set in motion here. The hucksters intervene as middlemen, integrating the peasantry in national and international networks not controlled by Geest and the DBGA. Yet such integration remains marginal, in part because of the small size of the international markets involved, in part because of its questionable legality: "exportable" bananas are legally DBGA property and the net revenues of hucksters who use the legal channels are meager.

The collection of rejects imposes upon members of the community one more self-evaluation. Producers try to pick up their rejected bananas in the most inconspicuous manner, unless the volume or the apparent quality clearly justifies the operation. Yet privacy and anonymity being rather difficult in the open space at Londonderry, others call for the attention they know to be coming anyway. Calling on the crowd to witness, they emphasize that it was "nonsense" for an arrogant or ignorant selector to reject such beautiful bananas. At any rate, a sense of shame pervades the operation as if one was being judged negatively according to the amount of rejects he or she collects.

I have so far presented the events of a banana day in the sequence that most individual producers experience them when they choose to harvest. Yet one must keep in mind that more than a hundred producers bring their fruits to Londonderry in a particular day, and that each of them enters into the process at a different time of the day and is likely to follow the sequence at his or her own rhythm. Thus, in real time, some harvest while others load the pickups; some bring their fruits to Londonderry while others contemplate their rejects. Pickup trucks go back and forth between the village and the Bush, between the Bush and Londonderry, mixing their klaxon to the noise of the larger trucks that carry the boxed fruits to Portsmouth. The larger trucks speed through the Main Road almost as fast as the pickups, overloaded with cartons of bananas on top of which sit two or three young men who will help the driver unload or an occasional passenger enjoying a free ride. Some go with their cargoes as others return empty, to be loaded anew; and pedestrians know to step aside as they approach. Pedestrians themselves are more noticeable then than on any other weekday. Those who help and those who watch, those who comment and those who listen, children returning from school, housewives who have just served the midday meal, street vendors of fruits or bakeries, all add to the commotion.

As the day progresses, Londonderry becomes the undisputed center of that effervescence, the place to which pickups and trucks, drivers and producers, onlookers and vendors, all tend to converge, a gathering of the greatest number of people at any single moment. And it is only at the peak of this concentration that one may realize the dimensions of the event: the whole village transformed into an assembly line of gigantic proportions, cutting, transporting, separating, weighing, washing, and boxing bananas according to the rules specified by Geest Holdings through an agency of the Dominican government.

Yet it is also at that time that Wesley takes a measure of its internal relations. No other task, no other routine event requires such a collective effort, such accurate knowledge of what one's kin or neighbor is doing. The continuous formation and breakdown of small groups provide to the participant observers a mirror in which to perceive their own alignments. The evaluation of the bananas, the verbal and nonverbal exchanges between producers and selectors, the communication among the onlookers, the collection of rejects, and the payment of previous harvests, in turn, give individuals and families a sense of their economic and social worth, as measured against both the larger order and the community. But that consciousness itself may be put to use in the manipulation of those very same personal, social, and economic assets to reinforce, change, or stabilize alignments and evaluations. In short, we can argue, following Geertz's (1973: 451) analysis of the cockfight, that the banana day functions as a meta-event, a *text* in which the Wesley villager "forms and discovers his temperament and his society's temper at the same time." But, in contrast to Geertz, rather than simply emphasizing the discovery inherent in that process, we must insist on the influence of structural factors and on the individual's constant efforts to expand his or her margins of maneuver. For the scene at Londonderry is a "play" in more than one way. It is a performance, a drama, yet one in which the actors improvise within certain limits. It is also a "play" in that sense of the word which evokes action, motion, as in the play of imagination. It is also a play in the sense of movement, or space for movement, as in the play of mechanical parts. In short, mediation, as it occurs, on the ground, is, inherently, a play of structural constraints.

Mediation, Time, and Spatiality

The critical observation of the Londonderry scene does not exhaust the ethnography of the banana day as a moment of mediation. Social and economic exchanges continue outside of Londonderry long after the closing of the plant. Street vendors still carry food items through the streets of the village, or simply sit on their porches, waiting for passers-by. Items range from pieces of sugarcane cultivated in a local garden, or mangoes brought by an amateur entrepreneur from outside of the Wesley area, to homemade cakes and cookies. Profits remain small, and one may even lose one's meager investment on any single venture. Indeed one must be in a particularly entrepreneurial mood to even think of the venture, and nobody would consider permanent engagement in such petty trading. Months may pass before the same individual attempts to hit the streets again. Yet everyone knows that on fig day the village itself is in the mood to buy.

One must differentiate between those occasional vendors and other part-time entrepreneurs who act more systematically as agents of mediation, offering the same commodities on a weekly or daily basis. Both groups are important but in different ways. Yet as petty as the occasional activities may seem, they do link the buyers and the sellers of the day around economically trite objects which nonetheless function as important instruments of mediation. The buyer and the seller may both belong to families deeply engaged in banana production through the peasant labor process; yet differences of age, sex, religious denomination, and residential area may have kept them almost unaware of each other's existence. The brief exchange on an early fig day evening may be the first close encounter between a little boy selling his mother's cakes and a hitherto unknown woman crossing the intersection. It establishes a bond, however tenuous, between two people whose similarity may reside only in their common structural position vis-à-vis Geest and the DBGA.

These occasional activities and the objects themselves also add to both the extent and the domains of the exchange between banana producers and nonproducers, since anybody can participate in any way he or she chooses, and since ingredients, if not the items themselves, are usually brought from town. More important, perhaps, such activities are instances in which a family or an individual may develop, use, or simply take the measure of personal talents. A single mother may use the opportunity to test her talents at making delicacies, improve her children's talents as sellers, and augment at the same time her family's income. She may also admit privately that this sale is the only way she can afford to give cookies to her children.

When the occasional vendors retire after sunset, the shops, especially those licensed to sell rum, remain vibrant with life. To be sure, these shops function every day as spatially fixed elements of mediation, but their role is much more obvious on the evening of a fig day. To start with, many shop owners depart then from their regular schedule. Some open late because they also grow bananas and use their morning hours to deliver their own harvest to Londonderry. Others own pickup trucks and find it more profitable to spend the bulk of the day providing transport services to producers. Few own larger trucks and carry bananas from Londonderry to Portsmouth for the DBGA. All generally agree that business is slow on the morning of a fig day since many potential buyers are at Londonderry or on their way there. Activities increase in the afternoon at about the time that most occasional buyers walk about the village, and many shop owners wait until then to open their doors. In the late afternoon and in the evening, when producers who delivered the previous week start collecting their returns, the rhythm accelerates and the volume of sales quickly surpasses that of a whole ordinary day. On any fig day, all shops close late; but rum shops close even later.

An unusually large number of people (almost exclusively males) gather at the rum shops in the evening of a fig day, especially if the second day of collection falls on a Friday or Saturday. Some drink alcoholic beverages, others play dominoes, some simply sit and watch. The owner rarely, if ever, tries to make a nonbuyer feel uncomfortable: there is no explicit purpose outside of the encounter itself, and one is more welcome for his participation in the conversation and in the games than for his buying power. To be sure, many of the customers in the crowd accumulate heavy drinking debts during that single evening, but shop owners and richer clients may also pay for an occasional round. Draughts and domino players gamble sometimes, but always at their convenience, according to the mood and the decision of the majority.

It is among that evening crowd at the shops that we find a group of agents of mediation highly visible throughout the day but neglected so far in the ethnography: the truck owners whose vehicles carried the bananas from Londonderry to Portsmouth. A number of them own shops and need only walk down the stairs from their living quarters to join the crowd. Yet whether they own a shop or not, they become quite evident on the evening of a fig day. They occupy a position similar to that occupied earlier by the owners of the smaller pickups at Londonderry, but in contrast to the pickup drivers who spent their entire day in the area, the owner-drivers of the larger trucks bring news of the outside, commentaries about the harvest as it affected not only Wesley but also other banana districts of the North and perhaps the nation at large. They likewise use the occasion to boast about the additional income they drew from the association in return for the use of their trucks or for their personal services, though they are not likely to mention specific figures. Still, we know that the association spends more than $300,000 a year on the "trucking of bananas" (DBGA, 1976–82), most of which goes specifically to the private truckers who help carry the bananas to the two national depots, and that Londonderry has long been a most important production district. As agents of mediation, the truck owners contribute to the inflow of cash within the village, sometimes quite directly, since they occasionally hire a few hands. Yet, on fig day evenings, their presence at the shops is more a reminder of their role and status, a way to both measure and consolidate the networks at the center of which they stand. On the one hand, truck drivers can spend more and monopolize the conversation more often than other people; on the other, the general permissiveness, facilitated by the absence of women, acts as social equalizer among the males, reinforcing solidarity. Thus at the very time that they are showing their larger income, the result of their differential integration, truck drivers become closer to their fellow Wesley people.

In conclusion, the ethnography of mediation verifies in numerous examples of various dimensions that a village such as Wesley creates its reality in the interplay between the structural constraints inherited from the international order and the mixture of local initiative and local response. Dominicans themselves have a neat choice of words to describe a reality that they consider to be muddled or changing. They often say: "It's neither here nor there." The phrase is not always pejorative though it tends, nowadays, to take a negative connotation when used by or in reference to members of the House. Yet it can apply to people, actions, or objects. From the point of view expanded here, it applies as well to the village itself.

Wesley is turned into itself, but its inward tendencies are only one aspect of a dual movement that also forces it into the nation and the world. The most important of its physical markers, those that define it as a space, all testify to its integration in a larger order. The two weekdays that require its most sustained concentration of human and material resources are dictated by outside forces; yet it is during those days, more than at any other time, that it acts as one village, that it secures its internal ties. It discovers itself way beyond its apparent boundaries at times when internal competition supposedly reaches its peak. Yet that discovery, in turn, makes sense only in light of what occurs at the Four Road, in the Bush, in the homes of Residential Wesley. In short, Wesley has more than one dimension. The past history inscribed in the fields of

Plantation Wesley, the centrifugal forces springing out of Residential Wesley, the centripetal influence of Central Wesley, the commotion of Londonderry, and the sustenance of the peasant labor process in the Bush, all combine to create a sociospatial entity that none encapsulates by itself. The changing reality of Wesley partakes of the very intermingling of its various subparts. As Wesley people might put it, "It's nida hir no dah."

CHAPTER 11

The Impact of the World: Hard Cash and Small Change

"Can't you see the banana trees bent with the weight of their bunches?"
"Yes, yes."
"Can't you see the vegetables and the ripe fruit?"
"Oui! Oui!"
"You see all that wealth?"
She opened her eyes. "You've made me dream! What I see is poverty."

—Jacques Roumain, *Masters of the Dew*

Routine is the cornerstone of social relations. Despite the play inherent in any exchange between individuals, the routine repetition of certain practices leads to the formalization of relations that the actors experience as steady. That apparent steadiness, far from being a veil, is an indication of the importance of the processes that sustain those relations. In the course of their daily routine, individuals do affect the social structure, but they also discover, if only implicitly, the structural boundaries within which they operate. They express that discovery through explicit or implicit categories.

Native categories are thus not the expressions of the alleged false consciousness of the masses. Rather, they are the language of routine;

and routine itself is both cause and consequence of the process of structuration. Native categories of social differentiation are products of recurrent relations sustained by the most important processes of social life. They are indexes of the importance of the processes that sustain them. The task of the social scientist is to go to the roots of the steadiness that those categories imply. If the integration of the Wesley peasantry is vital to the reproduction of that peasantry, native categories will express, even if indirectly, the importance of that integration.

To be sure, emic and etic categories need not overlap. Categories proposed by the social scientist need not match an exact counterpart within the native vision. However, they must make sense in the native world, even if only after a proper translation. If the processes that tie Wesley to the larger world are as important as I claim, the routine practices they foster are likely to crystallize in emic categories that are, themselves, the precipitates of the relations that the processes sustain and reproduce. In short, my categories should make sense to Wesley people even if they do not always match theirs.

The categories that best help us differentiate among Wesley people are not all part of the native vocabulary of differentiation. Some of them were coined by the villagers; but others were coined by this writer after months of observation. However, they all make sense within the native discourse, as I verified repeatedly. It is then telling that they all reflect the impact of the larger order. Differentiation within Wesley is, in an important way, a byproduct of the village's integration in the nation and in the world economy.

The categories expose two major mechanisms of differentiation: (1) the peasant labor process and (2) the mechanisms of integration in the sphere of valorization. The ties that bind Wesley to the larger order are at least as vital to our understanding of the village's internal structure as those that bind Wesley people to one another. Key among those mechanisms of integration and differentiation is the subsumption of the peasant labor process in the worldwide process of valorization. Hence, we can differentiate Wesley people (1) according to the extent of their participation in the peasant labor processes, and (2) according to the mechanisms that integrate them in the process of valorization.

The categories produced along those two axes are our best proofs of the impact of the world on local relations, especially if they fit the people's perception of themselves. They show that the most consistent sets of relations within the village are not the direct products of local trends, but complex precipitates of the encounter between Wesley and the world.

The two mechanisms of differentiation allow us to classify Wesley people into three large classes:

1. those individuals and/or households with little if any direct engagement in the peasant labor process and who do not depend on that engagement for their sustenance;
2. those who are dependent on the peasant labor process only in part, and whose integration into the process of valorization occurs through multiple means (including, though, peasant production of bananas for the benefit of Geest); and
3. those who fully and almost exclusively depend on their engagement in the peasant labor process, not only for the production of food crops but also for the bulk of their cash income.

The last class includes a majority of Wesley people, and its integration in the process of valorization and its reproduction occur mainly through the mechanisms put forth in chapter 7.

Historical origins, sources and level of income, native perception, and participation in processes of mediation will help us differentiate further within those three broad classes.[1]

The Outsiders

Not all the individuals who live in or around Wesley are peasants. In fact, a small but visible minority are not cultivators at all. These are people who never engaged in agricultural labor in Wesley though they benefit from the existence of the peasantry and affect it. I call them the "outsiders." In 1979–81, the group consisted of two families of estate owners (the proprietors of Eden and Londonderry), a resident Catholic minister, four Protestant ministers, three policemen, and a group of Roman Catholic nuns managing a lumber mill on the fringes of the Woodford Hill Estate.

I think of the outsiders as a separate category because their total nonparticipation in the peasant labor process fully distinguishes them from Wesley people. In fact, the villagers themselves do not consider any of the outsiders as Wesley people. Significantly, all were born outside of Residential Wesley (if not outside of Dominica altogether). All except the ministers and the policemen live outside the boundaries of Residential Wesley. In sharp contrast to most residents born elsewhere who came to work on the estates and are now engaged in the peasant labor process, the people I call outsiders do not intermarry with Wesley natives. Neither do they socialize with the villagers. Some of the outsiders are white, and almost all are "lighter" than Wesley people.

The presence of the outsiders influences village life, but only sporadically. All in all, they provide occasional employment to some thirty people, usually in menial, domestic, or agricultural tasks. Once in a great while an estate owner might gather a large group of boys to pick up his ripe coconuts from the ground in return for a pittance. Yet only the domestics, the half-dozen villagers who work for the nuns' mill, and a couple of watchmen on the estates enjoy a semblance of employment security.

As employers, some outsiders benefit from their workers' dependence upon the peasant labor process. Workers supplement their income through peasant work activities that provide them with food or cash; therefore, outsiders pay only minimal wages. But this transfer represents a relatively small drainage of village resources if compared to the surplus extracted through banana production or through peasant purchases of commodities. Rather, the most important economic impact of the outsiders' presence in and around Wesley is on the price of land. Indeed, the owners of Eden and Londonderry sell plots to their former workers or tenants at quite exorbitant prices (up to $4,000 E.C. an acre at 1979–80 prices). Land speculation became the estate owners' main source of income after the peasantry established its supremacy in the labor process, forcing estate owners to curtail their engagement in banana production. Estate owners also benefit from the surplus labor of their remaining tenants on the fields intercropped with coconuts.

Yet with the rise of the yeomanry the estate owners lost the social control they exerted on the whole of Wesley, and even their remaining tenants do not treat them with the deference that characterized the better days of Eden or Londonderry. The economic dependence on the outsiders does maintain an ideological and social submission on the part of the workers, their families, and their friends, but that dependence is waning. An outsider may dictate to a permanent worker the church in which to marry, and refusal may cost the worker his or her job. The policemen, in turn, do not have any employees or workers, but they settle local disputes, and can exert unrestricted power on most Wesley residents. The extent of abuse is largely a matter of each policeman's temperament. The influence of the ministers likewise extends beyond those few individuals who work for them, and I will return to that point later, when I discuss recent religious developments in Wesley.

In summary, the presence of the outsiders testifies to the complexities of Wesley's ongoing transformations. Despite marginal or potential benefits (the lumber mill could turn into a viable import substitution strategy and benefit the whole of Wesley if not all Dominicans), the outsiders' presence is a costly one. The marginal advantages they bring do not justify their social influence. They are not accountable to Wesley people but to superiors or creditors in town or abroad. Because of their own origins and their mode of livelihood they need not take into consideration the wishes or the interests of the Wesley people. Yet they necessarily benefit from the reproduction of the peasantry. Their presence is often exploitative, sometimes illegitimate, always unsolicited. It is, at best, a tolerated imposition.

However, the influence of the outsiders on Wesley's daily routine remains limited. The priest, the nuns, the ministers, the estate owners, and even the policemen could very well reside elsewhere, and visit the area weekly or monthly to attend to their affairs, and most Wesley people would not notice the difference. This observation does not contradict the point that the outsiders are indexes of the world's intrusion into Wesley's life. Rather, it indicates that they are not the primary agents of that intrusion. It verifies the contention that the integration of the peasant labor process in the process of valorization is now the fundamental mechanisms behind Wesley's encounter with the world. The peasantry's conquest of the work process isolated the estate owners, and the physical impact of the outside manifests itself through objects much more than through individuals: churches, schools, commodities, bananas. Now, the most visible agents of mediation and, indeed, the individuals who stand at the top of the village social hierarchy come historically from the mass of Wesley people.

The Big Farmers

Wesley people do not identify with the outsiders partly because of the latter's total lack of participation in the peasant labor process. In fact, most peasants do not have a single label for the category of outsiders: they do not consider them as part of their immediate social hierarchy. Rather, when asked to rank Wesley people, a majority of informants placed at the top of the village socioeconomic ladder one of the six or seven individuals whom they often refer to as big farmers.

Wesley's big farmers can be seen as something of a cross between the kulaks of the classical literature on peasantries and capitalist farmers.

Wesley people identify with them in ways in which they will never relate to any of the outsiders. In contrast to the outsiders' absolute lack of personal engagement in the peasant labor process, big farmers come from peasant families and are always one generation removed from full-time agricultural work on estate or peasant land. Many peasants clearly remember the time when some of those now important men were in working situations not too different from their own. A few kulaks still participate in garden work; others help, quite occasionally, to produce the ground provisions they consume. More important, while no single member of an outsider's household might be capable of digging a yam hold, climbing a coconut tree or deflowering a banana plant, each big farmer has some close kin, living under the same roof, who share in agricultural labor on a regular basis. Finally, three among those farmers, including one who lives alone, do a fair amount of agricultural work themselves.[2]

Hence, big farmers may at times be engaged in the peasant labor process. However, they differ fundamentally from most peasants because such engagement is not necessary to their immediate reproduction. For them peasant work activities constitute a supplement of income beyond the cost of reproduction. Many Roseau residents draw less cash income than some of those Wesley farmers and fully maintain a viable standard of living (in the Dominican context) without the supplement of home-grown provisions. In the mid-1970s, whereas the per capita Gross Domestic Product was below U.S. $400 per year, some of those farmers cashed banana vouchers worth more than U.S. $5,000 in one single year.

To be sure, not every one of those seven or eight individuals generally recognized as big farmers grosses so much. Banana incomes fluctuate yearly. More important, one needs to look at the whole household to understand fully the dynamics of the big farmers' reproduction. It could be argued that other members of their households are peasants inasmuch as they work full time on the family plot. However, those members do not perform the supervisory functions of the typical principal laborer, even though they may work much more than the farmer in whose name the bananas are delivered. The big farmers' households, then, depend much more on a symbiosis of exploitation and redistribution under the same roof than on a collective engagement in the peasant labor process. All big farmers are males, and power relations determine the member in whose name the bananas will be delivered. Yet part of the extra income trickles down to other members and benefits the household in general, say, in the form of a physically more comfortable living environment or greater buying power. Further, even though a kin, or the farmer himself, may take part in agricultural work, one of the distinguishing features of a big farmer is that the most arduous tasks on the land he controls, such as digging banana holes and harvesting, are performed by poorly paid task workers, mostly single males, engaged for the day.

The lack of dependence on the peasant labor process and the cyclical hiring of workers markedly differentiates big farmers from most Wesley people. Big farmers often control larger holdings. The typical Wesley big farmer is a male head of household, or an adult son whose actual control extends to between twelve and thirty acres of productive banana land. However, land, as such, is not the determining variable: a few peasants do control as much as ten acres of land, that is, almost as much as some big farmers actually cultivate. Further, some big farmers control aggregate family holdings that are not necessarily their individual property. To be sure, the total acreage planted is probably not so broken up into parcels as that of a peasant.

Still, the major difference lies in the work process itself: the much higher ratio of inputs (fertilizers, pesticides, etc.) used by the farmers and their allocation of labor, especially the use of occasional "gangs" of young male laborers for the most arduous tasks. The farmer occasionally participates in cultivation; but more often than not, his role is a supervisory one. Thus access to cash (the ability to acquire more inputs and to pay the workers) is more important than the actual holding size. In fact, variations in acreage influence only slightly net banana returns among the big farmers themselves, and some do as much with twenty acres as others do with thirty.

Efforts to diversify (especially coconut production and animal husbandry) also differentiate big farmers from most Wesley cultivators who cannot afford to wait long for the return of their investment. All big farmers own a motor vehicle (pickup, jeep, or full-sized truck) which they normally use to transport bananas for a fee, either from the peasants or from the association, in the manner described in the preceding chapter. A minority among them also own shops, and family members may act as occasional hucksters, buying rejected bananas or ground provisions to be shipped and sold in town or abroad. Together with the estate owners, big farmer families hold an oligopoly on red meat. This control affects the whole of Wesley except the richest yeomen. The high price of red meat, artificially raised by the local oligopoly, has contributed to the increased consumption of imported chicken parts. Thus, not only do big farmers benefit from the maintenance and reproduction of the rest of the Wesley people through the peasant labor process; many also serve as economic agents of mediation.

Except for one or two cases, though, Wesley people do not consider big farmer behavior exploitative, partly because of the Wesley work ethic: many villagers believe that an individual's economic situation is by and large the result of his or her own hard work, and that hard and consistent work eventually brings economic improvement. More important, they witnessed the rise of the big farmers, their slow ascension out of the peasantry. Indeed, most of them (or their parents) emerged from the group of yeomen who gained control of their land during the depression of the 1930s or at the very beginning of the banana expansion, at times when an acre easily sold for 150 to 300 dollars. The actual consolidation of their plots came later. Their greater access to cash derives from the accumulation they managed from 1953 to about 1965, when a majority of Wesley people were paying more than nominal rent to the estate owners, and when a substantial minority still engaged in wage labor. Big farmers are, in short, former peasants who benefited from the banana explosion. As such, they contributed to the transformation of Wesley into a banana-producing village substantially independent from the estates. Wesley people see them against the background of that still growing independence. Indeed, the big farmers even benefit from Wesley people's tendency to view the outsiders, especially the estate owners, as wicked people. I suspect that the way in which the big farmers sometimes mistreat their workers will become more evident as memories of the estates become less vivid. Meanwhile, despite their conservatism (big farmers generally "don't mix"), they look like Wesley people, speak like Wesley people, and eat like Wesley people. They naturally fill part of the social void created at the top by the decline of the estate owners. Their influence on public opinion and behavior, though limited, is second only to that of a minister. Their membership in a particular church brings respectability to that denomination. Their sexual behavior sets standards (though often "double standards") of morality in a community in which many profess some form of puritanism. Their political adherence to a party immediately ensures a certain number of followers.

The ideological ambivalence inherent in Wesley people's perception of the big farmers stems from the very processes that demarcate this category. As mentioned before, big farmers belong to households who were fully engaged in the peasant labor process and who count members who still perform agricultural labor. However, the big farmer himself, usually the male head of a household, rarely engages in that process. Further, his or other members' limited engagement in that process is not necessary in the sense that it provides a surplus that allows all the members to enjoy a material standard of living way above that of most Wesley people. Most big farmers enjoy yearly banana incomes of six to ten thousand Eastern Caribbean dollars a year, four to six times that of many peasants. Nonetheless, big farmers, like most Wesley people, and contrary to the outsiders, derive a substantial part of their income from bananas. Like all Wesley people, they must deliver their bananas to the DBGA. That some of those farmers are now allowed to box their fruits in their own field does not erase the fact that their bananas are useless to them unless they acknowledge Geest's rights over production. In short, big farmers prey on neighbors and kin, but they remain structurally part of Wesley people and are recognized as such.

The Entrepreneurs

Though big farmers are tolerated, few people spontaneously express affection for them. In contradistinction, the seven men who firmly belong to the category that I label entrepreneurs are generally liked and admired by their fellow villagers. Wesley villagers do not use a generic word to refer to those entrepreneurs, but they frequently named one of them in reference to the wealth of one of the big farmers. The usual comment is that the entrepreneur "has more bucks" though he is "not playing big," or, simply, that he is a nicer individual.

Entrepreneurs are well-to-do villagers who do not derive the bulk of their income from the land. Rather, they all have a major asset used in the delivery of services: a full-sized truck regularly carrying commodities, a van used for transportation of villagers to Roseau, a major shop in Central Wesley, or a combination of any two. Additional assets may include a bakery or a pickup truck. All entrepreneurs own banana lands, though the size of holdings varies widely. Some also cultivate coconuts. However, except for two individuals who fit both the entrepreneur and farmer categories, the entrepreneurs have much less land than the big farmers. The basis of an entrepreneur's success is not agricultural.

Thus, an entrepreneur's independence from the peasant labor process is quite similar to that of a big farmer, though for very different reasons. All entrepreneurs are male heads of households, and none of them works the land regularly. Other members of the household produce the staple provisions used in the daily family meals, and grow some bananas for delivery to the DBGA. Yet, this engagement is no more necessary to the entrepreneur's household than it is to that of the big farmers. In fact, since most entrepreneurs gross larger incomes than the big farmers, the parallel with urban households able to maintain themselves on lower net incomes without any involvement in peasant work activities is even more appropriate. Thus, within the local context, what fully demarcates the people I call entrepreneurs from other Wesley villagers is not so much their ownership of a particular means of service, but rather the household's freedom from the necessity of maintaining itself through peasant work because of this ownership.

The distinction is capital: it helps us separate these entrepreneurs not only from full-time peasants but also from other families or individuals who may also provide those kinds of services but remain dependent upon peasant production of both bananas and home provisions. Significantly, Wesley people never compare smaller entrepreneurs (small shop owners, petty entrepreneurs relying on a bakery or a pickup) to the big farmers, though they are likely to pick one of the major entrepreneurs as "the richest man in the village." Whereas some bakers or small shop owners cannot afford to drop out of banana production, entrepreneurs can. Further, owners of pickups are quite directly affected by any sudden cessation of deliveries at Londonderry in ways unknown to the entrepreneurs. They lose not only their own necessary banana income but also the profits made from carrying other people's fruits.

Those differences manifested themselves quite strongly in 1979–80, in the aftermath of Hurricanes David and Allen. Whereas most Wesley people, including pickup owners, lost their major source of cash for periods ranging up to six months after each hurricane, entrepreneurs were partly shielded because they were not primarily dependent upon banana production. Peasants continued to purchase basic commodities from those entrepreneurs, or to pay for passenger transportation, depleting their meager prehurricane savings or increasing their debts. Entrepreneurs registered a more modest fall in income, but that fall was more because of the decline in the purchasing power of their clientele than because of the entrepreneur's own inability to harvest bananas.

Finally, though small entrepreneurship is usually one individual's supplementary strategy within a peasant household, full-fledged entrepreneurship is generally a family affair. The wife may tend to the shop while the husband drives the truck on weekdays. The son may use that truck for early deliveries to Londonderry to be replaced by the father in the afternoon for the Wesley-Portsmouth trips. In short, most members of the household contribute to the production of services, and the total returns on the services suffice for the reproduction of the household. The household's engagement in the peasant labor process is then, as in the big farmer's case, a supplement above the cost of its reproduction. However, since all entrepreneurs work full time, and since most members of the household share in the production of services, entrepreneurial households show much fewer signs of internal tension than do major farming households.

The entrepreneurial households project a positive image of united families. Wesley people regard the entrepreneurs as self-made men who deserve credit for the past labor and long hours they spent to accumulate their capital and to keep that capital productive. Some of the entrepreneurs are returned migrants who invested their savings into a vehicle or a small shop; others are former yeomen who expanded from a land base. Their success is almost always more recent and somewhat more astonishing to villagers than that of the big farmers. A few entrepreneurs tried to expand their agricultural base in the 1960s and '70s, but since 1979–80 they abandoned this approach in part because of the increase in the price of land and the fall of banana prices, in part because Hurricanes David and Allen reminded all Dominicans of the vulnerability inherent in agricultural production. That retreat, in turn, saved the entrepreneurs from labor conflicts with their fellow villagers. Thus though outsiders (especially estate owners) are thought to be "wicked people," and big farmers are simply "big men," entrepreneurs are seen as "good people," or "hard-working men." The efforts of the male head of the household are usually responsible for this evaluation, though individual case histories reveal that the wives or close kin of some entrepreneurs secured the household reproduction, guaranteeing food or supplemental income while the initial debts were being paid off.

To be sure, the whole household benefits from favorable perception of the senior male by fellow villagers. Further, entrepreneurs' families work hard to maintain a delicate balance between friendliness and businesslike behavior which guarantees them a steady flow of paying customers for their shops or their transport services. Precisely because they owe their livelihood to the peasantry's gross cash income, they are more interested than the big farmers in an improvement of the yeomen economic situation and resent more the fluctuation of banana prices. Indeed, whereas big farmers can fall back on alternative crops (coconuts, grapefruits), animal husbandry, or may simply expand their actual banana acreage in periods of low prices, entrepreneurs know that their success depends, in part, on the welfare of Wesley as a village of independent banana producers. Their prosperity parallels the growth of the yeomanry, whereas the big farmers' success slightly preceded that growth. Further, entrepreneurs who experienced social life in different settings or are younger than the big farmers cling less to the old ways and more willingly espouse democratic ideals. Still, because they have recently established their position, because they control few workers, because they tend to be ten to twelve years younger than most big farmers, and in principle, treat every villager on the sole basis of supply and demand, entrepreneurs do not yet have the social and ideological impact necessary to counterbalance the conservative influence of the outsiders and the big farmers.

The positive evaluation of the entrepreneurs by fellow villagers, their long working hours, and their genuine sense of belonging to a community should not obscure their role as the most important economic agents of mediation in Wesley after the DBGA. As agents of mediation, the entrepreneurs routinely collect a substantial part of the peasantry's cash income, a portion of which they transfer to the banks, to the state and, ultimately, to the industrialized countries which produce the vehicles they use or the commodities they sell. Their position is as ambivalent as that of the big farmers; but that ambivalence has a different base. Entrepreneurs are both cause and effect of Wesley's integration in the larger order. Their relative wealth does not come from agriculture but from the global integration of the village in the world economy. Yet, the most important mechanism of integration, the production of bananas for Geest, affects them only indirectly.

The Peasants

In contrast to outsiders, entrepreneurs, and big farmers, the overwhelming majority of Wesley people (about 80 percent) live in households that depend primarily on the peasant labor process for their reproduction. In contrast to both outsiders and entrepreneurs, they are connected to the world economy primarily through the production of bananas monopolized by Geest through the DBGA. One can add to that already impressive majority another 10 percent who depend almost equally on the peasant labor process and on some involvement in nonagricultural simple commodity production. Craftsmen, seamstresses, and some bakers belong to the intermediate category of "part-peasants." I will return to them later, but suffice it to say now that their varying dependence on the peasant labor process reinforces the general impression that most Wesley people engage in the same activities. Most Wesley people are peasants. Most are primarily banana producers. Most are integrated in the process of valorization first and foremost through the mechanisms set and controlled by Geest and the DBGA.

It is no wonder, then, that the number of banana growers registered in the Wesley District by the DBGA comes close to the total number of Wesley households.[3] Similarities and differences within the Wesley peasantry can indeed be organized in terms of variations among banana producers. Table 11.1, reproduced from DBGA files, offers a preliminary outlook on the average annual income of the banana producers and the size of the holdings they control. However, those figures are at best a gross generalization and could be misleading if used indiscriminately. Neither the DBGA nor any other agency has direct knowledge of the actual size of most Dominican banana fields. The DBGA does have precise and reliable figures on the volume of bananas it accepts from, and the cash payments it makes to, each individual in whose name the bananas are delivered. Yet the practice, common throughout the Windward Islands, to estimate individual acreage on production figures, is a shot in the dark. Conditions of production vary so widely from one enclave to another, from one plot to the next, and from one season to another, sometimes within the same plot, that the average yield per acre is anyone's guess, econometric fads not withstanding.[4]

Still, the DBGA figures can tell us with near perfect accuracy the number of growers in whose names bananas were delivered in a given

Table 11.1. District 17, Wesley Area: General Outlook on Banana Production and Income, 1976–80

Year	Number of Growers	Estimated Acreage	Accepted Production (Pounds)	Yield Tons/ Acres (Estimate)	Price ($ E.C. per pound)	Total Payments ($ E.C.)	Individual Incomes in $ E.C. (Average)
1976	445	1,040	8,621,021	3.70	.0881	759,799	1,707
1977	437	864	7,389,640	3.81	.1181	872,791	1,997
1978	483	884	11,208,912	5.65	.1455	1,631,709	3,378
1979	467	864	4,977,655	2.57	.1335	664,753	1,423
1980[a]	460	873	2,685,635	1.37	.1900	510,271	1,109

Source: DBGA files.

[a] Data available for only six months of the year.

banana district, during a specific year, the total production accepted from those growers, and the total cash they received in return. Those are useful starting points in our efforts to differentiate among the mass of Wesley yeomen and tenants who draw almost all of their cash income from the delivery of bananas to the association.

DBGA executives and consultants, including their resident statistician, are aware of the gross generalizations implicit in the figures reproduced in Table 11.1. For instance, they know for a fact that about one-fourth of the growers in District 17 (the Wesley area) fall way below the area's mean, whereas a substantial minority collect twice as much. Unfortunately, the breakdown still follows the practice of classifying producers according to estimated acreages, even though the most reliable figures are the amounts of bananas accepted from, and the amounts of cash paid to, registered growers. This breakdown is nevertheless a useful step from the generalizations of Table 11.1. Table 11.2 presents an illustration for the years 1977 and 1978.

I have chosen those two years simply because the first is, by and large, a normal year, while the second was exceptional both in terms of production and prices. Thus, despite the uncertainty inherent in the estimated acreages as a basis for classification, both years present similar patterns of distribution of the growers. We can place in a special group the growers who grossed about three times the mean incomes for those two years and hold more than ten acres according to DBGA estimates: they represent the bulk of the category I described as big farmers. Likewise, the growers estimated to hold "under one acre" (20 to 22 percent of the total population) roughly correspond to laborers and tenants likely to be engaged in other activities or living way below Wesley standards. We are left with the DBGA's two middle categories, the people who contribute the bulk of the accepted production.

Despite the uncertainty of the estimated acreages, the DBGA breakdown strongly corroborates the image of a typical Wesley banana producer, one who fits roughly 70 to 80 percent of the growers, depending on fluctuations of production. That is not to say that Wesley banana growers are a totally homogeneous mass but rather that the bulk of the production accepted by the DBGA comes from a majority of the villagers whose similarities are, at least, as important as their differences. That point should be kept in mind, and for many reasons. First, Wesley people themselves are aware of the existence of this core group and the factors that both tie and divide its members. Second, the existence of a middle mass points to the internal economic stability the peasantry

Table 11.2. Average Banana Incomes of Wesley Growers Grouped according to Estimated Acreages in Bananas, 1977–1978

	1977			1978		
Estimated Acreage	**Number of Growers**	**Accepted Production (in Pounds)**	**Gross Individual Income ($ E.C.)**	**Number of Growers**	**Accepted Production (in Pounds)**	**Gross Individual Income ($ E.C.)**
Under 1 acre	84	817,463	1,149	106	1,446,487	1,986
1 to 4.75	313	5,531,280	2,087	339	8,235,142	3,535
5 to 9.75	35	802,678	2,708	33	1,146,378	5,054
10 to 19.75	5	238,219	5,627	5	380,905	11,084

Source: DBGA files.

Note: Acreage projected from production.

gained when it conquered the units of production. The 250 or so yeomen households that comprise the majority of Wesley people form together a buffer against the potential rapaciousness of outsiders and big farmers alike, increase the competition among the entrepreneurs, and constitute an occasional resource for poor tenants and laborers. Despite its marked inequalities, the part-society of which the yeomanry forms the core is not pyramidal, but widely inflated at the center.

Trends within the Peasantry

One needs to look at the peasant household in Wesley both diachronically and synchronically to realize its role in differentiation. From a diachronic viewpoint, it contributes to the differentiation of segments of the peasantry but, when perceived in synchronic terms, it also seems to be part of an informal network that partly reduces differentiation. At any point during the three distinct phases of its life cycle, a household may contribute to or draw from the network, and the impact of that exchange can strongly reduce differentiation. We can follow the life cycle of the common Wesley household by way of a modified version of Chayanov's classic model.

Chayanov (1967: 57–58) starts his now classic table of the peasant household's life cycle with a married couple of twenty-five and twenty years of age. He assumes that they have one child every four years, and tries to determine the balance between producers and consumers over a twenty-five-year period. Each adult contributes a full unit of work; each child over eight contributes a half unit. Within this scheme, the greatest strain on the family is in its fourteenth year with a consumer/worker ratio of 1.94, but strain exists also at the very beginning. The couple starts with a deficit, so to speak: within a year or so, the first child already counts as a nonproductive consumer.

What strikes the ethnographer in Wesley, as in many other Caribbean villages, is that the local model avoids Chayanov's first downswing phase. In Wesley, until recently, a woman had her first child by seventeen or eighteen, but she remained in her parents' household. Cohabitation with a man, who may be the children's father, started rather late, ideally when the woman reached thirty, and the man was thirty-five. Further, children follow each other faster than in Chayanov's Russia, roughly at two-year intervals, especially the first three. Finally, it seems to this observer that Wesley children contribute a half unit of labor only in their early teens.

That contribution increases rapidly between twelve and thirteen, and the fourteen to fifteen year old is expected to share the equivalent of an adult load, even if only in specific tasks.

Thus, our ideal household (Type One) starts with five members representing nearly three full units of labor against a total of five consumers (Table 11.3), quite a safe beginning. Within a year or so, when the first child is fourteen or fifteen (especially if a male) he fully participates in the most arduous tasks of banana production (digging, harvesting, loading). A female of the same age is likely to take over many household chores. Thus, the household enjoys about ten years during which the ratio of producers to consumers is quite favorable (and can lead to savings) even if the children go to school and work on the field only during weekends. If one assumes that the children are all female, the greatest strain will come around the tenth year of the household's life, when at least six unproductive grandchildren of the founders would be residing within the unit. If the first children are male, the crunch comes much later.[5]

At that point, the household enters into its second phase, largely a transitory one, when strategies are constantly devised to restore the balance. The household may seek for the addition of a productive member (a nephew, a godchild), reduce the number of unproductive members, or provide alternative sources of income to members not needed in the peasant labor process. One of the couple's female children might be placed as a domestic, in town or with an outsider; another might be pushed into marrying early or finding a job in town. It is also during that phase that migration to foreign lands appears the most attractive. Nowadays, males in their late teens or early twenties are strongly encouraged by peers and relatives to apply for visas to the United States. The period of expectation and preparation may last as many as ten years, perhaps from fifteen to twenty-five. Chances of success vary, of course, according to a logic that remains obscure, at least to most peasants. Be that as it may, and regardless of the children's gender, the decade that follows the twelfth year is often one of readjustment, when household composition changes fast, according to opportunities. Since opportunities and recognition of opportunities vary greatly, one cannot summarize household composition during that decade in a table. Suffice it to say that Type Two is a transitory phase between Type One and Type Three, marked by the constant reformulation of strategies.

If strategies are successful, after its twenty-second year, the household enters into a third phase, and its character changes profoundly. Some of

Table 11.3. Producer/Consumer Ratio in a Type One Household

Year of Household's Existence	Couple's Age		Children's Age			Grandchildren						Producers	Consumers	C/P[a] Ratio	P/C[b] Ratio
	M	F	1st	2d	3d	1st	2d	3d	4th	5th	6th				
1	35	30	13	11	9							3.0	5.0	1.7	0.6
2	36	31	14	12	10							3.5	5.0	1.4	0.7
3	37	32	15	13	11							3.5	5.0	1.4	0.7
4	38	33	16	14	12							4.5	5.0	1.1	0.9
5	39	34	17	15	13							4.5	5.0	1.1	0.9
6	40	35	18	16	14	1						5.0	6.0	1.2	0.8
7	41	36	19	17	15	2						5.0	6.0	1.2	0.8
8	42	37	20	18	16	3	1	1				5.0	8.0	1.6	0.6
9	43	38	21	19	17	4	2	2				5.0	8.0	1.6	0.6
10	44	39	22	20	18	5	3	3	1	1	1	5.0	11.0	2.2	0.4

[a] C/P = Consumer/Producer.
[b] P/C = Producer/Consumer.

the children have left to form households of their own. However, several members of the third generation are still cohabiting with their grandparents, and they contribute labor in the house or in the field. Their own parents may or may not be members of the household. Indeed, one finds in households of that type children whose parents have migrated to town or to foreign lands. Still, in that third phase of the household's life, at least one member of the second generation remains with the founders, most often a woman with children of her own. In cases in which a male child of the founders remains, his own mate may move in, especially if they have children in common. Young men more rarely move in with their in-laws, whether or not the union is legalized. Beyond those variations, we can define a Type Three household as a multigenerational household in which the producer/consumer ratio is largely favorable because of the presence of the founders' grandchildren. Table 11.4 illustrates the point: even though it includes only one member of the second generation and only one sexually cohabiting couple, the original founders of the household, the producer/consumer ratio remains quite favorable for almost a decade. If more than one member of the second generation remains, or if the mate of one of the children moves in, the ratio might become more advantageous.

Anthropologists have repeatedly suggested the existence of a pan-Caribbean rule of household composition according to which the domestic unit should include only one sexually cohabiting couple. Even though they agreed that the rule was not always applied in practice (Mintz 1984: 238–40), they rarely questioned its general validity (but see Price 1970, for an exception). The Wesley data qualify further the assumptions about household composition. The majority of households with more than seven members in Table 10.1 tend to include more than one couple. To be sure, the ideal remains a Type One composition. According to this pattern, the man establishes the cohabitating union only when he can set his own independent household. This preference may explain why young men are less willing to move in with their in-laws. Cohabiting with the wife's parents implies that he has not yet reached full adulthood. Nevertheless, many Type Three households include more than one sexually cohabiting couple.

To be sure, Type Three households are less common than Type Ones. Further, their internal composition varies more freely than that of Type One, though not nearly so much as the composition of Type Two households, which are constantly changing. However, households of the third type are not a variation of the first type. Their peculiarity and their role

Table 11.4. Producer/Consumer Ratio in a Type Three Household

Year of Household's Existence	Founders Age M	Founders Age F	Second Generation Members	Third Generation Members			Fourth Generation Members			Producers	Consumers	C/P[a] Ratio	P/C[b] Ratio
22	56	51	32	16	14	12				5.5	6	1.1	0.9
23	57	52	33	17	15	13				6	6	1	1
24	58	53	34	18	16	14				6	6	1	1
25	59	54	35	19	17	15	1			6	7	1	0.8
26	60	55	36	20	18	16	2			6	7	1	0.8
27	61	56	37	21	19	17	3			6	7	1	0.8
28	62	57	38	22	20	18	4	1		6	8	1.3	0.7
29	63	58	39	23	21	19	5	2		6	8	1.3	0.7
30	64	59	40	24	22	20	6	3	1	6	9	1.5	0.6
31	65	60	41	25	23	21	7	4	2	6	9	1.5	0.6
32	66	61	42	26	24	22	8	5	3	6	9	1.5	0.6

[a]C/P = Consumer/Producer

[b]P/C = Producer/Consumer

appear most clearly when observed synchronically. First, a Type Three household is likely to last until the original founders pass away; thus its life-span is as long as that of Type One. Its initially high ratio of producers guarantees its own survival and prepares for the retirement of the founders. More important, a synchronic overview indicates that this household type does not exist by itself. That is, diverse units go through a Type Three composition while others are in their first or second phases (Types One or Two). It is the duplication of households of that third type that alleviates the burden of Type Two households, or reduces the plight of single parents who may be preparing to enter into a Type One household.

In conclusion, when we look at household composition both synchronically and diachronically, two basic tendencies emerge. On the one hand, beyond multiple variations, individual household trajectories reveal a tendency to move toward Type One or Type Three. That tendency might explain the high number of eight-member households in the 1979 survey (Table 10.1) since both types reach their full equilibrium around that number and since both types face imminent danger immediately past that point. On the other hand, if we look at the whole system at any single moment, and freeze, so to speak, the individual histories, we realize that the types partly complement each other. Type Two households are precarious, but they are the result of broken-down Type Ones, or they are on their way to Type Three. More important, they depend upon households of the first or, especially, the third type to compensate somewhat for their own productive weakness. Hence, it is the coexistence of related households of different types that maintains the system. Success and failure are shared beyond household boundaries. Each household can be seen as a member of a multicentered network that comprises all three major types and possible variation.

There are times, however, when the exchange between related households or the transition from one type to the other does not operate fast enough. These long-lasting differences settle in, and total banana incomes drop drastically or fail to reach expected levels for periods long enough to affect fundamentally the fortunes of present or future members. The discrepancies inscribed in the DBGA vouchers are, by and large, long-term consequences of failures to pass from one stage of the cycle to the next. That is to say, not all peasant incomes are equal, and labor seems to be the most important factor shaping those differences.

Differences in income among the vast majority of Wesley peasants, yeomen and tenants alike, are experienced primarily in terms of the value of their DBGA vouchers for a determinate period. That value itself depends on the volume of accepted bananas that they can claim to have delivered, mainly at Londonderry and Constant Spring. The basic data are available: the DBGA maintains extremely well-kept records of the total weight accepted from each grower and the cash amounts they receive. Those records are entered in computerized form, and it is possible to retrieve the data at any point. (Again, it is a pity that these data are not used so adequately as they could be, and that the distributions are couched in terms of acreage.) Some peasants (and big farmers), in turn, systematically saved their vouchers over long periods, and I have been able to retrace yearly amounts that antedate the DBGA computerization. To be sure, members of the same household, working on the same plot, under the same main activator may sell bananas under different names, weekly or seasonally rotating the registration of the vouchers among themselves in order to build credit for individual members of the family, to avoid certain DBGA charges, or simply to make it more difficult for strangers to determine the household's final gross income. More rarely, a poor kin, working on his or her own plot, may add a few bunches to someone else's load, and two different producing units then enter the DBGA computerized file as one. Ethnography becomes crucial here: intimate knowledge of the households can indicate whether it is necessary to treat two or three registered names as one, whether gross figures actually encompass more than one unit, and whether the amounts should be divided among two or more households.

I selected vouchers from the growers I knew best, that is, individuals whose conditions of production I was intimately familiar with, having visited their holdings, observed the work process, and heard repeatedly about who did what and when. Going back to the vouchers (and the final incomes), I then asked: What factors most influenced the outcome? What determined the total volume of bananas produced by a household?

The first step was to explore the range of variations expressed through final income. Since the DBGA data already offered a statistical overview (Tables 11.1 and 11.2), I found it more fruitful to look at particular cases rather than to refine the aggregate figures. Table 11.5 illustrates the differences in banana income among three yeomen between 1976 and 1979, computed from their actual vouchers, and verified in DBGA files. The figures reveal a consistency, except for 1977–78, when yeoman Y2's field was gravely affected by disease (leaf spot).

Yeoman Y3 represents a minute and dying segment of the Wesley yeomanry. He is now over seventy years old, and by 1979–80, he decided

Table 11.5. Banana Incomes of Three Yeomen, 1976–1979 (in $E.C.)

Year	Y1	Y2	Y3
1976	4,926	2,714	499
1977	5,732	2,577	321
1978	8,078	593	432
1979	2,117	1,748	83

Sources: Individuals' vouchers; DBGA files; author's interviews.

to withdraw completely from commercial banana cultivation. He produces mainly coconuts (for cash) and ground provisions. He works his plot all by himself; and from his viewpoint, coconut production requires more consistent but less physically demanding labor. His additional cash income from coconuts and the occasional sale of provisions is, in a good year, slightly more than his highest banana returns. Hence, his total cash income is usually less than half of that of yeoman Y2. This is not to say that his material standard of living is necessarily low: he also raises chickens and other animals in small numbers for his own consumption, and systematically avoids using cash as much as possible. Crucial to the understanding of his personal history is a second marriage to a much younger woman which prevented a smooth transition to a Type Three household.

Yeomen Y1 and Y2 are much more representative of male heads of household who own their land and use the bulk of it for banana production. However, one's income is consistently twice that of the other, even though both claim to work on three acres of land divided in two plots. Yeoman Y1 lives in a variant of a Type Three household with four adult children, including two sons who fully participate in the peasant labor processs. Yeoman Y2 lives in a variant of a Type One household with his current mate, but the only child residing with him is too young to work, and his other children are abroad.

Observation and analysis of a number of cases verify, beyond individual idiosyncrasies and the differential relevance of secondary factors, the crucial role of labor in shaping income differences. First, and partly to my surprise, when one compares the incomes of both yeomen and tenants, actual ownership matters much less in Wesley than in many other rural situations. For instance, Yeoman Y2's income is close or equal to that of many cultivators who do not work exclusively on their own land, but work both on land legally owned by them or their family and plots rented from the estate owners.

Security of tenure does affect final income, but the extent of that impact varies widely. Yeoman Y1, for instance, accumulated the bulk of his savings while working on a plot (originally uncleared or reforested) that was part of the Eden Estate. He claims that he was evicted on short notice and some of his young bananas were taken over by the owner. But he acknowledges with satisfaction that he had saved enough to buy himself a second plot, more accessible than the one he kept fallow while working on the Eden holding.

I have emphasized before that tenants pay only a symbolic cash rent. Their bananas are intercropped with the estate owners' coconuts and their surplus labor is extracted indirectly: a substantial part of their inputs and labor power benefits the owners' coconut production. In that context, the speed at which one can dig, harvest, and load and the consequent volume of bananas guaranteed by each of those steps in a specific period determine one's final income. A principal laborer who can rely on the labor of three adult males may decide to dig more banana holes, and plant bananas six feet apart (as opposed to eight), betting on gross weight rather than on the size of individual bunches. By his fifth cutting, he may be able to deliver an average of seventy bunches every two weeks from a single acre of land. If labor power is available in great quantity, and the tenant family holds more than one acre, it may be able to draw enough from the land before the maturation of the owner's plants. Again, I do not suggest that ownership does not matter: yeomen do tend to use more inputs than tenants, and tenants, in turn, manifest much less enthusiasm to work when it is clear to them that the coconuts are consuming the bulk of their labor. Still, given the tenants' total control over the labor process in the production of bananas, for the purpose of discussing that production, we may treat them as quite similar to the yeomen if we keep in mind their insecurity of tenure.

That insecurity itself is partly reduced by the natural speed of the banana cycle, which is almost equal to the minimum duration of a tenancy contract (a year). To be sure, property rights and the extent of actual control over the entire intercropped field influence the final outcome. Some tenants are evicted illegally, as yeoman Y2 claims to have been some twenty years ago. The presence of the coconuts can force the tenant into temporarily accepting yields one-half to two-thirds less than that of most yeomen. Yet, as mentioned before, tenants are quite aware of the implications of the race against the coconuts, and try to move out to new plots when their disadvantages reach a certain threshold. The ideal, of course, is not so much to rent a new plot, but to accumulate enough savings to escape the tenancy cycle all altogether. Estate owners know this strategy and try to turn it to their advantage: as mentioned before, land sales have become their major source of income. Still, in terms of net cash income from bananas, a tenant household using four full units of labor on a two-acre field recently cleared, or planted with young coconuts, grosses more cash at the end of the year than a yeoman household using two full units on a plot of the same size. If the producer/consumer ratio is much more advantageous in the tenant household, or if the yeoman household has to meet bank payments on the land, the discrepancy is even greater. Of course, in a relatively short time span, the successful tenant is likely to purchase land, and may end up paying, in the form of a purchase price, more surplus than was actually extracted from him or her during the tenancy years. In conclusion then, differences among tenants and yeomen are not so pervasive or so fundamental as one would expect: they are strongly qualified by the principal laborer's ability to muster labor from within the houschold.

A second and related surprise, at least to this observer, was the small impact of individual ownership within the yeomanry. People work on family land (registered sometimes in the name of a deceased parent), on land legally held by spouses or kin, with the same degree of perceived security as they would if they were the registered owners.[6] Again, it is not that ownership does not matter. Rather, when the issue of the identity of the principal laborer (the activator of the peasant labor process who plans the productive cycle and decides in whose name the bananas will be delivered) is in doubt, the individual less likely to prevail simply restrains from working on that plot. Here, the head of household usually has the final word, especially if he is a male between twenty-five and fifty-five. He may decide to deliver bananas under the name of his choice. One example I keep in mind is that of a married man, working on his sister-in-law's land: he sold bananas under his son's name because he felt that the registered income would enhance the boy's chances to obtain a visa to the United States.

Contrary to the suggestions of most analysts of the Windwards' banana industry (who, incidentally, deal with gross figures rather than the individual returns favored by an ethnographer), I discovered from looking at particular production histories that acreage itself matters secondarily. Households controlling fewer than one and a half acres of land usually gross less than $1,500 E.C. a year and constantly face grave financial difficulties. They might be placed in a subcategory of their own, regardless of the actual property rights, though the difficulties increase for the tenants whenever coconuts are planted in the field. Likewise, households controlling more than eight acres tend to live comfortably by local and national standards, and might be placed in another category. Also, when total acreage exceeds six or seven acres, the family tends to own most if not all the land and is more likely to experiment with a variety of crops around the banana field proper. Differences in plot size thus seem to affect field techniques and total harvest, and result in differences in income between the families holding fewer than two acres and those holding six, seven acres, or more. Yet, above two acres and below six or seven, land size alone does not account for major differences in income.

Indeed, my observations in the Wesley area suggest that the marginal productivity of land in the banana-producing peasant unit grows quite fast between one and two acres, increases at a slower pace between two and four acres, to reach its point of diminishing return somewhere around six acres. Past ten acres, family labor may not suffice, and at fifteen acres, one needs paid laborers from outside the household for both digging and harvesting, and the unit best functions as that of a big farmer. Land thus serves to differentiate systematically between only two categories of peasants: those with fewer than two acres (most often tenants or part-tenants) and those with more than six acres (most often yeomen). The bulk of the bananas produced in the Wesley area comes from households controlling between two and six acres, that is, within the very range in which actual acreage is rarely the determining variable.

Now, few households in Wesley control six contiguous acres of land. Few individuals have rights (customary or legal) over six acres altogether, and most banana plots are said by their cultivators to measure between one and a half and three acres. The net banana acreage may be unknown even to the main activator of the peasant labor process because of intercropping (on estate land), or because the actual portion of a plot planted in bananas varies and is never actually measured by the peasants. In that context, the manner in which the total acreage controlled by a household is divided into different parcels and the number and size of those parcels influence considerably the net volume of bananas produced. It matters much to the producers whether the four acres they control are divided in two plots, whether those plots are of equal size, or whether one is three times that of the other. In general, the greater and the more unequal the parceling, the lower the volume of bananas produced and the lower the subsequent income. A yeoman who controls four acres in two parcels is likely to produce fewer bananas than one who owns three acres in one piece.

The distribution of the total acreage into separate parcels matters particularly when it implies distance and differential access, which, in turn, influence labor. The principal laborer usually spends the working day on one plot, and chances are that he or she will not visit a second one until the task at hand is complete. With time, one plot is likely to take precedence over others, especially if the distance between plots requires a long walk or if one is clearly more accessible from the house. Some peasants organize their schedule so as to harvest two plots alternatively. Easy access to a vehicle does facilitate planting and harvesting more than one plot throughout the year. Since the vast majority of peasants neither drive nor own a vehicle, many deliberately neglect a second plot if work on that plot can hinder the volume of bananas gathered from their more important holding. In fact, even vehicle owners easily agree that not all their holdings receive the same attention.

The importance of a parcel itself depends not only on size, topography, and soil, but also on access from the house (by way of the tracks) and, most important, to the nearest feeder roads. Most unacceptable bananas are bruised *after* harvest, while being loaded on the pickups, or during transport to Londonderry. Further, the harvesting itself and the loading of the vehicle require a fair amount of labor to be expended in a short time. And finally, as mentioned before, the trip to Londonderry is conceived as a race, both because of DBGA and Geest regulations and because of the vehicle owners' desire to carry as many loads as possible. Again, distance does not influence the price, but it does influence a driver's propensity to commit himself to a particular grower. Thus from the producers' viewpoint, a field from which the bananas can be harvested, loaded, and delivered in the shortest possible time, with the amount of labor usually available to the household, has much more value than a field of equal or even larger size where those tasks are accomplished with more difficulty. Distance and access, for instance, contribute to the high price of estate lands in contrast to forested Crown lands way up in the Bush: estate lands are usually closer to the major roads. All in all, parceling does influence final income, especially inasmuch as it places increased demands on labor.

Hence, within most peasant households, a conjunction of factors, including ownership, land size, topography, and distribution of acreage, influence the total output of bananas and the subsequent income. However, the comparison of different units of production strongly suggests that labor is, most often, the primary variable, the one that most strongly determines success or failure. The impact of the other factors increases when these factors increase the demands on labor or, conversely, when they directly reduce its efficiency.

The point might seem simple but is important in light of what has been said of Dominican peasant labor in preceding chapters. When we put together what we now know of the integration of the Dominican peasantry in the world economy and the mechanisms of differentiation within Wesley, it appears that, *ceteris paribus*, a typical peasant household's income is proportional to the amount of labor units that it provides to international capital. "Success" at the local level is contingent upon the amount of labor a household sells to Geest Holdings, the integration of its activities within the sphere of valorization. The more a household can muster labor for the specific purpose of planting and harvesting bananas, the greater its income, but at the same time the more its members work for the benefit of international capital. Wesley's integration within the world economy contributes not only to differentiation between peasants and nonpeasants but also to differentiation within the peasantry itself.

A Woman, Alone and Scrunting

Wesley's encounter with the world thus demarcates villagers in varying ways. It demarcates peasants from nonpeasants inasmuch as they are integrated in different ways in the process of valorization and collect substantially different incomes from their labor. It demarcates different subgroups within the peasantry inasmuch as their net income depends on the amount of labor they can muster to produce bananas. It also differentiates villagers along gender lines. That differentiation operates among members of different households who may belong to the same socioeconomic category, but it increases the inequality also between men and women living in the same household.

To say that banana production recently increased gender inequality is, of course, to suggest that such inequality existed before the imposition of the peasant labor process in the production of the island's main export commodity. Yet before the advent of bananas, Wesley experienced gender inequality mainly through the processes of household formation (and transformation) described earlier. Women were (and still are) most likely to head households that never reach the ideal types described. That reality and the villagers' awareness of it were certainly the most important manifestations in Wesley, even if not the only ones, of the universally known phenomenon of male domination. My argument then, is not that bananas or cash relations created female subordination, but rather, that the general imbalance enshrined in female-headed households is aggravated and is now being reinforced by the increasing subordination of females within households of the ideal types.

To proceed with the argument, one needs to look at the socioeconomic cost of the system described earlier, a cost disportionately paid by a small number of households. In that system, the emergence of a new unit and, particularly, the transition from a provisional Type Two to a Type Three household require the discharging of a number of individuals from existing units. Most of these individuals successfully enter a unit that conforms or comes close to one of the ideal types (Type One or Type Three); many linger in the transitional Type Two for more than the expected decade. However, a significant minority of the people discharged enter into households that systematically fail to achieve a new balance between producers and consumers. Those households disproportionately bear the social cost of the system.

The anomalous or failed households come in many sizes and shapes; but the 1979 survey reveals that one of those forms is prevalent enough to be considered a specific, even though marginal, subtype, which carries an unequal share of the system's cost. It is the female-headed household with one or two dependent children too young to contribute any labor. Its producer/consumer ratio is likely to remain unfavorable for twelve to fifteen years and may never be fully reversed if the offspring leave early, or if the mother or her daughter face subsequent pregnancies. I estimate that about 10 percent of Wesley households belong to that category.

The head of household was identified by gender in 207 of the 456 households covered in the 1979 survey. The 207 sample is amply representative in statistical terms: it equals more than 40 percent of the total number of Wesley households. Also, those 207 households come from the subsections of the village that I know best: Eden Road and Phillips Avenue where I lived in 1979 and 1981–82 (ninety-nine households), Priest's Gutter, Hunt, Hill, and Poor Man's Corner. Thus ethnographic observation greatly increased my understanding of the reality suggested by the numbers. I can strongly affirm, for instance, that in practice as well as in the projections based on the household types (Table 11.3 and 11.4), households with fewer than five members tend to have a difficult time making ends meet.

The 207 cases in which the head of household was identified reveal that many more households are headed by males (65 percent) than females (35 percent). The sample also indicates that as many as 73 percent

Table 11.6. Population of 207 Households according to Gender of Head of Household

	Female-Headed Households (FHH)	Male-Headed Households (MHH)	Total
Number of households	73	134	207
Population	314	842	1,156
% of households	53.30	64.70	100
% of population	27.20	72.80	100
Average number of members	4.3	6.3	5.6
Households with fewer than 4 members	36	39	75
Individuals living alone	14	21	35
Households with 2–3 members	22	18	40

of the village population live in male-headed households (Table 11.6). Further, male-headed households (hereafter MHH) also tend to have more members than female-headed households (FHH). The average numbers are six members for MHH versus four members for FHH. Hence, even in broad statistical terms, units differentiated by the gender of the head of household seem to present specific tendencies.

The differences between the two types become even more striking if one looks at the residual group of seventy-five households with fewer than four members. The numbers suggest a much greater chance for a man than for a woman to be the head of those households. However, while we look at the numbers, we must remember the analysis of the producer/consumer ratio: given the patterns of household formation, households with more than one but fewer than four members are likely to have many more consumers than producers. Within that context, we can safely suggest that women are disproportionately heading households in which the producer/consumer ratio is unfavorable.

To verify that proposition, we need to eliminate the thirty-five households of the sample composed of a single adult living alone. We are left with forty households with two or three members, twenty-two of which are FHH against eighteen MHH. A tiny minority of the MHH is comprised of single males living with one or two dependent offsprings; but, as a rule MHH with two or three members include an adult woman who may or may not be the mother of the third member. In contrast, FHH of that size are generally composed of a single mother living with her dependent offspring. Thus, about 10 percent of the households in Wesley are composed of single mothers and dependent children who face one of the most unfavorable producer/consumer ratios experienced in the village. Further, about 30 percent of all FHH are of that type. In short, there is a much stronger chance for a woman to find herself heading a household that cannot make ends meet for some twelve or fifteen years.

To be sure, from a statistical viewpoint, those numbers are not exceptional. The proportion of Wesley women who find themselves in that situation is still lower than, say, that of black women in the United States. However, this is no consolation for the Wesley women themselves. Further, the inequality does not deserve less attention for at least three reasons. First, those FHH bear disproportionately the cost of maintaining the system's general equilibrium. Their formation, which eventuates from the discharging of individuals from the transitional Type Two, guarantees many other households' successful passage to a balanced Type Three. Second, even though many single mothers living with their children receive occasional help from relatives, neighbors, or the children's father, such help is limited if only because of those individuals' objective limitations. Hence, those women find themselves at the very bottom of the economic ladder in a context in which most families live a relatively precarious existence. Wesley people recognize that fact: they are much more likely to say in reference to a household of this type: "Rose and her children are scrunting." Third, and more important perhaps, even though such women are in a minority because the gap between their households and the majority of Wesley people is so wide and because a Type One household typically starts a decade at least after the birth of the first child, the threat of "scrunting" looms large in the minds of most Wesley females. Few can predict what will actually happen between the birth of the first child and the period at which they and the father are expected to establish a new household. In many cases, indeed, the relationship will not last, and the Type One household is established with another man. However, that second mate himself is not likely to enter into a cohabiting union without a child of his own. Hence, a second pregnancy is often a woman's tenuous guarantee that she will enter into a Type One household. Yet, at the same time, second and third pregnancies increase the possibility of "scrunting" (if the second relationship does not mature).

Here, statistics and local perception emphasize strikingly different aspects of the same reality. The numbers do indicate that only a minority of women ultimately find themselves in those economically weak households. Yet the threat itself is rightly perceived as a general one: the possibility of finding oneself in that situation affects most Wesley women. Parents use the threat of "scrunting" to monitor their daughters' relationships. Siblings and friends make the adolescent female aware of the dreadful possibilities. Hence the young Wesley woman perceives male/female relationships (though, not necessarily sexual activity itself) against the background of that generalized fear. From her mid-teens to her early or mid-thirties, she perceives her future and that of her children as dependent upon a man's willingness to form a Type One household with her. The perception of that dependence diminishes with time, either after the household is firmly established or because the woman herself has abandoned all hopes of a cohabiting union. But by then, she is at least in her mid-forties and her own daughters have already inherited the fear of "scrunting" themselves.

Female Crops and Male Cash

The generalized fear of "scrunting" accentuated the imbalance of power between men and women in Wesley long before the advent of bananas, but many older women point to socioeconomic features that, until recently, mitigated complete male domination within the household. First, peasants occasionally sold provisions to hucksters who carried them to Portsmouth, and women who entered a cohabiting union with a holding of their own had much to say about the timing and the volume of those sales. Their varying power was due in part to the then lesser value of cash exchanges and in part to many villagers' view that provisions were "female" crops; women had the power of decision vis-à-vis the products and were not excluded on the basis of gender from any step of the work process that led to those products. Likewise, they fully participated in the processing of cassava, whether the farine so produced was for sale or for home consumption.

Second and more important, the occasional availability of estate labor made it possible for women to gather independent cash income, part of which (at least) they could use at their sole discretion. Many female interviewees clearly remember occasions when they worked a day or two, harvesting limes on estate land, or when they increased the number of tasks they performed because they felt the need to buy an item that their mate judged (or could have judged) superfluous. To be sure, they did not accumulate much cash, with the ongoing price for filling a whole barrel of limes set at twenty to twenty-four cents. Estate labor was (and still is) considered to be a more typically masculine occupation, probably because men always received higher wages. However, when in dire personal need, a woman could bring a sister or even a young child to help her complete her tasks faster, filling more barrels, and collecting more cash for the day. More important, the men who performed the heavier tasks did not earn much more, nor was their employment more secure. Thus, despite the generalized fear of "scrunting" alone and the subordination entailed in every woman's dream to enter an ideal Type One household, women could rely on modest forms of economic independence and partly contest male domination once the union was safely established.

Seen against that background, the advent of bananas appears to have increased gender inequality both directly and indirectly. First, the decline of estate labor and the marginalization of the sale of ground provisions—two side effects of banana production—removed the most important basis from which women could challenge male domination within the household. Second, the mechanisms of banana production and distribution themselves directly increased the power of adult males. They did so by sharpening the differences between collective and individual participation and rights, first in the labor process itself, and then in the control of the cash income.

I suspect that the peasant labor process always requires what I call an activator, an individual who is not necessarily in charge, but does have a greater say in certain key decisions concerning the nature of field activities, their timing, their ordering toward specific goals. I have never seen or heard of a field where any household member could go and do anything at will and at any time; and it is hard for me to imagine one. Some descriptions of vanilla production on squatted Crown lands in the mountains around Wesley come closest to my sense of the agricultural anarchy of a peasant labor process without activator, but the witnesses are quick to point out that vanilla did not survive and, more important, that the peasants of the area who relied heavily on vanilla did not plant it in a hazardous manner.

The activator may then be a character who always coexists with the peasant labor process even though his features are not always the same. The individual filling the function need not be the principal laborer as he tends to be in Wesley. I know cases in Wesley in which an older male continues to plan field activities while his son consistently performs much more labor on that same field. Likewise, the activator is not necessarily the head of the household. A single female head of household might relinquish all control over the labor process to an elder child, or even to a nephew or cousin whose presence in the household helps redress the producer/consumer ratio. Hence, the status and power of the activator may vary according to the specifics of the labor process itself (the crop, the type of field, the techniques used, etc.), but also according to the household as well as the larger sociocultural environment.

Bananas' emergence as a dominant export commodity produced through the peasant labor process considerably increased the power of the activator in most Wesley households. In contrast to ground provisions or vanilla, which could be harvested at any time, and sold in different degrees of maturation, bananas can be cut only if they meet DBGA standards. Further, they require immediate postharvest delivery. Timing is important in such a context, as is the individual doing the planning. Moreover, as mentioned before, the tasks that mark the beginning and end of the banana cycle (digging and harvesting) require intense labor. At harvest time, for instance, heavy bunches must be lifted by hand and carried to the vehicles on the roadside. Women may dig banana holes, but they contribute to the harvesting only if the labor available from the male members of the household is not sufficient. Finally, in part because males are already present at harvest time (cutting the bananas and loading the vehicles), in part because of the need to influence selectors, men tend to bring bananas to the boxing plant even if women have been active in other steps of the labor process. The heavy male participation in the final tasks of the cycle often leads to men's perception of the bananas as their individual property, especially if one individual combines the functions of principal laborer and activator of the peasant labor process. That attitude exists even in cases in which the male combining those functions is not the head of the household.

The increasing distinction between household and individual rights, duties, and responsibilities implied by the widespread application of the peasant labor process in the production of bananas for export is further upheld by the mechanisms of distribution and payment set by the DBGA. As mentioned before, at the time of delivery, the producer receives a voucher which supposedly identifies the individual "owner" of a particular load of bananas. Yet there is no way to verify the bananas' origins or the actual identity of the legal holder of the plot from which they came. In practice, bananas are registered under any name, generally at the discretion of the head of the household. I have witnessed bananas delivered under the name of people who had left the island long before I first went to Wesley. Still, DBGA vouchers bear a single individual's name regardless of household contribution to the labor process. To be sure, many names can be used consecutively (or alternately) by one household, but in cases of conflict the head of the household, often male, prevails, and the more so if he also acts as principal laborer and activator of the labor process. Hence, the distinction between household and individual rights in the labor process brought by bananas is furthered by the contractual relationship implied in the DBGA procedures.

Finally, just as the recorders present vouchers to anyone who delivers the bananas, so do DBGA cashiers convert vouchers to cash for those who present them at DBGA headquarters in town after the required delay, or at Londonderry a week later. Typically, the male who picks up the vouchers at the time of delivery does not relinquish them and ends up collecting the cash. This is not to suggest that Wesley men use that cash without consideration of the household's needs. However, the tendency to view the bananas as theirs, regardless of origins or conditions of production, makes it much easier to perceive the cash itself as an individual compensation. Hence, most men feel they have the right to make immediate decisions about the sums they collect prior to any eventual discussion of household budget. Few women, in turn, would contest that right. No Wesley male would think twice about stopping at a rum shop on the way back from Londonderry and disposing of the money as if it all belonged to him. The amount used in drinks or in petty gambling is restricted only by his own sense of responsibility. Likewise, the male who collects the cash in town may return with a new item of clothing for himself, bought on the spur of the moment. Even though he may also bring back a gift for his wife or an item much needed for household use, he still exercises discretionary power over some of that cash prior to the woman's participation in budgetary decisions. In contrast, the woman must present her individual needs to the man's consideration after or (more prudently) before he collects the cash. I emphasize that this prerogative does not at all suggest that most Wesley males spend banana money selfishly, without concern for the needs of their family. In fact, the opposite is more likely to be true. Further, the play inherent in relations among individuals is much greater than this generalization can indicate. Yet the generalization is no less valid: the commodification process does increase the imbalance of power between men and women within the household.[7] In fact, adolescents internalize the inequality at quite an early age. I have more often heard of a young male who returned home from town with a radio, a watch, a case of soft drink bought with banana money than of a young woman who dared to "break" the sum for the purchase of a dress or a pair of shoes. In short, not only are Wesley women more likely to head failing households but their power of decision is quite unequal to that of their male counterparts even in the most successful households regardless of their labor contribution.

Cash and Christianity

A much more complex case is that of the recent emergence and increasing appeal, in Wesley, of a number of Christian churches, in addition to the traditional Roman Catholic and Methodist denominations. One cannot isolate the new economic relations spurred by the spread of bananas as the main determinant, or even the immediate trigger, of the religious phenomenon, but it would be equally wrong to dismiss those relations in trying to account for the success of the churches. Here, more than in the case of female domination, economics and cultural tradition, world trends and local response merge in such a way that the ethnographer can only deal with the entire combination of factors rather than a causal sequence, however complex.

The facts can be summarized quite briefly. Traditionally, a majority of Wesley people have been Roman Catholics, but since the early nineteenth century Methodism drew a substantial number of followers and made an impact on the educational system. Up to the first half of this century, villagers belonged to one of those two churches. Since the 1950s, and particularly since the early 1970s, the emergence and growth of other denominations (mostly Christian fundamentalist churches) have substantially changed the numbers of Catholics and Methodists in Wesley. Most observers (including local residents, this writer, and the Roman Catholic rector of the Wesley parish) tend to agree that the newer churches drew substantially more Roman Catholics than Methodists, even though their growth affected both groups. Nowadays, nearly two-thirds of Wesley people identify with or practice Catholicism or Methodism, and the Catholic Church still attracts the greatest number of professed members. Some eight hundred people are divided among the Seventh Day Adventist Church, the Christian Union Mission Church, the Baptist Church, the Pentecostal Church, the numbers descending more or less in that order. About a dozen villagers associate with other fundamentalist denominations, such as the Seventh Day Church of God, or the Jehovah Witnesses, but do not have a fixed place of worship.

The recent advance of Protestantism in its more fundamentalist manifestations is not unique to Wesley or even to Dominica. It is a side effect of both the growing cultural influence of the United States on the former British colonies of the Caribbean and of relative shifts in the balance of ideological power within the United States itself. However, the timing of the fundamentalist penetration, its greater increase in the Wesley area, its greater impact on the Roman Catholic congregation, and its stronger appeal to certain segments of the peasantry, all suggest a convergence of local, national, and international trends.

The spread of the more recent religious groups coincides with the expansion of United States cultural influence on the British Caribbean, but it also overlaps, in time, with the physical and cultural opening of the Wesley area to the rest of Dominica and to the world at large. During this period the influence of local and foreign radio programs on Wesley people has been growing particularly because of the coming of electricity to parts of the village and the spread of cheap transistors bought with banana money. Today it is possible, and in some cases necessary, to travel weekly or biweekly to Roseau or Portsmouth, an unthinkable proposition for most Wesley people just fifteen years ago. Nowadays, nonresident (and foreign) preachers can reach Wesley by road fifteen minutes after landing at Melville Hall Airport or two hours after leaving the capital. Not surprisingly, even though the fundamentalist presence started to manifest itself with the arrival of the Seventh Day Adventists in the 1950s, most fundamentalists are recent converts who abandoned the Roman Catholic or the Methodist church less than twelve years ago.

One needs to see the recent religious trends in light of Wesley's history. Wesley's past had been markedly different from that of the rest of Dominica in its linguistic and religious dimensions. The early visibility of the Methodists and their outstanding contribution to formal education had already accustomed Wesley's Roman Catholics to religious pluralism, the benefits of which they could not deny. Wesley's Methodists, in turn, had accustomed themselves to being a demographic minority, even if a very proud one. Partly because of the isolation of La Soye, both groups had learned to coexist (more or less) peacefully through at least a century of conversions and intermarriage. In short, Wesley people, as a group, were more inclined to religious tolerance than most other Dominicans.

They easily listened to different hymns especially if the new tune was in English, the native language of all the foreign-born missionaries who conducted the first regular services of the new churches. As mentioned before, even now all the ministers (residents and nonresidents alike) who practice in Wesley are outsiders. Further, all except the Roman Catholic priest are native English speakers. Not surprisingly, many of them perceive the linguistic peculiarity of the Wesley-Woodford Hill-Marigot area as an advantage even though the continuing normalization of English throughout the island now makes it possible to proselytize in English everywhere in Dominica. Missionaries from Antigua, Barbados, or the United States feel more comfortable in a linguistic environment such as that of La Soye where the presence of the Lesser Antillean Creole is negligible. In contrast, I have heard some of the new converts make fun of the Catholic rector's heavy French accent.

Yet none of those factors solely accounts for the stronger impact of the new churches on Roman Catholics, nor can one find an explanation in the important fact that the resident Catholic minister is the only white preacher practicing permanently in the area. Most Protestant ministers do not live in the village, and even those who establish residence there for a few months are perceived as outsiders despite some phenotypical and cultural similarities. Neither do the physical opening of the area or its religious and linguistic particularities explain that most fundamentalists enjoy material conditions superior to those of many Roman Catholics and nearly equal to those of the Methodists.[8] Why are the fundamentalists attracting more Roman Catholics? And why do long-time fundamentalist families seem to be better off than Catholic families? Both questions call for a variety of answers. However, they are also linked to the persistent peasant dilemma of balancing production and consumption, especially in an economy in which the availability of cash strongly influences the level of consumption of the household. I suggest that, *ceteris paribus*, the conversion from Roman Catholicism to almost any of the fundamentalist denominations drastically reduces the size of what Wolf (1966: 7) calls the ceremonial fund of the peasant household, hence immediately improving its usual standard of living.

The cost of the First Communion may be the most important cash expenditure spared if a household converts from Roman Catholicism to any one of the fundamentalist denominations. Roman Catholic First Communions require more elaborate festivities than similar rituals in Protestant churches. Further, within the Roman Catholic denominations, First Communions are generally more costly than baptisms (if only because the child is baptized at an early age), and a First Communion can use up one-third of the annual income of an average household. Some informants admit that it took them years to pay back the debts accumulated for the festivities that are an integral part of the ritual. Since First Communions are likely to follow one another at intervals that duplicate that between the children's births, the conversion to another denomination often eliminates a pattern of indebtedness.

The timing of the ceremonial expenses across religious lines may be as important as their total costs. The Roman Catholic baptism is a much more individualized ceremony, which households face one at a time while the child is still in infancy. Hence households must go through a costly public exhibition for a member who is not likely to be productive for the next ten years. A succession of such rituals creates a large hole in the household's consumption fund, even if each ceremony requires less expense than a First Communion. A Roman Catholic household with three children is barely out of this pattern before it must look forward to the First Communion of the oldest child. Expenses of a First Communion vary, but they generally exceed that of the baptism-christening, and they are likely to hit the Roman Catholic household at a time of weakness, when the balance between producers and consumers is quite unfavorable. And again, they are likely to repeat in too rapid a succession.

In sharp contrast, fundamentalist rites of passage (including baptism) tend to be collective. Each participating household receives less public exposure and entertains fewer guests; hence cost is reduced. Second, the baptism and the First Communion are perceived as stages of the same step: the member's entry into the congregation. Therefore, fundamentalists tend to focus on one ceremony, not two. Third, and most important, this dual celebration occurs at a time when the child contributes at least half a unit, and often a full unit of labor, and after the household has moved out of its most critical phase. Finally, the festivities that accompany those religious ceremonies among fundamentalists are much less ambitious than those financed by both Catholic and Methodist families, and their modesty is socially approved. An inexpensive party after a Roman Catholic christening would mark the parents and godparents of the child as "cheap"; a similar function, costing the same amount, would indicate how "Christian" a fundamentalist family is. Further, in the latter case, the prohibition against alcoholic beverages implies that a sizable expense is avoided and that equal display in terms of social recognition can be achieved at nearly half the cash cost. Parents do not consciously make such calculations in changing religious allegiance, but families with large numbers of children, especially those with a single parent (or only one fully productive parent), seem more prone to join the new churches.

Further, an overwhelming majority of the recent converts joined the fundamentalist church of their choice at a time when the household to which they belonged was experiencing a downswing, most often the result of an unfavorable balance between producers and consumers. The life histories of the earliest converts particularly indicate that the shifts occurred at a time when "things were bad." The elimination of the major ceremonial expenses, conservative patterns of food and drink consumption, and the prohibition against alcoholic beverages contributed to increase the cash available for productive investments, particularly among Seventh Day Adventists. Subsequently, the rapid improvement of some early converts' basic consumption fund in turn increased the appeal of their denominations to friends and relatives who remained in the Catholic or Methodist ranks.

The sudden spread of the fundamentalist churches revived religious discourse in Wesley and increased the influence of all ministers. Methodist and Catholic leaders, lay and clerical alike, now want to influence the daily choices of their brethren at least as much as the fundamentalist preachers influence their own. They are now likely to present an official church position on issues about which they spoke less directly in the recent past: government programs, family planning, production, education, electoral politics. Villagers of all denominations affirm that the public association of the local and national Catholic clergy with the Freedom party was the determining factor in the election in 1980 of that party's candidate as representative of the Wesley constituency (which includes Calibishie and Woodford Hill). Some viewed the priests' public endorsement as interference; some viewed it as positive influence. A few people abandoned the Catholic Church in the aftermath of the elections. All agree that the church made a difference.

Yet the most important impact of the fundamentalist advance may well be on household composition and gender inequality. The premarital pregnancies tacitly accepted by Catholic and Methodist leaders for more than a century now bring public condemnation on the parents and expulsion from the fundamentalist churches. However, the unwed mother and her immediate relatives bear a heavier share of that condemnation. A young unmarried mother finds it more difficult to reintegrate socially than the father of her child, and her parents penalize her for their disgrace. The public condemnation of those pregnancies by members of the new church influence the rest of the Wesley population as well. Not surprisingly, unsafe abortions and infanticide seem to be on the increase. Likewise, the marrying age is dropping drastically, even among

Catholics, and many new households now comprise only a young couple (with or without young dependent children), a tendency that partly accounts for the high numbers of households with three or four members in the 1979 survey (Table 10.1). The new households, which bring Wesley closer to the "normal" patterns of the Christian West, start with a precarious producer/consumer balance, if not with a deficit. Their growing presence is likely to influence the system described earlier, though their final impact will depend on the readjustments and modifications made by Wesley people.

CHAPTER 12

Peasants, Part-Peasants, and Change: The Banana Children

Jamais nous ne pourrons vous rassurer.
Nous les derniers des paysans
A nos arbres sacrifiés
Nous ne savons ce qui nous retient . . .

—Kateb Yacine, *Le Cadavre encerclé*

The renewed encounter between Wesley and the world triggers and modifies so many trends that what the ethnographer observes is, ultimately, history in the making. Even if one could predict Dominica's economic future, no one knows how aggregate individual decisions will skew the relevance of the social and ideological tendencies observed at the microlevel. Those decisions, in turn, will likely influence the routine of village life and the direction of the nation, even if only in the long term. Hence, the selection of any recent development as an indicator of impending change is an ambiguous and limited exercise. The justification for taking that big leap falls somewhere between the desire to demonstrate the vitality of local response to national and international influences and the hope that such demonstration may add to the analytical arsenal of those Dominicans concerned with greater social justice. I share that concern. This chapter reformulates (even though it may not answer) some of the most salient questions put to me, in the field, by the many "banana children" who became friends.

The Part-Peasants

The integration of the peasant labor process in the capitalist process of production creates a tension between the logic of reproduction of the household and the mechanisms of the larger economy within which the household is integrated. Modern peasantries are characterized by the ever-increasing intrusion of the sphere of valorization in the daily life of the household. Consequently in many rural contexts the bulk of household production is exchangeable (Chevalier 1983: 118–22). Likewise anything that the household needs and does not produce could be acquired through the market. However, given the household's reliance on the peasant labor process for its reproduction, the need to balance consumption with production, the availability of cash, and the conditions prevalent in most Third World countries, only a few commodities actually enter or leave the peasant household. Hence, many items fully integrated in the sphere of valorization do not actually change hands. We may want to call them "unrealized" commodities, as opposed to "concrete" commodities, commodities that have physically been exchanged.

The tension between concrete and unrealized commodities is exacerbated by the greater impact of outside forces than household members on the actual exchanges that take place. We can state that whatever the household needs is physically available on the market and that household members may purchase it if they have enough cash. However, we cannot make the opposite generalization, at least not in the exact same sense. Many household assets are not realized as commodities in the outside world even though they are exchangeable. This observation applies to what Chevalier (1983: 118–19) calls "subsistence commodities"; it is also true of labor power. Thus the degree to which commodities produced outside realize themselves within the household and, alternatively, the degree to which commodities produced within the household (including labor power) realize themselves on the outside depend not only on the peasants' production/consumption balance, but on the effect of outside forces on the household. Regardless of the amount of extra yams a Wesley family produces above its consumption needs, those yams will not actually be exchanged—they will not be realized as commodities—if nobody purchases them.

The point seems simple enough; but it becomes crucial when we realize that most, if not all, of the peasantry's labor power is exchangeable, and that not all of that available labor power is necessarily used within the household. Quite often, the land/labor ratio within the household is such that there is more labor power than can be used within the unit even though the household cannot meet some of its basic consumption needs. The principal laborer and his or her most constant assistants may produce enough starch to keep the household way above starvation; they may, in addition, adequately cultivate the small banana field they control, and still not manage to acquire other necessities.

Hence, it would be a mistake to take the deployment of labor outside the unit of production as an indication that the household is living above subsistence level, that even all food needs have been met. In the case of Wesley and, I suspect, most of Dominica, the opposite is often true: many of the people who engage in nonagricultural activities for remuneration live in households precariously close to the subsistence level.[1] Those households would barely be able to manage without that outside involvement; but, more important, they would practically disappear without their general reliance on the peasant labor process for a minimum of food and cash. It is that continuous dependence on the peasant labor process for a minimum of food and cash that characterizes part-peasants.

Part-peasants then tend to reach out for work on the outside because their labor power cannot be used within the unit of production controlled by the household, even though that household is close to (or below) the subsistence level and remains dependent on the peasant labor process. Unfortunately, outside employment is not easy to find: it depends on conditions over which the peasantry has little impact. Many individuals try to bypass this difficulty through self-employment by becoming nonagricultural petty commodity producers.

About seventy-five Wesley people (60 percent of whom are males) neatly fit in this category. More than twenty-five men who describe themselves as builders, masons, carpenters, electricians, or plumbers, and do function as such when the opportunity presents itself, remain both physically engaged and economically dependent upon the peasant labor process. In fact, some of them act as principal laborers within their household. So do three fishermen in their late fifties, whose occupation the younger generation never learned and most men of their own age have abandoned since the cultivation of bananas became a more profitable enterprise. Seven to ten younger males who describe themselves as chauffeurs and sometimes work in that capacity for a big farmer or an entrepreneur, an equal number of mechanics, a dozen seamstresses, and fifteen to twenty part-time and full-time domestics also fit this category. So do most of the hucksters, and an indeterminate number of other small entrepreneurs.

The difficulty of fixing an exact number to these subgroups points to an inherent characteristic of the part-peasant category: its boundaries fluctuate as much as those of the peasantry itself, though usually in opposite directions. When a particular household meets its consumption needs through the production of cash crops and provisions, but does not generate a substantial excess of either food or cash, individual members who participate in the peasant labor process are less likely to experiment with outside employment unless the projected income clearly exceeds their net productive contribution. At such times, a single absence may threaten the balance between production and consumption and jeopardize the whole household, even though that absence might imply an increase in cash income. On the other hand, when the marginal productivity of labor has reached its point of diminishing return within the peasant unit, individual laborers whose help is less crucial to the activator of the labor process might take the most menial jobs.

The chances of success of any individual engaged in outside activities are often dependent on the general state of the yeomanry within the enclave or within the village itself. Natural disasters, drops in the prices of agricultural products, including, of course, bananas, affect builders, seamstresses, electricians, and small shopkeepers more directly and often before they affect the larger entrepreneurs. The activities of part-peasants engaged in petty commodity production or small trading can rarely survive a sudden decrease in their expected clientele. When this fieldwork first started in 1979, there were many more small shops in Wesley than there are now. Some of them were unlicensed, others carried only a few cans of evaporated milk, a few candles, some sugar and some kerosene, and other common articles. In the aftermath of the extraordinary banana harvest of 1978, which paralleled an increase in the price paid to the producer, many yeoman families had accumulated enough cash income over their minimal reproduction cost to invest a small amount of capital in such ventures. More important, the majority of Wesley people had increased their cash incomes just enough to expand their daily purchases in such a way that they all contributed to support these new ventures. By 1981, after the national strike of 1979, two hurricanes, and a sudden fall in the price paid to the grower (artificially maintained by the

DBGA in 1979), more than half the small shops had disappeared. The circumstances that determine the eventual size of the part-peasant group hence depend on a conjunction of factors: (1) the marginal productivity of labor within the peasant units of the village, (2) the relative importance of particular individuals to the peasant labor process within their households, (3) the general purchasing power of the yeomanry, and (4) the perceived range of outside opportunities.

The Lumpen Peasantry

Outside opportunities are not always readily available. In the case of Wesley, or that of the neighboring villages of Woodford Hill and Marigot, the craftsmen, seamstresses, or fishermen involved in petty commodity production can survive because cash incomes from bananas are much higher here than in most Dominican villages. Hence, besides relying on their home-grown provisions and a minimal cash income from their own bananas, the nonagricultural petty commodity producers have learned to depend on a minimal cash flow within the villages. However, as suggested above, any sudden decrease in that cash flow presents them with an immediate and considerable threat. Moreover, even when the cash flow remains stable, some workers still cannot make ends meet, often because the demand for the skills they possess remains low. The few young mechanics of Wesley, although talented, use their skills only occasionally, not because vehicles do not break down, but because the total number of vehicles is simply not enough to sustain even semipermanent self-employment. Likewise, Wesley's only part-time photographer emigrated to Guadeloupe after the yeomanry's condition declined in 1980.

The situation is much worse in many other Dominican villages. If the land base of individual households is too small or unreliable (as on the dry segments of the western coastal strip), or if the cash flow remains excessively low (as in the Southeast), the petty producers do not have much of a clientele. If population increase is combined with relatively low access to productive land and a relatively large flow of cash coming from the outside, individual craftsmen face an extremely harsh competition (as in the areas surrounding Grand Bay or Mahaut). As mentioned above, straightforward wage labor on a permanent or seasonal basis, never a strong characteristic of Dominica, has now dwindled to the point of irrelevance in most of the countryside. Hence, a substantial amount of labor power unused in the production of food for the household or of commodities for the national and international markets remains idle even with the existence of nonagricultural commodity production. Many of the nonagricultural petty commodity producers are thus *underemployed*; many who have not learned a craft or who cannot use the craft they acquired are fully *unemployed*. They rely on starches produced within peasant households, and occasional cash from their banana-producing kin; but their labor power is useless within the units, given the available land base. They constitute the lumpen peasantry, a group of part-peasants who continue to depend upon the existence of the peasant labor process, but whose labor power remains an unrealized commodity.

The lumpen peasantry is relatively weak in Wesley: many people move in and out of it. I became aware of its demographic importance in the field during brief visits in other villages and, later, while trying to make sense of the results of the 1980 Census. Hence, it is hard for me to judge fully its social momentum. It is clear to me, though, that the lumpen peasantry is leaning toward a more active political participation in the affairs of the nation, and not only because the people who constitute that category are generally younger and have more idle time to use than the average tenant or yeoman. As most part-peasants, the lumpen peasantry is at the crossroads of social change. Its members cannot engage in full-time agricultural work, yet they depend on the permanence of the peasant labor process. Indeed, they differ from most unemployed town dwellers inasmuch as the peasant production of goods guarantees them a minimal caloric intake. Many refuse to migrate to Roseau or Portsmouth because the risk of starvation is greater than the chance of finding employment. At the same time, prevailing conditions in the society at large, and especially in the countryside, prevent their engagement in wage labor. In short, many of them are dissatisfied young adults and they are forced to seek alternatives.

Not surprisingly, one alternative is ideological evasion; young idle men gather for hours in front of a radio or under a street light to "talk nonsense." Many are even more prone to gambling than the generally older yeomen who gather at the rum shops in the evening. Others are likely to spend the occasional dollars they acquire from the performance of a menial task on an item of limited used which is, for them, a luxury: a radio, a watch, a sweatshirt. Most seriously consider emigration, but opportunities are few. Others look to political patronage as a means to obtain a government job. However, a substantial number is willing to pay attention to political discourses that speak of fundamental change.

In Wesley itself, and probably in the rest of Dominica, the seriousness with which they consider political alternatives is likely to depend, at least in part, on the direction taken by another group of part-peasants, the banana children.

The Banana Children

The people whom I call banana children are part-peasants inasmuch as (1) they rely on the peasant labor process for part of their sustenance, and (2) their labor power remains (or remained until recently) an unrealized commodity.

To say that labor power remains an unrealized commodity is equivalent to saying that the individuals who carry that labor power are unemployed. When one deals with peasants, the main advantage of the first formulation is that it brings labor to the forefront. That labor power was produced. It is still maintained however inadequately. In societies such as Dominica, with minimum social services and no transfer payments, individual peasant households bear almost totally the cost of that production. Labor power, as a commodity, is a byproduct of the peasant labor process, and it continues to draw on that process for its maintenance as long as it remains unrealized or underused.

The combination of physical and intellectual capacities that we call labor power expresses itself in terms of time and energy allocation. Unemployment may mean having a lot of time to do nothing; but it may mean having the time to use one's capacities in nonremunerative activities. Hence, complete idleness and petty commodity production are not the only alternatives to wage labor. If a minimum caloric intake is guaranteed, adolescence may expand, masking the actual reality of unemployment. The capacities that compose the unrealized labor power may then be used to further the individual's education, as in many Western societies: France and especially Italy for example. However, the use of the educational system as a temporary parking lot for the unemployed should not mask the structural issue of the nonrealization of labor power as a commodity. In that light, many of Wesley's banana children are structurally closer to the lumpen peasantry or to the nonagricultural petty commodity producers than to their own parents.

The people I call the banana children have their counterparts throughout Dominica, but in no rural area is their presence as visible as in the villages of Wesley and Marigot. The category is quite arbitrary but nonetheless important. By banana children I mean a distinct group of Wesley people who share the following characteristics:

1. they were born after 1953, that is, after the rise of bananas to preeminence among the export crops;
2. they grew up in households that were, in varying degrees, dependent upon their members' engagement in the peasant labor process both for the production of their food staple and for that of bananas delivered to the DBGA;
3. they completed (or nearly completed) high school between 1971 and 1979, that is, before the current crisis of the banana industry, brought by Hurricanes David and Allen and the (unrelated) fall of prices in the international market; and
4. they went to high school outside of the enclave, in Roseau or in Portsmouth, before the 1979 opening of the Londonderry-based Saint Andrew secondary school, which now serves the whole southern part of La Soye.

The emergence of this generational subgroup exemplifies the villagers' determination to use local assets in the 1960 context characterized by the physical opening of the area and the subsequent increase in daily interchange with the nation and the world at large. The cumulative weight of individual decisions made in the recent past and attuned to both local history and the national context leads to a continuing restructuring.

What empirically demarcates Wesley's banana children from many in the lumpen peasantry throughout Dominica, or even from their own younger siblings, is not so much their attendance at school but the time they went. They emerged from schooling early enough to harvest some of the fruits of the national growth generated by the expansion of the banana industry and the continuous flow of grants from Britain before the 1978 Independence. That timing itself hinged upon a major development totally outside the peasantry's control: the physical opening of the village, especially after the construction of the Trans-Insular Road and the rebuilding of the road to Portsmouth. The yeomen understood that the idle time and the unused capacities of their growing children, who had become old enough to work but were nor needed permanently on the small banana fields, represented an asset, especially in light of La Soye's unique history.

The quick development of bananas in La Soye was due in part to the relative weakness of Plantation Wesley as a lime-producing area from the time of William Davies's death in 1916 to the end of World War II. Foley and Band's purchase of the Woodford Hill Estate to start the first banana plantation of Dominica, the revitalization of Eden and Londonderry, the commercial cultivation of bananas in the Bush by yeomen and squatters alike, all meant a sudden influx of cash in the Greater Wesley area. This cash spread throughout an enclave where the bulk of the population had been living below national standards for at least three decades. For those who had accustomed themselves to a meager life style during years of depression, part of that cash did seem to be an excess over the usual cost of maintenance in the locality. Some older yeomen recall with nostalgia the 1950s when they used to make "good money," selling some labor to the estate, some vanilla to merchants in town, and some bananas from their own land to the association. Others quickly mastered techniques of banana cultivation well enough to sell plants to the estates. Road construction and especially the building of the Melville Hall Airport provided additional cash in the 1950s and '60s.

That cash contributed to secure titles for Crown lands already occupied in the Bush or to buy plots closer to the village from estate owners. But as the seventies drew closer, most of the people who had secured themselves a minimal land base (and some who had worked only on estate land) still maintained the lifestyle of the late 1950s. Wesley people work harder and save more than most Dominicans. How much of this is due to the early Protestant influence or to the greater impact of the plantations is not clear to me. At any rate the sudden influx of cash was not spent on luxuries. Likewise, few families tried to extend their holdings beyond three or four acres, in part because they perceived the low marginal productivity of land beyond five acres, in part because of the high prices imposed by the estate owners. Rather, many more combined the cash with the assets they saw in their otherwise underemployed children and invested heavily in the children's education.

The reasons why Wesley people looked to education as a preferred investment are quite understandable. Even before the end of slavery, literacy contributed to the social promotion of some freedmen. In the nineteenth century, members of the Mulatto Ascendancy used their formal education to threaten the European-born plantocracy and then traded their political independence for profitable positions in the state apparatus. In the twentieth century, as the number of white colonial officials declined throughout the British Caribbean, the bureaucratic machinery (set up by the Colonial Office partly to accommodate Britons who could not find a better niche at home) was slowly taken over by natives who often did not need more than a high school diploma, and who, like many of their foreign predecessors, could not find a better niche. But in a country in which the official language never was the language of the majority, in which the most important school was opened by the colonial government with the specific goal of preparing native youngsters for clerical positions in the administration, in which there were no clear chances for the emergence of a strong merchant or industrial class able to provide alternative employment, the choice of investing in education was even more obvious.

Wesley people themselves were well placed to seize the opportunity. Since the 1830s, the continuous presence of the Methodists in La Soye had familiarized the laborers with primary education. After the 1870s, the Catholic-run primary school only reinforced that advantage. Second, both Methodists and Catholics achieved their relative success because the majority of the La Soye residents spoke English or a language lexically derived from it. In the 1950s and '60s the villagers of Wesley and Marigot rightly understood that their greater familiarity with both English and formal education gave their children better than average chances to pass through the secondary school system. The opening of the Trans-Insular Road which linked Marigot to the leeward coast reduced both the time and the money needed to reach Roseau (until then accessible only by sea to the people of the Northeast). Government scholarships had always been available on a competitive basis, and some yeomen whose children did not qualify for the free tuition could even afford the low fees of another secondary school in town. The cost of secondary education was slowly rising, but the pace of the increase was closer to that of inflation in the Roseau enclave, whereas the cash flow in the Greater Wesley area was improving at a faster pace. Because of the pioneering role of their own enclave in the expansion of banana cultivation, Wesley people had started on the road to recovery before the majority of Dominicans. Even though banana prices did not rise substantially between 1953 and 1964 (and, indeed, dropped drastically in 1965) peasants in the Northeast were drawing more cash than most Dominicans at a time when the labor power of many of their growing children was threatening to become an unrealized commodity.

In 1971, the opening of the Portsmouth secondary school whose fees and standards of admission were lower made formal education even more accessible to Wesley children. If the young scholars remained in town or in Portsmouth for the week, the chief expense for parents was to meet the cost of room and board. The increased cash from bananas provided for that part of the boarders' food which was purchased and a substantial part of the daily meals of quite a few Portsmouth and Roseau homeowners. Home-grown provisions carried every week from Wesley provided the staples of the diet.

I have been able to list by name 123 people from the Greater Wesley area who graduated from high school or reached the level at which they could take the government-sponsored final examination between 1971 and 1979.[2] I tried to collect, with various degrees of success, age, sex, year of final examination, high school attended, religious denomination, present place of residence. Information about the parent or parents of these individuals (at least 7 were raised solely by a mother or a grandmother) included, when possible, source of income, form of land tenure and estimated acreage, and perceived economic status ("rich," "well to do" [people who "made it"], "average," "poor," and "very poor").

The education of at least 53 of the individuals on that list was financed almost exclusively by cash obtained for bananas and by home-grown provisions produced through the peasant labor process. About fifteen others were supported equally by relatives producing bananas and provisions in Dominica and relatives in England or the United States who sent remittances regularly to Wesley. Only 7 more graduates may have been financed exclusively by relatives living in foreign countries. At least 6 received support from a patron, a godparent, or a distant relative living in town or in Wesley itself, though that support seems to have been generally limited to securing lodging in Portsmouth or in Roseau. Parents still provided the staple food items. Ten more scholars came from big farmers' households or were related to a big farmer. Four were outsiders' children and 4 were the children of professionals working for the government. The source of support for the remaining 24 is not clear.

Admittedly, one may not be able to draw far-reaching statistical conclusions from such a list. Still, if we define as banana children those who made it through high school in the 1970s, in part or in whole because of their parents' or guardians' engagement in the peasant labor process in the production of bananas and provisions, then, more than two-thirds of these 123 individuals belong to that category.

A Reevaluation

From the time they left for secondary school, the banana children became important agents of mediation between Wesley peasants and the

Dominican nation. Lodging fees varied, but remained usually around \$30 E.C. a month for boarding and purchased food items. One can safely say that at least \$150,000 E.C. were so transferred from Wesley peasants to Roseau and Portsmouth homeowners during the 1970s. Town merchants benefited from the sale of cloth for uniforms, though the government provided book allocations to some students on the basis of scholarship achievement. The back-and-forth movement of the children from school to village on weekends reinforced contacts with the outside. Many parents who had rarely if ever ventured out of Wesley during the first decade of the Trans-Insular Road found their way to town to visit their children (or their temporary guardians), make arrangements for their comfort or meet with a school official. In the process, the children attending Roseau schools and their parents served as the first regular clientele of the truck owners who pioneered the use of the Trans-Insular Road. Likewise, those attending the Portsmouth secondary school greatly improved the income of the vehicle owners who already connected Portsmouth and Wesley. Many Wesley people suggest that one or another truck owner "made his money carrying children to school." The emergence of the banana children was vital to the consolidation of the entrepreneurs as a distinct group in Wesley. It increased considerably the demand for transport services and created new consumption patterns that benefited the shop owners.

The influence of the banana children in modifying consumption patterns in Wesley is only one example of their contribution to a reevaluation of the village. Only a few Wesley people had ventured farther than Marigot or Woodford Hill before the 1960s. Contacts with Portsmouth were by and large occasional and the rest of Dominica (including Roseau) and the world at large remained obscure entities for most villagers. In the 1970s the banana children changed behavior and values that had been shaped in part by that isolation. They came back to the village with an education that, for all its inappropriateness, made them aware that neither Wesley, nor Dominica, nor even Great Britain was alone in the world. Moreover, since they had all been educated outside of Wesley, their claims to a greater knowledge often seemed legitimate to many villagers: not only had the children read more, but they had seen more of the real world.

The reevaluation brought about by the return of the high school graduates touches on many aspects of Wesley life, and affects differently the various groups of villagers. The estate owners and big farmers, in particular, are losing some prestige and influence as a result of the graduates' permanent or temporary presence. Having experienced Roseau more intimately than many (if not all) big farmers, the banana children know the limited extent of the farmers' power in national terms. They react to the big farmers' group from a larger perspective and are willing to challenge them in the local context, sometimes with the support of other villagers. In short, circumstances have placed many banana children in potentially powerful positions of leadership. The case of the Village Council might illustrate the point.

The position of Chairman of the Wesley Village Council yields little political power per se. Traditionally, big farmers or outsiders succeeded themselves as chairmen. Yet in 1979 a recent high school graduate of yeoman origins, and sole laborer of his family's plot, defeated the son of a big farmer (part-farmer and part-entrepreneur himself) to become the youngest Village Council chairman in Dominica. The elected chairman himself readily admits that he succeeded in part because he was associated with a then prominent and quite popular national politician. His political opponents are also quick to suggest that the big farmers in the young man's party made him run for the chairmanship because "they had nobody else" or that the candidate himself entered politics because, contrary to many other banana children, he had no source of income other than his field. But such explanations only confirm the reevaluation that we are discovering. The perception of the village had so evolved that big farmers who, at other times, might have looked quite eligible are now perceived as unqualified for the position. In the meantime, a banana child who is not necessarily perceived as exceptional received enough support to overcome his lack of political experience.

The banana children do not simply question the legitimacy of certain people; their reevaluation also touches on activities that were thought to be both necessary and inevitable. Many of them strongly question, at times explicitly, the rentability if not the appropriateness of agricultural work itself. Most of the males among the banana children dutifully participated in peasant work during their weekend visits or during the summer months as necessary. Many of those who now hold government jobs but reside in Wesley, permanently or occasionally, still help the principal laborer to dig the field or to deliver bananas at Londonderry on fig days. The reevaluation which started in the 1970s is both more subtle and more fundamental than a mere rejection of all manual labor, and it affects men and women differently. First, field labor is unworthy of any female, because it is "hard" and "dirty" labor; though it is inevitable for some poorer or older women, it is particularly unworthy of women who went to school. Second, agricultural labor, as a permanent engagement, is also unworthy of males who went to school. Third, and more important, under the present conditions, permanent agricultural labor is also unworthy of any individual simply because it does not pay.

The first two statements generally fit the views of the parents of these children whereas the third one seriously questions the traditional Wesley work ethic. Many young villagers now suggest that their parents "wasted their time on figs" or worked for nothing. Some go as far as suggesting alternative occupations to their kin or emigration. To be sure, Wesley people have felt that agricultural labor was less rewarding than almost any other occupation, but they also assumed that individual success within any particular occupational category was a reflection and result of one's labor. Implicit in many banana children's contention that their parents worked in vain is the more fundamental insinuation that hard labor in agriculture is not worth the effort. This attitude in turn affects not only the parents who are still fully engaged in agricultural labor but also, especially, the members of the growing lumpen peasantry, contemporaries or juniors of the banana children.

The few young adults who now function exclusively as yeomen and may be averaging cash incomes not substantially lower than those of some of their high school classmates who perform clerical duties see themselves as "unemployed." They often register themselves as such in official documents, job applications, and so on. (Loan applications may be the only exception.) At times they extend that perception to their kin: "My father not working. He just planting his fig." In a few cases, this conceptual devaluation of particular forms of work includes all labor performed for the family or any private employer except banking institutions such as Barclays Bank or the Royal Bank of Canada which have branches in Dominica. "X is not working. He has a little job [with a private employer]. But he is not really working." Such devaluations have increased the banana children's disenchantment with the system, especially at the times when they themselves join the ranks of the unemployed, and many view emigration as their sole option. In short, personal motivations as well as the discovery of the national and international context within which Dominican peasants operate have led the banana children to a global reconsideration of the Wesley work ethic.

Evidence for that reconsideration also came from the children's observation of Wesley itself. Though the graduates of the 1970s witnessed the rise of most entrepreneurs, they are too young to remember the ascension of the big farmers whom they tend to perceive as people who "made it" without effort. Likewise, many would say of an estate owner: "All R. has to do is wait for his coconuts to fall." In Roseau or in Portsmouth, as residents or as civil servants themselves, the graduates learned that success within the state machinery is more often a measure of one's political connections and ability to join the right side at the right time than a measure of one's service to the nation.

Many now accommodate themselves with the systematic reliance on "bòbòl" (grafts), which plagues branches of the state apparatus. On the one hand, in Wesley, Portsmouth, and Roseau, people who did little collected the rewards; on the other hand, in the Greater Wesley, people who worked all their life collected little, if anything, worth mentioning. The combination was potentially explosive. For the banana children that combination has meant, so far, a fundamental reevaluation of the La Soye work ethic—itself a peculiar feature within the Dominican system of values and, perhaps, the combined product of Protestantism and the Plantation Wesley of Charles Leathem's days.

Needless to say, this reevaluation is not so unilineal, and secondary considerations qualify each of its tenets. None of the banana children would suggest, for instance, a reduction of his or her family's acreage or total disengagement from the peasant labor process. Most consider the production of provisions as a quite normal feature of Dominican life. That view may be due, in part, to the continuing dependence of the banana children on the peasant labor process for their staple food. Even those who spend most of their time in Roseau regularly receive provisions from the family land. For some, these provisions constitute an exchange, albeit perhaps an unequal one: they provide some cash to the Wesley household and consume a share of the provisions produced by the main activator and his regular collaborators. For others, both in and outside Wesley who draw more modest cash incomes, the provisions produced outside the sphere of valorization are almost as necessary as they are to the lumpen peasants. Thus, although the banana children are questioning fundamental aspects of the peasant labor process as they experience it in the Dominican context, most have remained part-peasants. They see the plight of the peasantry, but they do not fully share all of its concerns, in part because of their different assets, in part because of their different perception. Contrary to most civil servants or petty bourgeois from Roseau or Portsmouth, however, they readily acknowledge that the peasantry carried the Dominican nation without collecting its dues.

"Patois People Foolish"

The reevaluation occasioned by the return of the high school graduates of the 1970s does not stop at economics: it touches on many other aspects of social life, speech patterns, for example. Given the current level of competence in standard (British) English among Wesley adults under fifty years of age, one suspects that the official language had serious effects on the performance of Kòkòy long before the banana children started to come back from school. Most Wesley residents switch to an acrolectal form (that is, one closer to standard English) when addressing an outsider, and the ease of switching suggests long practice. What seems to be changing, in part because of the influence of the banana children, is the evaluation of the three languages spoken in Dominica.

Wesley people always thought that the language spoken in the heart of La Soye (Marigot, Wesley, Woodford Hill) was somehow superior to the French-based Creole common to the rest of Dominica. This contention rested, in part, on the assumption that their own language was a form of English whereas the French-based Creole was something less of a language, being neither French nor English. That evaluation was reinforced by other manifestations of local ethnocentrism, often condensed in the common expression "patois people foolish," an expression that many residents of La Soye do not see the need to justify.

The banana children discovered in the 1970s that their most common form of speech was not immediately intelligible to a standard English speaker. Moreover, Kòkòy itself was derided in the classroom not to mention the schoolyard or the boardinghouse, by some of those very same "foolish patois people." While other Dominican teenagers were speaking the Lesser Antillean language (despite their masters' warning), would-be Kòkòy speakers from Wesley and Marigot switched to English to avoid criticisms of both masters and peers. As a result, many of the high school graduates now tend to modify their speech to sound like Roseau people, or rather to sound the way they imagine that an Englishman would sound, on the basis of the patterns they learned in Portsmouth and Roseau. Syntactic, phonologtcal, and lexical modifications intended to bring Wesley speech close to standard English are constantly introduced, though not always with the expected results. The growing influence of radio (enhanced by the spread of electricity throughout the village) balances some instances of overcorrection, now that many residents listen daily to BBC World Service. More important, though, the basilectal forms most associated with Kòkòy, and still considered by many as the preferred forms in specific contexts, are now being ridiculed, at least by some residents, not all of whom are high school graduates.

The new trends are not all going in one direction and, here again, one needs to note secondary influences. Since the late 1960s, a minority of Dominicans (largely Roseau residents) have tried to rehabilitate the French-based Antillean Creole. "Ekspéryans Kréyòl" is an influential radio program broadcast on the government-run station, tolerated by the most conservative elements of the society but quite appreciated by a majority of the population. It broadcasts music from all Kréyòl'-speaking countries, most notably Haiti and Guadeloupe; it also broadcasts national and international news as well as interviews and discussions on various subjects. This rehabilitation of the national language in turn has pushed a tiny minority of banana children to reconsider their view of Kòkòy, and at times to try to learn the Antillean Creole themselves.

Hence, the reevaluation brought about by the rise of the banana children as a distinctive group in Wesley is not a unilinear one. The category *part-peasants* itself (to which the banana children belong) implies an inherent ambivalence which tends to intensify with the complexity of an individual's attachment to the peasant labor process. Part-peasants may side consciously with or against the majority of yeomen and tenants in diverse conflicts which often oppose the more traditional segments of peasantry to outsiders, big farmers, entrepreneurs or the state itself. But the importance of each of these decisions varies according to the larger context. Above and beyond that immediate choice, the individual's structural position (and the routine actions that this position implies) may affect the integration of the peasant labor process and the livelihood of those who depend upon it in unforeseen ways.

In some cases, structural constraints might ultimately push a group of part-peasants closer to the peasantry at large. A good example is that of the small entrepreneurs who, at times, side with the yeomanry and the tenants, not only because small entrepreneurs overlap with one of those two peasant groups themselves, but also because their rise within the entrepreneur category greatly depends on the purchasing power of those who are exclusively engaged in the peasant labor process. Yet at other times individual decisions contribute to throw the power of a distinct subgroup of part-peasants for or against the peasantry at large, as in the case of the banana children. Their origins, their education, their resources, their continuous dependence on the peasant labor process, and also the obstacles that stop many of them from reaching the socio-economic level they thought they were being trained for, place them at the crossroads of Dominican society. Only the sum of their individual decisions will determine their long-term influence on Wesley itself and perhaps on the Dominican nation.

One can suggest, without questioning the altruism of the Wesley-born graduates of the 1970s, that those individual decisions depend largely on what many banana children perceive as alternative strategies for themselves and how well they succeed in their implementation. Emigration and employment in the Civil Service are two perceived strategies that exemplify the dilemma of the banana children.

Emigration

The significance of emigration from Dominica predates the abolition of slavery. In the eighteenth and nineteenth century, the number of slaves who were taken out of the island yearly often came close to the number newly imported. Many former slaves left the island at the end of the 1830s. The pace of emigration remained steady in the second half of the nineteenth century, barely slowed down at the beginning of the twentieth century, only to reach new peaks in the 1950s and 1960s (Boromé 1972b, 1972c; censuses of Dominica, 1848–71; Welch 1968; Myers 1976).

Census figures suggest that emigration may have been less important in the Saint Andrew South enclave than in the rest of Dominica, even though the numbers were not negligible there either. People of the enclave never established the more solid links with the outside that characterized enclaves situated at the northern or southern tips of the island. Only Calibishie has a tradition of seafaring, most likely a recent one when compared to that of Vieille Case or Scotts Head. Still, as noted before, some of the banana children received regular support from relatives who lived abroad. Further, quite a few Wesley people joined the flow of migrants who went to England between 1950 and 1969. Some of the newest wall houses of Wesley belong to people now in Europe, who have not returned for at least a decade and who seem to be slowly preparing for retirement. Those who reside in the Caribbean (Antigua or Guadeloupe, for instance) do visit once in a great while partly because, in contrast to those in England, they can afford an occasional trip. The visit is often an occasion to prove to themselves and those they left behind that the trip was worth it, and not only in economic terms. The visitor is expected to spend lavishly, to distribute gifts, to narrate his or her adventures and describe the places visited, all with the new accent supposedly acquired abroad.

The first obvious difference between the earlier migrations (and returns) and the patterns that characterize the flight of the banana children and their brothers and sisters from the lumpen peasantry is a quantitative one. Between 1979 and 1981, 32 of the graduates in my list of 123 names (26 percent) were residing abroad permanently. At least 9 have left the island since for various expected durations, all extending beyond a year. Hence the proportion of high school graduates who emigrate is relatively high. A second and related point is that the banana children leave Dominica at an earlier age than most other migrants. Third, the destination of the new migrants also differs from that of their predecessors. A vast majority live in North America (Canada, the United States). Only 2 lived in another Caribbean country in 1979–81, and 3 to 5 were thought to be in England.

Though one cannot surmise all the long-term effects of that migration, the immediate economic loss for Wesley and Dominica is obvious. A substantial minority of those in whose future the Wesley peasantry heavily invested the meager benefits of its early start in banana production have left, and remittances or occasional visits will not reimburse that investment. Most of the migrants' future income will likely remain in the countries where they now work, as is the case of most other migrants. Few have returned for short visits and few send remittances, though some may continue to do so for years to come. By and large they maintain less contact with the village than many of the older migrants who went to England twenty-five or thirty years ago.

The banana children now abroad have fewer ties with Dominica, and Wesley in particular, and fewer reasons to touch base, as it were, than the earlier migrants. They knew, before they left, that Dominicans perceive differently the countries of migration: people who go to North America usually "make it" and do not need to verify the story of their success as much as do those who reside in Antigua, Guadeloupe, or even England where some Dominicans are still thought to be "scrunting." More important, because of their younger age at the time of migration, because of their previous stay in Portsmouth or Roseau (which partly severed them from daily life in Wesley), and because high school itself represented an achievement way beyond the reach of most villagers, banana children now living abroad do not have the audience in front of which they would need to verify their success, regardless of their actual country of residence. Correspondence is usually limited to siblings and parents, and remittances are likely to stop completely at the death of the latter.

The lack of contact in turn tends to magnify the success stories even more than it usually does in the case of other migrants. Thus many of the banana children now in Dominica (especially the unemployed ones and the cultivators, but also many of those engaged in the Civil Service) view emigration as their primary goal. Consequently, they consider Dominica as a temporary place of abode and one not to be too concerned with, for the future lies somewhere else anyway. Of course, few of those dreams are likely to come true but their impact on the majority of banana children who are still on the island is no less real.

The Civil Service

Emigration continues to attract the banana children and many younger high school graduates among the growing lumpen peasantry in part because of their disappointment with the Civil Service. Many went to school at a time when the bureaucratic apparatus was expanding, but many more finished too late to benefit from that expansion. In 1979–81, 53 of the 123 graduates on whom I focus (hence more than 50 percent of those who stayed in Dominica) worked for the government. Roughly half of them maintained dual residence in Wesley and in their job area, usually Roseau.

Teaching tops the list of occupations among both public and private employees, though most government teachers are men whereas the graduates who teach in nongovernment schools or preschool are women. Female graduates of the seventies who belong to the Civil Service are generally nurses or student nurses who perform nursing duties and received a government stipend. A small minority from both sexes belong to the police force. Most of the graduates whose jobs keep them outside Wesley for long periods still remain involved in Wesley's daily life. As noted before, almost all receive provisions from Wesley or contribute financially to their parents' household, and some maintain dual residence. More important perhaps, many of those now involved in health services or in education (an overwhelming majority) would prefer to work in the village if given the choice. In fact, most of the teachers now work in Wesley, though most of the nurses do not.

The penetration of the Civil Service failed to meet the banana children's expectations. A breakdown of the 53 graduates employed by the government reveals that few of the children exclusively supported by their parents' engagement in the peasant labor process actually entered the Civil Service. Most of those who joined the police force, who became nurses, or who are now teaching after training at the Teachers' College (as opposed to on-the-job training immediately after high school) received supplemental support in the 1970s from a patron or a relative already in the Civil Service. All in all, only half of the current government employees were primarily supported by parents or guardians engaged in the peasant labor process, and they usually occupy lesser positions in the state apparatus or do not enjoy full Civil Service status and the security and benefits attached to it. Thus from the point of view of the yeomanry, the Civil Service strategy has been only a half success.

The impossibility of achieving security within the Civil Service has now become obvious. Some 30 banana children and the vast majority of the post-1979 graduates in need of employment cannot even penetrate the state apparatus. The expansion of the state apparatus in the 1970s was short-lived, in part because of the reduction in British aid (especially after the 1978 Independence), but also because successive administrations dominated by the Dominica Labour party quickly saturated the lower levels of the state administration often with incompetent political clients in the name of a rhetoric meant to please the "little man." There is a point at which government simply cannot afford to hire indiscriminately and that point was reached in the seventies. Moreover, the conservative administration of the Freedom party (which came to power in 1980 after a campaign that promised better days to the civil servants) dramatically reversed hiring policy, perhaps to the extreme opposite. As a result of the policies of both parties for the last nine years, those with fewer connections in the bureaucracy or with less influential patrons made little progress in securing employment despite their high school diplomas and their "advanced passes" from the government-run final examinations. The banana children and their parents discovered that one's social reach and one's ability to serve the political patrons of the day matter at least as much as the years spent in high school. In view of the saturation of the Civil Service and more recent conditions imposed by the conservative government in conjunction with the IMF (International Monetary Fund) it is now impossible for the bulk of the unemployed or for those occupying marginal positions to "make it" in public administration solely on the basis of merit.

The impact of the private sector on nonagricultural employment has always been negligible and will likely remain so for a long time despite government promises to attract investors and the political affinity between the current Dominican and United States administrations. The Caribbean Basin Initiative gives low priorty to the Lesser Antilles. Even a change of emphasis in Washington might not produce immediate effects: government incentives to potential United States investors cannot overcome the difficulties inherent in Dominica's deficient infrastructure. In such a context, the banana children may be at the crossroads of social change in part because of the sudden reduction of structural outlets. Their individual choices as citizens issued from the yeomanry, and their attachment to it economically and emotionally might strongly influence the future.

How that influence will manifest itself is unknown, for the banana children face a dilemma. They were trained to be the Trojan horse, so the speak, of the peasantry in its long battle with the state. And indeed, because of their origins and their preparation, because of their past engagement in the peasant labor process or their continuous reliance upon it, they are better placed than any nonpeasant to understand the plight of the peasantry. Because of that training, their direct knowledge of life outside of Wesley, their familiarity with the Civil Service, their awareness of the world at large, they are equally well placed to formulate social, economic, and political reforms taking that plight into consideration. And some of them are starting to do so.

But the banana children's consciousness of the cultivators' exploitation by various outsiders, and their growing awareness of Dominica's dependent status in the world system and the consequent willingness to fight for the groups of their birth, are mitigated by an awareness of their own individual possibilities within the status quo. They are as well equipped as most Dominicans for a job in government; the possibility remains alive in the minds of many that, with the proper submissive attitude and the right connections they might circumvent, as individuals, the structural obstacles that stop many of their colleagues. They are better prepared to "make it overseas" than most of the earlier migrants. But they rightly see themselves as prisoners of a rigid socioeconomic structure which offers few opportunities to the categories from which they come. Their potential involvement in consciously trying to change the structure is limited by the choices they perceive for themselves as individuals. Thus, their individual decisions and their conscious siding with or against the peasantry are likely to be a determining influence on the survival of the peasant labor process and the livelihood of those who are still very much engaged in that process.

CHAPTER 13

Contemporary Peasantries: Illusions and Hard Choices

Both the methodological and substantive conclusions of this book extend far beyond the case of Dominica. They point to the need for a more sophisticated treatment of the relations between contemporary peasantries and capitalism, a treatment that would take equally into account systematic features and historical particulars. The conceptualization offered in these pages starts with the very notion of peasantry itself and ends with a necessary reformulation of issues in development economics, anthropology, and history.

The most persistent chimera that plagues discussions of peripheral countries characterized by a sizable peasantry is that of development, conceived as a linear progression on the path created by the industrialized West. Beyond its multiple, and often ingenious guises, the notion of development usually assumes a fundamental equality in the position of "developed" and "underdeveloped" countries within the contemporary world.

That assumption has been questioned since at least the 1950s (e.g., Kuznets 1958), and continues to be challenged with increasing sophistication (Frank 1967; Amin 1974; Cardoso and Faletto 1979; Foster-Carter 1985; Amin 1986). Peripheral societies differ from the industrialized West in terms of their internal structures, their integration within the world economy, and their immediate historical and cultural heritage. This book is an additional contribution to the critique of the development formula. Dominica is not underdeveloped because of its feeble ties with capital. On the contrary: its present condition, including its low material standard of living, is a byproduct of its forced integration within the world economy. Hence, one is likely to wait in vain for the island to take off on the capitalist path: it has been on that path for more than two centuries. That this observation was not always obvious stems from the failure of the social sciences—attributable, in part, to Eurocentrism—to conceptualize properly both peasants and capital. The dominant tendencies in the related (multidisciplinary) literature have been to see peasants as a "type" and capital as a "thing." A major lesson of this study is the necessity to adopt conceptualizations rooted in process rather than essence, and in the experience of the world rather than the experience of Europe. This dual shift in perspective—from essence to process and from Europe to humankind—permits clarifications of the ties that bind contemporary peasantries and world capitalism, and hence a better approach to issues of development. The underdevelopment that characterizes so many societies with a large population of small-scale cultivators may very well be due to the nature of their relation with capital rather than the alleged gap between their economic activities and an ahistorical capitalist mode of production.

The Dominican case also demonstrates that one cannot treat relations between developed and underdeveloped countries as if they were the results of trade imbalances. Terms of trade are not irrelevant, but they must be treated as expressions of deeper structural inequalities inherited from a history in which power played and continues to play a crucial role. The issue is not so much that Geest seems to buy cheaply the bananas produced in the Windwards, but *why* it can do so. The conclusions of chapters 7 and 8 are eloquent in that regard: what appears to be an imbalance in the terms of trade can occur because Geest does *not* actually buy the bananas.

It follows that compromise solutions aimed at changing only the terms of trade, such as those adopted by the Organization of Petroleum Exporting Countries or the neocolonial states actively seeking a "New Economic Order," are not likely to work in such cases as Dominica. The inequalities are not restricted to the sphere of commercialization and exchange *stricto sensu*, but already loom large at the level of the production process. Even though Dominican peasants control the labor process in which they are engaged, that process itself is embedded in a process of production that is controlled by transnational capital.[1]

The unequal terms of trade are not only expressions of structural inequalities on the world scene; they also express socioeconomic divisions and the distribution of power within the peripheral nation-states themselves. To wit, not all classes within a peripheral area would be willing to modify those terms, and not all classes are likely to benefit from a simple change of those terms. The ineffectiveness of WINBAN suggests that this observation might be relevant to the entire Windwards. The history of Haiti, the Guyana of Forbes Burnham, and recent developments in Jamaica and Trinidad also suggest:

1. that the internal weaknesses that allow the imposition of unfavorable terms of trade upon Dominica are shared by the larger Caribbean territories and many non-Caribbean nation-states as well;
2. that the success of a more rewarding trade policy hinges partly upon the United States and IMF dictates, and the general distribution of power in the interstate system; and
3. that the peasantry may not benefit even if such a policy meets with partial success (Girault 1981; Manley 1982; Sandoval 1983; Stephens and Stephens 1984, 1985; Thomas 1984; Trouillot 1985a).

In short, the imbalance of the terms of trade also reflects both the configuration of the world economy and the neocolonial class structure of a particular periphery.

The failure of policies aimed at improving the terms of trade hence corroborate the view that we cannot treat the coexistence of peasants and capital as a simple exchange of goods between two discrete economies. There is not, and there never was, a peasant economy in Dominica. From the days of slavery down to the present routine of a yeoman-dominated village like Wesley, cultivators engaged in the peasant labor process always belonged to a larger order, the logic of which cannot be explained at the level of the unit of production. With the possible exception of some nineteenth-century squatters, the existence of the small-scale cultivators always presupposed the economic system to which they were tied. Dominican peasants, as their counterparts elsewhere, have always constituted a part-economy.

Peasants are part-economies not in any empirical sense but inasmuch as the type of work they engage in characterizes only a distinct level of a socioeconomic structure, that is, the labor process. And in the contemporary world, the relations between system and parts are always influenced, even if not determined, by the imperatives of capitalist accumulation on a world scale.

This influence has practical consequences for millions of peasants and policy makers, but also theoretical and methodological implications for peasant studies. Studies of contemporary peasantries cannot remain, either descriptively or analytically, at the level of the peasant farm. Nor can they focus only on the village or on the nation-state. Only an unquestioned (empiricist) tradition has led to the acceptance of those units of analysis as methodological isolates (Wallerstein 1974; Wolf 1982). Descriptions of work relations, village politics, or family life, however extensive, cannot delineate the structural limits within which the peasantry produces both its livelihood and its understanding of itself. Ultimately, both the empirical and analytical limits of the research on any peasantry must remain open.

For the structure is not a bound entity: the primary relations that define contemporary peasantries extend beyond geographical and political borders (Alavi 1982). Thus both the description and the analysis must venture out of the traditional safeguards to explore and document, as needed, the extent to which peasants operate within a world of commodities (Bernstein 1979, 1981), the confrontation between the commodification imposed from the outside and the more traditional patterns of sociocultural life (Chevalier 1983; Grossman 1984; Trouillot 1986b), and the profitability of the system for capitalists based in the industrialized nations (chapter 9). In short, our primary unit of analysis must be the world.

This argument is not an injunction against the study of particulars. In fact, quite the opposite is true. To be sure, we need more studies with the empirical breadth that Wallerstein (1974, 1980), Frank (1978, 1980), Stavrianos (1981), Wolf (1982), Worsley (1985) have all demonstrated to be within the reach of a single researcher. But we need even more studies that detail the past and present conditions of particular peoples, specifiable in time and space, and the dreams and hopes they build, sometimes despite those conditions.

The issue is one of methodology rather than a matter of empirical breadth. It boils down to the isolation of the particulars to be studied in terms of their always imperfect and always changing integration within wider fields of forces. A major suggestion of this work is the systematic use of multiple units of analysis as a strategy to approach those fields. The move from the nation, to the world, to the village, the successive emphases on different fields and the different types of agency that this back-and-forth movement reveals allow us to see how apparently unrelated processes do, in fact, interdigitate.[2]

The systematic delineation of multiple units of analysis makes it possible for the observer to have different viewpoints on the same object of study. This multidimensional view, in turn, can be nicely reinforced by the deliberate positioning of the analyst at the crossroads of different disciplinary traditions. History and political economy as much as anthropology permeate this book, partly by personal choice, partly because of the questions left unanswered by definitional treatments of peasantry, partly because little or no reference could be made to previously published works on Dominica. From an anthropological perspective, the reevaluation of both history and political economy is not simply a practical necessity. It becomes also a theoretical leap forward (Wolf 1982). The units that ethnography and cultural anthropology best treat are not self-sufficient isolates, in analytical, empirical, or even existential terms. To state that the villagers of Wesley define themselves as Wesley people and tend to act as such in certain circumstances is to open but a small window on the worldview of some highly distinct three thousand individuals. Hence, groupings like the Balinese, the Chinese, the Hausa, the Hopi are at best statistical extrapolations presented without the however dubious support of a proper statistical inquiry. As soon as we turn the procedure to the West and start generalizing about the Spaniards, the Germans, the Canadians, let alone the New Yorkers, the Niçois, or the Londoners, both the positivist underpinnings and the methodological ethnocentrism become obvious.

There are three unequal solutions to the dilemma of carrying out ethnographic research in the contemporary world. First, we could return to the a priori division between hot and cold societies, despite the critiques (e.g., Balandier 1979) that exposed its moot methodological and epistemological status. Cold societies would be amenable to the strange statistical hermeneutics mentioned above, and the West would be left to a more blatantly positivist sociology. Second, since the first solution seems overtly ethnocentric, we could try to legitimize it and finesse the international division of labor and the unequal importance of politics within the interstate system. But then, the falling incomes, the political prisoners, the victims of progress and of war that characterize so many populations in the so-called Third World (Kidron and Segal 1981; Bodley 1975; Worsley 1984) would come back to haunt us. Third, we can bravely acknowledge the relevance of both history and political economy, at the very least, to delineate the boundaries of our units of analysis. In peasant studies, in particular, the third option seems to me unavoidable if we acknowledge that peasants cannot be analytically severed from the wider world because they always constitute part-economies.

The realization that peasants are part-economies also reveals how illusory it is to wait for them to die out on the pretext that their economic activities are ultimately incompatible with capitalism and will necessarily give way to capitalist "progress." It is the social scientists' own faith in the inevitability of this progress that encourages so many of them to read the record in that light. The replacement of peasants by proletarians is not so obvious to a more skeptical observer. To be sure, in many Caribbean countries, the increased pauperization of the countryside has lead to the rapid emergence of a centripetal spatialization, itself reinforced by the concentration of political power in the capital towns (e.g., Trouillot 1986a). Like Latin America, the Caribbean is becoming increasingly urban at a tremendous pace (Chernick et al. 1978; Hope 1986; Centre d'Études de Géographie Tropicale 1986). But there as elsewhere, this urban macrocephalia does not indicate the death of peasantries, though it may testify to their continuous agony. Nor does it imply necessarily a growth of the proletariat. The proliferation of urban slums throughout the world (Tolnai 1984: 8–10; Kidron and Segal 1984: 46; Granotier 1980) is no proof that peasants are becoming industrial wage laborers. Indeed, I take strong exception to theories suggesting a worldwide proletarianization of peasantries. Would that it were so simple. But if we take the word *proletarian* in its narrowest sense, it becomes difficult to suggest a worldwide transformation of tenants and yeomen into industrial (or even agricultural) wage earners. If we take the word to mean a worker whose labor power is realized as a commodity within the sphere of valorization (whether or not the worker receives a concrete wage) we must acknowledge that the labor power of most ex-peasants remains (and will remain for a long time) an unrealized commodity.

The myth of the worldwide proletarianization of peasantries is a costly one, both economically and politically, for it deters us from the most important issues, hence retarding possible solutions. To say that the peasants migrating to the cities are becoming unemployed wage earners is to take a somewhat teleological stance: we expect them to find work; meanwhile we call them unemployed proletarians. But despite our hopes—or theirs, for that matter—many remain unemployed or underemployed, just like their rural counterparts. Many join what we now call the informal sectors. Most never become proletarians at all, simply urban and poor. Hence, in quite a few countries (Dominica, Haiti, Saint Vincent,

Jamaica, Mexico, Ecuador, Venezuela, Bangladesh, Sri Lanka, and India come to mind), the dominant sociodemographic transformation is what we may more properly dubb the "lumpenization" of the peasantry. An increasing number of peasants, unable to become (or remain) activators of the labor process on plots that they control in tenancy or in freehold, become part-peasants in the countryside or simply head for the urban slums in the dim hope of greater cash opportunities.

Here again, Eurocentric attitudes, especially the uncritical espousal of the urban/rural dichotomy, have masked the fact that this lumpenization is not limited spatially to the urban sphere. The shanty towns, the *favellas*, and *bidonvilles*, which provoke the sensationalism of the Western media and the condescending compassion of the unprepared visitor, are but one scene of a more complex drama that begins in the countryside. Many of the part-peasants described in chapters 2 and 12 move in and out of the lumpen without leaving their village. Many fall irremediably into it. Others, including quite a few banana children, spend their lives avoiding being part of the lumpen, living close to its margins. Some protect themselves against the lumpen threat by becoming agents and servants of whichever political clique holds state power, reinforcing both political clientelism and the tendency to authoritarian rule. All are faced with the dilemma of bearing a labor power that remains, in whole or in part, an unrealized commodity.

The continuous capacity for growth of the new lumpen does not come from within, but from the daily dramas of the countryside. One can stop that growth only by changing the conditions of integration of the peasantry itself, not by being conveniently charitable vis-à-vis the new urban poors. For instance, development programs aimed at using the cheap labor power of this growing urban mass may often aggravate the situation, if only by attracting more lumpen peasants to the shanty towns. Further, given the international division of labor, the kinds of enterprises that can be geared to use that labor power are often detrimental to the nation altogether. The recent revival of export-oriented light industry programs throughout the Caribbean is an example of the misuse of the growing lumpen. The actual operations vary from one island to the next. However, the basic strategy, backed by North American investors and the United States administration (notably the enforcers of the Caribbean Basin Initiative [CBI]), resembles experiments carried on in Puerto Rico and in Jamaica in the 1950s, and repeated in Haiti in the 1970s, before the launching of the CBI. The formula is simple. It intends to draw on the unused labor power of the urban dwellers to produce artisanal and light industrial export commodities primarily for the United States. That solution is open to the general criticism of development formulas sketched a few pages earlier. Even some of its advocates see it as a momentary palliative. However, it may turn out to be a costly one. One of the most common consequences of an export-oriented light industry formula is a tremendous rise in the price of food. Let me briefly show why.

In Dominica as elsewhere, the unused labor power of the new lumpen does not originate from thin air. It is most often produced, reproduced, or maintained through the peasant labor process. Investors find it attractive because it is cheap; but it is cheap exactly because of the support it receives (or received) from the peasantry. However, the systematic use of that labor power in export-oriented production for wages contributes to raise the general cost of living if only by severing the lumpen peasantry from the peasantry. The midterm result is that the cost of maintenance of the workers rises and, consequently, the cost of labor also rises. That rise, in turn, deters at least some of the foreign investors who were attracted in the first place by the larger profits implied by the low cost of labor. Indeed, light industries have a way of disappearing fast in search of cheaper labor. Hence, inevitably, light industries rarely guarantee full employment in the long term. One could even argue that they can create unemployment. But more important, they create a new type of unemployed, a worker who may have lost all of his or her informal sources of support. Entirely severed from the peasant labor process, away from his or her network of kin, the hitherto lumpen peasant becomes, temporarily, a full-fledged proletarian whose survival now depends on the concrete exchange of all commodities. Temporarily only, since our hitherto lumpen peasant quickly finds himself, or most often herself, without a job. And the situation of severe unemployment or, at best, underemployment, is likely to continue for a long time as more people invade the urban labor market. However, the individual, now totally unemployed, reverts not to the lumpen peasantry but to the lumpen proletariat. The worker has lost the traditional guarantee of minimal food, and in a context in which food itself has become more expensive. In short, export-oriented policies of this sort rarely benefit peasant nations, but even if they do in a limited way, the long-term result is likely to be an increased reliance on imported food and a tremendous rise in the price of both imported and locally produced edibles.

This has been the case in Jamaica and Puerto Rico in the recent past, and the failures of "industrialization by invitation" did contribute to Puerto Rico's dependence on food stamps and to the proliferation of slums in Jamaica. Similar industrialization programs launched in the seventies are aggravating food shortages right now in Haiti (Latortue 1984; Trouillot 1985). The combination of new food habits and shortages, in turn, tends to increase dependency. In Puerto Rico's case, for instance, increases in the consumption of meat led to increased importation of animal feeds (Pringle 1984). In Dominica's case, the danger of creating a politically volatile lumpen, unable to feed itself, is as great as anywhere else in the region, especially given the current administration's propensity to support zealously any suggestion emanating from Washington.[3] Yet one can easily guess that Washington is not likely to compensate for Dominica's food deficit as it does in the case of Puerto Rico. Dominican starvation would be a quite ironic result of modernism: because of its rurality, its lushness, and the spread of banana cultivation, Dominica is one of the rare Caribbean countries in which most people, if not all, can obtain a daily meal, however unimaginative or deficient.

The disturbing monstrosities of the lumpenization process do not presage, however, the immediate disappearance of peasantries.[4] My own guess is that peasants are here to stay until, at the very least, the first few decades of the next century. The continuous absolute growth and the social resilience that such growth implies demand that we start reconsidering their role in strategies of development. Eurocentric perceptions of progress and empiricist assumptions in the social sciences have led many academics and politicians to see peasants as economic, if not always social, liabilities. Peasants were observed primarily in countries that were poor; hence the presence of peasants came to signify poverty. On the other hand, the West had few peasants; the West was developed; so the absence of peasantries became an index of progress. Recently, however, analysts have become more cautious (De Rouffignac 1985; Tolnai 1984; Grindle 1986). The sheer demographic survival of peasantries has attracted attention to their socioeconomic resilience. The spread of the "informal sector" in many urban areas has forced a reconsideration of the practices of petty commodity producers in general. And the blatant failure of development programs throughout the world, their inability to deliver the miracles promised by the politicians, also convinced many concerned observers to seek alternative solutions.

Alternatives usually require a change of perspective. First, we must come to admit that peasantries do not necessarily constitute a liability, no more than the growth of an urban population is inherently a sign of material improvement. Of course, most nations with sizable peasantries are obviously poor, and most poor nations do have sizable peasantries; further, problems of productivity are inherent in the peasant labor process. However, the case of Dominica strongly suggests that the economic backwardness of those nations is due less to the presence of those peasantries as such than to the conditions of their integration in the capitalist world economy. The burden of these nations is not that they have to carry their peasants but rather that the peasants have to carry themselves and the nonagricultural producers of their own nation through an international system that rewards them much less than it rewards most proletarians, especially Euro-American proletarians. If Geest's records prove anything, it is that peasants can produce wealth.

Not only should we stop thinking of peasants as inherent liabilities, but we should start thinking of them as potential resources. They have demonstrated their resilience despite a hostile domestic and international environment. In quite a few cases, including that of Dominica, their victories in the politics of production tell of the cultural and economic investment they made in their control of the labor process. I suggest that we look at those peasantries against the background of that past. Given their proven resilience, given the fact that they have been able to support the lives and wealth of so many others, local and foreign, for so long, it is time to start developing policies that take that contribution and the potential it reveals into account.

The issue is how to reshape relations of production so that the integration of the peasant labor process into the sphere of valorization becomes less detrimental (if not always profitable) to the peasantry itself and to the nation at large. In most dependent societies, peasant labor benefits foreign-based capitalists, noncultivating nationals, and the peasantry, in that order. The task at hand is to modify the mechanisms of integration so that this order is reversed. Peasant labor must first benefit the peasantry and, through it, the nation at large. The needs or desires of noncultivators within the nation or of merchants in industrialized countries should follow those of the peasantry itself. This approach implies that the new mechanisms of integration reduce drastically the rate of surplus extraction. It implies also national policies able to ensure that whatever surplus is extracted benefits primarily the peasantry and the rest of the nation, again in that order. In short, it implies a self-centered notion of development, and a rejection of the assumption that economic improvement can come only from the outside.

Traditional policies are extraverted in two ways. Within the boundaries of the nation, they force the peasantry into the orbit of the noncultivating classes. Within the boundaries of the world, they maintain dependent nations in the orbit of the industrialized countries which form the core of the capitalist world economy. In the first field, they impose upon the peasantry the cost of an ever chimerical national development. In the latter one, they base that national development on the perception of demand as created elsewhere. In both fields traditional development programs view increased relations with the outside, and especially increased participation in the market, as an inherent advantage. That is, in part, linked to the assumptions I criticized earlier in chapter 7: the more peasants sell to the market, the more they are viewed as living above subsistence. I have demonstrated how futile these assumptions are. But if they are not grounded, why should one expect policies based on them to work?

Peasant involvement in the market implies no inherent advantage whatsoever for the peasantry. Indeed, a fundamental lesson of the Dominican case is that the first tenet of a notion of self-centered development should be suspicion toward the market. Increased participation in the national or international market does not imply that the peasantry or the nation will accumulate greater wealth in the short or long terms. The opposite is often true. We have already seen the fundamental weaknesses of development policies based on changes in the terms of trade between peripheries and industrialized countries. Economist Paul Latortue (1984) recently pointed out that Caribbean applications of the so-called Taiwan model fail to recognize that Taiwan's saturation of its internal market and the development of its agricultural base preceded the success of it export program. A notion of self-centered development for any nation with a sizable peasantry implies that market relations be subordinated to the logic of an internal growth rooted in the productive capacity of that peasantry.

Indeed, the notion of self-centered development always entails some distancing, some form of "delinking" (Amin et al. 1982), some degree of "deconnection" (Amin 1986) from the sphere of exchange dominated by capitalist accumulation. This view does not mean complete autarky or total withdrawal from the sphere of exchange, but it does imply that trade relations with the outside become subordinated to internal necessities rather than the other way around (Amin 1986: 115). In the case of nations in which the majority of the population depend on the peasant labor process, the delinking should be dual. First and foremost, relations and contacts with foreign industrialized nations should be governed by the logic of internal growth rather than by outside needs. Second, the logic of the relations between peasants and the rest of the nation should weigh more in favor of the countryside than in favor of the minority of urban nonproducers.

These observations follow from the earlier demonstrations. The major issue is that of surplus extraction, one much more important than that of productivity inasmuch as it may dictate productivity.[5] Yet surplus extraction itself is fundamentally tied to the integration of the peasant labor process into the sphere of valorization, usually through the market. We have already seen that structural inequalities make it impossible for many dependent countries to influence the market. In the case of weak agricultural producers, like most Caribbean nations, structural inequalities are reinforced by the nature of the crops, the size of the countries, the complexity of the world market, their relatively unimportant share, and so on. However unusual the suggestion might seem, it follows from the above that the only way to limit the damage and aim for some form of local accumulation is to reduce one's involvement in that international market.

This suggestion may seem quite idealistic, but I believe that a program of self-centered development is within the reach of most peasant nations. Furthermore, I believe that it is their only option, everything else having failed miserably.[6] I do not mean that this program will produce miracles. I see it rather as a path, a gradual process of uneven dimensions. That is, its implementation is likely to proceed at an unequal pace in different domains because it will be subordinated to the modalities of the class struggle on the national front and to the inequalities of geopolitics on the international scene. Hence it is crucial that the first few steps of any delinking strategy be based on a correct assessment of local strengths, including the social and cultural strengths of the peasantry. This assessment is necessary, first, to sell the delinking package to the nation as a whole and, second, to implement it gradually.

In most cases, food production offers a solid point of departure for a self-centered development program. In Dominica, edibles now represent roughly 20 percent of the national import values. Few in Dominica benefit from those imports. Given the low buying power and the tiny size of the entire island population, one even doubts that those sales constitute a substantial turnover for town merchants. The bulk of the importers' profits come from nonedible commodities. Hence, merchant resistance to such a program is likely to be minimal. Further, the merchants as such have no political constituency and, apparently, no immediate aims of direct political participation as a distinct group in state politics. All in all, urban resistance would be moot, even if the terms of trade between the peasantry and the urban dwellers are skewed to favor the producers. Imported food is expensive anyway.

The strongest resistance is likely to come from the countryside. The estate owners who speculate on idle land, some of the rural entrepreneurs, and the segments of the lumpen peasantry who show more reluctance to engage in agricultural labor could try to boycott such a project. But this observer's sense is that there is enough underused land, now controlled by the state or by potentially sympathetic segments of the peasantry, for such a program to start without coercion of the estate owners. Likewise, I suspect that part-peasants would provide sufficient labor with the proper incentives. Many rural dwellers who abandoned meat and poultry production in the early days of the banana boom might return to such occupations with only a guarantee of minimal returns. Likewise, government incentives to establish modest fisheries would return many coastal villagers to an old tradition that many of them regard with nostalgia. Indeed, the whole thrust behind such an enterprise would be the systematic reappropriation of the nineteenth-century forms of production that kept many Dominicans alive and fed during the sugar crisis and the downward curves of limes in order to channel peasant resources toward a more varied program of small-scale food production for the local market. Finally, many women in the countryside might be easily convinced of the potential rewards of such a program. As suggested earlier, both married women and single mothers have great difficulties buying imported commodities, either because of lack of cash within the household or because they do not control such cash. A program of food sufficiency would benefit them in many ways, especially if their unused labor is put to work in such an endeavor and gives them a source of income independent of banana production for Geest.[7]

A project of self-centered development requires political mobilization in the best sense of the term and a keen sense of the cultural particularities of the local class struggle. The political adhesion of successive segments of the population to diverse aspects of the program would necessarily influence the rhythm of economic implementation. It is here that subgroups within the lumpen peasantry or crucial fractions of classes, such as the banana children, may offer a breakthrough: they partake of a wider social scope than both the traditional politicians and the traditional cultivators. As privileged agents of mediation, they are better equipped to win the confidence of the peasantry and to muster the broad national support that is necessary to give to the state the momentum that it will need on the international scene.

The inequalities of the interstate system may be harder to deal with than local class divergences in the pursuit of self-centered development. Unless a nation-state disposes of large reserves in labor or land, it is quite unlikely that it will be able to protect itself successfully against the market and the forces of capital. A minimum of international cooperation, especially from one's closest neighbors, will be necessary.[8] Power enters here, and with it the differential ability of various subpopulations of this world to affect varying processes.

Still, part of the solution, once more, rests on a nationalist government's ability to phase its long-term goals according to the always changing reality facing it. To stay with the Dominican case and the issue of food, it is, at the very least, possible for a nation such as Dominica to find outlets within the Caribbean for many edible items that it could produce in great quantity and with relative efficiency.[9] That possibility itself could win support within the region for a self-centered development program.

With minimal regional and strong national support, a Dominican government deeply committed to a program of food sufficiency could easily fight back international resistance, including that coming from the United States. The stakes seem too small to justify a steady and all-out opposition from North America: thirty million Eastern Caribbean dollars a year, not even the price of a decent fighter-bomber. One hesitates to think that the United States would launch one more invasion for such an amount, or that the paranoia in Washington has reached the point at which even such a program would be read as a sign of Soviet influence. This is not to say that the possibility of such an interpretation does not exist: similar programs in Manley's Jamaica did not necessarily please Washington; but they were part of a more ambitious package (Manley 1982; Stephens and Stephens 1984, 1985). Further, as mentioned before, the former British Caribbean, in its entirety, is now going through a crisis of neocolonial hegemony.[10]

The most important obstacle to self-centered development is not its economic feasibility, but the threat of power used for its own sake. I believe that one can bypass that threat, if not completely defuse it, if only by dealing with the international issues involved on a one-to-one basis according to the specificities of the case. Again, the key factor may be how the gradual process of self-centered development is phased.

To be sure, more impetuous critics might call this suggestion only a half-hearted solution to the structural problems engendered by the unequal coexistence of peasants and capital. I myself can certainly see the merits of a more brutal withdrawal from the capitalist world economy. Yet, in many ways, my proposal is influenced by traditional peasant strategies. It is a peasant answer to a serious problem; a modest long-term approach; a proposal rooted in the knowledge of a disadvantage. Still, it satisfies me for three important reasons. First, to set the record straight: everything else has failed. And miserably. Second, phased-out programs in self-centered development are immediately applicable at a lower economic and political cost than many other proposed schemes, and can only help a peasant nation in the long term. For instance, a program that reduces dependence on imported food can become a test case, or a first phase in a progressive delinking strategy. Finally, and more important for those who see the specter of starvation behind the postcard images that hide the plight of three continents: the children born today in millions of peasant households may not be able to wait for more flamboyant answers.

AFTERWORD

by Schuyler Esprit

When I began my academic career as a doctoral student in English at the University of Maryland, College Park, the name Michel-Rolph Trouillot was most often associated with his homeland of Haiti or with the practice of "History" writ large. As a young scholar, I encountered *Silencing the Past: Power and the Production of History* as a seminal text that served as a rite of passage for those of us studying questions of narrative and power in the Global South.

Years after I completed graduate school in 2011, I discovered a more intimate bond with Trouillot. I felt both kinship and frustration when I belatedly discovered that he had begun his academic career in my homeland of Dominica. Indeed, much of Trouillot's later meditations on the archive, power, and history can be traced to his comprehensive study of Dominica and the village of Wesley where he resided for the duration of his dissertation fieldwork. Still, it was a chance encounter with *Peasants and Capital* through a Google Books search query that brought our encounter full circle. In this moment, it became clear that Trouillot's analysis of peasant life in Dominica had unearthed its critical relationship with the political and economic development of the country.

~

Dominica had always been a difficult and enigmatic place for European settlers. It saw several battles between the French and English in the eighteenth century. Enslaved people in Dominica waged battles of their own, including a revolt of the 8th West India Regiment at Fort Shirley in 1807 that secured freedom for enslaved soldiers. The island's rough topography, the opacity of its greenery, the indigenous people, the Kalinago, whose efforts made it the last island to be colonized and who have survived to this day, and the persistent Maroons who challenged the British and French for autonomy with many wars—all crafted a colorful story of survival as well as a legacy of neglect, resentment, and indeed erasure by the British colonial system. In essence, the Empire treated Dominica as what Lisa Paravisini-Gebert calls "a forgotten outpost" (1999). Travel narratives of the nineteenth century, as well as later historical and anthropological accounts, all attribute this abandonment to the island's rugged terrain, which looks as if it just shot up straight into the sky from the center of the earth. Dominica is a powerful cannon of volcanic rock that demands attention, drawing every cloud in sight to stand guard over its mountains and wash the world anew with a daily rainfall.

This history has left a haunting of sorts: a country with nothing to show for its occupation, exploitation, and the legacies of slavery and violence. This is, at least, a common lament for Dominicans when the economy is bad, the government makes decisions and investments against the interest of the poor, or both of these conditions lead to higher crime rates in a small country with a population of about 70,000. This is to say, the systems left behind by colonialism have only limited our abilities to make life for ourselves beyond the fragmented and borrowed economic scaffolding bequeathed to us at political independence in 1978. The so-called modernity of the colonizing mission seems to have completely skipped over the island and left behind only broken systems that do more to elevate colonial ideals and ideas and engender anti-Blackness through what I call low national self-esteem—the feeling that everything outside of our tiny home is better or more valuable than our homegrown things. This is one way to read and experience Dominican history, until you've read Trouillot's intervention.

~

In 2013, I returned to Dominica after thirteen years in the United States. This return home was also a return to the familiar comforts of my grandparents' estate home in Belles, which lies a few miles southwest of the coastal village of Wesley. Belles and Wesley have much in common and these similarities were even more striking during the years that Trouillot conducted his fieldwork in the early 1980s.

Like many men in the post-World War II Caribbean, my grandfather traveled to the Dutch Antilles. He and my grandmother worked there for several years before returning to Dominica with two children and one on the way, after which they purchased a large property in the center of the island. Before his temporary migration, he had worked for a while as a teacher, opening a school in his home village of Campbell, a fishbowl peasant community inland of Mahaut, the coastal village where he would later live and sell the leftover produce from his Belles farm. My grandfather died in 1997 after an almost forty-year tenure as a small-to-medium scale banana and citrus farmer who sold to Geest on Thursdays and at the local market on the weekends.

It is this practice of making life that Trouillot encountered in Dominica's banana industry, where subsistence farming meets systemic agricultural export production. This belies the expectation of detachment from one's labor in the Marxist sense. The farm ideology was exactly as Trouillot describes. The economic driver of the family was as wide as the extended family network. My grandfather's employees comprised close and distant cousins, as well as neighbors, all of whom resided within Belles and the neighboring communities. The kinship ecosystem of the family depended on the leftover crops that fed our Belles home and the many family homes in the Mahaut and Jimmit area, in addition to the families of the relative-employees. This subsistence network was supported by the childhood hands of me and any number of my thirty-four first cousins during summer, Christmas, and Easter breaks. We were joined by our parents during these times and on select weekends, all under the astute management of resources by my grandmother, who also kept a special garden of fresh vegetables for daily consumption.

This is what my parents' generation met as the "banana children" Trouillot describes in *Peasants and Capital.* My grandparents had supported their children into university and the workforce. For the most part, their work took them far away from the business of agriculture. Moreover, their lives pointed away from the farm except for fellowship and leisure, a practice which they passed on to us. The variety and vast distance of their work (and ours) from having their hands in the soil seemed to be a marker not just of their success (and ours) but my grandparents' as well. Their logic presumed that previous generations labored in the soil so we wouldn't have to. Even my father, who came of age in the 1980s and experienced a promising opportunity to learn to run the farm working alongside his father, felt the decline of the industry which had already begun. The fears of bleak national and regional futures for agricultural trade and the mounting pressure of seeking stable wages as a young man with tiny mouths to feed led him by the mid-80s to the start of a career in construction. My understanding of my family history reads my father's exit as a reflection of the death knell of the industry—our family estate another instance of its collateral damage.

~

When "banana day done," what comes next? My family has asked that question for a long time. In the 1990s, before Banana died, Dominican Prime Minister Dame Eugenia Charles had called for diversification of the agriculture industry, bringing in a host of new farming initiatives through a diplomatic relationship with Taiwan, including a prawn farm in Belfast and vegetable crops in the Stockfarm area, the place now occupied by Dominica State College. The irony is not lost on me that my onetime place of work in higher education has come to replace this space of agricultural possibility. Perhaps what the perfect storm of trade, capitalism, and geopolitics taught us in the Eastern Caribbean is that making life is antithetical to making money (in the GDP sense). Even now as we navigate new technologies including artificial intelligence that further alienate people from their work, the expectation of overproduction and overperformance for economic growth still persists. Agricultural uncertainty continues to exacerbate a fracture in Dominica's development and its economic promise, even as it did then.

Despite the peculiarities of Dominica's underdevelopment in some key areas, including road infrastructure and health systems, I often must remind myself and my countryfolk that we are not alone in this quarrel with colonialism. The Caribbean region is indeed a new world, always in the process of making and remaking possibilities out of the legacies of slavery and colonialism, conquest, oppression, and vulnerability of its peoples. In the era of the digital, this is no different: digital code and technologies provide space for engagement amidst the realities of ongoing planetary crises—climate, disease, and continued colonialism.

As the granddaughter of "Big Banana," I represent the loss of agricultural continuity in Dominica that Trouillot so presciently foresees in *Peasants and Capital*. On my return to Dominica, I worked for some time as a lecturer at Dominica State College and eventually served as Registrar and Dean of Academic Affairs at the same institution. Symbolically and materially, I had achieved the dream of many small farmers who had gone into the banana industry in the 1960s and 1970s. However, my return to the region to make a new life was a disheartening yet catalyzing moment. I began to rethink how my training may not take my hands into the soil, but may provide a space to reimagine why and how our relationship to our land, water, and foodways help us make sense of our Caribbean identities. What if we uprooted and replanted our silenced, buried, and looted local knowledges and they grew into more beautiful shapes, wavelengths, flowers, ideas? What would happen if they stayed close to the ground and carpeted the earth or stored energy in their stocky bits like mushrooms, serving as food, as stimulant, as poison, all at once? What if we could, indeed, grow libraries from the roots of our labor and our nourishment?

The digital has allowed me to expand the network of knowledge production and activism in the region. I employ the metaphor of the rhizome as proposed by Caribbean theorist Édouard Glissant, whose work is a blueprint for Caribbean relation and the formation of networks and discourse in the region's historical and cultural context. In Glissant's writing on the poetics of relation, he charts the social and cultural process through which the Caribbean (and Caribbean people) confront and move past histories of slavery and colonialism. This transformative process—an encounter with oppression, suppression, and reflection, and then alchemy and emergence of new identities—inhabits the logic of the rhizome and the substance of relation, "the world's newness" (Glissant 1997: 177). Marisa Parham provides the best synthesis of this rhizomatic theory, describing it as "social configurations and cultural productions that offer insight into an individual's sense of rootedness in them, even as these configurations clearly grow, thrive and transform both towards and away from an otherwise untraceable location or origin" (2015: 132). To interrogate rhizomatic theory in my work as founder and Director at Create Caribbean Research Institute, the first digital humanities center in the Caribbean, I think about the power of the rhizome as a lens through which I work to engender these relations at the levels of pedagogy, digitality, and cultural production. The work of the Research Institute is to essentially produce an almanac for Caribbean (digital) futures via its commitment to planetary responsibility, sustainable living, and community accountability through teaching, research, and community engagement.

I often ask myself: What if my students and collaborators never enjoy access to some of the books and information that have formed my education about the region, in all its nuance and texture? Some of the critical texts that informed my worldview and scholarship include the large library of *Farmers' Almanacs* that my grandfather collected for decades and housed at Belles as reference texts for all—those whose hands were in the dirt and those, like me, whose heads were in the sky. What if the books, the materiality of their learning, were to disappear or change form? How else could they engage and contend with history? For me, root crops are the best symbols for the merging of the ecological and narrative of the Caribbean in digital time. Root crops like cassava, dasheen, yams, potatoes, and ginger belong to a broad family of buried production and sustenance. By virtue of their formation, they can grow and flourish out of sight and out of harm. They extend their lives beyond the materiality of their original form. After they are harvested and consumed, their leftovers spark the beginnings of new processes and outcomes.

I think of the root crops that have been staple foods across the Caribbean and the African diaspora for centuries and remain a testament to the labor, resilience, and resistance of their people in the face of scarcity and poverty created through colonial and neocolonial excavation. I extend the logic of the rhizome to consider the other formations of rootedness that take shape in the context of the making, sharing, and preserving of Caribbean knowledge production. Not only do networks grow toward and away from the origin of local knowledges, they also grow back into the earth, and layer onto and within each other. They also multiply and extend the longevity and generational promise of knowledge production. I see the pedagogy of play and experimentation at Create Caribbean mimicking the logic of the corm. As students learn through the values of digital scholarship proposed by Paige Morgan, their interest in their own histories and cultures emerge. Digital humanities becomes the methodology through which they undertake a radical reeducation in Caribbean studies.

The research conducted by and with students at the Institute are the layers that build a bridge between their current lives and the broader and deeper self-knowledge they seek through the acquisition of history. Through the logic of the bulb's growth, history is our story and research is "we-search." Contrary to recent debates over empiricism and political neutrality sparked by the leadership of the American Historical Association, our practice centers the political restorative work that takes place when students do humanities work that centers the silenced and invisible histories of their lives.

The programs at Create Caribbean are, at their core, for, by, and with the country, region, and world which the students and teachers inhabit. We are the audience for our work. We are the ones without a functioning library building and with an undervalued library system. We are survivors of hurricane trauma—of Hurricane David which interrupted Trouillot's fieldwork in 1979 and of Hurricane Maria which devastated Dominica in 2017—always awaiting the possibility of the next major disaster as climate conditions increase the frequency and intensity of these storms. Therefore, we must apply the logic of tubers and extend the reach of our work, ideas, questions, and dreams for our future. The rhizome is, at once, the source and the outcome of the three pillars of Create Caribbean. The cultural products exist because of these processes and networks and the networks are formed through the iterations and reiterations of culture in the making.

In the project "Heartland,"[1] I considered the ways that ecological, agricultural, and cosmological imperatives that governed my grandparents' commercial farm provide a map for a livable and sustainable Caribbean future despite the ever-present crisis of climate disaster. The Heartland project was an extension of the Carisealand project, through which Create Caribbean modeled sustainable Caribbean futures through mapping, digital storytelling, and ongoing speculative work that incorporates oral histories, climate justice theories, and augmented reality. Beyond the work of the environment and sustainability, the principles of rootedness extend to the cultural knowledge of the region. This sense of rootedness through the reclamation and reparation of the region's literary history guides our project "Visualizing Caribbean Literature" as well.[2]

Édouard Glissant reflects on the possibilities of new formations brought on by the democratizing effects of radio and television and notes,

> It is no longer easy to spot the possible influence of any group of individuals or works belonging to an "elite," except at the limited stage of some technical or scientific specialization that is tacitly recognized without verification. Proof by elite has ceased to count. The enormous divagation replacing it leaves no time for retreat or re-seizure. (Glissant 1997: 175–76)

Essentially, these mediums have become so fast and wide in reach, like the rhizome Glissant wrote of, that by the time the elite of industrialized

1. Schuyler Esprit. *Heartland* (June 16, 2021). ArcGIS StoryMaps. https://storymaps.arcgis.com/stories/d7e34a74695c4b54a55742e9e2d5bf93.
2. *Visualizing Caribbean Literature*. Create Caribbean Research Institute (n.d.). https://createcaribbean.org/vcl/

nations catch on, the languages, attitudes, and cultures of marginalized peoples have already taken root and forged relations anew.

Soon after he penned his *Poétique de la relation* in 1990, computer programs and the Internet completely transformed not only our ability to use global oral languages but the possibilities of knowledge production for the people empowered by this orality. Indeed, Glissant had anticipated this. The digital, in its mired present and futures, fulfills some of Glissant's imaginings for new beginnings in the Caribbean and the world. And the present calls out for new beginnings. Trouillot was proven right in many of his predictions about the direction of the banana industry. The professional class created out of the labor of small farmers has all but neutered the possibility of renewing large-scale farming in Dominica, even while Caribbean policymakers remain enchanted by the promise of technology and global development entities. Does *Peasants and Capital*—upon its publication in 1988 and republication 2025—propose an almanac of relation guided by the lives made possible by the peasant labor process? At the very least, with its cycles of teaching, research, and reflection with the community on what it needs and desires to be, this network of rootedness governs the shape and trajectory of Create Caribbean—an almanac for relation when banana day done.

References

Glissant, Édouard. 1977. *Poetics of Relation.* Translated by Betsy Wing. Ann Arbor: University of Michigan Press.

Paravisini-Gebert, Lizabeth. 1999. "'A Forgotten Outpost of Empire': Social Life in Dominica and the Creative Imagination." *Jean Rhys Review* 10 (1&2): 13–26.

Parham, Marisa. 2015. "Breadfruit, Time and Again: Glissant Reads Faulkner in the World Relation." In *Theorizing Glissant: Sites and Citations*, edited by John E. Drabinski and Marisa Parham, 129–38. London: Rowman & Littlefield International.

Notes to *Peasants and Capital*

CHAPTER 1. Peasants as Part-Economies

1. Kroeber, despite later conceptualizations based on his work (Redfield 1956; Foster 1965), did not define peasants, but legitimately used their case as one of many illustrations in a long discussion of dualisms, cultural and social polarities and symbioses (Kroeber 1948: 274–86). He only indicated a sociocultural divide that any comprehensive conceptualization, even if primarily centered around economic referents (e.g. Firth 1961: 87), should explain. Similarly, Marx's study of the French peasantry in the context dominated by Louis Bonaparte (Marx [1852] 1964) never claimed the programmatic value that Marx clearly saw in his later work on capital and the industrial labor process. It was the study of a particular social mix in a specific historical situation, the study of one manifestation of the peasantry's sociopolitical ambivalence. A conceptualization should be able to account for the nature of that sociopolitical ambivalence.

2. There are more extensive summaries of the different trends in peasant studies than this oversimplified sketch (e.g., S. Silverman 1979; Archetti 1979). Shanin's later work (e.g., Shanin 1982) has moved toward a greater complexity and a much finer understanding of the puzzle presented by the coexistence of peasants and capitalism.

3. The typology that followed Wolf's original call was in fact based on quantitative evaluations of cash sales (Wolf 1955). One wonders about the use of typologies at all at that level, as opposed to, say, a historical investigation of gradations and mixes of these economic and sociopolitical relationships. Mintz (1973) seems to adopt the latter position, though at

points he used the word *typology*; but his own historical categorizations are based on process rather than essence (1973: 95, 101; 1984: passim).

4. In the void created by the general dissatisfaction with rural sociology (Saunders et al. 1978) and divergences within the anthropological discourse on the "folk" (S. Silverman 1979), peasantries were to be conceived as an altogether different "mode of production" (Kerblay 1971; Harrison 1977) or merely as a guise or form of capitalism (e.g., Patnaik 1979; Ennew et al. 1977). Rey's (1973) illuminating suggestion that such noncapitalist modes can be articulated to capitalism and Alavi's (1965) concept of "colonial modes of production" should not blur the loss caused by the terminological intransigence of the mode of production debate.

5. To be sure, the long accumulation of questions and answers has not been in vain. Stimulating suggestions for further inquiries (Mintz 1973; Archetti and Assa 1978; Shanin 1982) could emerge only within a fertile climate.

6. Relations between size and complexity have been well explored, notably in an international symposium at which various scholars offered numerous suggestions on their possible implications for social analysis (Barth 1978a). But it is not certain that size implies complexity as Barth (1978b) suggests; smallness may mask complexity to an observer (Trouillot 1983). Moreover, Berreman (1978), in a paper originally delivered at the same symposium, so skeptically assessed the concept of "scale" that further studies must face the issues he raised.

7. Empirical "scale" may be retained as a variable (Gronhaug 1978) but it should be so retained at all levels of the analysis. As Wolf (1978) suggests, the repetition of techniques in different loci does not lead necessarily from a micro to a macro perspective (e.g., Steward et al. 1951). Likewise, the extreme restriction of empirical boundaries does not necessarily produce a shift from macro to micro.

8. I use the words *individual agency* to emphasize what I perceive as a common mistake in the social sciences: agency cannot be located a priori and exclusively at the level of the individual. I do not see why the notion should necessarily exclude other historical actors: classes, ethnic groups, nations, clans, bureaucracies, social forces, and so on. Still, individual agency seems to me more amenable to a microlevel analysis.

9. Extensive use of this criterion within a narrower scope is likely to produce categories that fall within the range of the two types usually treated as "middle" and "poor" peasants, precisely the range requiring further differentiation (e.g., Wolf 1955; Patnaik 1978; Bernstein 1979).

CHAPTER 2. Space: A Patchwork of Enclaves

1. Many geographers and historians distinguish "regions" within the larger political units; but such studies were originally meant to demonstrate the unity of the countries themselves (Capel 1981), and they seem to continue nowadays partly because of the difficulties inherent in handling large amounts of empirical materials.

2. Not all items so produced are "surpluses" from the point of view of that peasantry. Tomatoes, carrots, or poultry, for instance, are primarily produced for urban consumption. Thus, though economic and ideological dependence on the town takes a different character in the interior, it is no less important there than on the coastal strip.

3. The resurfacing of an extremely steep road, politicians' promises to bring electricity to the area, old issues of rivalries between Portsmouth and Roseau rekindled in contemporary guises may very well thrust this area into mainstream national life, but it is most likely that the peasant ways will survive for quite some time through diverse forms of integration.

4. One can hardly surmise the reasons why Vieille Case or Peineville peasants came to produce coffee or peppers that are in demand in the French islands whereas many others who could enjoy similar or equal access to those territories do not take advantage of their "contacts" in such manner. Still, the case of this enclave suggests that prior mechanisms of integration in the valorization process may affect later occurrences, even if the later mechanisms are structurally dominant.

5. That failure itself is significant and tends to reinforce my wider conclusions on the systematic co-optation of the peasant labor process through the apparent sale of major export commodities. Interestingly, banana acreage actually decreased in the early days of the cooperative, but banana production regained impetus and now overwhelmingly dominates the Castle Bruce area.

6. Though most houses are erected less than half a mile from the sea, the steepness of the coast precludes the development of fishing, and few villagers dare to brave the high windward waves with the frail crafts most common throughout Dominica. The repeated destruction of the Saint-Sauveur School, which stands on one of the few flat spots of that coastal stretch, reminds one of the harshness of the elements on that segment of the windward shore. More people simply and safely walk from one village to the next, as in the rest of Dominica; but communications with other enclaves or with the capital, are perhaps more limited than in

many other areas. In 1980 and 1981, any mechanical breakdown of the old and only truck that regularly made the long journey to the capital on Mondays, Wednesdays, and Fridays forced residents to postpone urgent business.

7. I have left out as many as perhaps six villages of the interior. Some stand alone on the roads between some of the enclaves described (e.g., Bellevue-Chopin and Pichelin on the road from Roseau to Grand Bay, Bells at the southern tip of the Central Forest Reserve). Others lay isolated at the end of secondary paths (e.g., Grand Fond). I visited these villages with a few friends from Wesley in 1981, but a description that would do credit to the originality of each one is outside the scope of this writing. Finally, I never visited two or three villages (Robinson, Gueule Lion) because lack of resources or sheer exhaustion at times forced my native companions and me to change our plans and head back to town or "home" to Wesley.

And, obviously missing so far is Wesley itself and the enclave to which it belongs, the southern part of Saint Andrew Parish, otherwise referred to as the La Soye (or La Soie) District. This area is the banana belt of Dominica, the region where I conducted most of my ethnographic fieldwork, and the primary focus of this book's third and last part.

CHAPTER 3. Time: An Island in the World Economy

1. Likewise, the recent and quite dramatic rise of coconut byproducts on the export lists is linked to social and political trends. It is not coincidental that the rise of coconuts (an estate crop) occurred after the coming to power of the conservative Freedom party, a party traditionally controlled by estate owners. One cannot yet suggest that Dominica is moving toward a new preeminence, but some of the signs are there. However, the continuing increase of banana exports, even though at a much slower pace than coconut byproducts, is a good sign for the yeomanry. One wonders, of course, how much the government will support banana producers if and when coconuts top the export lists.

CHAPTER 5. Factions and Strategies

1. Glenelg's instructions curiously anticipate the published work of Edward Gibbon Wakefield, at times almost word for word. Marx (1967: 768) quotes Wakefield's treatise on colonization: "Where land is very cheap and all men are free, where every one who so pleases can easily

obtain a piece of land for himself, not only is labour very dear, as respects the labourer's share of the produce, but the difficulty is to obtain combined labour at any price." Marx (1967: 772) goes on to expose Wakefield's plan for "systematic colonization" as one in which "the price of the soil imposed by the State must be a 'sufficient price'—i.e., so high 'as to prevent the labourers from becoming independent landowners until others had followed to take their place.'" I thank Ashraf Ghani for calling my attention to those passages.

CHAPTER 6. "I Can Always Eat My Fig"

1. There is no record that Saint Lucia or Grenada, which were meant to become the major complements of Jamaican production, received similar grants.

CHAPTER 7. Working for Capital

1. The *Report of the Seventh Session of the Intergovernmental Group on Bananas*, based on meetings held at Rome in May 1980 (FAO 1980), provides us with some clues on the Windwards' marginality and on WINBAN's ineffectiveness. No representative of WINBAN is listed among the 126 participants, though an individual I know to be a WINBAN official took part in the session as representative of Saint Lucia. Grenada, Saint Vincent, and Dominica had no official say at all among the forty-one nation states gathered to guide the future of the world banana trade. Ironically, Dominica's future is much more dependent upon that trade than almost any of the producers represented at Rome. In sharp contrast, the procurement manager of Geest Industries sat among the six delegates from the United Kingdom.

2. Surplus is a central notion of classical distribution theory; but for the Physiocrats, it was what remained of the gross product after the subtraction of labor and technical inputs (Bharadwaj 1978: 159–60). Thus, even for the Physiocrats for whom surplus came closest to meaning excess (over necessary costs) the issue of the workers' subsistence level remained secondary. Thereafter, classical economic analysis emphasized the generation of surplus (Smith), the division of surplus into rent and profits (Ricardo), the relation of surplus, accumulation, and exploitation (Marx), rather than an alleged gap between surplus and subsistence levels as such (see Robinson 1979: 18–34, and also Marx 1963).

3. I fundamentally agree with Sen (1978) that too much has been made of the otherwise serious difficulties involved in the transformation of values into prices (Sraffa 1960; Steedman 1977). The labor theory of value is acknowledged here as a descriptive-explanatory device, not as an accounting procedure. Inherent accounting problems multiply tenfold when the theory is taken to predict prices on a world scale, especially for "primary commodities" (Robinson 1979: 64; but see Amin 1980, 1986).

4. This argument needs to be counterpoised with Chevalier's (1982: 118) illuminating notion of "subsistence commodities." The problem with Chevalier's stance is that it sets no limits to exchangeability. Everything becomes a commodity in potential. He writes: "Production for household consumption may have *nothing to do* with the preservation of a 'natural' economy" (1982: 119; emphasis mine). I do not wish to hold to the ideological implications of the "natural economy" notion, but it does seem to me that we need to know more of the internal logic of household reproduction (Evers et al. 1984; J. Smith 1984) before making of it a mere formal consequence of the valorization process. The transfer of surplus labor does not seem antithetical to the existence of subsistence commodities. It is a middle-of-the-road position (see Archetti 1978a; Amin 1986), but the safest one in my view, given our theoretical and empirical knowledge of the issues.

CHAPTER 8. The Making of a Transnational

1. Wailing van Geest & Sons is now a multimillion dollar empire in its own right, and its subsidiaries in England share members at the senior management level with Geest Holdings.

2. The most notable exception was W. Groom Limited, a timber and woodwork merchandizing firm originally founded in 1931 by a Spalding farmer, of which John van Geest became the chairman in the early 1940s (C.R.O. 257425). After its takeover, W. Groom went through a period of intensive capitalization quite similar to that of Geest Industries.

The handling of W. Groom by the Geest team confirms the periodization presented in this chapter. Prior to 1952, W. Groom was as important to the Geest brothers as Geest Industries, and went through an identical, though independent, process of capitalization. When Geest Industries picked up Antilles' banana contract, W. Groom became a subsidiary of Geest Industries (1952) and remained marginal for the twenty-year stretch of Geest Industries' expansion, providing services to the banana operations, notably boxes. In 1974, two years after the formation of Geest Holdings, W. Groom became Geest Industrial Group Limited, the spearhead of Geest's venture into agricultural engineering.

3. The market for bananas in the United Kingdom remains a "protected" one. This protection takes essentially the form of duties to banana imports from non-Commonwealth countries. Moreover, the final share of the market supplied by different former British colonies is determined, at least in part, by formal and informal arrangements of the importers under the watchful supervision of the British government. As suggested above, this protection greatly accounts for the expansion of the Windward Islands' production. Yet it is important to emphasize that this fact does not invalidate the basic argument of this chapter.

First, one could argue, along formal economic lines, that producing countries in the Caribbean are "enslaved by subsidies," (as the *Economist* recently suggested about some sugar-producing countries). Second, and more to the point, inasmuch as the protection facilitated expansion, it protected Geest, the ultimate beneficiary of that expansion. Import duties protected Geest against its British and foreign competitors which had the capacity to acquire bananas from non-Commonwealth areas long before Geest itself did. Formal and informal arrangements among British-based importers protected Geest perhaps from JAMCO and certainly from Fyffes. Caribbean peasants benefited from this protection only inasmuch as their continuous production of bananas was necessary to Geest's profitability.

4. The "net capital employed" is not always equal to the sum of assets minus the liabilities because of internal charges within the conglomerate, for example, the debt to parent company.

5. It became usual for the directors to mention only the most important affiliates in their annual reports because, as they often put it, "to include all other subsidiaries would require particulars of excessive length" (Reports of the Directors, Geest Holdings & Geest Industries, 1972–80; C.R.O. 1068048 and 308737).

6. The creation of the conglomerate itself required the participation of many more people than the Geest brothers and the small group of associates, solicitors, and businessmen who ran, and continue to run, most of the Geest enterprises. The first members of Geest Holdings included a number of insurance and finance companies, such as the Industrial and Commercial Finance Corporation, the Prudential Assurance Company, the Northern Assurance Company, and the Midland Bank Executor and Trustee Company. One member of the British Parliament sat on the Board of Directors. Geest's political contributions to the Conservative

party and the Economic League also point to contacts and ramifications way beyond the immediate personal relations of the two brothers.

7. The sectors of activities are not exactly coterminous with the four groups. First, not everything having to do with a type of activity fell under the group officially designated to carry that particular activity. For instance, Geest Industries owns Geest Foods, the company that supplies most of Geest's edible commodities to wholesalers and retailers in England. Yet, contrary to what one could expect, neither Geest Industries nor Geest Foods controlled Oval Eggs which was completely owned, rather, by Geest Associates (WINBAN 1980; Geest Associates, Reports of the Directors, 1977; C.R.O. 1060806). Second, some activities carried out by third-or fourth-level subsidiaries fall completely out of the main objects and purposes of any of the major group companies.

The expansion of the conglomerate entails four different processes: (1) diversification of activities, (2) consolidation of activities, (3) diversification of assets, and (4) asset consolidation. The form under which a subsidiary is integrated within the conglomerate at any time may reflect the primacy of any one of those four processes. Besides, senior management may have reasons of its own to place a newly acquired subsidiary within a particular group. Yet beyond these fluctuations, it remains true that each of the conglomerate's four groups specializes in one of its four major types of activities (Geest Holdings, Chairman's Statement, 1976; C.R.O. 1068048). WINBAN (1980) does offer an alternative presentation of the Geest empire in the late 1970s, but it does not conflict with the thrust of this one.

8. What was to become Geest Associates was registered only in July 1972 under the name Geest Management Services Limited (C.R.O. 1060806). Likewise, Geest's ventures in agricultural engineering started in the mid-1970s. The old W. Groom Limited was revived, at first, to produce boxes and pallets (presumably used in the transportation of bananas and produce); it became Geest Industrial Group Limited only in 1974. By 1976, it began to specialize in "industrial handling equipment, agricultural machinery and trailers" and to phase out its previous activities (Reports of the Directors, 1976; C.R.O. 257425). In 1980, it sold all its pallets and packing cases interests. Similarly, the fourth and last major subdivision, Geest Horticultural Group Limited (not to be confused with the original Geest Horticultural Products Limited) became important in terms of both turnover and profits only in the mid-1970s, even though it emerged earlier, from the 1968 takeover of Europa Horticultural Products Limited by the Geest brothers (C.R.O.

786805). Geest's international spread also dates from the 1970s (except for companies registered in the Caribbean). Clearly then, the expansion and diversification of the Geest empire postdates by two decades Geest's involvement in the Caribbean banana industry.

9. The disproportionate importance of bananas within the activities of Geest Industries and the poor performance of the Geest Horticultural Group suggest that bananas may constitute more than two-thirds of the so-called bananas and produce sector.

10. The alternative assumption (i.e., that these fellow subsidiaries performed those services at a loss) leads to two ridiculous conclusions. Since we already know that the Caribbean associations cannot verify the costs of those services (they cannot even verify the Green Market Price), a loss can only mean two things: either that Geest's senior management wanted to subsidize Caribbean peasants with the fruits of the labor of British workers or that they wanted the subsidiaries they had just created to go bankrupt. I assume that they are innocent of such charges.

11. For example, the records of the Geest Industrial Group for the year 1979 count among the branch's current assets 57,074 pounds "due from group companies," 5,866 pounds "due from Holding Company," and 167,000 pounds of "Group loss relief receivable." Likewise, the liabilities include 782,918 pounds "due to Holding Company" (down from one million in 1978), and 15,421 pounds "due to group companies" (Geest Industrial Group, Statement of Accounts, 29 December 1979; C.R.O. 257425).

CHAPTER 9. Wesley Ville La Soye

1. Occasionally, some publications broke away from the ethnographic triad and managed to remain comfortably within the mainstream of the disciplinary discourse (Lesser 1978; Nadel 1942; Benedict 1946; Steward et al. 1956). Yet theoretical inquiries on the nature of the link between the object of observation and that of analysis (e.g., Firth 1951, 1964; Lesser 1985, Wolf 1978) rarely questioned the epistemological necessity of the triad itself.

2. Even in cases in which more attention was paid to methodology, the results were not always worth the efforts. Julian Steward (1955: 79), one of the few anthropologists who faced the question of methodology directly, complained that, in practice, the culture area concept led many North American anthropologists to assume that it is "possible to write an 'ideal' ethnology which records ALL cultural data for the permanent

record" (Steward 1955: 79). Data accumulation became an end in itself and, once more, boundaries fell wherever they seemed most obvious to the writer. Steward (1955: 82) asserted: "Wissler divided North America into nine culture areas; Kroeber (1939) lists six 'grand areas,' twenty-one 'areas,' and innumerable 'sub-areas' for North America; and other scholars have divided it in still different ways. South America has been divided into twenty-four areas by Murdock (1951), eleven by Stout (1938), five by Wissler (1922), four by the Handbook (Steward 1946–48) and by Kroeber (1948), and three by Cooper (1942) and by Bennett and Bird (1949)."

3. Large-scale units of production still exist: specializing mainly in coconuts, they occasionally use wage labor. More often, the larger fields are divided among tenants who intercrop their bananas with the owner's coconuts. Such tenants freely dispose of the whole of their banana harvest and pay only a nominal cash fee, but the owner benefits from their general maintenance of the field: weeding, fertilizing, and so on. Still, by and large, estates are dead or dying. Most of the land that constituted the Geest Woodford Hill Estate is now held by independent peasant owners. Further south, large segments of the Londonderry Estate were sold in small portions along the years. Most of the remainder was occupied by tenants for a nominal cash rent (sometimes as low as $5 E.C. a year for an acre) at the time of this fieldwork, but have been sold since.

4. Langford Lovell owned 263 slaves concentrated on the property now referred to as the Londonderry Estate, a series of contiguous plots then totaling over one thousand acres, and originally granted by the Crown of England to one Patrick O'Connor. Lovell acquired the estate from Richard Oliver in 1812 (C.O. 152/293). On a continguous property, now shared by the Melville Hall Airport and the government-controlled Melville Hall Estate, John M. Melville controlled the third largest labor force of the area.

5. In the 1840s, Leathem was one of many white immigrant shopkeepers in Roseau, and an attorney for the Geneva and Berricoa estates. He first gained national notoriety because of his brutal treatment of cultivators during the 1844 Riots or La Guerre Negre. Governor Fitzroy then called him "the most inveterate enemy" of the blacks. In an abrupt turnabout Leathem later charged that the government had reacted with brutality against the cultivators involved in La Guerre Negre. Soon after, Leathem gained more visibility as the loser in the first legislative race won by Charles Gordon Falconer (the colored politician who was to become the leader of the Mulatto Ascendancy).

In 1856, Leathem bought the Londonderry Estate from Ann Lovell, Langford's daughter, and added to it the area now known as Hunt, an original Crown grant to one Rowland Hunt, adjacent to the properties held by the Burtons (CO. 152/293). By 1859, when Leathem took the second Assembly seat for Saint Andrew, he already owned or controlled most of the estates of Saint Andrew South: Blenheim, Eden, Londonderry, and Woodford Hill, in addition to the large Belfast Estate and Hartington Cottage, near Roseau, where he lived (*Dominica Almanac*, 1859, 1862, 1864; CO. 74/33; CO. 75/1). The 1,237 acres of Melville Hall escaped his control, but that estate was run by his friend William McIntyre, the only man besides Leathem to be referred to by his contemporaries as a "sugar king" of Dominica. It is no exaggeration to suggest that, by the mid-1860s, Leathem and McIntyre owned or controlled most of the Dominican estates (together perhaps with the powerful Garraway family who represented European merchant houses and held liens on a number of estates).

6. The November 1865 elections in Saint Andrew provide a good example of Dominican politics in the second half of the nineteenth century. The new constitutional arrangement of 1865 called for a bilateral Legislative House of seven elected representatives and seven Crown nominees. James Caffyn ran against Charles Leathem for the Saint Andrew seat. Leathem questioned Caffyn's qualifications, that is, his actual ownership of some commercial premises, but the electoral officer ruled against him and "at the close of the poll, Mr. Caffyn was declared duly elected *by a majority of one vote*" (C.O. 74/33; emphasis mine). After the opening of the new legislative session, Leathem brought to the Assembly a certificate of the registrar stating that there were no records of a deed or conveyance passing the said premises to Caffyn. The issue was to be decided on 25 January 1866. The Crown nominees were expected to back Leathem. The mulatto-dominated group of elected representatives was expected to back Caffyn. Since Caffyn himself could not vote, mulatto leader Charles Gordon Falconer tried to equalize the numbers by introducing a motion that was to prevent Crown nominee Alexander Robinson from voting on the Leathem-Caffyn issue on the grounds that Robinson worked for Leathem. With mulatto politician John Bellot absent from the House on that day, Falconer's motion was rejected. The House then requested the attorney general's opinion on Caffyn's legal ownership of the premises. The attorney general declined to comment. The House then asked Caffyn to produce his documents, and the mulatto elected representatives were forced to recognize publicly that the

documents that made Caffyn eligible for office (proofs of ownership) postdated his inscription as a candidate. On March 21, the attorney general ruled that Caffyn's election was invalid. New elections were ordered for April 5. Caffyn ran again and won. Leathem himself returned to the House on November of the same year as a Crown nominee.

7. As mentioned, alternative versions or modifications abound, and some need to be mentioned. Nevis and Saint Kitts are sometimes proposed as the place of origin, and Woodford Hill as the estate to which the immigrants first came. Likewise, some informants mention a transitional period during which the Antiguans or Nevitians stayed at Portsmouth until they were driven out by yellow fever or some other tropical sickness associated with the Portsmouth swamps. Religion sometimes enters the story as the estate owners' rationale for bringing in Antiguans on their Dominican estate. Though some informants simply suggest that the owners "liked Antiguans better," several claim that they did not trust the slaves of the French, and only a few suggest that Protestant slaves or English-trained slaves were better workers.

There is nothing in the official records consulted that would contradict the major tenets of that historical tradition or, for that matter, the many variations built upon it. The fundamental ambuiguity may be that of the legal status of the immigrants at the time of arrival. Though some informants refer to them as "emancipated slaves," they do not offer the time of arrival in pre- or postslavery terms: when pressed, speakers tend to provide an impromptu answer, one that seems forced upon them by a nagging interviewer. Likewise, only a minority suggest that the immigrants were Methodists. For most, religious differentiation is rather a contemporary issue.

8. The first census with precise religious classifications is that of 1844, and it indicates the Methodist presence in Saint Andrew. Unfortunately, one has to wait for the 1870 Census to see a systematic breakdown of birth places in Saint Andrew South itself. The 1870 Census reports 118 La Soye residents born outside Dominica, fewer than 50 of whom came from the British West Indies. Many of those immigrants came from Guadeloupe (44); 24 were from Africa. Among those born in the British West Indies, 15 came from Saint Vincent, 12 from Antigua, 6 from Barbados, 5 from Saint Kitts, 2 from Nevis, 1 from Trinidad, and 1 from the Virgin Islands. Later censuses report lower numbers of foreign-born residents in Saint Andrew.

The migrations recorded by the 1870 Census seem too little and too late to have made much of a cultural difference. Forty English speakers of different background could not have changed the linguistic landscape in an area that had counted 858 slaves in the 1820s. Further, the written record emphasizes a strong Methodist presence in Saint Andrew as early as the 1830s (ZHC1/1266), a presence confirmed by the 1844 Census. We may then assume that the Protestant immigrants came before the end of slavery, or during Apprenticeship at the latest.

9. The Reverend Thomas Coke visited Dominica in the 1780s, and his reports to John Wesley indicate the presence of only a few Methodists (Coke, 1787, 1788, 1789). Yet twenty years later, in his *History of the West Indies*, Coke (1808–11: 867) repeats a local preacher's claim that there were 900 Methodists in the whole island, about 600 of whom resided in the Portsmouth area. (Note the similarity with Wesley people's mention of a possible first stop in Portsmouth.) On the other hand, in 1817, Watson (1817: 69) reported only 170 Methodists in the whole island. The reality probably lay somewhere between those two figures. Given Watson's superficial overview, he may well have underestimated the Wesleyan population. On the other hand, the local Methodist preachers had good reasons to inflate the numbers they reported to Coke. At any rate, in 1826 the Wesleyans built a chapel at Layou; and in 1830 they rebuilt for the third time their church at Point Ruperts (Portsmouth) and immediately thereafter their first chapel at La Soye. That indicates a strong Methodist interest in the enclave more than a decade before the start of Apprenticeship.

The suggestion of a pre-Apprenticeship date for the original migration holds also on theoretical grounds. Afro-American languages seem to have solidified quite fast, after the early migratory waves (Mintz and Price 1976). It is unlikely that Kòkòy, or English for that matter, would have made such an impact on the enclave after the consolidation of the Lesser Antillean Creole.

A few Wesley people would strongly disagree with my timing of the migration. Two among my most reliable oral sources maintain that the Antiguans came "immediately after Emancipation." I have no way to disprove their timing; but if they are right, then the impact of Methodism on the area preceded the migration they are referring to.

10. Various censuses of Dominica help us quantify the relative decline in the number of Wesleyans in Saint Andrew South. A comparison of the figures reveals that the proportion of Methodists in the parish dropped from 38 percent in 1844, to 37 percent in 1871, 31 percent in 1881, 25 percent in 1911, 22 percent in 1921, to stabilize around 21 and 19 percent in the second half of this century. Separate figures for

the northern and southern parts of the parish suggest that the relative decline was *not* primarily because of the increases of Roman Catholics in the Peineville-Vieille Case enclave: the proportion of Wesleyans in La Soye proper dropped from 57.5 percent to 52.4 percent between 1871 and 1881. (My calculations are based on the Dominica censuses of 1844, 1871,1881, 1911, and 1921, and oral information.)

11. Average daily attendance remained low, at first, but not significantly lower than that of other schools elsewhere. A year later, in 1860, Castor registered 107 students (64 boys and 43 girls), an exceptional achievement in a district with fewer than 400 children of school age. Average daily attendance rose to 60, a higher proportion than in Portsmouth schools, and more than half of the average recorded at the Roseau Government School, largely attended by the children of the elite and middle classes (*Dominica Almanac*, 1861, 1862). Later on, the Wesley school grew to outperform even Roseau for attendance ratio and the reading ability of its students (CO. 74/33).

12. Significantly, in the petition presented to Commissioner Robert Hamilton (1894: 93) and quoted from at the beginning of this chapter, the Wesley villagers extended to the whole enclave attributes that fitted them more closely than the inhabitants of neighboring villages such as Calibishie or Marigot. To be sure, Calibishie (then Calibistrie) counted only 138 people, the village of Marigot had only 17 families and a total population of 78, and Woodford Hill was still the name of an estate, whereas Wesley had already grown into a striving village of more than 130 households and a total population of 457 (Dominica Census 1891).

13. The name of the village obviously reinforced the Methodist association though the descent line is not so clear as it first seems. Some village oral historians who shared their knowledge of the past with me kept insisting that the name *Wesley* was originally that of a person. I first assumed that they were referring to the Reverend John Wesley until Leslie Africa, realizing my misunderstanding, told me that this Wesley person was a Dominican. Later on, Fred Henry, whose knowledge of La Soye's past remains unequaled, told me in no uncertain terms that the name of the village came from a certain "Mrs. Wesley" who had a shop at the junction of Eden and the then growing residential agglomeration. Mrs. Wesley owed her fame to her unbeatable prices. Hence, people would walk relatively long distances to go a "Ma Wesley." Soon, by extension, the whole residential area was referred to as "Wesley."

Health reports for the year 1866, entered in the 1867 Minutes of the Legislative Assembly, verify the existence of a Mrs. Wesley, then living on Eden. Her three-year old child, suffering from "glossite" (glossitis), was cured in the summer of 1866 (CO. 74/33). Hence, Mrs. Wesley was alive—and, I presume, well—at the time "Wesley Ville" first appeared in the written record. One would like to know when and where "Mrs. Wesley" got *her* name. Yet, without the rather benign inflammation of a three year-old child's tongue, written history might have omitted the existence of Ma Wesley.

14. That decline was not simply the result of Leathem's death, nor did it occur only in Plantation Wesley. It fitted a general pattern of national and international dimensions, caused ultimately by the fall of sugarcane throughout the world. Yet because of Leathem's grip on Saint Andrew South, because of the importance of that enclave in the Dominica of the 1860s, and because of the importance of Plantation Wesley within the enclave, the impact was perhaps greater there than elsewhere on the island.

15. William McIntyre may have acted as attorney for the Leathem estate (CO. 152/293) though he had passed formal control of Melville Hall to W. G. Ellis, at some time in the mid-1870s. At any rate, some of the land formally controlled by Leathem's heirs reverted to forest, some was used for pasture, and the rest may have been planted in diverse crops (including sugarcane) on small units controlled by renters and squatters who sold their harvest to Melville Hall. Major changes occurred inevitably at the level of the labor process, affecting the relations of production in that part of the enclave.

16. The planters were Colin McIntyre and William Callendar. One witness, W. G. Marie (who read and handed in a letter) was identified as a "proprietor" but specifically spoke in the name of "small owners." Another one was identified as a "labourer." The four remaining witnesses were all specifically identified as "peasant proprietors." Two among those peasants presented petitions to Hamilton. The first petition, labeled "Petition from Peasant Proprietors from St. Andrew's South," was read by Nathaniel Powell and endorsed by nine other signatories. It is a short but precise list of seven collective claims or grievances. The second one, read by David Barnes Leslie and endorsed by twenty-nine signatures or marks, outlined seventeen points that it later covered in detail (Hamilton 1894: 39–40; 93–97).

17. Twenty-two years before Hamilton's visit, the 1871 Census had counted only nine "petty cultivators" in southern Saint Andrew. Ten years later, in 1881, census takers listed eleven petty cultivators; but mention of twenty hucksters and eleven shopkeepers already suggests

an occupational independence not incompatible with the presence of a larger yeomanry (or, at least, squatters). One would like to know how many of the people involved in various independent occupations in the year 1881 also worked more or less regularly on their own gardens.

18. The testimonies indicate that the small proprietors wanted to maintain the production of provisions for the local market, but also that they aimed at producing for export. W. G. Marie in particular (who claimed to represent "a large number of the people of this parish") repeatedly emphasized the plight of "owners of small lots of land who dispose of their produce locally, and cultivate only provisions for home consumption" (Hamilton 1894: 93–94).

The records also point out the outstanding political priority of the yeomanry: the abolition of the taxation system erected by the government, merchants, and planters between 1856 and 1893. The land tax is the first issue raised in all three lists but peasants also demanded the abolition or the reduction of all taxes, licenses, or duties pertaining to the possession of boats and animals, the production of rum, or the maintenance of roads. The agenda also included the reestablishment of export duties in lieu of the land tax, a coastal steamer that would carry agricultural products outside of the district, the provision of Crown lands to people willing to work on them, greater political power to the elected and electorate alike, and, as noted, special representation for La Soye apart from Saint Andrew North on grounds of cultural and economic differences.

The yeomen grievances overlapped some points made by the only laborer heard by Hamilton in Wesley, and they also touched on many claims made by wage earners elsewhere in the island. Yet more surprisingly perhaps, they coincided with grievances made by planters in La Soye and elsewhere. In short, the visibility of La Soye's small yeomanry, already marked by its cultural singularities, was further intensified because they saw themselves as small proprietors halfway between planters and landless cultivators.

19. One can barely guess at the reasons that might have pushed Davies to buy Melville Hall in 1887, especially since, at that time, he was leading, in Roseau, the Mulatto Ascendancy's fight against the governor, Viscount Gormanston, and the Colonial Office. Political control of the La Soye District might have figured among his aims. On the other hand, Davies might have thought that the numerous proposals he was to present for establishing modern means of communication between La Soye and the rest of the country would have turned the area into the most valuable district of Dominica.

20. Some evidence of Davies's vain efforts to implement this economic scheme still lies in the mill's ruins on the Melville Hall Estate, but C. O. Naftel (1898: 65–71) provides us with a solid description of the property in 1897. An efficient use of resident laborers and villagers otherwise engaged in the peasant labor process counterbalanced Davies's massive use of funds for technological improvements. Naftel (1898: 68) writes:

> [There are] in the forested parts [of Melville Hall] acres of tenants' gardens where they grow bananas, yams, sweet potatoes, &c., &c., under three years' agreements. The custom here is to prop up these gardens with limes, cocoa, or Liberian coffee, which the tenant takes care in lieu of rent. When the proprietor's products approach the age of bearing he takes over the garden and roots up what remains of the tenant's provisions. This method does not, of course, result in the evenest of clearing, but it has the merit of being a cheap way of getting the land planted up.

Davies supplemented the small resident labor force with villagers, notably from Wesley and Marigot. He used laborers of both sexes and all ages though he paid them quite unequal wages. Adult males were paid ten shillings a day, adolescents eight to nine shillings. Weeding was "done by women and children by task, for which the former [received] 6 d. and the latter 2 d. to 4 d." (Naftel 1898: 71).

21. The intellectual arrogance of the ascendancy alienated many voters in Saint Andrew South who could have been their allies. Many of the party's members (including Davies himself), well known for their anticlerical stance, had joined in the House to block the funds traditionally granted to schools run by religious congregations. The Melville Hall and Hampstead Wesleyan schools suffered. The Wesleyans turned against Davies and his protégé, D. O. Riviere, the mulattoes' candidate for Saint Andrew South. With little else to show to counterbalance their arrogance, the mulattoes lost the La Soye seat: the Wesleyans (and many Catholics) successfully supported the election of white planter J. C. McIntyre, the owner of Hampstead (Boromé 1972c).

22. Though shipping facilities of Marigot never improved enough to match Davies's expectations, though the railroad never materialized by the time of Davies's death, the jetty he built for Melville Hall, the viable bridle path from Hatton Garden to Layou, the new bridge across the Melville Hall River (which linked the two parts of the estate), all meant a marked improvement in communications; Wesley itself benefited only indirectly because of its more central position.

23. New estates emerged south of La Soye, such as Concord, a property of 257 acres that Davies cut out of Melville Hall before selling the larger estate. Experiences with diverse crops (e.g., limes and coconuts) may not have been quite successful at first, but they were more promising than similar trials on the estates around Wesley.

CHAPTER 10. "Neither Here nor There": The Ethnography of Mediation

1. This typology is nothing but an empirical point of entry into the study of the encounter between the village and the larger order, but an important one, I believe. Looking at traditional ethnographies, one is often surprised by how much they can miss the objects, the persons, the relations through which the nation or the world daily intrudes on village life. The prior classification of the elements of mediation should help us perceive at the time of fieldwork, or when analyzing ethnographies, objects, persons and relations that often escape our attention. Likewise, an a priori classification may call our attention to the role of certain elements which, though they might at first appear to be natural components of village scenery, testify to the encounter between the village and the world.

2. Even shopowners who primarily sell liquor by the drink maintain some sugar or canned milk on their shelves and a barrel of oil or kerosene on the floor as if to justify the enterprise. Such shops function mainly as places of encounter but they would not do so without the groceries, and certainly not without the drinks.

3. H. Henderson Henry, then health inspector for the Wesley District, conducted this survey. I thank him for sharing his results with me.

4. One suspects that within three to five years the involvement of native Wesleyans in estate labor will become altogether insignificant unless an estate-produced export crop, like coconuts, completely displaces bananas.

5. Recent relative drops do not necessarily reflect a decrease in Wesley's production: quite a few producers are now engaged in field packing, bypassing Londonderry, Constant Spring, and DBGA boxing plants.

6. Few villagers explicitly state the decrease in competition as the goal of this schedule. They often relate it to the physical process of maturation of their bananas, suggesting that bananas that are much too young to be cut in any given week are young enough to wait another fourteen days. Many mention also the necessity of avoiding too many costly trips to the plant within a single month. Fewer producers voluntarily mention a

link between their cutting schedule and the heavy labor requirements of harvesting. No one ever suggested to me that this schedule roughly cuts in half the weekly demand for motor vehicles though most informants readily admitted that fact when I brought it to their attention.

7. Let me quickly dismiss two possible interpretations of that exchange. First, one must not get the impression that harvesting peasants approach vehicle owners, some of whom are peasants themselves, with any pretense of humility. Both parties are aware that the demand is reinforced by allusions to social ties of one kind or another, but both are equally aware that it is a demand for services that will be paid in cash. Second, the encounter is not defined by the parties as a pure economic transaction, however. One rarely mentions money, since the prevailing price is known to everybody. The vehicle owner rarely goes beyond a recognized ceiling, though he may lower his price in quite exceptional cases at his own discretion. The producer formulating the request himself rarely suggests a different price. The understanding is that the ongoing transportation fees for all the bananas carried on a fig day are collected when the DBGA pays for the accepted part of the harvest one or two weeks later. Thus the entire conversation securing the driver's commitment may take place without any mention of money if the producer is one of the driver's regular customers, yet in such a manner that its economic basis cannot be severed from the whole verbal exchange. The harvesting peasant is seen as placing a request, partly because there are many more producers than available vehicles and also partly because there is much symbolic gain in one's ability to secure a vehicle early.

8. To be sure, not all drivers work on every fig day; not all producers lose a third of their harvest at selection; not all bunches of bananas accepted at Londonderry weigh thirty-five pounds. Still, this model is a projection based on the production history and returns of three different banana producers and the figures listed on their vouchers from 1975 to 1981 (in one case from 1972 to 1981) and on my participant observation which occasionally included riding with a particular driver for a whole fig day.

Given the general worsening of conditions (especially the fall of banana prices), one suspects that things may have changed since then.

CHAPTER 11. The Impact of the World: Hard Cash and Small Change

1. Ethnographic observation suggests different occupational priorities within households otherwise dependent upon the labor process for their reproduction. Needless to say, then, that the socioeconomic categories

through which we can classify the people of Wesley can only be middle-level abstractions: some of the indivduals or groups they refer to may, at times, share strong similarities with others placed in different categories. Within any category, one may need to emphasize either the household or one of its members. At other times, the gray area between individual engagement and household reproduction may turn out to be the crucial characteristic of a category.

2. In the course of my fieldwork, I identified seven male heads of household who are recognized as big farmers by almost all Wesley people. An additional case is that of a father and son living in the same household: both control independent properties. Two or three other individuals can be added to the margins of that list, as they share one or more characteristics of the big farmers: more systematic use of inputs, occasional hiring of laborers, diversification of cash crops. Yet they remain much more active in the peasant work process. They are much closer to the category usually described as rich peasants. Finally, two other individuals functioned equally as big farmers and entrepreneurs and one big farmer functions as a professional politician.

3. In the late 1970s, the DBGA accepted bananas from about 470 growers in the Wesley area. Wesley then counted about 550 households. However, not all registered growers represent an independent household, and the figures for Distnct 17 also include a few Marigot villagers. Still, one can safely suggest that the number of registered growers for District 17 represents more than two-thirds of Wesley's households.

4. Most observers agree that banana yields vary greatly throughout Dominica, but most social scientists, economists, local and international agencies persist in suggesting an average yield per acre for the island, or even for all the Windwards (Baker 1973, 1975; Beckford 1967, 1974; DBGA 1976–80; Maillard, 1969, 1983; Persaud 1967; Yankey 1969). Those suggestions are meaningless for many reasons:

1. the actual acreage cultivated in bananas by a particular grower may vary from one season to the next;
2. bananas are almost never intercropped with root crops, but they are often intercropped with coconuts, and no one knows for sure the area planted in bananas or the impact of the presence of coconuts on banana yields;
3. not all the bananas delivered by the grower come from the same field;
4. not all the bananas delivered by a grower come from a field registered under the grower's name; and

5. the actual distance between banana holes on a particular plot varies, even though the grower may state an ideal figure (6 × 6 or 8 × 8 feet).

5. Table 11.3 simplifies Chayanov's projections in two ways. Chayanov counts the couple as 1.8 units of labor. I upgrade that figure to two full units to reflect the woman's much greater participation in household chores. Chayanov also suggests a gradation in the consuming power of the children: they consume more as they grow older. My own observation, both as an anthropologist and as a parent, is that, though an infant or a young child needs smaller volumes of food than an older sibling, the additional care and the special items they require for feeding and clothing may add up to more cash expenses than those needed to maintain the older child, or an adult for that matter.

Table 11.3 also projects a worst-case scenario. I assume that the children are all female, and that each of them becomes pregnant at seventeen, and gives birth to one child every two years. However, though one full-time worker planting both bananas and root crops can barely maintain a family of two at the level socially acceptable in Wesley, two working members feed and clothe fairly well a family of three. On the basis of this and similar observations, I estimate that the socially acceptable level of consumption is easily reached at 1:1.8 producer/consumer ratio (or below), or a 1:0.55 consumer/producer ratio (or above). For example, three working members can feed and clothe five consumers, eight consumers can be fed and clothed by five full-time workers, and so on. Even in the worst case scenario sketched in Table 11.3, the Type One household enjoys nine full years of a positive balance.

6. On family land in the Caribbean, see Besson 1984.

7. See Whitehead (1981) for a similar argument.

8. Traditionally, the average Methodist household fared better economically than its Catholic counterpart, essentially because of the evolution described in chapter 10. First, many of the first yeomen were Methodists. Second, though the Methodists' impact on formal education benefited all Wesley people, Methodists benefited much more than Catholics both socially and economically.

CHAPTER 12. Peasants, Part-Peasants, and Change: The Banana Children

1. Most Wesley housewives fill their cooking pots with enough bananas, plantains, or tanias to satisfy their children's hunger; and few people literally starve in Dominica, as opposed, say, to Haiti or Jamaica.

However, few manage to place more on the table than the boiled provisions spiced up with some fish sauce.

2. The list may not be exhaustive, but I suspect that not more than fifteen individuals could have been unaccounted for. Even now that the yearly number of expected graduates is much higher, the prestige attached to a high school diploma makes it fairly easy to identify all the candidates. The 1971–79 list was compiled from four shorter lists, kindly drawn from memory by two males and two females who themselves graduated during that period. The longer list was modified according to data gathered from the files of the Wesley Village Council and from interviews or informal conversations with twenty-eight other graduates known to me on a first-name basis. Additional information came from relatives and friends and from direct observation.

CHAPTER 13. Contemporary Peasantries: Illusions and Hard Choices

1. First, beyond the inherent limitations of those strategies (Girvan 1976; Amin et al. 1982), it is unlikely that any peripheral nation-state will now be able to improve significantly its terms of trade. Core countries have learned from the experiences of the 1970s and reacted accordingly. Second, size, infrastructure, natural resources, and demography, the types of commodities that Dominica can produce and the minimal amounts that it can place on the world market will prevent it from reaching a level of bargaining power similar to that of a nation-state with oil and mineral reserves.

My observations on the world banana trade corroborate the point. The Windward Islands' total output is so dismal in terms of world demand, that Dominica, Saint Lucia, Saint Vincent, and Grenada have no joint impact on the market, even under the WINBAN umbrella. Further, WINBAN's own ineffectiveness stems in part for the respective Windward governments' inability to exercise pressure on the parent body.

2. One can envision different strategies in the construction of those units, depending on the subject matter and on the researcher's training and interest. The most obvious strategy would be a downward spiral from the level of the system at large to, say, that of the household or the unit of production, a strategy I first proposed in the study of plantation slavery (Trouillot 1981, 1982). But the order of exposition need not be the logical order of the analysis or the broken order of empirical discovery. The expository procedure that I followed for this book emphasizes,

in turn, the nation, the world, and the village—with the Dominican enclaves, the British empire, and the Caribbean, as intermediate units of varying importance. My methodology has been to carve out multiple units of analyses.

3. The danger of a violent outburst of the new lumpen is not unique to Dominica. In the entire English-speaking Caribbean, the problems created by the new lumpen are exacerbated by the uneasy transfer of control over the former British possesions to the United States. This geopolitical reshaping is itself made more difficult because it overlaps a "crisis of the state" which reaches to the whole region and the circum-Caribbean parts of the continent (Ambursley and Cohen 1983). In the former British colonies, the search for independent models of society was cut short by the brutal invasion of Grenada in 1983, a clear indication that the United States is once more willing to impose by force its Pax Americana as it did earlier in Puerto Rico and Cuba (1898), in Haiti (1915), in the Dominican Republic (1916)—before the revolutionary birth of the Soviet Union provided an easy rationale for imperial adventures. At the same time, many Caribbean nationalists look with suspicion at Cuba's economic, if not always political (W. Smith 1985), dependence on the Soviets. Likewise, it is commonly acknowledged that Guyana's experience with so-called cooperative socialism has not improved the lot of its peasantry. Meanwhile, some rulers from the newly independent states have quickly joined others in the region in seeking improbable favors from Washington. The Caribbean has rarely looked so internally aimless since perhaps the end of the sugar crisis.

4. In fact, insofar as census categories can be trusted, the number of peasants throughout the world continues to increase. The absolute growth of the world's rural population was about three-quarters of a billion between 1950 and 1979. Even in Latin America, where the urban macrocephaly is at its worst, the rural population increased by thirty-two million during the same period (Tolnai 1984).

5. The mechanisms of surplus extraction overpower problems of productivity inasmuch as technological improvements in the labor process may end up being much more beneficial to capitalists in the core than to the peasant producers in the periphery. Technological improvements in banana production in the Windwards, albeit limited, did not result in larger benefits for the Caribbean peasants. That is not surprising: to the extent that the increase in surplus extraction remains higher than the increase in productivity, that productivity cannot fully benefit the peasant-producer. Conceivably, it can even be detrimental to the producer.

Again, only Eurocentric assumptions about "progress" lead us to think that higher productivity is always beneficial to the nation at large, or to the sum of individual producers.

6. Only ideological blindness prevents more observers from seeing the dimensions of these failures and the unlikelihood that the Windwards, Dominica in particular, will revive the banana industry. Regardless of national or pan-Caribbean efforts, the banana industry will soon not be able to contribute to Dominica's national wealth in the proportions of the recent past. The long-term downward trends in international prices will continue to afflict Dominica much more than it hurts most producing countries, partly because of the small net volumes that the island exports, partly because of its greater reliance on such exports. Changes within the European Common Market will continue to gnaw at the effectiveness of formal protections if not lead to their total disappearance. Further, Geest is likely to deal with the Windwards in the very same way Britain dealt with its former colonies: having exhausted their resources for its purposes, it will increasingly turn to newer pastures. Last, no amount of wishful thinking on the part of Dominicans or promises from United States officials will give Windward bananas a share of the North American market, now dominated by the most powerful fruit-specialized transnationals in world history.

7. Actual realization of a program of food sufficiency would require, among other things, a convergent import policy and a family planning program tuned to the cycles of the peasant household. Still, such a program is within the reach of any Dominican government willing to invite peasant participation in both the planning and execution phases.

8. In the case of the Caribbean, for instance, delinking cannot be an individual island strategy; but it need not be a fully pan-Caribbean strategy. To be sure, a fully Caribbean solution that would take into account the assets, needs, and weaknesses of the various nations of the region, across languages, colonial histories, local cultures, and political formulas might seem the most desirable; but the realization of that dream remains far away. What I am suggesting does not require cooperation on that scale, but a minimum of both will and awareness.

9. Many Caribbean peasants, part-peasants, and urban dwellers have not waited for governments to suggest patterns of trade and cooperation. Dominican higglers, for instance, are taking advantage of the higher cost of edibles in Guadeloupe and Martinique. Haitian and Saint Lucian market women are now operating at the level of the region. In this regard as in many others—one could think of informal support systems,

education, energy-saving practices, and so on—government officials are likely to learn a lot by observing the economic, social, and cultural rationales for the practices of the common folk.

10. See note 3 in this chapter. The Dominican example is telling: Dominica now sells about 50 percent of its total exports to Britain, but buys less than one-third of its imports from the former metropolis. In contrast, Dominica now acquires 15 percent of its imports from the United States, whereas the United States does not acquire any more Dominican goods than say, Guyana, Trinidad, or Jamaica. The decline of British international hegemony, verified by two world wars, has finally reached the Caribbean. Now that Britain has little use for those former colonies, the most ancient of its dominions, the United States, is fast moving to impose its domination on every few square miles of land that bears an independent flag.

Bibliography to *Peasants and Capital*

A. Documents

Public Record Office (PRO)

The Public Record Office (Kew Gardens, London) provides the largest and by far the most valuable collection of documents on Dominica's remote and recent past. Not all the PRO materials that informed this book have been cited in the text, though documents quoted or relied upon for specific data were identified with their PRO class and piece numbers. The following Colonial Office documents were most useful:

C.O. 73/ . . . Dominica Acts, 1830–1889

C.O. 74/33 Dominica. Minutes of the Legislative Assembly from January 1860 to January 1880

C.O. 75/1 Dominica. Official Gazette, 1865–1868

C.O. 152/ . . . Leeward Islands. Correspondence, Secretary of State [for the Colonies], Administrator of Dominica, Despatches, 1903–1934

C.O. 441/ . . . West Indian Incumbered Estates (which includes descriptions of Dominican estates in the nineteenth century, and papers related to their history before the 1860s).

Public reports consulted at the PRO, but available elsewhere in printed or typed form, are listed in the Reports section below under their authors' names (e.g., Hamilton 1894; Naftel 1898) with the class number under which they are registered at the PRO.

For the sake of convenience, a document crucial to my understanding of the expansion of the peasant labor process in the immediate aftermath of slavery has been repeatedly referred to in the text by its PRO number "ZHC1/1266," although it is available in the Parliamentary Papers (PP).

The full citation to this material as published is: *Accounts and Papers*. 8. Colonies, West Indies; &c. Leeward Islands . . . Session 5 February–27 August 1839. Volume 37, 1839. *Papers Relative to the West Indies,* part 3. *Papers on the Condition of the Labouring Population, West Indies.*

British Library

Documents consulted in the British Library were generally of a legislative nature. They included the *Laws of Dominica,* the *Freeport Regulations* of 1766, the 1771 *Proclamation* on French names in Dominica and other regulations.

Foreign and Commonwealth Office Library (FCO)

Documents consulted at the FCO include all the censuses of Dominica from 1849 to 1921 and a rare copy of the first proposal to export bananas from the island (Nicholls 1890).

Companies Registration Office (C.R.O.)

The microfiches of "Companies House" provided a wide range of information about importers and wholesalers of bananas in the United Kingdom including Geest Holdings Limited and more than fifteen past or present Geest affiliates and subsidiaries. My reading of the more than three thousand pages of Geest reports strongly influenced the argument of chapter 7. The numbers in chapter 8 refer to the company number of the C.R.O.

Dominica Banana Growers Association (DBGA)

The DBGA files contained the most important unpublished documents consulted in Dominica. I have relied heavily on three files:

File 1-02-02. Cutting Notices 1979 (the file also includes material from 1978 to 1981)

File 1-02-06. Green Market Price. Price Payable to Growers. January 1980–November 1981.

The Production Books, 1976 to 1981 (November).

Dominica Archives at the Public Library

The National Archives of Dominica were not accessible to the general public at the time of this fieldwork. Copies of the *Dominica Alamanac* were consulted at the public library in Roseau.

Miscellaneous

Papers of various Wesley families (including banana vouchers, land titles, rental agreement, etc.). Baptism and marriage records of the Wesley Catholic Church. Records of the Wesley Village Council (including a comprehensive voters' list with occupations of more than 1,000 individuals).

B. Serials and Periodicals

Dominica Almanac (spelling varies), 1814–1879. Annual. Roseau, Saint John (Antigua). Included in *Antigua Almanac* in 1852, and in *Leeward Islands Almanac* in 1879.

The New Chronicle. Roseau.

The West Indies and Caribbean Yearbook, 1929–1979 (title varies). London and Montreal.

C. Reports and Official Publications

Baker, Cynthia

1973 "Some problems of the banana industry of Dominica. An interim report . . ." FCO, Overseas Development Administration, and University of Swansea.

1975 "Economic and social aspects of banana production in Dominica." Ministry of Overseas Development Administration, Great Britain.

Dominica

1963 *The Laws of Dominica.* London: Eyre & Spottiswoode. Limited printing for the government of Dominica.

Dominica. Legislative Council

1928 *Exportation of Fruits Ordinance, 1928.* Roseau: Government Printing Office.

Dominica. Ministry of Finance. Statistical Division

1980a *Statistical Digest, 1978.* Roseau: Government Printing Office.

1980b *Annual Overseas Trade Reports, 1978–1978.* Roseau: Government Printing Office.

1980c *1980–81 Estimates of the Commonwealth of Dominica.* Roseau: Government Printing Office.

Dominica Banana Growers Association (DBGA)

1976–1980 Annual Reports. Roseau.

Dominica Banana Growers Association et al.

1977 "An Agreement, dated 29th March 1977, between . . ." Roseau.

FAO (Food and Agriculture Organization of the United Nations)

1980 *Report of the Seventh Session of the Intergovernmental Group on Bananas to the Committee on Comodity Problems.* Rome: FAO.

Great Britain. Colonial Office

1845 "Copies or Extracts of Despatches Relating to the Disturbances in the Island of Dominica." Colonial Office, Downing Street, 17 March 1845. G. W. Hope. Printing ordered by the House of Commons. PP, 31 (146). West Indies.

Great Britain. Colonial Office

1889–1898 "Leeward Islands Annual Report." PP, House of Commons Papers, various years. (PRO, ZHC1/5337, 5338, 5541, 5656, 5869, 5973, 6084, 6197).

Great Britain. Colonial Office

1950–1965 *Colonial Reports on Dominica.* London: His (Her) Majesty's Stationery Office (HMSO).

Great Britain. Imperial Economic Committee

1926–1927 *Report of the Imperial Economic Committee on Marketing and Preparing for Market of Foodstuffs Produced in the Overseas Parts of the Empire.* 8 vols. London: HMSO.

Great Britain. Imperial Economic Committee

1927 *Third Report—Fruit.* London: HMSO.

Great Britain. Royal Commission

1884 "Report of the Royal Commission Appointed in December 1882 to Inquire into the Public Revenues, Expenditures, Debts, and Liabilities of the Islands of Jamaica, Grenada . . ." PP, 46 (C. 3840 II).

Great Britain. Royal Commission

1894 See Hamilton (1894).

Great Britain. Royal Commission. West India Sugar Commission

1897 "Correspondence Relating to the Sugar Industry in the West Indies." PP, 61.

1898a "Report of the West India Royal Commission . . ." PP, 50.

1899b "Report . . ."Appendix C. Volume 3 containing parts 6 to 13. Proceedings, Evidence, and Documents Relating to the Windward Islands, the Leeward Islands, and Jamaica. PP, 51 (part 9, Dominica).

Hamilton, Robert

1894 "Report of the Royal Commission (Appointed in September 1893) to Inquire into the Conditions and Affairs of the

Island of Dominica and Correspondence Relating Thereto." Presented to both Houses of Parliament by the Command of Her Majesty. August 1894. PP, 57 (PRO, ZHC1/5667).

Jones, G. A. (assistant curator and chemist)

1916 "Report by Agricultural Department on Damage to Estates, 28 August 1916." Confidential. (MS, privately held, Roseau, Dominica.)

Morris, D.

1898 "Subsidiary Report by D. Morris on Agricultural Resources and Requirements." Appendix A to the Report of the West India Royal Commission. PP, 50.

Naftel, C. O.

1898 "Report of the Agricultural Capabilities of Dominica." Presented to the House of Commons, March 1898. PP, 59. Accounts and Papers. (PRO, ZHC1/6084.)

Prestoe, Henry

1875 *Report on Coffee Cultivation in Dominica.* Printed for the Government of the Leeward Islands. Trinidad: Government Printing Office. (PRO, C.O. 74/33.)

Watkins, Frederic Henry

1924 *Handbook of the Leeward Islands.* London: West India Committee.

Watts, Francis (government analytical and agricultural chemist for the Leeward Islands)

1902 "Report on the Soils of Dominica." (Typescript consulted at the Free Public Library in Roseau, marked "Copied by A. L. Blanchard, Caretaker, Victoria Museum, Roseau, 1950.")

1927 *Report on the Agricultural Conditions of Dominica with Recommendations for Their Ameliorations.* Antigua: Government Printing Office. (PRO, C.O. 152/398 and Roseau Public Library.)

WINBAN (Windward Islands Banana Association)

1980 *A Report on Geest Banana Operations in the West Indies and in the United Kingdom.* Castries: WINBAN Head Office.

Wood, E. F. L. (parliamentary undersecretary of state for the colonies)

1922 *Report . . . on His Visit to the West Indies and British Guiana—December 1921–February 1922.* Presented to Parliament by Command of His Majesty. London: HMSO.

D. Books, Theses, and Articles

Alavi, Hamza

1965 "Peasants and revolution." In R. Miliband and J. Saville, eds., *The Socialist Register.* London: Merlin.

1973 "Peasant classes and primordial loyalties." *Journal of Peasant Studies* 1(1):23–62.

1975 "India and the colonial mode of production." In R. Miliband and J. Saville, eds., *The Socialist Register.* London: Merlin.

1982 "The Structure of peripheral capitalism." In H. Alavi and T. Shanin, eds., *Introduction to the Sociology of "Developing Societies."* New York: Monthly Review Press.

Althusser, Louis et al.

1973 *Lire le capital.* Paris: Maspéro.

Ambursley, Fitzroy, and R. Cohen

1983 *Crisis in the Caribbean.* New York: Monthly Review Press.

Amin, Samir

1973 *Le développement inégal.* Paris: Les Éditions de Minuit.

1974 *Accumulation on a World Scale: A Critique of the Theory of Underdevelopment.* New York: Monthly Review Press.

1978 *The Law of Value and Historical Materialism.* New York: Monthly Review Press.

1986 *La déconnexion.* Paris: La Découverte.

Amin, Samir (ed.)

1975 *L'Agriculture africaine et le capitalisme.* Paris: Anthropos.

Amin, Samir, and Kostas Vergopoulos

1974 *La question paysanne et le capitalisme.* Paris: Anthropos.

Amin, Samir, Giovanni Arrighi, Andre Gunder Frank, and Immanuel Wallerstein

1982 *Dynamics of Global Crisis.* New York: Monthly Review Press.

Anonymous

1764 *Some Observations, Which May Contribute to Afford a Just View of the Nature, Importance, and Settlement of Our New West India Colonies.* (Available at the British Museum.)

Archetti, Eduardo P.

1983 (1978) "The growth of capitalism and the peasant economy: Some problems on the transference of surplus." In Joan P. Mencher, ed., *Social Anthropology of Peasantry,* 87–103. Bombay: Somaiya Publications PVT. (Paper originally presented at the Tenth International Congress of Anthropological and Ethnological Sciences. Lucknow, India.)

Archetti, Eduardo P., and Svein Aass

N.d. "The concept of feudalism: A critical discussion." Mimeo. Oslo, International Peace Institute.

1978 "Peasant studies: An overview." In H. Newby, ed., *International Perspectives in Rural Sociology.* New York: John Wiley & Sons.

Archetti, Eduardo P., E. Fossum, and P. O. Reinton

N.d. "Agrarian structure and peasant autonomy." Mimeo. Oslo, International Peace Institute.

Atwood, Thomas

1791 *The History of the Island of Dominica.* London: J. Johnson.

Bagchi, Amiya Kumar

1982 *The Political Economy of Underdevelopment.* Cambridge: Cambridge University Press.

Balandier, Georges

1979 "Tradition, conformité, historicité." In Jean Poirier and François Raveau, eds., *L'Autre et l'ailleurs. Hommages à Roger Bastide,* 15–38. Paris: Berger-Levrault.

Banaji, Jairus

1977 "Modes of production in a materialist conception of history." *Capital and Class* 3:1–44.

1978 "Capitalist domination and the small peasantry." In A. Rudra et al., eds., *Studies in the Development of Capitalism in India.* Lahore: Vanguard Books.

Barth, Fredrik

1963 *The Role of the Entrepreneur in Social Change in Northern Norway.* Oslo: Universitetsforlaget.

1978 "Introduction and conclusions." In F. Barth, ed., *Scale and Social Organization.* Oslo: Universitetsforlaget.

Barth, Fredrik (ed.)

1978 *Scale and Social Organization.* Oslo: Universitetsforlaget.

Bastien, Rémy

1985 (1951) *Le paysan haitien et sa famille.* Paris: Editions Khartala.

Beaver, Patrick

1976 *Yes! We Have Some: The Story of Fyffes.* Cutting-Hill, England: Publications for Companies.

Beckford, George

1967 *The West India Banana Industry.* Studies in Regional Economic Integration, volume 2. Mona, Jamaica: Institute of Social and Economic Research, University of the West Indies.

1974 "Issues in the Windward Jamaica Banana War." In N. Girvan and A. Jefferson, eds., *Readings in the Political Economy of the Caribbean.* Kingston: New World.

Benedict, Ruth

1946 *The Chrysanthemum and the Sword.* Boston: Houghton Mifflin.

Benet, Francisco

1963 "Sociology uncertain: The ideology of the rural-urban continuum." *Comparative Studies in Society and History* 6(1):1–23.

Bennholdt-Thomsen, Veronica

1982 "Subsistence production and extended reproduction: A contribution to the discussion about modes of production." *Journal of Peasant Studies* 9(4):241–54.

Benveniste, Émile

1969 *Le vocabulaire des institutions indo-européenes.* Paris: Éditions de Minuit.

Bernstein, Henry

1979 "African peasantries: A theoretical framework." *Journal of Peasant Studies* 6(4):421–43.

1981 "Concepts for the analysis of contemporary peasantries." In Rosemary E. Galli, ed., *The Political Economy of Rural*

Development: Peasants, International Capital, and the State, 3–24. Albany: State University of New York Press.

Berreman, Gerald D.

1978 "Scale and social relations." *Current Anthropology* 19(2):225–46 (with *CA* comment).

Berry, Sara S.

1975 *Cocoa, Custom, and Socio-Economic Change in Rural Western Nigeria.* Oxford: Clarendon Press.

Besson, Jean

1984 "Family land and Caribbean society: Toward an ethnography of Afro-Caribbean peasantries." In Elizabeth M. Thomas-Hope, ed., *Perspectives on Caribbean Regional Identity.* Liverpool: Centre for Latin American Studies, University of Liverpool.

Bettelheim, Charles

1972 Preface, in A. Emmanuel, *L'Échange inégal.* Paris: Maspéro.

1976 (1970) *Calcul économique et formes de propriété.* Paris: Maspéro.

Bharadwaj, Krishna

1978 "Maurice Dobb's critique of theories of value and distribution." *Cambridge Journal of Economics* 2:153–74.

Bhaskar, Roy

1979 "On the possibility of social scientific knowledge and the limits of naturalism." In J. Mepham and D. H. Ruben, eds., *Issues in Marxist Philosophy.* Volume 3, *Epistemology, Science, Ideology.* Brighton (Sussex), England: Harvester Press.

Bodley, John Harry

1975 *Victims of Progress.* Menlo Park, Calif.: Cummings Publishing Co.

Boromé, Joseph A.

1972a "Spain and Dominica." In D. Taylor et al., eds., *Aspects of Dominican History,* 67–79. Roseau: Government Printing Division.

1972b "The French and Dominica, 1699–1763." In D. Taylor et al., *Aspects of Dominican History,* 80–102. Roseau: Government Printing Division.

1972c "Dominica during French Occupation, 1778–1784." In D. Taylor et al., *Aspects of Dominican History.* Roseau: Government Printing Division.

1972d "How Crown Colony Government came to Dominica by 1898." In D. Taylor et al., *Aspects of Dominican History.* Roseau: Government Printing Division.

Bradby, Barbara

1975 "The Destruction of the Natural Economy." *Economy and Society* 4:127–61.

Braudel, Fernand

1967 *Civilisation matérielle, économie et capitalisme, XVe–XVIIIe siècle.* Paris: Armand Colin.

1979a *Civilisation matérielle, économie et capitalisme, XVe–XVIIIe siècle.* Volume 2. *Les Jeux de l'échange.* Paris: Armand Colin.

1979b *Civilisation matérielle, économie et capitalisme.* Volume 3, *Le Temps du monde.* Paris: Armand Colin.

Brockway, Lucile H.

1979 "Science and colonial expansion: The role of the British Royal Botanic Gardens." *American Ethnologist* 6(3):449–65.

Burawoy, Michael

1984 *The Politics of Production. Factory Regimes under Capitalism and Socialism.* London: Verso Editions and New Left Books.

Capel, Horatio

1981 "The institutionalization of geography and strategies of change." In D. R. Stoddart, ed., *Geography, Ideology and Social Concern.* Totowa, N.J.: Barnes & Noble Books.

Cardoso, Ciro F.

1979 *Agricultura, esclavidad y capitalismo.* Petrópolis: Ed. Vozes.

Cardoso, Fernando Henrique, and Enzo Faletto

1979 (1971) *Dependency and Development in Latin America.* Berkeley and Los Angeles: University of California Press.

Chace, Russell

1983 "Protest in post-emancipation Dominica: The Guerre Nègre of 1844." Paper presented at the Fifteenth Conference of Caribbean Historians. Mona, Jamaica, 15–20 April 1983.

Charlesworth, Neil

1985 *Peasants and Imperial Rule: Agriculture and Agrarian Society in the Bombay Presidency, 1850–1935.* Cambridge: Cambridge University Press.

Chayanov, Alexander V.

1966 (1923) *The Theory of Peasant Economy.* Edited by D. Thorner et al. Chicago: Irwin. Published for the American Economic Association.

Chevalier, Jacques M.

1982 *Civilization and the Stolen Gift: Capital, Kin, and Cult in Eastern Peru.* Toronto: University of Toronto Press.

1983 "There is nothing simple about simple commodity production." *Journal of Peasant Studies* 10(4):153–86.

Chernick, Sidney E., et al.

1978 *The Commonwealth Caribbean: The Integration Experience.* Baltimore: Johns Hopkins University Press. Published for the World Bank.

Clairmonte, Frederick

1977 "World banana economy: Problems and prospects." *Economic and Political Weekly,* Annual Number, February 1977.

Clarke, S. St. A.

1967 "Some aspects of the banana industry in Latin America." In K. Leslie, ed., *Proceedings of the Second West Indian Agricultural Economics Conference,* 2–34 (with comments). Saint Augustine, Trinidad: University of the West Indies, Department of Agricultural Economics and Farm Management.

Claval, Paul

1982 "Les grandes coupures de l'histoire de la géographie." *Hérodote* 25:129–51 (May–July 1982).

Cliffe, Lionel

1977 "Rural classes formation in East Africa." *Journal of Peasant Studies* 4(2):195–224.

Coke, Thomas

1787 *A Journal of the Rev. Dr. Coke's Visit to Jamaica, and of His Third Tour on the Continent of America.* London: J. Paramore.

1788 *A Farther Continuation of Dr. Coke's Journal: In a Letter to the Rev. J. Wesley*. London: J. Paramore.

1789 *Some Accounts of the Late Missionaries to the West Indies, in Two Letters . . . to the Rev. J. Wesley*. London.

1808–1811 *A History of the West Indies* . . . 3 vols. Liverpool and London: Nuttal, Fisher, & Dixon.

Cooper, Frederick

1980 *From Slaves to Squatters. Plantation Labor and Agriculture in Zanzibar and Coastal Kenya, 1890–1925*. New Haven: Yale University Press.

Dallas, George

1982 *The Imperfect Economy: The Loire Country, 1800–1914*. Cambridge: Cambridge University Press.

Dallemagne, Jean-Luc

1978 *L'Économie du "Capital."* Paris: Maspéro.

Dalton, George

1974 "How exactly are peasants 'exploited'?" *American Anthropologist* 76:553–61.

Davies, P. N.

1978 *Sir Alfred Jones. Shipping Entrepreneur par Excellence*. London: Europa Publications.

Davy, John

1854 *The West Indies before and since Slave Emancipation*. London: W. & P. G. Clark.

Day, Charles William

1852 *Five Years' Residence in the West Indies*. 2 vols. London: Colburn & Co.

Deerr, Noel

1949–1950 *The History of Sugar*. 2 vols. London: Chapman & Hall.

De Janvry, Alain, and Frank Kramer

1979 "The limits of unequal exchange." *Review of Radical Political Economics* 114:3–15.

De Rouffignac, Ann Lucas

1985 *The Contemporary Peasantry in Mexico. A Class Analysis*. New York: Praeger.

De Silva, S. B. D.

1982 *The Political Economy of Underdevelopment.* London: Routledge & Kegan Paul; Singapore: Institute of Southeast Asian Studies.

Dupre, Georges, and Pierre-Philippe Rey

1978 (1968) "Reflections on the relevance of theory of the history of exchange." In D. Seddon, ed., *Relations of Production.* London: Frank Cass.

Durrenberg, E. Paul, and Nicola Tannenbaum

1979 "A reassessment of Chayanov and his recent critics." *Peasant Studies* 8:48–63.

Emmanuel, Arghiri

1972 *L'Échange inégal.* Paris: Maspéro.

Emmanuel, Arghiri et al.

1973 *Un débat sur l'échange inégal.* Paris: Maspéro.

Ennew, Judith et al.

1977 "Peasantry as an economic category." *Journal of Peasant Studies* 4(4):295–322.

Evers, Hans-Dieter et al.

1984 "Subsistence reproduction: A framework for analysis." In Joan Smith, Immanuel Wallerstein, Hans-Dieter Evers, eds., *Households and the World-Economy.* Beverly Hills, Calif.: Sage Publications.

Farley, Rawle

1964 "The rise of village settlements in British Guiana." *Caribbean Quarterly* 10:52–61.

Faure, Claude

1978 *Agriculture et mode de production capitaliste.* Paris: Anthropos.

Findlay, G. G., and W. W. Holdsworth

1921 *The History of the Wesleyan Methodist Missionary Society.* Volume 2. London: Epworth Press.

Firth, Raymond

1957 (1936) *We, the Tikopia.* Boston: Beacon Press.

1961 (1951) *Elements of Social Organization.* Boston: Beacon Press.

1964 *Essays on Social Organization and Values.* Boston: Beacon Press.

Foster, George M.

1965 "Peasant society and the image of limited good." *American Anthropologist* 67:293–315.

Foster-Carter, Aidan

1985 *The Sociology of Development.* Ormskirk: Causeway.

Foucault, Michel

1972 (1969) *The Archaeology of Knowledge.* New York: Harper Torchbooks.

Frank, Andre Gunder

1967 *Capitalism and Underdevelopment in Latin America.* New York: Monthly Review Press.

1978 *World Accumulation, 1492–1789.* New York: Monthly Review Press.

Friedman, Harriet

1978 "Simple commodity production and wage labour in the American plains." *Journal of Peasant Studies* 6(1):71–100.

1980 "Household production and the national economy: Concepts for the analysis of agrarian formations." *Journal of Peasant Studies* 7(1):158–84.

Galli, Rosemary E.

1981 "Rural development and the contradictions of capitalist development." In Rosemary Galli, ed., *The Political Economy of Rural Development: Peasants, International Capital, and the State.* Albany: State University of New York Press.

Gardiner, J.

1976 "The political economy of domestic labour in capitalist society." In D. Leonard Barker and S. Allen, eds., *Dependence and Exploitation in Work and Marriage.* London: Longman.

Gatrell, Anthony C.

1983 *Distance and Space.* Oxford: Clarendon Press.

Geertz, Clifford

1973 *The Interpretation of Cultures.* New York: Basic Books.

Giddens, Anthony

1979 *Central Problems in Social Theory: Action, Structure, and Contradiction in Social Analysis.* Berkeley and Los Angeles: University of California Press.

1985 *The Constitution of Society: Outline of the Theory of Structuration.* Berkeley and Los Angeles. University of California Press.

Girault, Christian A.

1981 *Le commerce du café en Haiti: Habitants, spéculateurs, exportateurs.* Paris: Centre National de la Recherche Scientifique.

Girvan, Norman

1876 *Corporate Imperialism: Conflict and Expropriation. Transnational Corporations and Economic Nationalism in the Third World.* New York: Monthly Review Press.

Godelier, Maurice

1977 (1979) *Perspectives in Marxist Anthropology.* Cambridge: Cambridge University Press.

1978 "Infrastructures, societies, and history." *Current Anthropology* 19(4):763–71 (with *CA* comments).

Goodridge, Cecil

1972 "Dominica: The French connexion." In D. Taylor et al., *Aspects of Dominican History.* Roseau: Government Printing Division.

Granotier, Bernard

1980 *La planète des bidonvilles: Perspectives de l'explosion urbaine dans le liers monde.* Paris: Seuil.

Green, William E.

1976 *British Slave Emancipation: The Sugar Colonies and the Great Experiment, 1830–1865.* Oxford: Clarendon Press.

Grindle, Merilee S.

1986 *State and Countryside: Development Policy and Agrarian Politics in Latin America.* Baltimore: Johns Hopkins University Press.

Gronhaug, Reidar

1978 "Scale as a variable in analysis: Fields in social organization in Herat, Northwest Afghanistan." In F. Barth, ed., *Scale and Social Organization.* Oslo: Universitetsforlaget.

Grossman, Lawrence

1984 *Subsistence Ecology, and Development in the Highlands of Papua Guinea.* Princeton: Princeton University Press.

Hall, Douglas

1978 "The flight from the estates reconsidered: The British West Indies, 1838–42." *Journal of Caribbean History* 10–11:7–24.

Harris, Marvin

1959 "The economy has no surplus?" *American Anthropologist* 61:185–99.

1968 *The Rise of Anthropological Theory: A History of Theories of Cultures.* New York: Thomas Y. Crowell.

Harrison, John

1973 "Political economy of housework." *Bulletin of the Conference of Socialist Economists* 3(1):35–51.

Harrison, Mark

1977 "The peasant mode of production in the work of A. V. Chayanov." *Journal of Peasant Studies* 4:323–36.

Harriss, John

1982 *Capitalism and Peasant Farming: Agrarian Structures and Ideology in Northern Tamil Nadu.* Bombay: Oxford University Press.

Harvey, David

1982 *The Limits to Capital.* Chicago: University of Chicago Press.

Higman, Barry

1976 *Slave Population and Economy in Jamaica, 1807–1834.* Cambridge and New York: Cambridge University Press.

1984 *Slave Populations of the British Caribbean, 1807–1834.* Baltimore: Johns Hopkins University Press.

Himmelweit, Susan, and S. Mohun

1977 "Domestic labour and capital." *Cambridge Journal of Economics* 1:15–31.

Hope, Hempe R.

1986 *Urbanization in the Commonwealth Caribbean.* Boulder, Colo.: Westview Press.

Huggins, George, T. Henderson, and F. Nunes

1978 *Rural Transformation Initiatives in Dominica: An Evaluation of Selected Agricultural Cooperatives.* Roseau: Management Consultants.

Imray, John

1848 "Observations on the character of endemic fever in the island of Dominica." *Edinburg Medical and Surgical Journal* 70(177):253–87.

1864 (1862) "The useful woods of the island of Dominica." *Dominica Almanac, 1864.* Reprinted from *The Technologist* (1862).

Kahn, Joel S.

1980 *Minangkabau Social Formations: Indonesian Peasants and the World Economy.* Cambridge: Cambridge University Press.

Karasch, Mary

1979 "Commentary on 'Slavery and the rise of peasantries' by S. W. Mintz." *Historical Reflections* 6(1):248–51.

Kepner, Charles David, and J. J. Soothill

1935 *The Banana Empire: A Case Study of Economic Imperialism.* New York: Vanguard Press.

Kerblay, Basile

1967 "A. V. Cajanov: Un carrefour dans l'évolution de la pensée agraire en Russie de 1908 à 1930." In A. V. Cajanov, *Oeuvres Choisies,* 17–66. Volume 1. Paris: École Pratique des Hautes Études, Sorbonne, and S. R. Publishers, Johnson Reprint Corp., and Mouton & Co.

1971 "Chayanov and the theory of peasantry as a specific type of economy." In T. Shanin, ed., *Peasants and Peasant Societies.* Harmondsworth: Penguin Books.

Kidron, Michael, and Ronald Segal

1981 *The State of the World Atlas.* London: Pluto Press.

Klein, Marin A. (ed.)

1980 *Peasants in Africa. Historical and Contemporary Perspectives.* Beverly Hills, Calif.: Sage Publications.

Kroeber, Alfred

1948 *Anthropology.* New York: Harcourt, Brace.

Kuznets, Simon

1958 (1954) "Underdeveloped countries and the pre-industrial phase in the advanced countries." In A. N. Agarwala and S. P. Singh, eds., *The Economics of Underdevelopment,* 135–53. Delhi: Oxford University Press.

Laborie, P. J.

1798 *The Coffee Planter of Saint Domingo: With an Appendix Containing a View . . .* London: T. Cadell & W. Davis.

Latortue, Paul R.

1984 "Thoughts on the possibilities of Haiti as the new Taiwan of the Caribbean." Paper presented at the conference "New Perspectives on Caribbean Studies," Hunter College, City University of New York, and Research Institute for the Study of Man, 28 August–1 September 1984.

Lepkowski, Tadeusz

1968–1969 (1964) *Haiti.* 2 vols. Havana: Casa de las Americas.

LeRoy Ladurie, Emmanuel

1969 *Les Paysans de Languedoc.* Paris: Flammarion.

1972 "Structures familiales et coutumes d'héritage." *Annales* 4–5:825–46.

Leslie, K. (ed.)

1956 *Proceedings of the Second West Indian Agricultural Economics Conference.* Saint Augustine, Trinidad: Department of Agricultural Economics and Farm Management, University of the West Indies.

Lesser, Alexander

1939 "Problems versus subject matters as directives of research." *American Anthropologist* 41(4):574–82.

1978 (1933) *The Pawnee Ghost Dance Hand Game.* Madison: University of Wisconsin Press.

1985 *History, Evolution, and the Concept of Culture. Selected Papers by Alexander Lesser.* Ed. Sidney W. Mintz. New York: Cambridge University Press.

Lévi-Strauss, Claude

1963 (1958) *Structural Anthropology.* New York: Basic Books.

Levy, Claude

1980 *Emancipation, Sugar, and Federalism. Barbados and the West Indies, 1833–1876.* Gainesville: University of Florida Press.

Lim, Teck Ghee

1977 *Peasants and Their Agricultural Economy in Colonial Malaya, 1874–1941.* Kuala Lumpur and London: Oxford University Press.

Lodbell, Richard

1985 "British officials and the West Indian peasantry, 1842–1938." *Caribbean Societies* 2:54–61. Collected Seminar Papers, No. 34. London: Institute of Commonwealth Studies, University of London.

MacFarlane, Dennis

1964 "The future of the banana industry in the West Indies," *Social and Economic Studies* 13(1):38–93.

McLennan, Gregor

1981 *Marxism and the Methodologies of History.* London: Verso Editions.

MacPherson, John

1976 *Caribbean Lands.* London: Longman Caribbean.

Maguire, Robert Earl

1975 "Coast or Interior? Changing perceptions of land use in Dominica, West Indies: 1870–1970." M.A. thesis, University of Florida.

Maillard, Jean-Claude

1969 "La banane en Jamaique et dans les Windward Islands." *Études de Geographie Tropicale* 3:1–12.

Malinowski, Bronislaw

1967 *A Diary in the Strict Sense of the Term.* New York: Harcourt, Brace.

Mandle, Jay R.

1974 *The Plantation Economy. Population and Economic Change in Guyana, 1830–1960.* Philadelphia: Temple University Press.

Manley, Michael

1982 *Jamaica. Struggle in the Periphery.* London: Third World Media in association with Writers and Readers Publishing Cooperative Society.

Marshall, Woodville K.

1979 "Commentary on 'Slavery and the rise of peasantries' by S. W. Mintz." *Historical Reflections* 6(1):243–51.

Marx, Karl

1963 (1862–1863) *Theories of Surplus-Value.* 3 vols. Moscow: Progress Publishers.

1967 (1867) *Capital: A Critique of Political Economy.* New York: International Publishers.

1971 (1863–1866) *Un Chapitre inédit du "Capital."* Paris: Plon.

1973 (1857–1858) *Grundrisse.* New York: Vintage Books.

1974 (1852) "The Eighteenth Brumaire of Louis Bonaparte." In D. Fernbach, ed., *Surveys from Exile.* New York: Vintage Books.

1976 (1863–1866) "Results of the immediate process of production." Appendix to *Capital,* volume 1. New York: Vintage Books.

Mathieson, William Law

1926 *British Slavery and Its Abolition, 1823–1838.* London: Longmans, Green & Co.

1932 *British Slave Emancipation, 1838–1849.* London: Longmans, Green & Co.

Mencher, Joan P. (ed.)

1983 *Social Anthropology of Peasantry.* Bombay, Madras, New Delhi: Somaiya Publications PVT.

Mintz, Sidney W.

1953 "The folk-urban continuum and the rural proletarian community." *American Journal of Sociology* 59:136–45.

1961a "Pratik: Haitian personal economic relationships." *Proceedings of the 1961 Spring meeting of the American Ethnological Association,* 54–63. Seattle.

1961b "The question of Caribbean peasantries: A comment." *Caribbean Studies* 3:31–34.

1973 "A note on the definition of peasantries." *Journal of Peasant Studies* 1(1):91–106.

1974 "The rural proletariat and the problem of rural proletarian consciousness." *Journal of Peasant Studies* 1(3):301–25.

1977 "The so-called world-system: Local initiatives and local response." *Dialectical Anthropology* 2:253–70.

1978 "Was the plantation slave a proletarian?" *Review* 2(1):81–98.

1979 "Slavery and the rise of peasantries." *Historical Reflections* 6(1):213–42.

1982 "Afterword: Notes on a discovery." In R. P. Weller and S. E. Guggenheim, eds., *Power and Protest on the Countryside.* Durham: Duke Umversity Press, Duke Press Policy Studies.

1983 "Reflections on Caribbean peasantries." *Nieuwe West-Indische Gids / New West Indian Guide* 57(1)1:1–17.

1984 (1974) *Caribbean Transformations.* Baltimore: Johns Hopkins University Press.

Mintz, Sidney W. (ed.)

1985 *History, Evolution, and the Concept of Culture: Selected Papers by Alexander Lesser.* New York: Cambridge University Press.

Mintz, Sidney W., and R. Price

1976 *An Anthropological Approach to the Afro-American Past: A Caribbean Perspective.* Philadelphia: Institute for the Study of Human Issues.

Mallard, Amédée

1977 *Les paysans exploités: Essais sur la question paysanne.* Grenoble: Presses Universitaires de Grenoble.

Mourillon, V. J. Francis

1978 *The Dominica Banana Industry from Inception to Independence, 1928–1978.* Roseau: Tropical Printers.

Murphy, Robert

1971 *The Dialectics of Social Life: Alarms and Excursions tn Anthropologtcal Theory.* New York: Basic Books.

Myers Robert Amory

1976 "I Love My Home Bad, But ... ": The Historical and Contemporary Contexts of Migration on Dominica, West Indies. Ph.D. diss. in Anthropology, University of North Carolina at Chapel Hill.

Myint, Hla

1958 "The 'classical theory' of international trade and underdeveloped countries." *Economic Journal* 68 (June):317–37.

Nadel, S. F.

1942 *A Black Byzantium.* Oxford: Oxford University Press.

Newby, Howard (ed.)

1978 *International Perspectives on Rural Sociology.* New York: John Wiley & Sons.

Nicholls, H. A. Alford

1890 *The Cultivation of the Banana in Dominica.* Roseau: Office of the *Dominican.*

Paget, Hugh

1964 "The free village system in Jamaica." *Caribbean Quarterly* 10:38–51.

Patnaik, Utsa

1978 "Class differentiation within the peasantry: An approach to analysis of Indian agriculture." In A. Rudra et al., eds., *Studies in the Development of Capitalism in India.* Lahore: Vanguard Books.

1979 "Neo-populism and Marxism: The Chayanovian view of the agrarian question and its fundamental fallacy." *Journal of Peasant Studtes* 6(3):375–420.

Paul, Edmond

1876 *De l'impôt sur le café.* Kingston: Cordova.

Pearson, Harry W.

1957 "The economy has no surplus: Critique of a theory of development." In K. Polanyi et al., eds., *Trade and Market in the Early Empires: Economies in History and Theory.* New York: Free Press.

Persaud, B.

1967 "Economic problems of the Windward Islands banana industry." In K. Leslie, ed., *Proceedings of the Second West Indian Agricultural Conference,* 35–55. Saint Augustine, Trinidad: University of the West Indies, Department of Agriculture and Farm Management.

Phillips, W. J.

1973 "Some interpretations of banana statistics relating to the EEC markets and the Commonwealth Caribbean industry." A paper prepared for the EEC Commodity Workshop (Bananas) of the Eighth West Indian Agricultural Economics Conference, Trinidad, 1–7 April 1973.

Pouillon, François

1976 "La détermination d'un mode de production: Les forces productives et leur appropriation." In F. Pouillon, ed., *L'Anthropologie économique: Courants et problèmes,* 57–95. Paris: Maspéro.

Price, Richard

1970 "Studies of Car:ibbean family organization: Problems and prospects." *Dédalo,* Revista do Museu de Arte e Archeologia da Universidade de São Paulo 3.

Pringle, George

1984 "Puerto Rico: A deficit food-producing area." *Revista de Ciencas Comerciales* 6(1):23–28.

Redfield, Robert

1960 (1955–1956) *The Little Community: Peasant Society and Culture.* Chicago: University of Chicago Press.

Rey, Pierre-Philippe

1973 *Les alliances de classe: Sur l'articulation des modes de production.* Paris: Maspéro.

1977 "Le transfert du travail de la paysannerie au capitalisme." *L'Homme et la société* 45–46:39–49.

Reynolds, Philip Keep

1927 *The Banana: Its History, Cultivation, and Place among Staple Foods.* Boston: Houghton Mifflin; Cambridge, Mass.: Riverside Press.

Riviere, Emmanuel W.

1972 "Labour shortage in the British West Indies after emancipation." *Journal of Caribbean History* 4:1–30.

Robinson, Joan

1979 *Aspects of Development and Underdevelopment.* Cambridge: Cambridge University Press.

Roseberry, William

1976 "Rent, differentiation, and the development of capitalism among peasants." *American Anthropologist* 78(1):45–58.

1983 *Coffee and Capitalism in the Venezuelan Andes.* Austin: University of Texas Press.

Sahlins, Marshall

1969 *Tribesmen.* Englewood Cliffs, N.J.: Prentice Hall.

1974 *Stone Age Economics.* New York: Tavistock.

Salama, Pierre

1982 (1975) *Sur la valeur.* Paris: Maspéro.

Sandoval, José Miguel

1983 "State capitalism in a petroleum-based economy: The case of Trinidad and Tobago." In F. Ambursely and R. Cohen, eds., *Crisis in the Caribbean*, 247–68. New York: Monthly Review Press.

Saunders, Peter, et al.

1978 "Rural community and rural community power. In H. Newby, ed., *International Perspectives in Rural Sociology*. New York: John Wiley & Sons.

Schaff, Adam

1976 (1971) *History and Truth*. Oxford and New York: Pergamon Press.

Scott, C. D.

1976 "Peasant, proletarianization, and the articulation of modes of production." *Journal of Peasant Studies* 3(3):321–41.

Seccombe, Wally

1974 "The housewife and her labour under capitalism. *New Left Review* 83:3–24.

Sen, Abhijit

1981 "Market failure and control of labour power: Towards an explanation for 'structure' and change in Indian agriculture." *Cambridge Journal of Economics* 5:201–28, 327–50.

Sen, Amartya

1978 "On the labour theory of value: Some methodological issues." *Cambridge Journal of Economics* (2):175–90.

Sewell, William G.

1861 *The Ordeal of Free Labour in the West Indies*. London: Sampson Low.

Shanin, Teodor

1971a Introduction to T. Shanin, ed., *Peasants and Peasant Societies*. Harmondsworth: Penguin Books.

1971b "A Russian peasant household at the turn of the century." In T. Shanin, ed., *Peasants and Peasant Societies*. Hardmondsworth: Penguin Books.

1973 "The nature and logic of peasant economy." *Journal of Peasant Studies* 1:63–80, 91–106; 2:186–206.

1982 "Class, state, and revolution: Substitutes and realities." In Hamza Alavi and T. Shanin, eds., *Introduction to the Sociology of "Developing" Societies.* New York: Monthly Review Press.

Shenton R. W., and L. Lennihan

1981 "Capital and class: Peasant differentiation in Northern Nigeria." *Journal of Peasant Studies* 9(1):47–70.

Silverman, Marilyn

1979 "Dependency, mediation, and class formation in rural Guyana." *American Ethnologist* 6(3):466–90.

Silverman, Sydel

1979 "The peasant concept in anthropology." *Journal of Peasant Studies* 7(1):49–69.

Smith, Carol A.

1979 "Beyond dependency theory: National and regional patterns of under-development in Guatemala." *American Ethnologist* 5(3):574–617.

1984a "Does a commodity economy enrich the few while ruining the masses?" *Journal of Peasant Studies* 11:60–95.

1984b "Labor and international capital in the making of a peripheral social formation." In C. Bergquist, ed., *Labor Systems and Labor Movements in the World-Capitalist Economy,* 135–56. Beverly Hills, Calif.: Sage Publications.

1984c "Forms of production in practice: Fresh approaches to simple commodity production." *Journal of Peasant Studies* 11:201–21.

Smith, Joan

1984 "Nonwage labor and subsistence." In Joan Smith et al., eds., *Households and the World-Economy: Explorations in the World-Economy,* 64–89. Volume 3. Beverly Hills, Calif.: Sage Publications.

Smith, Landel

1981 "Elections and politics in the Eastern Caribbean: July 1979 to August 1980 . . ." *Caribbean Quarterly* 27:42–62.

Smith, Wayne S.

1985 *Castro's Cuba: Soviet Partner or Nonaligned?* Washington, D.C.: Woodrow Wilson International Center for Scholars.

Soiffer, S. M., and G. N. Howe

1982 "Patrons, clients, and the articulation of modes of production: An examination of the penetration of capitalism into peripheral agriculture in Northeastern Brazil." *Journal of Peasant Studies* 9(2):176–206.

Somers, M. R., and W. L. Goldfrank

1979 "The limits of agronomic determinism." *Comparative Studies in Society and History* 21:443–58.

Sraffa, Piero

1960 *Production of Commodities by Means of Commodities: Prelude to a Critique of Economic Theory.* Cambridge: Cambridge University Press.

Stavrianos, Leften S.

1981 *Global Rift: The Third World Comes of Age.* New York: Morrow.

Steedman, J.

1977 *Marx after Sraffa.* London: New Left Books.

Stephens, Evelyn Huber, and John D. Stephens

1985 *Jamaica's Democratic Socialist Experience.* Washington D.C.: Woodrow Wilson International Center for Scholars.

1985b "Bauxite and democratic socialism in Jamaica." In Peter Evans, Dietrich Rueschemeyer, and Evelyn Huber Stephens, *States versus Markets in the World-System,* 33–66. Beverly Hills, Calif.: Sage Publications.

Steward, Julian H., et al.

1956 *The People of Puerto Rico.* Urbana: University of Illinois Press.

Sutton, Paul

1984 "From neo-colonialism to neo-colonialism: Britain and the EEC in the Commonwealth Caribbean." In A. Payne and P. Sutton, eds., *Dependency under Challenge: The Political Economy of the Commonwealth Caribbean,* 204–37. Manchester: Manchester University Press.

Tanzi, Vito

1976 "Export taxation in developing countries: Taxation of coffee in Haiti." *Social and Economic Studies* 25:66–76.

Taylor, John G.

1979 *From Modernization to Modes of Production: A Critique of the Sociologies of Development and Underdevelopment.* London: Macmillan

Thomas, Clive Y.

1984 *Plantations, Peasants, and State. A Study of the Mode of Sugar Production in Guyana.* Los Angeles: Center for Afro-American Studies, University of California Press; Mona, Jamaica: Institute of Social and Economic Research, University of the West Indies.

Thompson, Edgar T.

1975 *Plantation Societies, Race Relations, and the South: The Regimentation of Populations.* Durham: Duke University Press.

Thorner, Daniel

1971 (1962) "Peasant economy as a category in economic history." In T. Shanin, ed., *Peasants and Peasant Society,* 202–18. Harmondsworth: Penguin Books.

Thornton, Robert

1983 "Narrative ethnography in Africa, 1850–1920: The creation and capture of an appropriate domain for anthropology." *Man,* n.s. 18(3):502–20.

Tilly, Charles

1981 *As Sociology Meets History.* New York: Academic Press.

Tolnai, Gyorgy

1984 *The Role of the Peasant Small-Scale Commodity-Producing Sector in the Third World.* Budapest: Institute for World Economy of the Hungarian Academy of Sciences.

Tomich, Dale

1976 "Some further reflections on class and class conflict in the world-economy." Mimeo. Binghamton: State University of New York: Fernand Braudel Center.

Touraine, Alain

1984 *Le retour de l'acteur.* Paris: Seuil.

Trouillot, Michel-Rolph

1980 Review of *Peasants and Poverty* by Mats Lundahl. *Journal of Peasant Studies* 8(1):112–16.

1982 "Motion in the system: Coffee, color, and slavery in eighteenth-century Saint Domingue." *Review* 5(3):331–88.

1983 "The production of spatial configurations: A Caribbean case." *Nieuwe West-Indische Gids / New West Indian Guide* 57(3/4):215–29.

1984 "Labour and emancipation in Dominica. Contribution to a Debate." *Caribbean Quarterly* 30:73–84.

1985a *Nation, State, and Society in Haiti, 1804–1984.* Washington, D.C.: Woodrow Wilson International Center for Scholars.

1985b "Between moles and visionaries: Notes toward a theory of ethnography." Paper presented at the annual meetings of the American Ethnological Society and the Canadian Ethnology Society, Toronto, 10 May 1985.

1986a *Les racines historiques de l'État Duvaliérien.* Port-au-Prince: Editions Henri Deschamps.

1986b "The Price of Indulgence." In "Capitalism and the Peasantry in South America: The Chevalier-Taussig Controversy: A Critical Review Symposium." *Social Analysis* 19: 85–90.

Valles, Jean-Paul

1968 *The World Market for Bananas, 1964–72.* New York: Praeger, Special Studies in International Economics and Development.

Verdery, Katherine

1983 *Transylvanian Villagers: Three Centuries of Political, Economic, and Ethnic Change.* Berkeley and Los Angeles: University of California Press.

Vergopoulos, Kostas

1977 *Le capitalisme difforme et la nouvelle question agraire: L'Exemple de la Grèce moderne.* Paris: Maspéro.

Vincent, Joan

1982 *Teso in Transformation. The Political Economy of Peasant and Class in Eastern Africa.* Berkeley and Los Angeles: University of California Press.

Wallerstein, Immanuel

1974 *The Modern World System, 1: Capitalist Agriculture and the Origins of the European World-Economy in the Sixteenth Century.* New York: Academic Press.

1980 *The Modern World System, 2: Mercantilism and the Consolidation of the European World-Economy, 1600–1750.* New York: Academic Press.

Watson, Richard

1817 *A Defense of the Wesleyan Methodist Missions in the West Indies.* London: Thomas Cordeux.

Webster, Steven

1982 "Dialogue and fiction in ethnography." *Dialectical Anthropology* 7:91–114.

Welch, Barbara

1968 "Population density and emigration in Dominica." *Geographical Journal* 134(2):227–35.

Whitehead, Ann

1981 "'I'm hungry, mum': The politics of domestic budgeting." In Kate Young, C. Wolkowitz, and R. McCullage, eds., *Of Marriage and the Market: Women's Subordination in International Perspective,* 88–111. London: CSE Books.

Williams, A.

1972 *A Chance for a Change, Development through the Transformation of Agriculture: The Case of Castle Bruce.* Roseau.

Williams, C. N.

1975 *The Agronomy of the Major Tropical Crops.* Kuala Lumpur: Oxford University Press.

Wilson, Peter J.

1973 *Crab Antics: The Social Anthropology of English-Speaking Negro Societies of the Caribbean.* New Haven: Yale University Press.

Wolf, Eric R.

1955 "Types of Latin American peasantry: A preliminary discussion." *American Anthropologist* 57:452–71.

1966 *Peasants,* Englewood Cliffs, N.J.: Prentice Hall.

1978 "Remarks on the people of Puerto Rico." *Revista Interamericana* 8(1):17–25.

1982 *Europe and the People without History.* Berkeley and Los Angeles: University of California Press.

Worsley, Peter

1984 *The Three Worlds: Culture and World Development.* Chicago: University of Chicago Press.

Yankey, Joseph Bernard

1969 "A study of the situation in agriculture and the problems of small-scale farming in Dominica." Ph.D. diss., University of Wisconsin.

Index to *Peasants and Capital*[1]

Abolition of slavery, 88, 104–105, 122
Acreage and production, 293–95; of average holidings in 1920s, 112–13; of average holdings in 1946–61, 159; of banana fields, 281–82; of cultivated land in Dominica, 33; of lime estates in 1916, 227; of peasant farms, 275
Activator. *See* Labor process
Agency, 19–22, 61, 163–65, 336–37, 358n8
Agents of mediation. *See* Mediation
Alavi, H., 82, 288, 358n4
Amin, S., 183, 187, 333, 343
Anthropology, 20–21, 212–14, 336–38, 358n4, 365n2
Antigua, 120, 122, 128, 135, 220, 328, 329
Antilles Products Ltd., 152–53, 167, 196
Apprenticeship, 88, 117, 121–25
Arrowroot, 110, 128
Assembly (House of), 118, 122, 126–27, 136–37
Banaji, J., 13
Banana Act of 1959, 167
Banana children, 317–32
Banana Contract of 1977, 167–69
Bananas: acreages, 319, 376n4; and peasant diet, 153–59; boiled, 156; British market for, 196; cultivation requirements of, 154–55, 245, 248–49, 285, 302; early exports of, 148–50; in Europe and North America, 156, 184; export values of, 184; incomes from, 274; introduction into Dominica, 148–49; pricing system, 169–72, 175–77, 204; recent exports, 60, 74, 159; rejects, 261–62; in Saint Andrew, 216, 226–30; shipping, 173–74; transportation, 255–58, 374n6; Windward Islands production, 196–97; world market for, 149–50, 184–85, 360n1(ch3); yields, 281–82, 374n5. *See also* "Boxing plants"; "Fig days"; Vehicle owners

1. This index to Trouillot's book has been modified, but not redone.

Banks, 324
Baptism, 308
Baptist Church, 236, 238, 304
Bell, H. H., 131–32, 139, 160
Bernstein, H., 6, 15
"Big farmers," 273–77, 322–23, 325, 376n2
Botanic Station, 146
"Boxing plants," 174–75, 252, 374n5. *See also* Londonderry Boxing Plant
Brown Privilege Bill, 117
Bush, the, 243–45

Cacao. *See* Cocoa
Cambridge Computer Services, 201, 205
Canada, 67, 149, 152, 329
Capitalist farmers. *See* "Big farmers"
Capucine, 45–46
Caribs, 32, 33, 49, 55, 61, 217
Castle Bruce, 49–51, 56, 359n5
Catholicism, 35, 47; and literacy, 221, 320; and politics, 308; in Wesley, 221, 235, 238, 304–309
CBI (Caribbean Basin Initiative), 339
Census riots, 118–20
Central Wesley, 235–39
Ceremonial fund, 306
Ceylon, 142
Chamberlain, Lord J., 142, 149
Charles, J. B., 146
Chase, R., 119
Chayanov, A., 4–5, 9, 284, 377n5
Chevalier, J., 15, 179, 312, 362n4
Christian Union Mission Church, 304
Churches, 233, 235–37, 304–309
Circulation. *See* Commodity
Civil Service, 121, 137, 181, 328, 330–32
Cocoa, 45, 65, 68, 69–70, 72, 74–75, 99, 100, 101, 111, 128, 142, 156, 157
Coconuts, 37, 45, 72, 227–29, 249, 272, 277, 279, 291–93, 325, 360n1(ch3), 366n3, 374n4. *See also* copra
Coffee, 62–65, 74–75, 97, 117, 128–29, 155, 156, 217
Colebrooke, G., 88, 122
Colihaut, 43
Colonial Office, 72, 115, 117, 121, 125, 128, 129, 132, 135–36, 139, 142, 144, 146–48, 151, 153
Color, 272. *See also* "Coloreds"
Colored population during slavery, 116–17
"Coloreds," 116–20, 135–39; ambiguity of the term, 116–17, 138
Commodification, 312, 336
Commodities, 10, 155–56; concrete, 312; imported commodities, 237, 238, 344–45; unrealized, 312
Copra exports, 64
Council (Board of), 117, 122, 123, 135
Creole language. *See* Lesser Antillean
Crown colony rule, 135–36, 141–43
Crown lands, 80, 102–109, 123–24, 228, 229–30, 244–45, 295, 301. *See also* Three Chains

Dasheens, 158, 187
Davies, W., 97, 127, 138, 224, 225–26, 373n20

DBGA (Dominica Banana Growers Association), 37–38, 166–69, 277, 278, 280–82, 289–90, 303; and banana collection, 258–62; performance of, 172–75; and pricing system, 175–77
DBS (Dominica Broadcasting System), 174, 234, 252
Delinking, 343–45, 380n8. *See also* Food sufficiency
De Silva, 178–79
Development: theories of, 333–34, 341–42
Diet, 156–58, 275, 240–41, 377n1
Differentiation among peasants, 18–19, 271–309 passim, 359n4; according to income, 283, 291; and household composition, 284–89; and labor, 291, 295–96; and native categories, 269–70; mechanisms of, 270–71. *See also* Gender
Disciplinary traditions, 337
Domestic labor, 186–88
Dominica: as unit of analysis, 31–32, 57; environment, 32–34, 124, 132, 154–55; Gross Domestic Product, 274; occupational categories in, 35–38; population of, 35; population by parish, 41, 56
Dominica Banana Association, 151–52. *See also* DBGA

Eden Estate, 101, 126, 152, 211–30 passim, 292
Education (formal): 219, 220, 221, 222, 224, 318, 319–22. *See also* Catholicism; Methodism; Schools
Elders and Fyffes, 149–50. *See also* Fyffes
Elements of mediation. *See* Mediation
Emancipation. *See* Abolition of slavery
Emic/etic, 270
Emigration, 43, 316; in Saint Andrew South 328–30; after slavery, 133, 328; during slavery, 328
Emmanuel, A., 183
Enclaves, 31–57, 165
English language, 220–22, 320, 326–28
Entrepreneurs, 264, 277–80
Estate laborers: after Apprenticeship, 90–97, 121–25; in 1910s, 143; in nineteenth century, 223
Estate owners: after Apprenticeship, 88, 101, 115; and land speculation, 271–72, 345; in Wesley, 227–29, 271–74; marginalization of, 273
Estates: revitalization at the turn of the century, 142–44; in second half of twentieth century, 159; after slavery, 121–25; around Wesley, 250; in 1879, 128–29
Ethnographic trinity, 21, 365n1
Ethnography, 211–15, 231–32, 290, 336–37

Falconer, C. G., 119, 120, 128, 137, 138, 219, 366n5, 367n6
Family land, 294
"Farine manioc," 128, 157
"Fig Days," 174–75, 250, 252, 254–56, 258–63; as critical moments of mediation, 251, 256, 263, 266

Finance capital, 198–206
First Communion, 306–307
Fishing, 16–17, 38, 45, 49, 345
Food prices, 340–41
Food sufficiency, 344–46, 380n7
Formal subsumption, 12–19. *See also* Labor process
France and Dominica, 61–63, 69, 216–17
Frank, A. G., 4, 333
Freedom party, 308, 311, 360n1(ch3)
French planters, 128
Fruit trade, 146. *See also* Bananas; Imperial Economic Committee
Fundamentalism, 304–308. *See also* Churches
Fyffes, 153, 169, 183. *See also* Elders and Fyffes

Geest Associates, 202, 205, 364n7, 364n8
Geest Holdings Limited, 37, 166, 168, 191–207 passim; affiliates, 201–202, 363n6; in Banana Contract, 167–68; and control of production process, 174–78, 259, 277, 334; creation of, 200, 363n6; payroll, 212
Geest Horticultural Group, 204–205, 364n8
Geest Horticultural Products, 195, 364n8
Geest Industrial Group, 201, 202, 204, 364n8
Geest Industries Limited: capital, 197; evolution and growth, 191–93; financing of, 198–99; profits, 197; take-over of Antilles Products Ltd., 191, 196; vessels, 199
Geest, J. van, 168, 193–95, 362n2
Geest, L. van, 193–95, 200
Geest, van (family), 194
Gender: and adolescence, 300, 303–304; and cash, 302–304, 345; and color, 116; and occupation, 17, 300–301, 323, 330, and religion, 308
Gender inequality, 299–304
Geneva Estate, 55
Glenelg, Lord, 88, 125–26, 360n1(ch5)
GMP (Green Market Price), 169–72, 204
Grand Bay, 55–56, 143, 315
Grapefruits, 147, 157, 177, 248, 279
Greater Wesley, 319
Ground rent: disappearance of, 188
Guadeloupe, 33, 34, 35, 45, 47, 233–34, 327, 368n8, 380n9

Haitian Revolution, 120
Harris, M., 179–80
Harriss, J., 6, 13
History, 57, 164, 212, 231, 333, 337
House. *See* Assembly
Household: composition, 239–41, 284–89, 296–300; contribution to labor process, 245, 248–49; exploitation within, 274–75; female-headed, 296–300; household labor in the West, 186–87; networks, 289; population, 223, 240–41; reproduction, 278–79, 312–13
Houses, 239–40
Hucksters, 44, 111, 234, 262, 300, 314, 371n17
Hurricane Allen, 278, 279
Hurricane David, 278, 279

IMF (International Monetary Fund), 331, 335
Immigration after slavery: of Africans, 132; of white planters, 132, 141–45, 146
Imperial Economic Committee, 146–51
Imray, J., 65, 70–71, 127
Incumbered Estates Commission, 99
Industry, 339–40
Intercropping, 292–94

Jamaica, 64, 149–53 passim, 196, 339, 340–41, 346
JAMCO (Jamaican Producers Marketing Company Limited), 169

Kòkòy, 216, 220, 221, 326–27, 369n9
Kulaks. *See* "Big farmers"
Kroeber, A., 5, 358n1, 364n2

Laborers. *See* Estate Laborers; Estates
Labor market, 143. *See also* Unemployment
Labor power: as unrealized commodity, 312–13, 316, 317, 339; reproduction of, 316, 340
Labor process, 6–8, 83, 335; limitations of concept, 10–12, 206–207; subsumption of, 12–19
Labor relations, 87–88, 94
Labor theory of value, 362n3
La Guerre Negre. *See* Census riots
Land acquisition, 109–10, 125, 130, 143–44, 244–45, 295
Land/labor ratio, 313
Land prices, 272, 295
Language. *See* English language; Kòkòy; Lesser Antillean
La Plaine, 53–54, 56
La Soye. *See* Saint Andrew South
Layou River, 42–43
Leathem, C., 120, 126–27, 218–19, 222–23, 224, 227, 325, 366n5, 367n6, 371n15 and 16
Leeward Islands Federation, 128, 136–37, 145
Legislature, 86, 134, 135. *See also* Local government
Lepkowski, T., 82
Lesser Antillean, 35, 47, 48, 219, 306, 326, 361
Licenses. *See* Taxes
Light engineering, 203
Limes, 68, 70–74, 133, 142, 157, 225, 227–29
Lloyds Bank, 170
Local government, 117, 135–39, 141–42. *See also* Assembly; Council
Londonderry Boxing Plant, 233, 250, 251–52, 290; "fig days" at, 252–55, 258–63
Londonderry Estate, 126, 152, 211–30 passim
Lumpenization of peasantries, 339–41, 379n3
Lumpen peasantry, 42, 315–17, 339–40, 379n3
Lynch, W., 88–89, 90, 97, 103–104, 109

Mahaut, 39–41, 43, 55, 315, 377
Manumission, 116
Marginal productivity of land/labor, 292–94, 314, 319

Marigot, 157, 216, 217, 219, 220, 225, 226, 242, 306, 315, 317, 320, 326, 370n12, 373n20
Maroons, 33, 80
Martinique, 33, 34, 35, 38, 53, 55, 71, 380n9
Marx, K., 4, 6, 11, 12–13, 14, 177, 182, 357n1, 360n1(ch5)
Means of production (ownership of), 177
Mediation: agents of, 232–35, 280, 321, 345; critical moments of, 250–66; elements of, 232–35, 374n1; as a process, 232–33, 245
Mediators, 233–35
Melville Hall Airport, 34, 250, 305, 319
Melville Hall Estate, 126, 152, 154, 218, 220, 222, 223, 226, 250, 367n5, 371n15, 373n20
Metayer System, 98–102. *See also* Sharecropping
Methodism: and literacy, 221–22, 320, 370n11; and politics, 373n21; in Wesley, 219–222, 236, 238, 304–309, 369n10, 370n13
Methodology, 211–12, 335–38
Metropolitan control. *See* Colonial Office
Microlevel analysis, 20–22, 211–12, 214, 311
Migration (internal), 142–43, 316. *See also* Emigration; Immigration
Mintz, S. W., 6, 23, 79, 81, 83, 104, 357n3
Mulatto Ascendancy, 115, 120, 135–39, 181, 219, 319, 372n19
Mulattoes. *See* "Coloreds"
Musaceae, 148, 156

Native categories, 269–71

Oral history, 153–54, 157–58, 220–21
Outsiders, 271–73

Part-peasants, 280, 312–32, 339; inherent ambivalence of, 327
Patchouli, 158
Patois. *See* Lesser Antillean
Pearson, H., 179
Peasant Adviser, 147
Peasant Information Bureau, 147
Peasant labor process: activator of, 245, 301–302, 303; definition, 6–10; domains of, 78–79; and exports, 139, 145–48, 160; historical configurations of, 78–81; household contribution to, 292, 301; and production of commodities, 78–79, 96, 155–56; reactions to emergence of, 145; and slavery, 81–88; subsumption under capitalist relations, 135, 159, 181–82, 206, 270–71; and valorization, 164, 166–67, 193, 207
Peasants: and capitalism, 4, 12–19, 24–28, 164, 188, 207, 333–34, 338; in the Caribbean, 25–28; emergence in Dominica, 88–89; as national resources, 342; proprietors, 275. *See also* Differentiation among peasants
Peasant studies, 3–5, 193, 213, 357n2
Pentecostal Church, 304
Petty commodity production. *See* Simple commodity production
Plantains, 148–49

Plantation labor process, 83, 157, 224
Plantation Wesley, 211–30, 318–19
Political economy, 212, 336–37
Politics of production, 164–65, 206–207
Portsmouth, 33, 35, 43–45, 225, 318, 320–22, 325, 326, 368n7
Positivism, 337
Preventive tactics, 121–25
Principal laborer, 245–50, 292, 293, 313
Production/consumption balance, 8–10, 156, 284–89, 291–93, 312–14
Proletarianization of peasantries, 338
Protestantism, 48, 216, 319. *See also* Fundamentalism; Methodism; Seventh Day Adventists
Provision grounds: after slavery, 88 90; during slavery, 81–88
Provisions, export of, 129
Puerto Rico, 339, 340–41

Quebec Steamship Company, 149

Radio, 174, 175, 234, 252, 305, 316, 326, 327
Rastafarianism, 33, 42
Recorders, 259, 303
Relations of distribution, 18, 87
Relations of production, 11, 17–18, 87, 98, 108, 133, 216, 342
Rent. *See* Ground rent
Residential Wesley, 239–43
Rey, P. P., 187
Roman Catholicism. *See* Catholicism
Rosalie, 51
Roseau, 33, 38–44 passim, 68, 72, 116, 126, 137, 143, 146, 149, 189, 226, 252, 274, 316, 318, 320–30 passim
Routine, 269, 311
Rum, 35, 65–67, 117, 126, 127, 254, 264, 364

Saint Andrew (parish), 47, 89, 216–18; nineteenth-century politics in, 367n6
Saint Andrew North, 47–48, 217
Saint Andrew South: early history of, 215–18; education in, 219–22; Methodism in, 369n9; lime production in, 227; migration in, 369n8; oral history of, 220–21; peasantry in nineteenth-century, 222–24; slavery in, 217–18
Saint David (parish of), 49
Saint George (parish of), 38–43
Saint John (parish of), 43–44, 136
Saint Joseph (parish of), 43
Saint Luke (parish of), 38–43
Saint Mark (parish of), 38
Saint Paul (parish of), 38–43
Saint Peter (parish of), 43
Scale, 19–20, 358n7. *See also* Units of analysis
Schools, 45, 221–22, 319–21, 330; Dominica Agricultural School, 146; Dominica Grammar School, 137; Portsmouth Secondary School, 320, 322
Scotts Head, 38
Selectors, 254, 259–61
Self-centered development, 343–47
Seventh Day Adventists, 236, 238, 304, 305, 308
Seventh Day Church of God, 304
Shanin, T., 5, 357n2

Sharecropping: after Apprenticeship, 93–94, 97, 98–101; in Saint Andrew, 228–29
Shops, 233, 237, 238, 264–66, 314–15
Simple commodity production, 12–19, 313–14, 341
Size. *See* Units of analysis
Slavery, 26, 59, 78–88, 217–18
Slaves: food of, 83–87; types of activities of, 64
Slums, 338–39
Spain and Dominica, 61
Spalding, 195
South Africa, 132, 142
Squatters, 335. *See also* Crown lands
State politics, 160
State power, 124, 206–207. *See also* Colonial Office; Local government
Structuration, 270
Subsistence: critique of the concept, 9, 178–81, 312–13
Subsumption. *See* Labor process
Sugarcane, 63–68, 90–94, 128–29, 224–25
Sugar crisis, 129
Surplus: concept of, 178–80, 276, 359n2, 361n2; extraction of, 167, 182–89, 379n5
Surplus labor, 187–88
Surplus value, 187–88

Taiwan model, 343
Tanias, 158
Tanzania, 206
Taxes, 126–35; export duties, 127–30; import duties, 134; indirect, 133–34; licenses, 126–27; real estate taxes, 128–31; Road Tax, 130
Teachers, 330–31
Tenants, 284, 291–93. *See also* Sharecropping
"Three Chains," 105–106, 129
Trade imbalances, 334–35
Trans-Insular Road, 318, 320, 322
Truck owners, 225–26, 277–78, 322
Turkey, 205, 206

Underemployment, 315–16, 340
Unemployment, 36, 313–17, 331, 338, 340
"Unequal exchange", 122, 167, 183–84, 187–88
United Fruit, 149–50
United States, 142, 147, 149, 150, 152, 233, 285, 293, 305, 329, 332, 339–40, 341, 346, 379n3, 380n6, 381n10
Units of analysis, 20–25, 31–32, 213–15, 335–37, 365n1, 378n2(ch13)
Units of production, 7–10, 78–79, 83–83, 92–93, 115, 122, 159, 335
Urban macrocephalia, 338

Valorization, 10–12, 17–19, 22, 47, 193, 312, 342
Value: of labor power, 182–83; labor theory of, 182, 362n3
Vanilla, 72, 74–75, 152, 154, 156, 157, 228, 301, 302, 319
Vegetable Growers Association, 154
Vehicle owners, 255–58, 265, 375n8. *See also* Truck owners
Vieille Case, 47, 48, 359n4. *See also* Saint Andrew North
Village: as unit of analysis, 213–14
Village Council, 215, 323

Wakefield, E. G., 125, 126, 360n1(ch5)
Wallerstein, I., 1, 21, 336
Walter Groom Limited, 362n2, 364n8
Watts, F., 112–13, 147, 160
Wesley (village of): in 1893, 127, 211, 223–24; peasants in nineteenth century, 372n18; population, 240–41; registered banana growers, 281–82; relations within, 241–43; relations with the outside, 237–39; as unit of analysis, 214–15, 231–32, 266–67; work ethic, 276, 319, 323–25
WINBAN (Windward Islands Banana Association), 151, 166–68, 169, 171, 172
Windward Islands, 150–53, 281, 293, 334–35
Wolf, E. R., 5, 9, 11–12, 21, 306, 357n3
Women. *See* Gender
Woodford Hill (village of), 216
Woodford Hill Estate, 126, 152–53, 189, 211–30 passim, 319
World economy, 333–34
World system analysis, 21
World War I, 142
World War II, 157

Yeomen, 36, 79, 109–13, 222–24, 275–76, 284, 290–92. *See also* Land acquisition; Peasants, proprietors